MARKETS WITH BUREAUCRATIC CHARACTERISTICS

THE MIDDLE RANGE

THE MIDDLE RANGE SERIES

Edited by Peter S. Bearman, Emily Erikson, Christopher Muller, and Catherine Turco
Co-Founding Editor: Shamus R. Khan

The Middle Range Series promotes studies that link theory to richly textured empirical contexts to produce innovative paths of inquiry and new solutions to intriguing and substantively important problems.

The Middle Range, a term coined by and represented in the work of Columbia sociologist Robert Merton, is a style of social research that links theory with observation to produce empirically novel and theoretically generative research. This approach yielded significant advances in the social sciences over the last half century. The Middle Range series builds on that tradition, publishing works that are as innovative theoretically as they are empirically.

The series is most interested in projects that seek explanations of substantively important, intriguing phenomena and puzzles from the real world, whether contemporary or historical. Exemplary projects tend to span micro and macro levels of analysis, incorporate qualitative and quantitative data, and engage theory with richly textured empirics. The series supports authors attempting to discover innovative new paths of inquiry and creative new solutions to old problems.

Markets with Bureaucratic Characteristics: How Economic Bureaucrats Make Policies and Remake the Chinese State, Yingyao Wang

Judge Thy Neighbor: Denunciations in the Spanish Inquisition, Romanov Russia, and Nazi Germany, Patrick Bergemann

Trade and Nation: How Companies and Politics Reshaped Economic Thought, Emily Erikson

The Corsairs of Saint-Malo: Network Organization of a Merchant Elite Under the Ancien Régime, Henning Hillmann

Working for Respect: Community and Conflict at Walmart, Adam Reich and Peter Bearman

Concepts and Categories: Foundations for Sociological and Cultural Analysis, Michael T. Hannan, Gaël Le Mens, Greta Hsu, Balázs Kovács, Giacomo Negro, László Pólos, Elizabeth Pontikes, and Amanda J. Sharkey

The Conversational Firm: Rethinking Bureaucracy in the Age of Social Media, Catherine J. Turco

Markets with Bureaucratic Characteristics

HOW ECONOMIC BUREAUCRATS MAKE POLICIES AND REMAKE THE CHINESE STATE

Yingyao Wang

Columbia University Press
New York

Columbia University Press
Publishers Since 1893
New York   Chichester, West Sussex
cup.columbia.edu

Library of Congress Cataloging-in-Publication Data
Names: Wang, Yingyao, author.
Title: Markets with bureaucratic characteristics : how economic bureaucrats make policies and remake the chinese state / Yingyao Wang.
Description: 1 Edition. | New York : Columbia University Press, [2024] |
Series: The middle range series | Includes bibliographical references and index.
Identifiers: LCCN 2023039189 (print) | LCCN 2023039190 (ebook) |
ISBN 9780231214780 (hardback) | ISBN 9780231214797 (trade paperback) |
ISBN 9780231560467 (ebook)
Subjects: LCSH: China—Economic policy—2000- |
China—Economic conditions—2000- | China—Politics and government—2002-
Classification: LCC HC427.95 .W3678 2024 (print) |
LCC HC427.95 (ebook) | DDC 330.951—dc23/eng/20230821
LC record available at https://lccn.loc.gov/2023039189
LC ebook record available at https://lccn.loc.gov/2023039190

Cover image: Noah Arlow
Cover image: Shutterstock

CONTENTS

Introduction   1

PART I. GENESIS

Chapter One
The Socialist Circulators and the Bureaucratic
Origin of China's Economic Reform   35

Chapter Two
Balanced Development or Decentralized Growth?
Elite Reformers in the 1980s   63

PART II. CONSOLIDATION

Chapter Three
The Rise of Technocrats: Market Rationalization
and the Macrocontrol Paradigm   85

Chapter Four
National Champions and the Organizational Approach
to Enterprises and Markets   118

PART III. EFFERVESCENCE

Chapter Five
The Remaking of Public Finance in China and the
Financial Approach to Economic Control   149

Chapter Six
The Ascent of the Industrial View: Industrial Policy for Making a
Manufacturing Superpower   181

Conclusion   215

LIST OF ABBREVIATIONS   233

ACKNOWLEDGMENTS   235

NOTES   239

REFERENCES   269

INDEX   285

MARKETS WITH BUREAUCRATIC CHARACTERISTICS

Introduction

In the wake of the 2008 global financial crisis, countries around the world were forced to reevaluate their assumptions about financial systems and economic development. Advanced economies needed to determine how their policies failed and revise their development priorities accordingly. Chinese officials watched the crisis closely as it transpired and continued to track its impact long afterward. As they watched not only from Zhongnanhai, the royal palace where top leaders reside and work, but also from the state ministries and departments, they contemplated how the crisis could create opportunities for them to advance the agendas that were already on their desks. Technocrats at the Ministry of Industry and Information Technology (MIIT) observed that advanced economies in North America and Europe reacted to the crisis by pivoting away from finance and dedicating resources to reindustrialization. They believed that this shift in the West should spur China to reground itself—to strengthen manufacturing capabilities and indigenous innovation. They urged that China seize what they saw as a once-in-a-lifetime opportunity as a new wave of technological advances created shortcuts for late developers like China to join the league of economic and technological superpowers. According to the officials at the MIIT, the changes in economic development then taking place around the world were indications that the techno-industrial policy the ministry and its technocrats had been promoting was more relevant and necessary than ever.

In the years leading up to the Thirteenth Five-Year Plan (2016–2020), ministries in Beijing were anxiously devising their own agendas and proposing initiatives in the hope that these would find their way into the plan, boosting the profiles of their authors. With this goal in mind, the MIIT teamed up with the Chinese Academy of Engineering to produce a detailed blueprint of their manufacturing power strategy, presenting it to the State Council in 2013. The ministry's Bureaus of Equipment and Development Planning were at the forefront of the drafting efforts, assisted by partners from the academy and a wide range of consultants, researchers, and managers. The proposal, if implemented, vowed to launch China from its position in the third tier of manufacturing powers to the second tier by 2025. The strategy attracted great interest at the State Council and ultimately became a national initiative.

This vignette illustrates the origin of what is widely known as China's most ambitious development plan in recent years—*Made in China 2025*. Defying the common perception that such a plan must have been top-down and tied to the paramount leaders and their geopolitical ambitions, the reality is something altogether different. Rather, it was a middle-out plan developed in the economic bureaucracy by ministry- and bureau-level economic bureaucrats who interpreted the world events around them through the lenses of their particular backgrounds, specialties, and career experiences. As this book shows, Made in China 2025 turns out to be the result of one of many times when the particularities of the economic bureaucracy gave rise to major shifts in economic practice and policy. Beyond the rise of techno-industrial policy, there are other marked policy movements that this book identifies as having bureaucracy-related origins: macroeconomic centralization in the early 1990s, public-sector restructuring and the building of "national champions" in the late 1990s, the financialization of public finance, and the pursuit of debt-driven development starting in the early 2000s. Even the very inception of economic reform was associated with the efforts of bureaucratic incumbents. That is, major policy shifts were intrinsically tied to the interests and visions of the Chinese bureaucrats.

The Chinese bureaucracy is the world's oldest bureaucracy. It is characterized by state longevity, an age-old civil service system, and relative cultural continuity. But for centuries, or even for millennia, the Chinese bureaucracy was not geared toward markets or economic development. Rather, it was committed to maintaining the stability of the imperial regime. In the Mao period, the state bureaucracy was highly ideologized under one-party leadership. The economic bureaucracy was part of the planning machine and revolved around managing a command economy. Yet just four decades ago, the same economic bureaucracy was abruptly put in charge of generating growth and overseeing market transitions. Since then, the economy has grown to nearly three hundred times its size in the late 1970s and lifted seven hundred million people out of poverty. How has the world's oldest bureaucracy come to manage what is now the world's second-largest economy while supervising what is allegedly one of the fastest market expansions in human history?

More surprisingly, the Chinese bureaucrats didn't just take over this mission reluctantly. They embraced it with much ardor, creativity, and self-preservation. Markets greatly expanded without undercutting the power of the economic bureaucracy. In fact, economic bureaucrats frequently used the market, or a simulation of it, as an essential tool to strengthen bureaucratic control and authority. As a result, the bureaucracy that is in charge of the economy has grown in its capacity, its sophistication, and, as this book shows, its internal competition. This phenomenon may not surprise classical political economists such as Karl Polanyi who argue that market expansion and state expansion always happen together, that market building has a state origin and ends up strengthening the sovereign power of the state.[1] Yet the Chinese case still cries for a more nuanced account. Where did Chinese bureaucrats' economic ideas come from, given their isolation in the socialist period? How did incumbent bureaucrats adapt to managing a marketized economy? How did the bureaucracy accrue power in spite of relinquishing the socialist-style control over the economy in favor of markets?

In spite of the importance of the Chinese economic bureaucrats in shaping history, they have largely been excluded from the public limelight and scholarly scrutiny. To outside observers, Chinese bureaucrats often appear faceless, even necessarily so, in a system that aggrandizes leaders at the pinnacle of the polity. Public fanfare does not exalt the ministries, bureaus, and agencies. We know little about the men and women who direct the state apparatus other than the fact that they spend long working lives inside state administration, biding their time and climbing the ladder. As the following chapters show, it is precisely in these ostensibly lifeless domains that big ideas are born, critical situations are redefined, and momentum is built up, all against a background of intense competition for policy authority and bureaucratic turf. This book thus uncovers the profound but neglected role that China's economic bureaucracy has played in shaping the lives of billions in China and beyond.

That said, bureaucrats do not control every aspect of the Chinese economy. Nor can they precisely steer the entire economy in a particular direction. What has sustained China's growth model is wide-ranging development coalitions that include the private sector, state-owned enterprises (SOEs), local governments, foreign firms, middle-class consumers, a disciplined and repressed workforce, and others far beyond the confines of state ministries. Nevertheless, this book finds that in *formulating* economic policy, economic bureaucrats played a disproportionately large and, in some cases, determinative role. And I propose that the level of influence that Chinese economic bureaucrats exert is at what Thomas Kuhn calls the level of "paradigms."[2] Paradigms are not technical or isolated policies. Nor are they megaprojects or collections of initiatives that catch media attention. Instead, paradigms are integrated approaches to the economy and markets: worldviews on what the goals of economic development should be, how economic problems should be defined, and how state-economy relations should be formatted. In turn, paradigm development affects consequential decisions on the ground such as where to invest, what sectors to develop, what role the central and local governments should play, and how to define and strive for competitiveness. Through instituting policy paradigms, Chinese economic bureaucrats effectively use the prism of their own means when representing, addressing, and communicating with the leadership and the public about the structural pressures placed on the Chinese economy. This is the ability I refer to as *policy authority*, an understudied dimension of power in Chinese politics but essential for understanding the rules of the game the economic bureaucrats play.

To trace the origin of policy paradigms, this book develops a social and dynamic understanding of the bureaucratic state. On the surface, the Chinese state consists of organizations that exist in walled buildings and mission statements. The economic bureaucracy, for instance, comprises two dozen commissions, ministries, and agencies performing policy functions associated with taxation, central banking, macroeconomic management, market regulation, agriculture, industries, construction, trade, statistics, and so on. Examined across time and through the people who staff it, however, the state is constituted of small "societies"—defined by career movements, generational shifts, and social networks—that evolve within the state and across organizational boundaries. These little societies are the flesh-and-blood manifestations of bureaucratic organizations, and as these societies change, policy areas become unstable and their boundaries fluid. Supported by a body of qualitative and quantitative biographical data, this book attends systemically to how the configuration of these social elements supplies impetus, solidarities, and entrepreneurship and gives rise to large-scale changes in China's economic policy. Over the course of the book, I identify the specific groups of bureaucrats responsible for originating each economic paradigm and uncover the tactics they used to coordinate action and exert supraorganizational influence.

THE POWER OF CHINA'S BUREAUCRATIC STATE

China is a strategic case for examining the role of the bureaucratic state in economic development. A number of factors associated with the Chinese polity and history are poised to structure the power balance between the state and society in favor of the state. The configuration of state-society relations in the context of economic development should constitute our baseline understanding of bureaucratic power in China.

First, traditional economic elites were weak or had been weakened prior to and during the economic take-off. As such, no major opposition to state economic action could be effectively mounted by social elites. The indigenous bourgeois class was historically weak because of its dependence on colonial power and the exceptional feebleness of the industrial capitalists in its midst. The Communist Revolution further depleted their already feeble existence along with that of other traditional elites. Sweeping land reform eliminated the landed class and uprooted the old gentry in rural societies. Labor movements were incorporated into the socialist state early on and then essentially demobilized to become a corporatist wing of the production machine. That is, the social forces that would otherwise serve to counterbalance the top-down imposition of bureaucratic will in other national contexts were weak to nonexistent in China.

Second, China started its pursuit of capitalism without capitalists, and the continuous grip on power over the state by a single party prevented the formation of powerful economic classes.[3] Make no mistake, economic reform introduced potent market forces and fierce economic competition into most segments of the Chinese economy, but it did so without giving political power to the newly created market actors. Private entrepreneurs, the middle class, and the workers were either given carefully delimited zones of action or largely incorporated into the orbit of state policies.[4] Party control also set limits on the privatization of the public sector. Granted, the ways in which state enterprises were unraveled were functions of policy decisions, and these are explained in my analysis. The speed at which SOE privatization happened from the late 1990s to early 2000s, for instance, was nothing short of a smaller version of Russia's and other post-communist countries' shock therapy. Still, the ability of the state to retain the "strategic" state sector served to maintain the state's control over the economy. The state sector has been an important vehicle for the state, enabling it to influence the parameters of the economy and provide a training ground for state managers.

Third, the starting point of China's transition to markets—the socialist command economy—preserved a vestige of the bureaucratic command of the economy, a power that would only later be repurposed for market building. Previously, the economic bureaucracy ran the planning machine and gave bureaucrats what scholars of state socialism call a redistributive power in allocating resources.[5] Granted, China never practiced the planned economy with the same rigor as the Soviet Union. Nevertheless, the old machinery supplied organizations, tool kits, capacities, and, equally importantly, a planning disposition—the idea that one can design the economy according to a central vision. These structures and ideas were carried over through intergenerational diffusion, organizational memories, and biographical circulation and were retooled to engineer economic modernization and, as this book shows, even to build markets.

Taken together, in many aspects, the Chinese bureaucratic state greatly resembles the East Asian "developmental states" exemplified by Japan, Korea, and Taiwan. In these countries, too, the state was able to impose a transformative strategy on society and fend off resistance from capital or labor. With strong state capacity and autonomy, they were able to maintain control and order while remaining unswervingly committed to high growth in the name of the nation. Their bureaucrats were also immersed in a long-standing bureaucratic tradition, recruited through highly selective processes, and strongly committed to long-term careers in the state.[6] If anything, China's political system and its history extended all the elements and markers associated with the developmental states and carried them to extremes, outstripping China's neighbors in its commitment to and cohesion in developing its economy.

In spite of its resemblance in terms of bureaucratic power and ethos, China's bureaucratic state did not produce the kind of corporate coherence that was often expected to occur within developmental states. Instead, the Chinese state bureaucracy was frequently cited for producing fragmented authoritarianism, with policy coordination fractured along territorial and vertical functional lines.[7] This fragmentation is quintessentially manifest in elusive attempts at summarizing the China model. Different parts of the elephant showcase different aspects or dimensions of the economic reality and lead to inconsistencies in declaring what makes China work or not work. Some scholars, for this reason, recognize that China is a system of systems and its development approaches were nothing but plural or even "paradoxical."[8] This book, too, points to changes of direction and juxtapositions of paradigms that reveal irreconcilable incoherence among them and therefore complicate any appeal to the one-model narrative.

THE SOCIAL CHARACTER OF THE BUREAUCRACY

To reconcile high state capacity/autonomy on the one hand and policy incoherency on the other, one needs to look deeper into the bureaucratic state to see if it is the source of heterogeneity. If the comparative studies of neoliberalism are any indication, we should expect that the type of state actors put in charge of executing (neo)liberal transformations will matter a great deal.[9] In France and Mexico, it was the state technocrats who instituted revolutions from within and put in place a pragmatic version of neoliberalism aligned with a larger pursuit of modernization. In Britain and Chile, neoliberal policy makers rose from marginal status through new party movements. They ended up implementing highly ideological and dogmatic versions of neoliberal policies.[10] In spite of the policy makers' shared project, their differing positions sent their countries off on different trajectories of development. To account for the Chinese case, a more fine-grained model is needed to draw connections between the backgrounds of the policy makers and the policy outcomes.

To that end, we need to sociologically unpack the bureaucracy and understand its dimension of heterogeneity. In this regard, Max Weber's classic account of the rational bureaucracy reveals as much as it obscures. Weber rightly argues that bureaucracy organizes authority in ways that differ from authority in traditional organizations. The array of organizational features of the bureaucracy—the installation of hierarchy, division of labor, technical specialization and standardization, and formal rules—is meant to reduce personal idiosyncrasies and increase institutional durability.[11] Yet Weber also overextends the construction of his ideal type by removing personhood and sociality from his characterization of bureaucratic lives. This tendency results in a temptation to focus on the structures and not the people when it comes to analyzing the bureaucracy and, as a result, to reduce the interests and identities of bureaucrats simply to those of the organizations they serve.

Weber's depiction of the bureaucracy in the image of a rational machine has inspired a perennial dread that aspects of the celebrated bureaucratic ethos, such as impartiality, routinization, and the separation of office and individual, can also turn into alienation, lack of creativity, and inertia, collectively comprising a form of modernity's iron cage.[12] In this model, the most faithful bureaucrats also risk being divorced from social reality and the people they serve. They lack sympathy and flexibility in going about their business. James Scott's account of why large projects of high modernism in human history have failed is largely built on this assumption about the nature of bureaucratic decision-making. Bureaucratic intelligentsia, technicians, planners, and engineers, Scott explains, disregard local knowledge and the creativity of frontline actors. Instead, they see situations like a state does—from high above—and govern the complexity of social process through abstraction and standardization—enforcing a machine-like operation.[13]

While the bureaucracy may be an ensemble of rationalized structures, scholars demonstrate that it is also an institution inhabited by human agents.[14] Paying attention to the lived experiences of bureaucrats enables a closer approximation of how real-world bureaucracies operate, uncovering the experiences situated between idealized traits and downright self-serving corruption. Ben Schneider, in his studies of the Brazilian state, for instance, encourages an insider's perspective on the bureaucracy. In particular, he points to the centrality of careers in organizing bureaucratic lives. Where outsiders see durable state structures revolving around organizations, he posits that insiders see mobile careers extending behind and before them.[15] Careers organize various interests and orient bureaucratic pursuits over time and across issues. Bureaucrats devise policies in conjunction with their career interests.[16] Chinese career bureaucrats, too, are not exactly fixed cogs in one part of a machine; rather, they are mobile agents of the state. During their tenures, they travel through various parts of the state and typically serve in multiple organizations. I calculated rates of mobility using a biographical database I assembled on elite-level Chinese economic bureaucrats (vice ministers and above). On average, elite bureaucrats spent 36.7 years in the Chinese government and changed organizations every 7.1 years.[17] While this number may indicate less personnel turnover compared to other national cases, it does convey the fact that career transfer remains common in China's economic bureaucracy, with its implication rarely investigated.

Attention to career mobility relaxes the assumption about the congruence between organizations and individuals and highlights instead career-based similarities and differences. Precisely because Chinese bureaucrats are career bureaucrats, many of them came from lowly positions; even the top leaders in China have worked their way up from the rank and file of the government.[18] In other words, bureaucrats at the elite level are sourced from different parts of the state where they had variable relationships with situations on the ground. Some of them are even equipped with local economic knowledge, drawn from a wide range of experiences while working in local governments, street-level agencies, state-owned factories, or frontline research. This arrangement challenges Scott's depiction of the enterprise of "seeing like a state," which is largely depicted as top-down and unified. Instead, bureaucratic solidarities may be built around small groups based on shared constellations of bureaucratic experiences.

In a similar spirit, an emergent scholarship on the Chinese bureaucracy has initiated a rethinking, in light of China's experience with reform, of the relationship between Weberian bureaucracy and efficiency. Scholars have noted that the Chinese bureaucracy has many mixed characteristics, exhibiting both classical Weberian and more social and informal ways of organizing authorities. The exercise of political charisma, for instance, remains a viable method of organization and control. In fact, bureaucratic organizations in China resemble charismatic organizations that are marked by goal commitment, informal structures, and charismatic mobilizations.[19] Bureaucrats are highly incentivized to perform by a mixture of moral mobilizations and routine performance evaluations. In addition to the blending of routine and charisma, the fusion of formal and informal institutions in the Chinese bureaucracy highlights its hybridity. Central policies are adapted locally, and local experiments with proven success are scaled up into national policies. Social networks, informal cross-organizational coordination, and rule malleability have all come together and bent bureaucratic rigidity to deliver results. Granted, this system has produced rampant corruption and rule breaking, but the same system has also produced bureaucratic entrepreneurship, flexibility, and risk-taking behavior during the course of economic reform.[20] When coupled with career incentives, these mixed features can be mobilized into powerful means to achieve larger goals. This is not to say that the Chinese bureaucracy is an unfinished Weberian project or that it has met Weberian standards halfway. Scholars make the opposite argument: that the mixture is an integral, institutionalized part of China's bureaucracy[21] and that this mixed system can settle into a social and historical equilibrium, generating unpredictability but also dynamism.[22]

To date, local governments are considered the main sites for generating bureaucratic entrepreneurship. Whether the central bureaucracy is imbued with similar experimental and entrepreneurial drives has gotten much less research attention. The received wisdom is that it is through the adaptation of central policy by local governments that bureaucratic creativity is most evident and prominent. The bureaucratic processes involved in the formulation stage of policy making in the central government remain a black box.

MOTIVATING THE CHINESE ECONOMIC BUREAUCRATS

To understand how their careers are organized and their interests defined in the economic bureaucracy, one needs to understand how economic bureaucrats are motivated. Chinese cadres are subject to rigorous and sometimes draconian evaluation regimes.[23] Yet the way central bureaucrats are evaluated is less obvious than it is for local officials. Local officials govern clearly bounded geographies and answer to identifiable indicators such as GDP. Central bureaucrats, in contrast, produce national policies whose immediate consequences are hard to pin down and whose ultimate results are affected by a host of intervening factors and confounding variables. In this section, I zoom out to situate the economic bureaucracy in the institutional milieu of the Chinese government. I propose that the central economic bureaucracy is not passive or unenterprising. Instead, the bureaucracy is a competitive stage where action and forms of entrepreneurship are necessary for success.

For starters, China's one-party political system blurs the line between political and bureaucratic elites. Party elites are all career bureaucrats; economic career bureaucrats are mostly party loyalists. The fusion politicizes the economic bureaucrats to a degree unseen in electoral regimes. Chinese economic bureaucrats are given viable career ladders to climb and a stake in "politics as a vocation."[24] This means that Chinese bureaucrats are not content with merely making technical decisions or implementing policies. Instead, they are driven by a desire to seek wide-ranging influence where they can demonstrate their contribution to the regime. This is very different from career bureaucrats in electoral systems, who tend to resign themselves to the exercise of technical skills and approach policies from narrow and detailed perspectives. This is because professional proficiency, construed in narrow terms, helps these career bureaucrats steer clear of politics and acquire the appearance of neutrality, which is the source of their authority. Career bureaucrats in China are animated politically. Policy is political not only because bureaucrats should toe the party line but also because policies can be used as instruments for grabbing power and advancing careers. Ministries in China host ambitious careerists who set their sights far above perfecting technical skills in a single organization. Many of them strive to be polymaths among specialists, developing a relatively broad set of skills for a mobile career in the Chinese state. That is, Chinese career bureaucrats are motivated to think beyond technical domains and formulate big-picture policies. To a large extent, the ability to devise policy programs that showcase a concern for the national situation and impact a broad spectrum of the economy is an expression of political acumen for economic bureaucrats.

This encouragement of big-picture thinking injects a measure of competitive dynamism into the economic bureaucracy. When commenting on why the Banking Regulatory Commission—a new and supposedly highly technical agency—would step on the toes of the long-standing Central Bank, Wu Xiaoling, the former vice governor of the Central Bank, reveals important clues about how economic ministries are motivated. "The way that the ministries are evaluated means that ministerial leaders hope they have a clear voice and good performance to show to the State Council.

Because of this, the Banking Regulatory Commission will not be satisfied with making micro-decisions and doing technical jobs but will also want to do things at the macro-level."[25] This is to say that economic ministries are under considerable pressure to take on large and comprehensive initiatives and engage with one another in a race of "competitive persuasion" in front of choosy leaders.[26] Because macrolevel aspirations almost inevitably lead to encroachment on one another's territories and increase the odds of jurisdictional competition, they have implications for interagency relations. The developmental state literature attributes one source of the state's effectiveness to the existence of a pilot agency in the economic bureaucracy that is instrumental in devising coherent strategies and coordinating investments. In China, the need for a nodal agency has been well recognized, but the problem is that under a competitive policy regime, there are many ministries vying for nodal status. Following the decline of the hegemonic State Planning Commission, many agencies—including the Ministry of Finance, the Ministry of Economic and Trade Commission, and the Ministry of Industry and Information Technology—have aspired to become comprehensive economic agencies (*zonghe jingji bumen*), a designation that would earn them a wide-ranging portfolio and coordinating power over other agencies.[27] The pressure to take on large initiatives is foundational in guiding bureaucratic behavior in the central government.

POLICY AUTHORITY AND THE CHINESE ECONOMIC BUREAUCRACY

Economic bureaucrats are able to use the generic power of all central bureaucrats as well as certain kinds of power specific to the economic bureaucracy. Economic bureaucrats surely have weak coercive power, as they do not possess any piece of the coercive machinery of the state. Their ability to enforce their will pales in comparison to that of local governments, which often wield undue influence over local courts, public security, and procuratorial organs. Economic bureaucrats need to consciously factor in this weakness in implementation when formulating policy programs. As one of the Chinese officials I interviewed confessed, central economic policy makers always needed to "cut the pork ribs at the right angle."[28] That is, their power needed to be wielded carefully and smartly. This point broadens our understanding of state power in China. The Chinese state is well-known for its possession and exercise of coercive power, but the operation of its symbolic power is less well understood.[29] Because economic bureaucrats lack coercive power and easily defined standards for evaluating their performance, it is more accurate to say that they wield soft power. Therefore, in lieu of *power, authority* may be the more fitting term, taking into consideration the performative space in which bureaucrats operate and the importance of the question of legitimacy. Specifically, I argue that Chinese economic bureaucrats are driven to seek policy authority, a recognized ability to speak authoritatively about a given policy issue.[30] Often this involves the ability to define the parameters of an economic situation—for instance, whether SOE debt is a financial-, managerial-, or production-related problem—and in the process rule out alternative explanations while prescribing legitimate courses of action.

China's economic bureaucracy and its decision environment have evolved in the reform era in ways that have pushed the importance of ideas, legitimacy, and institutions to the forefront of bureaucratic politics. Three factors are crucial for highlighting the relevance of policy authority to bureaucratic pursuits. First, economic policy is a relatively depoliticized policy area in the reform period. That is, the economic bureaucracy orients itself toward a distinctively depoliticized object of management—the economy. This is not to say that economic policy has no political implications. Yet the shift in the basis of legitimacy of the party from dominating political ideology to promoting economic growth severed the economy from political agitation and removed the class question—and thereby the question of distribution—from the discussion of economic matters. This could be considered a neoliberal move with Chinese characteristics that paralleled the intrusion of an economic style of reasoning into left-wing political discourse in advanced economies.[31] The Chinese economy is largely represented in nondistributive and growth-oriented terms. In effect, this representation delineates a value-free zone in which a particular type of economic discourse can flower and the importance of expertise in defining and managing the economy is enshrined. Against this background, the economic bureaucrats reassert themselves as agents of modernization who will steer China beyond its ideological baggage in a rational quest for modernity and international eminence.

Second, over the course of economic reform, agencies have brought on economic bureaucrats with a higher level of professionalization. This is reflected in their educational level, discipline concentration, and insulation from administration turnover. As table 0.1 shows, the shift across generations[32] points unequivocally toward an improved level of educational achievement, as seen in the steady rise in the percentages of both college and graduate degree holders among elite economic bureaucrats. The change in their disciplinary backgrounds is also stark. Economics has decisively replaced engineering as the dominant major for officials' highest degrees. In this regard, the third generation of officials, those who went to college in the reform era, defined the transition. The rising retention rate of ministers and vice ministers in the face of administration changes is another revealing indicator of the growing professional autonomy of the economic bureaucracy. When the Jiang Zemin/Li Peng administration assumed office in 1992, 21.5 percent of the economic ministers and vice ministers from the last administration were retained in their original positions. This rate climbed to 26.6 percent with the beginning of the Hu Jintao/Wen Jiabao administration and to 51 percent with the inauguration of the Xi Jinping/Li Keqiang administration.[33] The last number is especially striking, given the tightened political grip on many other aspects of Chinese government and society under President Xi. It suggests that the ability of the economic bureaucracy to maintain its own continuity in the wake of the rise of powerful political personalities is greater than many have thought. This is not to say that Chinese economic bureaucrats have become professional economists. They are foremost state bureaucrats and often attribute their knowledge to their career experiences and practical understanding of the economy, a far cry from the theory-heavy discipline of academic economics. Yet rising professionalization is still poised to

TABLE 0.1
Educational background and the rotation rate of elite economic bureaucrats

	College degree (%)	Graduate degree (%)	Top major	Minister retention rate (%)
Generation 1	62.5	3.8	Engineering (36.3%)	N/A
Generation 2	86.4	19.7	Engineering (33.3%)	21.5
Generation 3	83.1	53.8	Economics (24.4%)	26.6
Generation 4	92.0	66.0	Economics (32.5%)	51.0

Source: Calculated by the author from officials' CVs.

change the overall quality and orientation of the economic bureaucrats. It raises the entry barriers for newcomers, hardens the boundary between the economic bureaucracy and the rest of the government, and attaches generalized importance to knowledge-based legitimacy.

Third, high uncertainty in China's economic reform attaches importance to idea-based legitimacy in shaping policy outcomes and effecting institutional change. Economic ideas are powerful in moments of uncertainty because they are blueprints that "tell agents what to do and what future to expect." They reduce uncertainty and allow groups of actors to build coalitions around them.[34] The Chinese economic reform is composed of highly nonuniform events wherein China simultaneously pursued the twin agendas of economic restructuring and growth.[35] Institutional adjustments have been conducted with a keen eye toward generating rapid economic development. Using the language of Zhou Xiaochuan, China's long-time engineer-turned-central-banker, what Chinese economic policy makers do to the economy is a form of "online repair" (*zaixian xiufu*); China cannot afford to shut down the computer to fix it, so the economy has to keep running and expanding while institutional surgeries take place.[36] Many transitioning economies in a similar position have come up short on one of the two tasks, making them poor models for China to follow. The lack of an obvious model only adds to the uncertainty.

In addition to an uncertain transitology, China's status as a late and "compressed" developer enlarges the policy space and potentially intensifies the struggle for authority among policy makers. Compressed development introduces a diverse set of challenges for policy makers and enlarges the space for competitive policy making. As soon as the Chinese economy got back on its feet with the initial phase of reform, it forced itself into the rapids of economic globalization. By doing so, China joined other late developers that had to tackle the structural pressures of compressed development,[37] condensing development processes that normally would have been introduced over multiple stages into a short period of time. Compressed development coincides with these late developers' hastened course of integration into the global economy. This means that policy makers could be faced with diverse and sometimes mismatched development needs. For instance, China had to deal with challenges from unfinished industrialization while simultaneously trying to leapfrog in emerging technological domains and locking itself in competition with the most advanced economies. Similarly,

modernizing and protecting domestic manufacturing ran against a con-
current desire to liberalize finance and improve China's standing in global
financial and currency markets.

These complex challenges have decisively pushed economic policy
making beyond merely affirming local experiments (e.g., private-sector
development) or capitalizing on existing endowments (e.g., labor-intensive industries), for which early reform had already been credited. Instead,
intensified compression required creative and correspondingly compressed policy responses, encouraging different personnel with different
ideas to respond to pressures coming from all fronts and to a competition
to determine China's development priorities. As such, compressed challenges have contributed to the widening of the economic policy spectrum
in China. We see that propositions for financial liberalization and arm's-
length macroeconomic adjustment coexist with those for structuralist
management. In a compressed decisional environment, old economic
ideas and tool kits, such as those associated with industrial planning,
were not displaced outright but found their way back to serve new
purposes—market creation and technological development. As a result,
China's economic bureaucracy resembles a living world-historical museum
in which a wide range of modes of economic management can be observed
all at once. An enlarged policy space reduces the odds of consensus
and tends to instigate competition over which mode of management is
most desirable.

The struggle around policy authority has had visible impacts on the
ways in which economic bureaucrats organize their claims. It has carved
out a space for arguments, justifications, and self-promotion that is
uncommon in a nomenklatura system where personnel decisions seem to
be orchestrated top-down in secretive fashion, leaving little room for self-
advocacy. Given the centrality of careers in defining bureaucratic interests,
a substantial part of the struggle for policy authority revolves around cre-
dentialing one's career experiences in light of their usefulness to economic
policy making.[38] Prior work experiences, even those remotely connected
to economic policy, are often explained in terms of how they can be a
source of the knowledge and information needed to manage a national
economy. The cooptation of local generalist knowledge by the economic
bureaucracy is an example of this. Since the 1990s, the economic bureaucracy has recruited a growing number of local generalists to run central

economic affairs.[39] The potency of the economic bureaucracy is evident in its ability to transform localism from a potential centrifugal force into a form of economic statecraft. As soon as they arrived, local generalists swiftly subscribed to the new game in town—vying for policy authority— and made a broad case for how they could bring their local knowledge and connections to bear on crafting policy projects, arguing that they were well suited for efforts such as integrating national markets, restructuring SOEs, or making industrial policies.

MAPPING THE SOCIAL TERRAIN OF CHINA'S ECONOMIC BUREAUCRACY: LOCATIONS, CAREER TRAJECTORIES, AND NETWORKS

To understand the diversity of the lived experiences of bureaucrats and how these experiences inform their organized understanding of the economy, one needs to identify the group dynamics emerging within the bureaucratic state. To this end, the sociological analysis of the state provides a useful starting point for charting the social terrain of the Chinese bureaucracy and its elastic properties. Scholars have shown that states are not monolithic but rather are composed of many functions, organizations, purposes, and projects. Each of these may be sustained by different constellations of actors, organizational histories, and patterns of interaction with constituencies.[40] Metaphorically, it is useful to conceive the state not as a clenched fist but as many hands and fingers that, in grasping different aspects of social reality, may or may not cohere.[41]

In lieu of cohesion, winding bureaucratic histories, factions, and turf wars—factors related to the process of state building itself—may take over and fracture the state.[42] These historical and social lines of cleavage result in different ways of organizing the constellation of bureaucratic practice, affecting what bureaucrats see and do on the job as they collect economic information, assess situations, manage enterprises, mobilize constituencies, travel on inspection tours, write policy articles, and talk to economic actors on the ground. That is, instead of bureaucrats seeing like one state, as Scott suggests, their various lines of experience running through the Chinese state may lead them to see like many states through many lenses. The purpose of my analysis of the bureaucratic state is to identify these lenses that form the social and cognitive infrastructure of the Chinese state.

Overall, I observe that bureaucrats form groups in three ways that cannot be explained by simply appealing to their employing organizations: locations, career trajectories, and networks.

Locations

Location matters.[43] Bureaucratic locations are the positions occupied by bureaucrats from which they observe the economy. Bureaucratic locations affect which parts of the economy they see and what lenses they use. By mobilizing a constellation of epistemic resources and tools for intervention, locations make certain aspects of the economy legible, accessible, and susceptible to government policy. Locational resources include standpoints for observation, means of obtaining data, policy instruments for intervening in and regulating the economy, direct access to certain economic actors, and so on. Occupants of bureaucratic locations draw from these location-specific resources, both tangible and symbolic, to support their claims to a superior understanding of the Chinese economy. Economic policy views, as a result, are framed, enabled, and constrained by these bureaucratic locations.

Organizations can serve as one basis for bureaucratic locations, but locations and organizations are not all coterminous. Locations influence perspectives on the economy at a level that transcends organizational duties. A bundle of organizations can occupy the same location because of their shared relation to the economy. That is, locations can be collective. One group of China's first-generation reformers, for instance, served in disparate agencies in the socialist era, such as the Ministry of Commerce and the Ministry of Finance, but these agencies cohered due to their marginality to the central planning apparatus and their shared understanding of the economy as an integrated system of circulation. Thus, they shared a bureaucratic location that generated sensitivity toward macroeconomic fluctuations and sympathy toward markets that eventually inspired an advocacy for a large-scale market reform. Other examples of locational differences in the state concern, for instance, structuralist versus macroeconomic understandings of the economy and short-term management versus long-term planning. That is, locations are not just organizational points of view but also comprehensive perspectives on the economy.

Career Trajectories

When bureaucrats transfer across the state, they create career trajectories that involve more than one organization or career stage. As the following chapters repeatedly show, bureaucrats develop similar outlooks on the economy when they share career trajectories. Similar career paths indicate that bureaucrats may have occupied structurally equivalent positions in the government and interacted with comparable aspects of the economy in the same period. This combination of location and period effects exposes officials to similar sets of problems and in many cases leads them to gravitate toward similar diagnoses and solutions. For instance, the dysfunctional planned economy in the late half of the Mao period meant that across the nation managers overseeing state factories at the local level were exposed to common problems associated with the lack of supplies. Many managers of these enterprises alleviated shortages by getting around planning and linking up covertly with managers of other factories to exchange resources. On account of this experience, this group of managers-turned-bureaucrats developed a particular approach to the economy, one of thinking about the economy through the structure of interenterprise ties. In cases like this one, officials in equivalent positions stand in silent solidarity, without knowing each other personally, by virtue of their common career experiences. Early career experiences, in particular, have formative impacts on officials, sending them onto certain career tracks and exerting a lasting influence on how they relate to the economy and to their peers.

Shared career trajectories are also unifying experiences because of the similar *sequences* in which bureaucrats move through career phases or positions. This likely results in a convergence of strategies that bureaucrats use to align prior career experiences with their new positions. Using state factory managers again as an example, their shared career sequence—from managing local state factories, to becoming generalist leaders at the provincial level, and, finally, to overseeing the whole nation's industries at the national level—leads to a sequential increase in scale of the linking-up method, first as a provincial-level and then as a national-level development strategy. Lastly, shared career trajectories lead to similar outlooks and coordinated action because officials who have similar career backgrounds are more likely to concentrate in the same organization toward the later part of their careers. Bureaucrats may be promoted in concert with one another by virtue of their similar traits or experiences. The managers-turned-bureaucrats just mentioned were promoted by the vice premier Zhu Rongji to lead a new ministry in the State Council—the State Economic and Trade Commission. Zhu considered their combination of industrial and local experience desirable for overseeing the challenging public-sector reform with which the new agency was charged. In these instances, bureaucrats with similar career experiences had the opportunity to operationalize their policy views in a coordinated fashion with the backing of organizational resources.

Networks

Networking involves individual bureaucrats or agencies building horizontal relationships across the economic bureaucracy. This is considered a novel way of grouping because the rules of the Chinese government discourage liaisons across organizational boundaries. But precisely because the system encourages hierarchies much more than horizontal networks, the network-based structures that do exist often assume irreplaceable functions and reach a considerable level of cohesion. In an environment in which cognitive authority is highly desired, like-minded bureaucrats bonded with each other across organizational alleys to build communities of ideas and influence. As chapter 5 documents, the financial reformers who rose in the 1990s developed from an intellectual network, the Comprehensive Reform School, that formed in the 1980s when these future reformers were researchers at different state think tanks. Through their conferencing, publishing, and advising activities, members of this school created a favorable intellectual climate in the central government for disseminating their *comprehensive* version of economic reform. This network continued to supply solidarity even after the state think-tank researchers became important regulators and ministers in their own right.

Networking can also be a strategy used by ministries to build cross-organizational coalitions. While interministry collaboration coordinated by the State Council is common, it is much less common for such collaboration to be built horizontally, initiated by a ministry in a bid for authority. When ministries' views are not mainstream and their power is fragile, it helps to seek out those who might embrace a similar view or take a sympathetic stance. The Ministry of Industry and Information Technology provides just such a case. In order to claim a footing in the already crowded field of industrial policy, the agency enlisted an array of marginal but sympathetic agencies, striving to create synergies across its newly built policy network. Policy networks can spread beyond the boundary of the state to parastatal or nonstate actors. In the case of the MIIT, this lead agency formed a tripartite network with research institutions and business associations. Nonstate entities provided intellectual and personnel support to the lead government agency and also served as advocates for and implementers of that agency's policies. As a result, through the policy networks the MIIT constructed, the young agency was able to overcome its marginal status and build a policy movement across and outside the state. In this case, networking was an important means to expand ministerial policies into broader policy paradigms.

CROSSING THE RIVER BY FOLLOWING THE PARADIGMS

Locations, career trajectories, and networks are building blocks of the bureaucratic state and its officials' career backgrounds. Yet not all career backgrounds exert the same level of impact. Some career experiences never translate into influential policies. Others spawn only ad hoc or discrete policies that have no far-reaching effects. This book focuses on those policies that are escalated into policy paradigms. *Policy paradigms* are overarching frameworks, principles, and ideas used to characterize problems as well as to guide the search for effective policy responses.[44] Shifts in policy paradigms involve not only the mobilization of new policy instruments but also the reformulation of development goals, often depending on how economic reality is redefined. In the case of China's economic reform, in spite of a general consensus on the importance of investment and growth, major differences loomed over issues related to what type of growth was desirable, what sustainable means were available to achieve growth, how competitiveness should be defined, and how growth should be reconciled with competing goals such as macroeconomic balance, stability, or technological advancement.

In contrast to the narrative that China's economic reform simply "crossed the river by feeling for the stones,"[45] this book shows that Chinese reforms were not as ad hoc as the existing literature suggests. Instead, several major policy currents emerged and carried China's economic reform toward the other bank of the river on currents and cascades built up over time. Table 0.2 reports these paradigms and the timeline of their emergence. The most pronounced shift concerns the genesis of economic reform itself in the late 1970s, which unraveled the planned economy and introduced the market as a major mechanism for allocating resources. The socialist economy did not appear to be collapsing near the end of the Cultural Revolution. The beginning of economic reform was a function of power struggles in the state bureaucracy, and how and where these struggles started were associated with the socialist bureaucrats' ideas about markets. Other paradigm shifts have received less attention and are less frequently recognized as such. Market reform in the 1990s, for instance, profoundly reversed the decentralization approach to market development prevalent in the first decade of reform and reasserted the role of the central state in economic management. This round of state rebuilding and deepening market reform was associated with a technocratic movement in the Chinese state following the 1989 Tiananmen incident and a recognition of the need to advance economics and demobilize politics.

TABLE 0.2
Timeline for the emergence of economic policy paradigms

Period	Paradigm	Driving bureaucrats	Background of bureaucrats	Leading agencies
1978–1989	Decentralization	Circulators, local generalists	Finance and commerce, local governments	State Council Public Finance and Economic Commission, Ministry of Finance, presidents and premiers
1993–present	Recentralization	Central technocrats	Engineering and planning	Entire economic bureaucracy
1993–2002	Interenterprise restructuring	Industrial managers	State factories and local governments	State Economic and Trade Commission
2001–present	Financialization	Financial reformers	State think tanks	Central Bank, Ministry of Finance, development banks
2005–present	Industrial competitiveness	Industrial technocrats	High-tech SOEs and industrial ministries	Ministry of Industry and Information Technology

The centralization paradigm, while resetting the stage for China's economic policy since the mid-1990s, did not preclude other paradigms from ascending under its broad rubric. In the second half of the 1990s, economic reform made inroads into the heart of the socialist economy—the state enterprises. From the heyday of SOE reform there arose a conglomeration approach to improve enterprise efficiency, which eventually became an overarching method for rationalizing industrial structures and managing the macroeconomy. This approach was instituted by the industrial managers who had experience managing local factories in the Mao period and came of age in the 1990s during additional local industrial restructuring. While the state managers understood SOE inefficacy as the result of structural and organizational problems, a group of financial reformers ascended in the same period that understood SOE problems as those of corporate control and financial discipline. They proposed the development of financial markets to enhance the performance of the state sector. They also tackled a series of other issues of this period related to underinvestment and bank restructuring through similar financial mechanisms, which then spread into a general reliance on the use of credit expansion to reformat state assets and public finance. As this financial paradigm began to pick up steam in the mid to late 2000s, the desire to increase China's industrial competitiveness was gathering support in different corners of the state. This movement didn't become paradigmatic until a group of industrial technocrats who were previously scattered by rounds of administrative reforms were able to reclaim their collective voice and a new ministry to push for their agenda. This industrial competitiveness paradigm, as we retrospectively refer to it, not only redefined priorities of economic development for China but also initiated a chain reaction around the world that led to a global revival of industrial policy even at the core of advanced liberal economies.

Existing explanations of policy paradigm shifts maintain that an economic crisis is a necessary trigger. Exogenous shocks delegitimate existing ways of doing things and make room for maverick politicians and alternative ideas.[46] The Chinese case, however, does not fit with this crisis-based explanation. With the possible exception of the recentralization approach, which closely followed the 1989 Tiananmen movement, all other paradigms originated at times when no large-scale crisis was present. Strictly speaking, even the 1989 crisis, which broke out on the economic front in the form of inflation, does not qualify as an exogenous shock; it was rather an internal crisis partially triggered by the policy arrangements of the 1980s. This does not mean that crises are irrelevant. In fact, talk of crises is prevalent in the bureaucratic discourse on the economy. Yet whether economic problems are defined as crises is routinely subject to how policy makers interpret and present them. Chinese bureaucrats only selectively problematized some parts of the economy, made contingent connections between policy issues, and responded to some structural pressures instead of others. Even when facing the same problem, such as SOE inefficiency, the organizational and the financial approaches to public-sector restructuring, for example, offered different conceptualizations of the problem and proposed very different solutions.

This quick walk-through shows that the development of new paradigms is predetermined by structural shifts in the economy. Paradigm formation is an evolutionary and endogenous process in which new solutions and new careers bubble up into large-scale policy changes. How exactly do changes in career patterns scale up into paradigmatic changes in policies? This book shows that this leap depends on social movement–like bureaucratic entrepreneurship waged through key conflicts and opportunities for regrouping.[47] As the following chapters demonstrate in detail, policy paradigms are actively shaped and mediated by bureaucrats who act as powerful filters between the economic context and actual policies.[48] The formation of a new paradigm often takes a decade or two and is associated with the maturation of new groups of bureaucrats and their entrepreneurial efforts to advance policy approaches. The key junctures that move ideas into action and then action into paradigmatic influence involve instances of "emergence," in which shared career experiences are translated into collective action as bureaucratic groups seize organizational platforms, build coalitions, and project influence across more than one policy domain. That is, shared career backgrounds may have predisposed bureaucrats to cohere, but the articulation of an agenda depends on movement-making strategies to clear a path, animate interest, and engineer a favorable environment. This process is deeply collective, social, and often novel. In this process, career making and policy making are intertwined: Chinese bureaucrats build careers by making influential policies, and vice versa.

While the emergence of each paradigm is not exactly the same, they share similar patterns that warrant synthesis into a heuristic model. Next

TABLE 0.3
Pattern and stages in policy paradigm emergence

Convergence	Concentration	Expansion
Career experiences	Seizing organizations	Paradigm forms
• Locations		• Spanning policy domains
• Trajectories		• Localization of policy
• Networks		• Central leadership support
↓	↓	
Bureaucratic groups	Developing initiatives	

I summarize the stages of progression: what I term stages of *convergence*, *concentration*, and *expansion*. As Table 0.3 shows, the first stage, convergence, involves the alignment of novel social elements—new locations, career trajectories, and networks—to form bureaucratic collectivities. In the second stage, concentration, bureaucrats seize an organizational platform to advance their key initiatives. In the third stage, expansion, the moments of paradigm formation are defined. Signs that policies have obtained paradigmatic status include the growth of programmatic initiatives in one policy domain into an approach to economic development that affects multiple policy domains, the explicit support of central leaders for further expansion of the approach, and the incorporation of the approach into local development agendas by local governments. Although not every paradigm contains all three evenly developed stages, often shortening certain stages and lengthening others, in general this pattern is widely observed, signaling what it takes to build long-lasting policy influence in the institutional environment in which the Chinese economic bureaucrats find themselves.

DATA AND METHODOLOGY

This book employs an actor-based analysis to study state bureaucracy. This perspective is premised on the suppositions that bureaucrats have agency to actively shape state organizations in their favor and that the interests and perspectives of the state and its bureaucrats are not always interchangeable.[49] Focusing on bureaucrats makes it possible to attend meticulously to transformative periods when they made and remade the state. This has the explanatory advantage of detecting undercurrents within bureaucratic organizations and revealing how they operate in practice beneath their structured appearance. Following the footsteps and biographies of bureaucrats provides distinctive access to the Chinese state, exposing what is otherwise hidden in a black box, shielded behind stern faces, or distorted in rhetorical strictures. It foregrounds processes in which bureaucrats breathed new life into state agencies with their ideas, experiences, aspirations, and self-interest. This array of information would be easily lost if organizations were taken as explanatory starting points.

Focusing on bureaucrats allows for the possibility that the interests and views of Chinese officials are not always in accord with the interests of the state. Some swaths of Chinese bureaucrats started in government positions closer to society and didn't always identify with the technocratic mission of the central state. A broad identification with the state, as this book shows, can also take on a variety of meanings and needs to be unpacked to appreciate which parts of the state are being invoked. Appeals to the interests of "the state" or "the people" are commonplace in official rhetoric. Questions remain as to what represents the state economically, what forms of state intervention are advocated, and how the investigation of these questions reveals the particularities of bureaucratic motivations. Precisely because the Chinese state is constantly being made and remade by state actors, it is seldom a centrally programmed and well-coordinated machine. Its internal heterogeneity begs for analytical disaggregation of the state in order to better understand its many constitutive and moving parts. This book pursues such disaggregation by examining state actors and their connections and shared courses of action.

An agency-based approach guided my collection of materials. A core component of my data is a biographical database I constructed for elite-level economic bureaucrats, consisting of 281 individuals and based on the CVs of all economic bureaucrats ranked at the vice minister level or above in the reform period. It offers consistent biographical information on each individual— the birth year and place, schools attended, disciplines majored in, positions held, and time spent in each position. The majority of the officials' CVs are publicly available. When these were truncated or missing data, I pieced the information together from local chronicles, news reports of officials' activities, and memoirs. I applied basic statistical analysis to this data set to obtain an overview of bureaucratic careers, identify emergent career patterns, and track variations in educational credentials and career paths across generations, organizations, and policy domains. I also used network analyses to track how individuals moved across organizations throughout their careers. In this way, I obtained an agentic representation of interorganizational networks, which provides insights into the structure of the economic bureaucracy. The network method is applied to identify social circles such as coauthorship networks.

My interviews of Chinese officials provided access to stories and thought processes unobtainable through published records. I conducted forty-three unstructured interviews with officials at or below the vice minister ranking. Obtaining access to interview Chinese officials is notoriously difficult in a gated officialdom. My extensive fieldwork in Beijing provided hard-won and sometimes unexpected interview opportunities, an undertaking that warrants a sociological analysis of its own. Policy journal articles, of which I read more than two hundred, were another source of semiofficial or even unofficial information. Thanks to the lingering scholarly-official tradition, in which officials consider polished literary and intellectual skills an embodiment of personal qualities and a useful boost to their policy authority, economic bureaucrats publish extensively in policy-oriented and quasi-academic journals. Some of these publications offer rare glimpses of their personal views and, in some instances, detailed explanations of the rationales behind these views. I supplemented this array of information with chronologies, biographies, autobiographies, memoirs, diaries, and news reports of officials' activities that reveal streams of bureaucratic practices—that is, what officials did and what they said. Seemingly mundane activities, including to whom they talked and where they visited, sometimes convey unspoken messages about the kind of personnel and policies they endorsed and where their networks and partnerships could be found. This array of backstage information was then paired with the analysis of hundreds of "frontstage" products—decrees, directives, regulations, plans, government reports, public speeches, etc., mostly obtained from Wanfang Laws and Regulations Database—in an effort to make connections between the backstage production of policy views and regular practices and the final policy outputs. Equally important, all actions were examined in relation to those of competing groups of bureaucrats and to efforts that failed. Alternative lines of bureaucratic action served as counterfactuals, highlighting differences between successful and unsuccessful attempts and helping to explain why particular career trajectories and their associated policy formations prevailed.

AN OUTLINE OF THIS BOOK

This book is divided into three parts with a total of six chapters, followed by a conclusion. Each of the three parts seeks to capture a distinguishable phase in the course of China's economic reform wherein new policy paradigms emerged and the economic bureaucracy was reconfigured as a result. Part I, "Genesis," addresses the origin of China's economic reform and its association with bureaucratic experiences in the socialist era. This part comes to terms with the fact that China's economic reform was led by bureaucratic incumbents who were well entrenched in high-ranking positions in the socialist government. It shows that the way in which bureaucrats ran the socialist economy significantly informed their ideas about how to build markets. More than one group of bureaucrats was able to envision alternatives to central planning, nurturing these ideas on the margins of the planning-industrial core. To the extent that these unorthodox career experiences already differed in the socialist period, these differences carried over into the reform period and escalated into conflicts about how to approach market reform. Interbureaucratic competition in this period significantly shaped the dynamics of the reform government.

Specifically, chapter 1 identifies a key group of reformers who served in the central economic bureaucracy in the socialist era, those I term the *circulators*. They held positions in finance- and commerce-related agencies in the planning machine and conceived of the socialist economy in terms of movements of goods, credit, budgets, etc. The circulation perspective allowed these central bureaucrats to identify macroeconomic vulnerabilities in the socialist economy, convincing them of the usefulness of market forces and central regulation for correcting systemic "imbalances." Chapter 2 continues to show the potency of socialist careers in shaping the direction of China's economic reform by focusing on the transitory alliance between the circulators and a second group of incumbent reformers—the *local generalists*. The local generalists derived their reform capital from social proximity with local producers and an allegedly intimate understanding of hidden incentives in the Chinese economy. This microperspective on the economy informed a growth-centered approach to reform based on decentralizing economic decision-making and government authority. This approach clashed with the circulators' macrolevel concern for balance and fiscal prudence. Yet inattention to institution building by both reform camps gave a factionalist appearance to policy agreements in this period. Eventually, the local generalists' toleration of inflation and the Tiananmen movement shortened their political lives and led to a chilling period of retrenchment.

Part II, "Consolidation," characterizes the technocratic era, the 1990s, which saw a significant reordering of state-market relations. A new force arrived on the political landscape in this era, a generation of *technocrats* with engineering degrees and a commitment to push China further toward a market order. Their goals of installing market efficiency and administrative rationality significantly altered the playing field of the economic bureaucracy. While market building undermined the dominance of the State Planning Commission and opened up space needed for other ministries and modes of economic management to flourish, state building simultaneously armed those ambitious bidders with newfound resources and authority, leading to the ascendance of the ministries. As a result, centralized technocraticism breathed new life into the economic bureaucracy, turned it into a contested zone of power and ideas, and increased the ability of the central economic bureaucracy to absorb local interests and knowledge into forms of economic statecraft.

Concretely speaking, chapter 3 explores the connections between the engineering backgrounds of those in the post-Tiananmen administration and their technocratic approach to politics and the economy. The role of Zhu Rongji and his cabinet was especially central in demobilizing politics and instituting a panoply of measures—fiscal, monetary, and regulatory—to rebuild the central state in the service of liberalizing markets while controlling political and macroeconomic risks. Under the umbrella of this administration, economic bureaucrats who had previously been state factory managers ascended through the ranks, bringing with them an organizational approach to economic reform. They are the subjects of chapter 4. I show that the amalgamation of their managerial experience in state factories and their generalist experiences in local governments led them to use methods of interenterprise and interregional integration to reorganize the economic structure. This organizational approach was first employed to reform the ailing state sector by merging SOEs and constructing conglomerates. This approach was then extended to other policy domains—importantly, macroeconomic management—allowing this group of bureaucrats to build their ministry, the State Economic and Trade Commission, into a versatile organization with sprawling regulatory and managerial power, on par with the State Planning Commission.

After a decade of renewed state centralization, the economic bureaucracy was in a much stronger position to govern the economy. Power began to shift decisively away from localities and back to the central state at the dawn of the twenty-first century. In the process, this more potent economic bureaucracy became increasingly internally incoherent and competitive. Part III, "Effervescence," examines this transformative stage. As the central economic bureaucracy gained power over localities and authority over the economy, various groups of bureaucrats, then maturing in diverse career trajectories, came of age and looked to advance their policy visions and bid for ministerial power.

Chapters 5 and 6 investigate two distinct policy approaches—financialization and industrial competitiveness—that are often considered incompatible with one another in other development settings. Chapter 5 focuses on the emergence of the financial approach to economic management. This approach defined economic efficiency in financial terms and devised a range of financial solutions to solve governance problems. I show that the origin of this paradigm is associated with the development of a joint force of two intellectual movements in the research wings of the economic bureaucracy—the Wudaokou and the Comprehensive Reform Schools. Their influence grew as they developed credit-based solutions to solve problems related to public revenue constraints. Through overlapping career paths and networks, this new generation of financial reformers was able to mount a collective takeover of ministry-level positions in key agencies such as the Ministry of Finance and the Central Bank, significantly revamping the ways in which public revenues, state ownership, and local development were financed. Chapter 6 analyzes the causes and processes that led to the emergence of a completely different agenda from that of financialization. The industrial competitiveness approach to development defined a country's economic might in terms of the quality of its manufacturing sectors. I explain that the late recognition of the centrality of this agenda was related to the absence of bureaucratic forces that could acquire autonomy and jurisdiction for industrial policy.

The qualitative shift happened when bureaucrats with similar backgrounds in high-tech sectors concentrated in a new industrial policy agency, the Ministry of Industry and Information Technology, and fused their policy thinking with the new agency's ambition to establish a footing in the emergent and competitive field of industrial policy.

The conclusion of this book synthesizes major arguments and distills latent but important themes that gain clarity in retrospect. These are issues regarding the relationship between the state actors and the state, the pragmatic use of markets to achieve bureaucratic goals, and the filtered influence of global forces and ideas on China's decision makers. The conclusion addresses a host of timely issues confronting China related to the rise of political charisma and the inward turning of national economies in what appears to be a deglobalizing age. It discusses the way in which these developments will challenge and substantiate the bureaucracy-based explanation of policy change I propose in this book. I submit that the role of Chinese bureaucrats remains important in shaping the rise of China in a profoundly changed geopolitical environment.

PART I

Genesis

THE SOCIALIST CIRCULATORS AND THE BUREAUCRATIC ORIGIN OF CHINA'S ECONOMIC REFORM

In late 1978, following the death of Mao Zedong and the fall of the Gang of Four, the Third Plenum of the Eleventh Central Committee of the Chinese Communist Party installed a new slate of leaders, officially kicking off a new era in the history of the People's Republic of China (PRC) known as Economic Reform and Opening Up. A casual glance at the leadership of the reform government belies the conventional characterization of China's economic reform as a drastic change. The composition of political elites showed a remarkable continuity, rather than rupture, with the leaders of the socialist era. Notably, key economic bureaucrats responsible for building the command economy in the socialist era were among the avid supporters and key architects of market reform. Those in the top stratum of Deng Xiaoping's reform government who were in charge of economic policies were, without exception, holdovers from the Mao era. Continuity was also prevalent at the minister level of the economic bureaucracy. More than 70 percent of such elite bureaucrats were kept on in the same positions and in the same agencies through this epic transition. In particular, agencies related to finance, banking, and commerce saw the least turnover.[1] As scholars of post-Communist studies have noted, the transition of China (as well as that of Vietnam) is an outlier when compared with the transitions of other post-Communist countries because China's central bureaucracy retained a political monopoly on initiating economic reforms.[2] While the *effect* of reform without regime change has been thoroughly examined in the literature, questions as to why and how the erstwhile socialist bureaucrats initiated reform and where their reformist ideas came from remain underexplored.

This chapter tackles head-on the question of reform's origin. It identifies the specific group of incumbent officials who altered the course of socialism and examines the specific trajectories by which they arrived at reformism. Featured are three types of bureaucratic elites in the Mao era. The first group, whom I call the *circulators*, is represented by Chen Yun, vice president and director of the Financial-Economic Committee of the State Council in the reform era and once vice premier, minister of commerce, and director of the Financial-Economic Commission in the Mao era; Li Xiannian, vice president and vice director of the Financial-Economic Committee of the State Council in the reform era and once vice premier and minister of finance in the Mao era; and Yao Yilin, vice president and director of the State Planning Commission in the reform era and once minister of commerce in the Mao era. I find that this group of socialist reformers did not simply change their beliefs to "go with the flow," nor were they secret liberals all along, waiting for the right moment to throw off their camouflage. Instead, they were officials whose duties positioned them on the margins of the planning machine, where they developed alternative views of the socialist economy. Their initial argument for incorporating the role of the market was that it would make socialism more effective and responsive to pragmatic tasks related to state building.

The second group featured in the chapter is the planning-industry officials who controlled the central planning apparatus and its heavy-industry arms. Their authority peaked when the five-year plan was honored and carried through. The third group is the Maoist radicals, who were a mixed bag of central generalist officials, local leaders, and cultural officials. They were not economic specialists but nevertheless attempted to make claims to economic policy authority. They mounted populist challenges to the bureaucratic state and fortified the circulators' determination to reform the economy.

EXPLAINING THE ORIGIN OF CHINA'S ECONOMIC REFORM

Even reform led by incumbent elites who are attempting to prolong or reassert their power can bring economic, political, and social changes comparable in scale to those of outright revolution. China's economic reform is a case in point. It altered the criteria defining political legitimacy and social well-being; it transformed the ways in which the Chinese people organized their lives, families, careers, and communities; and it changed the valuation of many moral and intellectual goods in public life, including the importance of loyalty and scientific knowledge. When incumbent elites engineer such large-scale changes, it is hard to imagine that these elites were excluded from the deliberation process or that they failed to undergo change themselves. Understanding elite self-transformation is key to understanding the origins of elite-led reform.

Existing accounts of how and why elites chose reform are insightful but have their shortcomings. They excel at explaining the reform's environmental impetus but downplay the question of elite self-transformation. One explanation advanced by scholars focuses on the political environment and interelite dynamics.[3] It argues that, toward the end of the Cultural Revolution, the impossibility of reaching a reconciliation between Deng's faction and the Gang of Four and their supporters resulted in a life-or-death struggle between the two groups, compelling Deng's faction to push for policies diametrically opposed to those of the radical leftists. In this politics-centered explanation, economic thinking was a by-product of political competition.

Another explanation views the decision to reform as overdetermined by economic causes.[4] Scholarship in this vein points out that China suffered from a range of structural weaknesses that rendered Soviet-style planning much less feasible on Chinese soil. These innate shortcomings included the low point from which China would begin development, weak administrative capacity, scanty stocks of human skills, varied geography, and diverse local industrial structures. As a result, many chronic ills associated with the command economy, such as shortages of basic consumer commodities and missteps in material balance planning, had exaggerated consequences in China.[5] Viewed in this light, economic reformers were simply correcting the course of wrongheaded policies that were doomed to fail. In other words, the reformers were agents of structural economic determinants.

Both the political and the economic explanations highlight some of the structural pressures that the elites faced, but both fall short of discussing exactly how elites responded to these pressures and factored them into their own political concerns and intellectual comprehension. Instead, both explanations treat Chinese elites as "born-again" reformers who were converted to the reform cause with relative ease. We are left in the dark about where these new economic ideas originated.

The question of the source of elite self-transformation in China has remained a puzzle. Chinese reformers were deeply entrenched in the socialist regime, which also meant they were hermetically sealed off from most international influences. They had been the revolutionary founders and managers of the socialist economy, and their immersion in that social-ist economy was made more complete by the autarkic nature of the Chi-nese geopolitical economy. The country was basically shut off from foreign trade, capital, and ideas for most of the PRC's early period, limiting the Chinese bureaucrats' exposure to outside policy environments. Following the Sino-Soviet split in 1960, China became even more isolated. Beginning in the mid-1960s, however, it developed a rapport with the United States and other Western countries that caused a geopolitical reorientation of the Chinese leadership. Yet at that point, diplomatic ties with these countries resulted in hardly any concrete guidance on how to turn around the social-ist economy, to which Chinese elites remained committed. In short, without identifying the sociological conditions that enabled the decision makers to develop transformative outlooks and engage in strategic reconsiderations, we risk missing the opportunity to move beyond the demise of state social-ism to explain why economic reform took place in the ways it did. Deter-mining the origin of China's economic reform boils down to discovering how that reform was associated with the ways in which the incumbents experienced the socialist economy, its bureaucracy, and its politics.

CURRENCY STRUGGLES AND THE MAKING OF THE COMMUNIST ECONOMIC SPECIALISTS

The founding experiences of a regime often leave a long-lasting imprint on the configuration of the new government. My first analytical step is to trace the source of personnel in China's fledgling economic bureau-cracy during its founding period as well as the circumstances in which the first groups of economic bureaucrats came into existence. As the PRC rose through revolution and war, its founders were largely revolutionaries and generals. They earned their credentials in the field and were general-ists not yet wedded to particular aspects of government work. This found-ing circumstance impacted the knowledge portfolio of the PRC's new government and depressed its degrees of specialization and "expertness." Where economic policies are concerned, some scholars contend that it was the Communist Party's pre-1949 revolutionary experiences and guerrilla-style warfare that exerted oversized influence on its approaches to economic governance for decades to come. In particular, the party's ability to adapt to changing economic environments and adopt impromptu governance methods to fit local conditions harkens back to the early political and military experiences of the party, which were passed down through multiple generations of officials and became an institutional tradition.[6]

While it is worth pursuing the question of how noneconomic traditions influenced the parameters of China's economic policies, this chapter draws attention to an overlooked line of bureaucratic development that was at least equally consequential. Economic specialization took place early on within the party and had both immediate and far-reaching consequences for the new government. In a sea of generalists, a group of economic specialists emerged in the late 1930s. Certainly, the "economic specialists" in this case did not hold degrees in economics. Formal education in general was a luxury, given the low literacy rate of the population and the largely peasant origin of the party. Even if begun, education tended to be disrupted by active participation in the revolution. Rather, economic specialization in this context means a concentration of work experiences in financial and economic work (*caijing gongzuo*) whereby bureaucrats learned on the job and developed formative understandings of the economy. Because this financial and economic work was deeply tied to the party's immediate objective at the time—to support territorial consolidation and the construction of a new state—the early cultivation of economic expertise was geared toward meeting subsequent military and political needs. Therefore, analytically, it is essential to pay attention to how the development of economic expertise coevolved with the exigencies of state building.

Curiously, in spite of their aspiration to build a socialist China, the first economic specialists were not planners. They were market builders and "money doctors" and had operated for many years in an economic environment that remained a market or semimarket economy, having not yet undergone Communist reconstruction. In this environment, territorial consolidation could not happen without market integration and some centralized forms of macroeconomic control. In addition, the Communist Party inherited a war-torn economy, rampant with competing monetary regimes, runaway inflation, and fragmented markets, all of which boded ill for achieving even a minimum degree of political centralization. The construction of the new state required that the party drive out contesting monetary claims, exercise some forms of financial centralization, and stem inflation. In addition, as the Communists were still fighting to expand the frontiers of the areas they controlled, resources needed to be extracted and channeled from "liberated areas" to the battlefields. Yet the Communists up to this point had limited means of extraction at their disposal. They could neither resort to an extensive system of taxation, which was yet to be established in the territories they had seized, nor fully control bases of industrial production. The only option left was monetary in nature: the party needed to swiftly establish a widely accepted, stable currency to drive out other monetary claims over resources and in this way establish the purchasing power of the new regime.[7] Restoring monetary order would address two urgent purposes simultaneously: stabilizing the economy and seizing control of resources. Thus, those who came to specialize in economic affairs needed to become self-taught money doctors.

Prior to the establishment of a central government, the field governments in regions controlled by the party functioned as proving grounds where the economic specialists' effectiveness at restoring monetary order could be observed and compared. Across the five regions the Communists seized, the new field governments faced similar challenges, which they identified as the "currency struggles."[8] Moneys issued by Japan and the Chinese Nationalists continued to flood the Communist-controlled areas. The conversion of these paper currencies into resources caused the exodus of supplies and undermined Communist efforts to support continuing battles on the frontiers. The influx of paper money also caused the monetary supply to soar and prices to inflate, leading to a sharp decline in standards of living and widespread complaints. If left unaddressed, economic chaos and popular grievance would certainly threaten the credibility of the new government.

Now facing similar problems, those who had excelled at stabilizing regional economies and restoring market activities quickly established their reputations as economic experts in the party. Chen Yun and Xue Muqiao stood out for their work in the northeastern and northern regions, respectively. At regular intervals, they both carefully sampled the quantities of key commodities and paper currency in circulation in the markets to see how the two compared. To stabilize the value of the Communist-issued money, they issued bank notes and backed them with physical resources possessed by the government, such as grain, cotton, cloth, and peanuts. They were ready to sell off these resources to withdraw currency from circulation if prices rose and to buy more resources to add currency to circulation if prices dropped.[9] A series of monetary operations like this gradually established the creditworthiness of the Communist-issued money, stabilized prices, and eventually drove out competing currencies.

This maneuvering was unlikely to have been the result of studying economics textbooks or foreign models. As Xue explained, the discovery of monetary rules of thumb was a product of firsthand observations and calculation,[10] for the prevailing global norms associated with monetary regulation had been developed in the context of a gold standard and provided little guidance for managing a fiat money that was backed by neither specie nor foreign currency. The primitive nature of the Chinese local economies in the 1940s made it easier to track the price movements of key commodities. The more relevant point here is that the discovery of what resembled monetarism, which Milton Friedman would formulate two decades later, had a formative impact on how this group of economic specialists thought about public finance. It heightened their sensitivity toward inflation and led them to believe monetary oversupply was invariably a grave hazard.

Following the establishment of the central government in Beijing, the regional economic specialists who ascended through the currency struggles formed a critical pool from which central economic bureaucrats were drawn. For his outstanding work in stabilizing the northeastern regional economy, Chen Yun was widely acknowledged to be the supreme economic expert and the helmsman of the economic bureaucracy. Joined by Jia Tuofu from the northwestern field government, Zeng Shan from the eastern, Li Fuchun and Ye Jizhuang from the northeastern, and Xue Muqiao from the northern, Chen put together the Central Financial-Economic Commission (Central FEC) to centralize finance and economic policy making at the national level. Chen's team was put to immediate use, as inflation and financial speculation continued to plague the coastal areas—the economic powerhouse of the nation. Commercial centers like Shanghai were hardhit and closely watched by skeptics to see whether the Communists would be up to the task of repairing the economy after their military triumph. Domestic and international political rivals raised widespread doubt about the Communist Party's ability to run a peacetime economy.

For the regional-turned-national economic managers, previous experience integrating local economies proved to be instrumental in stabilizing the economy at the national level. To fend off financial speculation fanned by the domestic capitalists who were resisting Communist rule, Chen and his Central FEC again tethered the circulation of renminbi to major commodities controlled by the government. In Shanghai, where the force of speculative capital was most powerful, they stockpiled and tracked the circulation of "two whites (rice and cotton) and one black (coal)," the three essential goods found to have systemic importance in the market in Shanghai.[11] They also didn't shy away from utilizing newly established state-owned trading firms as hubs for accumulating reserves and creating channels of distribution in order to strategically sell and buy these major commodities. In the face of pervasive suspicion, Chen's team succeeded in unifying financial management, curbing inflation, and saving an economy on the brink of collapse. With this major economic victory, the economic specialists awed the regime's doubters and impressed their fellow Communists, including Mao himself.[12] They swiftly established their specialist reputation among the generalist majority within the party. The tireless recounting of this segment of history in almost every memoir by those who participated in this economic battle reveals the foundational importance of the experience in forming their identity.[13] Further, they emphasized with pride that their methods were mostly market oriented rather than political. This difference set their efforts apart from the later policy practices of the planning-industry officials, who relied on administrative means to control the economy.

MARKET STIMULATION AND STATE-BUILDING PRAGMATISM

With the macroeconomy stabilized, broader issues thrust themselves onto the table of the economic managers: taxes needed to be raised, credits allocated, and markets integrated on a national scale. These action items were indispensable to promoting a vibrant national economy and establishing the fiscal foundation of the central government. The imperative of raising government revenues as expeditiously as possible to ensure the basic capacity of the new state led the economic specialists to adopt a pragmatic attitude toward the relationship between socialism and markets. While the party generalists were in a hurry to fulfill the promise of a socialist revolution by taking over private commerce and nationalizing industries, the economic specialists recognized the importance of stimulating the market to maintain a high level of economic activity so that jobs would be created and tax revenues would grow and flow to the new government.[14]

One year into the socialist transformation, the private sector was already struggling to make profits in a market space increasingly squeezed by state-owned firms. Inventories accumulated, factories shut down, and urban unemployment shot up, all of which threatened the health of the economy and jeopardized government revenues. To breathe new life into the economy, the economic specialists attempted to build markets that would benefit both the private firms and the growing state sector. They used state contracting to private business to stimulate demand and sought to form markets by reviving trading relationships between disconnected regions.[15] This latter policy idea has a biographical origin. It stemmed from the specialists' years as regional economic managers, where they noted that wars and political turbulence had, regrettably, disrupted the age-old commercial ties between towns and the countryside.[16] To restore urban-rural exchanges, the national economic managers encouraged the production of cash crops, nonstaple foods, and other subsidiary products in the countryside and helped farmers connect with urban buyers through commercial brokers and government procurement officials.[17] The growing money income of peasants in turn increased the demand for industrial products and revitalized the ailing private urban factories.[18]

To the economic specialists, market revitalization was a necessary means to bump up economic output and build the new state. It was by no means a sign of their acceptance of the market as a chief organizing principle of the economy. Instead, building markets was meant to be pragmatic—to facilitate an organic integration of national territories and encourage taxable economic activities. The bottom line for the specialists was that leaving productive capacity idle was a waste in an economy already defined by scarcity and poverty, regardless of the ownership status of those underutilized capacities. The specialists had neither the intention nor the power to halt the project of nationalization that had already begun in earnest. In fact, subsequent history shows that this early scramble to build the state and revive the economy proved to be brief—at most, a transitional stage that would end as soon as its original objectives were fulfilled. As the fiscal condition of the new state improved, finance was centralized and the macroeconomic situation stabilized. The socialist transformation from markets to central planning proceeded faster than anticipated, facilitating the rapid rise of the planners and heavy-industry officials.[19]

Yet the early period of state building was preserved in the career experiences of a generation of economic specialists. It proved to be a formative and fundamental moment, providing these specialists with tangible and intangible career outcomes. Their early success in handling financial and economic work earned them a set of finance-related positions in the new administration, covering the policy areas of commerce, public finance, and macroeconomic regulation. These official posts granted them formal authority and a range of policy tools with which to regulate the macroeconomy. Other payoffs were less visible at this point. These included reformist credentials, which proved to be valuable and on which they could capitalize as soon as opportunities arose. Their experience with finance work in the period immediately before and after the founding of the PRC accorded them unplanned exposure to market environments. This window of exposure promptly closed for other economic bureaucrats, as the Chinese economy rapidly became a command economy. As China launched its market reform in the late 1970s, knowing how to work with the market, not against it, was an important qualifier for economic leadership.

Another intangible career asset was that this transitional period in the run-up to the installation of a full-scale socialist economy served as a development model for a mixed economy in its own right.[20] As the need for reforming the socialist economy was widely acknowledged, this group of economic specialists reimagined this period as a historical experiment worthy of reference. It became an example of how to create a new type of economy different from either a laissez-faire market or central planning.

THE CIRCULATION PERSPECTIVE ON THE SOCIALIST ECONOMY

Certainly, assuming finance-related positions did not insulate the economic specialists from central planning. Public finance, banking, and commerce were supposed to be incorporated into the five-year plan and the plan's provisions properly implemented. That being said, these policy areas supplied those who oversaw them with a different vantage point from which to understand the socialist economy—what I term a perspective of *circulation.* This perspective was markedly different from that of the planners, who were mainly concerned with issues of investment, extraction, and accumulation. Commerce work, for instance, in its attempt to substitute central coordination for market mechanisms in allocating goods, was nevertheless concerned with creating horizontal exchange relationships between regions and sectors. This line of policy is very different from the top-down allocation of goods and materials in central planning per se. Public finance became another policy ground for honing circulation thinking, even granted its strong distributive aspect and its hierarchical mechanisms. Yet tax collection and budget redistribution in essence involved the conversion of resources into monetary metrics and therefore were inevitably tied to the circulation of money and credit in the economy. Thus, financial and economic work allowed bureaucrats to see the flows in the economy in both material and monetary terms. This way of perceiving the economy was very different from a focus on the pockets and reservoirs of accumulation revolving around large heavy-industry projects.

The larger implication of the circulation perspective is that, through it, the circulators cast the entire economy in a different light—as essentially a connected and interdependent system. As a result, they asked a different set of questions than did the planners or the heavy-industry managers; the circulators wanted to know how the circulation of money and the circulation of goods were interconnected, how the supply of raw materials was linked to final economic output, how production and consumption were related to each other, and how financial flows constrained material flows, to give a few examples. Yao Yilin, the minister of commerce, maintained that the inventories held at the Commerce Department were a barometer of economic health.[21] He observed that whenever basic construction projects expanded, workers' wages rose, or agricultural loans were extended, these inventories dropped, raising the risk of shortages in consumer goods. State budgeters gravitated toward a similarly holistic understanding of the economy. Although budgeting was a fiscal instrument of the five-year plan, any imprudent budgeting and deficit spending would trigger inflation and shortages, eventually plucking the nerves of the entire economy and undermining the feasibility of material planning. Li Xiannian, the minister of finance and one of the key circulators, was keenly aware of how this distinctive perspective had honed a collective disposition among the circulators. In a self-mocking tone mixed with a hint of pride and self-defense, Li confessed: "Those of us who do finance and commerce work tend to see more problems and difficulties. [This is because] we look at things from the perspective of distribution and circulation and feel that there are many difficulties facing us. This could be our own 'occupational hazard.'"[22]

The planners and heavy-industry officials had the privilege of focusing on large construction and capital projects and requested that the rest of the bureaucratic apparatus concentrate on capital accumulation. The circulators, however, played the role of night watchmen, on constant lookout for the fiscal and macroeconomic impacts these large undertakings had on the rest of the economy. They dubbed any mismatch between constitutive parts of the economy caused by the five-year plan as a symptom of "imbalance," reflected in telling signs such as budget deficits, investment overgrowth, and shortages in raw materials and consumer goods. All of the symptoms simmered in the 1950s during the rushed implementation of the first five-year plan.[23] By offering this diagnosis, the circulators implicitly appealed to some sort of inviolable and objective law to which a balanced economy would have to adhere and to which the circulators had unique access due to their positions.

To achieve balance, the circulators developed a set of policies that could put the circulation perspective into practice. They needed to revitalize sectors or segments of the economy that were suppressed by an accumulation-based economy. Consumption, for example, was long held down. To the circulators, increasing consumption was vital for raising fiscal revenues and stimulating production. Relatedly, the underdevelopment of agricultural markets, as Li pointed out, failed to incentivize peasants to grow economic crops and produce for markets. As a result, these underdeveloped markets failed to generate demand for light-industry products that would be used in agricultural production and eventually resulted in an under-realized purchasing power of the peasants.[24] Small shops and peddlers made up still another area that had yet to be developed. These seemingly insignificant "private" sectors, made illegal in 1956, could act as tentacles and outposts of the circulation system that the Ministry of Commerce was trying to design. Small-scale markets could serve remote rural areas that the formal system could not reach.[25] In sum, the circulators were adamant about the newfound role they could play in the socialist economy, which was to develop light industries, agricultural products, and consumer markets to reinvigorate and balance the economy.

MARGINALITY AND GROUP COHESION IN PRESERVING
BUREAUCRATIC EXISTENCE

To the chagrin of the circulators, their remedial proposals to balance the economy were never fully incorporated into the management of the planned economy. To the contrary, even the mere preservation of the circulation perspective required tremendous effort. China's central planning was modeled on the Soviet system and left little flexibility to develop consumption and incorporate the presence of market mechanisms. As a later and poorer developer than the Soviet Union but also one with an outsized ambition to catch up, China tolerated an even larger share of heavy industry in its economic output than did the Soviets, squeezing even more tightly the margin for improving the living standards of the population.[26] As a result, consumer-goods shortages turned out to be more severe in China. Ideologically, Chinese Marxism attached far more importance to transforming means of relations than to improving productive forces in economic development. This belief rendered the Chinese Marxists unsympathetic to the circulators' pragmatic attitude toward increasing government revenues, stimulating market demands, and stabilizing the macroeconomy for productive gains. Instead, the Chinese Marxists criticized the circulators for being antisocialist. In short, neither the prevailing development focus nor the dominant political ideologies supported the circulators' propositions.

Against such odds, the circulators worked to maintain their bureaucratic existence and prevent their perspectives and bases of expertise from being completely absorbed into the hegemony of planning. The Ministry of Commerce (MOC) provides a good example of institutional self-preservation. The MOC occupied an awkward position in the socialist economy. On the one hand, the population often blamed it for goods shortages, as resource allocations were strongly biased toward heavy industry and against light industries and the consumption sectors. The MOC was left scrambling to procure materials from factories and handicraft workshops for consumer-goods production and was often unable to meet its targets. On the other hand, the planners did not perceive shortages to be a problem and lacked incentives to address the issue. They saw shortages as evidence of the superiority of the socialist economy, a sign of the people's robust purchasing power that required no structural remedies. Shortages could even be seen as a cause for celebration. Having failed to sway the planners, Yao Yilin, the commerce minister, insisted on keeping two books going forward: one for industry and the other specifically for commerce. In the book for commerce, the MOC developed its own assessment of the purchasing power in the economy, taking into account the availability of supplies and the amount of cash in circulation.[27] By establishing the MOC's own accounting existence, its officials sought to lay bare what to them were the objective and insurmountable constraints on the supply of consumer goods.

Aside from claiming some forms of statistical independence and record keeping, the circulators attempted to retain their personnel. The dominance of industrial planning was reflected in the transfer of finance and banking functionaries to departments of industrial planning and management. This phenomenon was especially prominent at the level of local governments, where bureaucratic specialization was less clear and weakly enforced. The reassignment of finance officials to industrial departments alarmed the circulators in the central government.[28] They worried that this threatened the functional integrity of finance work and also risked losing generation-specific memories and identities. The local finance and banking officials, just like the central circulators, had gained their expertise during the period of state building and shared similar indigenous expertise with inflation control.[29] To halt this poaching of talent, the central circulators had to tighten vertical control over the financial system and draw clearer organizational lines between finance and industry at the local level. Unable to push through their policy programs and expand their own power, the circulators nevertheless kept alive an alternative viewpoint on the economy through the maintenance of their bureaucratic pedigrees.

From a sociological perspective, the upside of maintaining marginal autonomy under the hegemony of the five-year plan is that it may have helped sustain the integrity and solidarity of the circulators. To assess whether the circulators coalesced in their career concentrations, I have used network analysis to track their career movements in relation to other bureaucratic peers in the same administration. Two agencies form a tie if there is an individual official who moved across them. Figure 1.1 provides a visually intuitive understanding of how organizations are connected with one another based on their knowledge portfolio and social proximity enacted through shared employees. As we can see, the typical circulation agencies—represented by MOF (Ministry of Finance), PBOC (People's Bank of China), MOFCOM (Ministry of Commerce), FTOSC (Finance

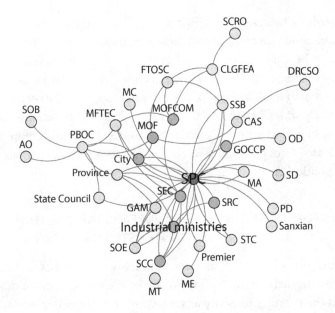

FIGURE 1.1. Personnel networks of first-generation elite economic bureaucrats. *Source*: Compiled by the author from elite economic bureaucrats' CVs.

and Trade Office of the State Council), and MFTEC (Ministry of Foreign Economic Relations and Trade)—are not tightly connected to the core of the network centered around the SPC (State Planning Commission). They not only remain on the periphery of the network but also are closely connected with one another. In other words, the circulators formed a cluster of their own and concentrated their core area of expertise in what was otherwise a centralized bureaucratic field. Such career clustering played a role in preserving the integrity of their collective views on the economy such that these views would not be easily diluted or coopted by the logic of planning.

In addition to the concentration of their careers within a small set of institutions, interpersonal relationships among circulators enhanced group solidarity. The circulators shared a leader, Chen Yun, who attracted followers like a magnet thanks to his reputation and the extensive collegial ties he developed throughout the bureaucracy. To establish the central economic bureaucracy, he brought a team of economic officials to Beijing from the northwestern field government he once oversaw. In Beijing, Yao Yilin, the minister of commerce, worked with Chen "shoulder to shoulder"

and regarded Chen as his economic mentor.[30] Li Xiannian, a local generalist who became vice premier and finance minister, formed a strong nexus
with Chen because his jurisdiction as vice premier also covered finance,
commerce, and banks—areas where Li had his own portfolio and credentials. According to his account of their relationship, Li felt he clicked almost
immediately with Chen thanks to their shared views.[31] In sum, the circulators were bound together by a leadership core and a sizable group of loyal
subordinates. Group cohesion was a crucial survival strategy in an inhos-
pitable political environment.

THE POPULIST CHALLENGE TO BUREAUCRATIC AUTHORITY AND THE CIRCULATORS' EXISTENTIAL CRISIS

The circulators did not face an existential crisis in the era of central planning, despite their subordination to the priority of accumulation. They
retained their formal authority as servants of the central bureaucracy. The
opening third of the Mao period was characterized by a respect for central authority and a belief in the ability of the bureaucracy to execute the
five-year plan and develop the economy. In this climate, the circulators
joined the planners in running the economic bureaucracy. Both groups
of bureaucrats derived their authority from allocating input and output in
what Ivan Szelenyi and Eric Kostello called the "state socialist redistributive economy,"[32] although the circulators saw more room to improve the
redistributive system.

What came to fundamentally threaten the bureaucratic existence of the
circulators was the populist waves that attempted to tear apart the authority
of the economic bureaucracy in general. The Great Leap Forward (GLF)
(1958–1962) and the Cultural Revolution (CR) (1966–1976) were the crests
of these antibureaucratic waves. Before delving into the details of the two
movements, it is worth mentioning that Mao-style radicalism did not
appear in a vacuum; the attack on bureaucratic planning was not entirely
unanticipated. Among the rank and file of the party apparatus, discontent
with centralized control already simmered and led to passive resistance. In
fact, the party officials' suspicion of the center was rooted in the history
of the Chinese Communist Revolution and defines one of the key differences between the Russian and Chinese Revolutions. While the Russian
Revolution relied on cities and industrial workers, the Chinese Revolution

mobilized peasants and depended on the agricultural sectors for political and material support. This mode of revolution shaped the distribution of power in the Chinese government. Ministerial control—that is, the lines of authority (*tiao*)—never completely overshadowed the importance of territorial power (*kuai*). Localities remained important bases for political mobilization, and when it came to state-led industrialization, they often strayed outside the vertical organizations of industrial discipline. Not surprisingly, to defy planning and keep their control over local resources, provincial administrative leaders appealed to Mao's sympathy toward mass initiatives and decentralization.[33] Direct channels of communication between regional leaders and the ultimate leader, Mao, were already well used, even in the years leading up to planning.[34]

Against this backdrop, the GLF can be understood as an escalation of the antibureaucratic undercurrent in the party. As the economic bureaucrats furthered their power with the growing mandate of planning, this current of discontent rose to the surface. Mao was unhappy with the directives and constraints he received from the central economic bureaucrats, as they were justified on the basis of an expertise he did not possess.[35] He even started to show intolerance toward the principle of "being red and expert" in selecting and promoting specialist cadres, a personnel guideline that he had previously approved.[36] Instead, Mao challenged the need to reserve any policy space for the "experts" and denied in particular the existence of any "independent laws" that regulated economic activities.[37] Emboldened by a disgruntled Mao, the party generalists raised with him their concern that the central bureaucrats were "nationalizing local factories at will and constraining local development initiatives."[38] They teamed up with Mao to halt centralization and specialization, reversing what had once appeared to be an inevitable trend toward building a bureaucracy-led economy.

The Great Leap Forward and Its Populism

The GLF has not been identified in the scholarship as a populist movement; yet many of its features justify this view. Reconsidering the GLF in the light of populism—for its mobilization of charisma and "the people" and its disdain for bureaucratic institutions—is useful for understanding the jeopardies faced by the circulators. In general, the GLF was a party movement to counter the rise of technocracy.[39] It spurned experts, bureaucracy, and centralized authority and instead insisted on the centrality of political charisma—in this case, Chairman Mao—in directing society.

In terms of economic policy, the movement resorted to the mass line and people's initiatives to develop the economy. In a characteristically anti-institutional move, the party refrained from setting up any regular organizations to formulate or implement GLF economic policy. Instead, it appealed to Mao's vaguely formulated general line (*zong luxian*)—"to go all out, aim high, and achieve more, faster, and better economic results with less cost"—to inspire local initiatives. The general line conveyed a palpable impatience for any mode of development that smacked of careful planning or balanced thinking. Originally, the slogan did not contain the phrase "less cost." Central bureaucrat Li Fuchun suggested this addition to preserve a minimal concern for cost and feasibility.[40] Still, this vague guideline didn't specify any organizational plans to realize faster development. The ambiguity allowed Mao to serve as the ultimate judge. In the implementation of the general line, he also authorized a proliferation of agents who could interpret the principle in light of local conditions. This way of wielding authority empowered Mao's local followers as they resorted to the general line and overrode the experts in the name of Mao's authority. Any dissatisfaction with the party generalists' policies could be articulated as a violation of the general line, or Mao's will.

There were two lines of development in the GLF-inspired political economy that drifted even further away from the circulators' proposals in the era of central planning. The first concerns the GLF's conceptualization of "the people," and the second concerns local governments' frenzied investment in heavy industries. Thanks to the GLF, for the first time in the history of the PRC, "the people" became an indispensable ingredient in the formula for social and economic development.[41] This move was reflected in the way in which production was organized. In the countryside, communes were established to mobilize rural labor to undertake construction projects and provide social services. In urban factories, managers were asked to work with and even bow to the party bosses in making managerial and technical decisions. State-owned factories became sites of a battle between the bureaucracy and the party. Industrial experts were relieved of power, and party control was reinstated on the grounds that the party cadres represented the thinking of common men. The GLF also refused to acknowledge any role for material incentives or monetary rewards in configuring people's motivations. As a result, bonuses were eliminated in state sectors, and marketplaces in the countryside were completely shut down. Taken together, the idea of "the people" was both antiexpert and automatically antimarket.

On the question of who embodied the will of the people, GLF policy assigned local governments to serve as its proxies. This equivalence led to an economic program of decentralization. Under the sponsorship of local governments, small rural factories mushroomed. Most of them were iron and steel mills burdened with backward technologies and poor supplies of resources. Ironically, in a vow to create a vision of socialism different from that of the Soviet Union, the GLF instigated a massive steel drive and fanned a frenzy for promoting heavy industries that went beyond what had been imagined in the First Five-Year Plan. Consequently, the rate of investment in heavy industries soared. It meant, to the chagrin of the circulators, more aggressive extractions from agricultural surplus to support the industrial sectors and an increase in the imbalance between accumulation and resource supplies.[42] Reflected on financial spreadsheets, as the circulators predicted, budgets became reckless and spun out of control. Credit discipline immediately broke down.[43]

To a large extent, the CR was a continuation of the GLF, as it was launched under similar populist banners. The attack on the bureaucracy took place on a much larger scale and with greater force. Central bureaucrats across the administrative spectrum were all hard-hit, with bureaucratic operations kept to a minimum. The economic programs of the CR also extended those of the GLF. The central economic bureaucracy was further hollowed out from within, and the financial arm of the state took a big hit. Functions of public finance and banking were merged and their personnel greatly reduced. The number of specialists was slashed, leaving only one or two work teams (yewu zu) to house them.[44] The hollowing out of the central bureaucracy undermined the basic central state functions of collecting taxes and disbursing credits. This debureaucratization took place in conjunction with the decentralization of economic policy making and the reorganization of the public sector. Rural industries continued to flourish outside of the orbit of planning. With decentralization, regions were encouraged to become self-sufficient economic units.[45] Local governments were now in charge of collecting revenues and deciding how to spend them. More crucially, they took over the central planners' authority to allocate material resources, a right that had been at the heart of central planning.[46] As a result, by falling back onto regional circuits and economic fragmentation, the CR pushed the Chinese economy further away from the integrated national economy imagined by the circulators. Material incentives to motivate producers continued to be attacked across urban and rural sectors, with markets of all kinds eliminated.[47]

Unlike in the first decade, when the circulators coexisted with the planners in sharing the bureaucratic apparatus, in the following two decades the populist movements threatened the careers, if not the lives, of the circulators. This was reflected in both the direct stripping of the circulators' official power and the simultaneous unraveling of the bureaucratic fabric of which they were part. During both the GLF and the CR, the circulators were sidelined and humiliated and their policies vehemently criticized. In the run-up to the GLF, they were dubbed "rightists" and left out in the cold by Mao. The CR struck an even heavier blow to their official capacities. They were thrown out of their administrative positions and sent down to factories or farms in remote areas for extensive periods.

In place of the bureaucratic approach to economic policy, the populist movements instituted a different way of organizing the economy, starting with the ways in which information was collected, commands disseminated, and the input of the producers and workers solicited. In the 1950s, the economic bureaucrats had adopted an exhaustive approach to gathering economic information and creating statistics. This method consisted of producing periodic complete accountings. The circulators especially relied on this method to assemble comprehensive reports on the macroeconomy in a timely fashion in order to track trends and movements. Starting in the late 1950s, the ethnographic method of data collection gained momentum and replaced the exhaustive method. The ethnographic approach, an indigenous method widely used in the 1920s and 1930s by Mao and other Communist founders to study the Chinese peasants, encouraged researchers to place themselves in the middle of the people to arrive at a "typical" understanding of the situation on the ground.[48] This methodological transformation was not trivial, for it problematized issues such as what counted as truthful information and what kinds of access to society were considered valuable. The substitution of the ethnographic approach for the exhaustive approach was especially damaging to the circulators because it ceased to provide the macrolevel information they needed on a consistent basis to detect macroeconomic warning signs.[49] In any event, the ways in which information collection was altered reinforced the consequences of populist economic policy that redistributed policy authority from the central bureaucrats to the local political leaders, from the experts to the nonexperts.

POPULIST CRISES AND THE BUREAUCRATIC POWER OF EXCEPTIONS

The radicals, however, were unable to completely get rid of the money doctors. The decentralization policies championed by the populist movement strained the macroeconomic situation, and the circulators were nearly the only ones who allegedly had experience dealing with macroeconomic matters. For this reason, the circulators were not relegated to complete dormancy. They were periodically called back from political exile to bring the economy back on track. This practice granted the circulators a form of emergency power and was presumably one of the reasons why they were not purged outright.[50] Three years into the GLF, its disastrous economic consequences were already on full display. From 1961 to 1963, Chen Yun and other important circulators such as Yao Yilin and Li Xiannian resumed their control of financial policy and instituted a series of crisis-control remedies. They cooled down investment, eased strains on resource supplies, and assisted with the recovery of agriculture. Free markets were reopened to provide additional channels for peasants to supply food to cities and address food shortages in urban areas. Piece-rate wages and bonuses in industrial factories were reintroduced as well. Control over the economy overall was recentralized to restore order.[51] This retrenchment was replayed from 1972 to 1974, following another episode of "leaps" in industrial investment and decentralization in the CR.

Resuscitation, even when repeated, did not turn the circulators' emergency power into routinized duties. As soon as the economy showed signs of recovery, the circulators were dismissed, and their organizational home, the Central FEC, was dissolved. Paradoxically, the distance of the circulators from power shielded them with a sheen of heroism as the political tide turned. Their earlier dissatisfaction with the orthodox planning system had already distinguished them from traditional planners and heavy-industry officials. In the populist period, the fact that they often acted as fixers gave them a reputation as saviors possessed with the power to restore normalcy.

This is not to say that they never participated in planning. Neither does it mean that they were not complicit in at least indulging the populist ways of organizing the Chinese economy. Yet they were assigned a much smaller share of the blame associated with both central planning and, later, the radicalization of socialism. The kind of internal exile they had endured yielded a form of political capital, allowing them to present themselves as victims of the Mao era without ever having entirely lost their front-row view of the inner workings of the system and its ills. Equally important, their troubleshooter roles allowed them to accumulate substantial evidence from moments of exception and gave them confidence in their balance perspective. As the CR ended, they were able to spring back with relatively untainted reputations from the old era and a verifiable track record of cool-headedness and competence.

I have highlighted here the existential struggles that the radicals experienced in the wake of the populist takeover. Seen in this historical context, the launch of China's economic reform could be interpreted as a mission as much about liberalization as about rehabilitation of bureaucratic authority by the circulators and their allies. No evidence was more illustrative of the urgent need to restore bureaucratic normalcy than the fact that the circulators teamed up with the planners for this task. Both groups, despite their disagreements on policy, nevertheless felt the shared need to correct the course of decentralization and political radicalism. The central planners, too, had been edged out, especially in the later years of the CR, as the radicals' force began to threaten industrial production and core construction projects. They, too, were aware that the heart of the radicals' economic program—decentralization—would eventually lead to the unraveling of planning discipline and the basic state infrastructure needed for the five-year plans. With both the planners and the circulators facing existential threats, these strange bedfellows formed a temporary union.[52] A coalition, after all, was useful for fighting common foes.

As expected, this reform alliance between the planners and the circulators did not last long. Solidarity between them formed prior to and immediately following the military action against the Gang of Four. Yet before long, programmatic fissures from their preexisting differences highlighted the ephemerality of their alliance. In 1976, the planners asked for another chance to make planning work but failed miserably. Their failure was partly due to a wrongheaded projection of China's oil reserves, but the emphasis on oil was also characteristic of the planners' continuous insistence on a resource-intensive approach to development.[53] This colossal failure sealed the fate of the planners and fed the reputation of the circulators, who had always wanted to follow an alternative path that combined planning with the market.[54] From 1978 onward, the circulators advanced their vision of reform without looking back.

THE SOCIALIST CONSTRUCTION OF MARKET REFORMERS

In the preceding sections, I have discussed why the circulators, a group of socialist-era elites, were predisposed to reform the socialist economy. I have argued that this particular breed of economic bureaucrat understood the socialist economy from a perspective different from that of the orthodox planners and saw the need to harness the forces of the market in order to balance the economy and extract maximum outputs. I have further demonstrated that their resolve to reform was fortified by an attempt to restore the authority of the bureaucracy in the wake of power challenges from the populist radicals. What remains to be articulated is how the circulators actively tied their experiences in the socialist period to the making of reformist policies. It is one thing to have the right kind of political and professional credentials to lead the reform government but another to draw on career experience to devise concrete reform programs. My observation is that many of the reform policies were adapted from experiments, concepts, and perspectives developed by the circulators during the socialist era. When doing so, they did not shy away from emphasizing the origins of their ideas and the unique positions they once occupied that allowed the adaptations. The reincarnation took place on two fronts: programmatic and theoretical.

Programmatically, the circulators turned their experiments with a wide range of practices from the socialist period into official policies in the reform period. They implied that the socialist era *they* experienced was not "wasted" because many of the remedial measures they proposed to balance the socialist economy were trial runs of economic reform. They sought to combine mechanisms of planning with the market. Thanks to the unorthodox roles they played in the socialist economy, their "revisionist" policies—although brief, ad hoc, and small in scale in their implementation—were able to emerge in the cracks between orthodox planning and radical politics. The circulators implied that social learning took place on their part, so not only did they fully understand the reasons why existing forms of socialism failed but also they were already aware of the working alternatives.

Although the circulators avoided explicitly claiming credit, their characterization of the socialist period was clearly self-referential. Li Xiannian, a key circulator, explained: "Our idea of reform did not burst out of people's minds one morning. It is a decision made after 30 years of both positive and negative experiences, after repeated comparative studies, and careful consideration."[55]

The testimonies of the circulators should not be taken at face value, since the circulators emerged as the winners of the political struggles and may have glorified their experiences and obscured others. But there is still a kernel of truth to Li's remarks. The zigzagging road that Chinese socialism took produced a wide range of experiments that stretched the imagination of socialist bureaucrats. Conventional narratives, including China's own official historiography, portrayed the reform period as a product of grand discovery. Yet as table 1.1 shows, a comparison of the key "experiments"

TABLE 1.1
Reincarnation of socialist-era experiments as reform-era policies

Socialist-era experiment	Time of experiment	Official policy in early reform era
Legitimizing the role of private industry	Early 1950s	Encouraging the development of private business
Prioritizing the development of coastal cities and provinces	Mid-1950s	Carving out special economic zones in the coastal areas
Relaxing state monopolies and control over commerce and resource allocation	Mid-1950s	Downsizing the scope of planning and state control over economic activities
Reducing capital construction and developing light and consumer-goods industries to improve basic living standards	1959 to mid-1960s	Prioritizing the development of light and consumer-goods industries
Accepting household farming	1962	Implementing the household or contract responsibility system to boost agricultural production
Implementing piece-rate wages	1961 to mid-1960s	Extensively implementing wage and bonus systems according to individual performance
Allowing prices to fluctuate to reflect market-determined differentials	1965	Gradually liberalizing prices

Source: Compiled by the author.

involving the circulators in the socialist period and the signature policies of the reform period reveals a great deal of similarity and continuity. Concretely speaking, one set of experiments was attempted by the circulators to correct macroeconomic imbalances and later became a pillar of their development strategy in the reform era. These measures included reducing heavy-industry production, fostering the development of light industries and consumer-goods manufacturing, and prioritizing the development of coastal areas versus inland provinces. Another set of experiments revolved around permitting market-based allocation and private production alongside the five-year plan. In the socialist era, such tactics had been used to ease supply strains, absorb excess purchasing power, and increase government revenues; they later gained legitimacy in the reform era as formal, long-term policies. Additionally, the circulators were among the socialist bureaucrats who, in the face of the massive collectivization of agricultural production, tolerated and acquiesced to a series of bottom-up initiatives such as household farming. This array of practices was later made official and widely implemented on a national scale in the reform era. In short, economic reform came to legitimize many of the early transient measures and gave them proper names and justifications.

The socialist era not only informed concrete policies in the reform era but also sowed the seeds of an economic theory that the circulators insisted would be applicable to a marketizing economy. The balance theory was an indigenous economic theory developed by the circulators in the late 1950s to capture their experience in managing the macroaspects of the socialist economy. It was not an abstract, high-powered theory filled with analytics and math. Rather, it was a theorem consisting of stylized factors and loosely connected causal statements. Its function, however, was both substantial and symbolic. The circulators frequently referred to the idea of balance to serve as a reminder of the historical roles they played in pulling the Chinese economy back from the edge of crisis. Internally, the balance theory served as a social device, a shared language, and thus a rallying point to build solidarity between the circulators and their new followers.[56]

The substantial content of the balance theory was also devised in such a way that it accrued reputation and authority to its authors. Originally, *balance* was a concept of the command economy and specifically referred to material balance, a technique that planners used to compute the uses of individual commodities and balance the production and allocation of all supplies.[57] As discussed in the previous section, the major modification that circulators made to this narrow conceptualization of balance was to expand the physical understanding of the economy to include balances in financial and credit terms. The circulators posited that these kinds of balance, if upset, would eventually undermine material balance. Experimenting with this broad vision of *comprehensive balance* in the socialist era gave the circulators the confidence to elevate the policy guideline to an axiomatic status. When China's relationship with the Soviet Union soured, any direct borrowing from the Soviets became problematic and was criticized by the populists as "slavish dependency" on foreign ideas and technologies.[58] The circulators' indigenous balance theory, however, survived the criticism because it was developed out of these Chinese bureaucrats' own career experiences. Thus, it was viewed as having a considerable sense of indigenous righteousness and authenticity. The circulators claimed that in a reform economy, where material, financial, and monetary aspects would only be intertwined further, the balance theory would be even more useful in guiding macroeconomic management.

Another substantive feature of the balance theory elevates the importance of a practical understanding of the economy, a kind of knowledge that the circulators possessed. This has to do with the criterion for assessing balance. Early on, the Soviet orthodox planners prescribed a rule of thumb for achieving economic balance in China, expressed in the idea of *proportionate development*. These planners labored to determine the ideal proportions, the "magic ratios" for regulating relations among sectors—for example, between agriculture and industry.[59] The circulators, however, did not interpret proportionate development literally. They rejected the teleologically defined rules of proportionate development[60] and any numerical truth imposed from abroad. They insisted that ratios were difficult to pin down because they were subject to changes, with economic circumstances varying across different countries and periods. They believed that good proportional relations occurred when the economy found its balance as it evolved.[61] As such, the circulators promoted their balance theory as a form of situational knowledge that only practitioners like themselves could master. In doing so, they assigned exceptional importance to their cumulative experience of managing the economy through its ups and downs. In fact, they went so far as to argue that the pursuit of balance did not need to answer to any long-term objective but was, in its essence, a form of short-term cyclical management.[62] Only through short-term management on a yearly basis could real balance be achieved.[63] In brief, the circulators defined a balanced economy with considerable flexibility. They turned a previously rigid theory into adaptive guidelines for short-term macroeconomic management when Western macroeconomics had yet to be introduced in China. As soon as the reform unleashed the growth momentum of the economy, the circulators emphasized that "balanced development is the fastest development" and made a case for the importance of developing monetary and fiscal tools to iron out economic cycles.[64]

This chapter shows the potency of socialist careers in the initiation of China's economic reform. I argue that the group of reformers carried over from the socialist era was not innately liberal. Their perspective on the economy was tied to the specific ways their careers unfolded throughout the socialist era and to their collective intent to promote their expertise as an asset in economic reform. Equally as revolutionary, their early roles in fighting inflation, integrating national markets, and building the fiscal foundation of the state set them onto an economic and financial track in the new government and instilled in them a certain pragmatic attitude toward questions of markets and ownership. This formative experience evolved into formal roles in the planning apparatus, where they were in charge of managing aspects of the socialist economy related to public finance, banking, and commerce. The chapter demonstrates that these bureaucratic positions allowed them to develop an unorthodox understanding of the socialist economy, which I call the *circulation* perspective. This perspective informed a set of programmatic remedies to address weaknesses in central planning that later became formalized and extended into a paradigm of economic reform.

This chapter also demonstrates that intrabureaucratic struggle matters in understanding when and how economic reform started. While the circulators' economic outlook was gradually honed in the socialist bureaucracy, their ultimate impetus to transform such revisionist views into a paradigmatic quest for systematic reform was fortified by a three-way competition in the Chinese state among the populist radicals, the orthodox planners, and the circulators themselves. In the later years of the socialist era, populist movements purged market-tolerant talk and threatened the very existence of the central bureaucracy, which was the source of the circulators' authority. The push for reform, I argue, was triggered by elites' different views on the role of the central bureaucracy in Chinese politics and should be understood therefore as an attempt by the reformers to revitalize both the Chinese economy and the central bureaucracy.

By establishing the association between China's reform and the circulators' career experiences and economic outlooks, this chapter lays a foundation for understanding how this connection narrowed the historical possibilities for China's economic reform. Many of the early reform policies were in fact reincarnations of experiments originally intended to help socialism function. China's consistent intolerance for macroeconomic instability and inflation throughout the reform period was very likely rooted in the socialist era, inscribed in the circulators' memory, and expressed in their balance theory. Yet to the extent that careers are a crucial basis for bureaucratic groupings and a locus of contestation, it is not surprising to see that the circulators would face challenges from another group of officials who embraced a different career identity, giving rise to a new round of bureaucratic competition. The next chapter addresses these new challenges and the transformation of China's economic reform that ensued.

Chapter Two

BALANCED DEVELOPMENT OR DECENTRALIZED GROWTH?

Elite Reformers in the 1980s

China's economic reform has always been a collective political project. Those who rallied behind Deng Xiaoping were committed to correcting the existing course of economic policy. Yet a generalized commitment to reform is not necessarily sufficient to maintain cohesion among reformers throughout the reform process. The circulators were bureaucratic veterans and an established component of the reform government. Their previous collegial relationship with Deng and their familiarity with the central administration helped ensure a stable transition at the center without too much disruption. Yet the circulators were not the only socialist officials who supported reform. A reform government that vowed to depart from the past and recast the future was also open to recruiting from outside the pool of central bureaucrats and incorporating new blood into its organizational makeup.

This chapter features a second group of reformers—the local generalists. After regaining supreme positions in the economic bureaucracy, the circulators had to share authority in making reform policies with this newly risen group from the localities, and the chapter lays out the evolving relationship of the circulators and the local generalists during the early reform period.

Like the circulators, the local generalists were incumbent officials in the socialist government who had developed a penchant for reform, but they did so from a different career location than that of the circulators. From a local perspective, the generalists faulted orthodox planning for its centralism and also resisted the Maoist development method because it stifled producer autonomy and market activities. Such career differences between the circulators and the local generalists were stronger than their political alliance and became the basis of a political divide. This chapter shows that the division stemmed from their differing bureaucratic practices, rooted in their careers, in relation to observing the economy, collecting economic information, engaging with constituencies, and establishing bases of policy authority. The impact of their career origins was formative and dispositional. Even at the pinnacle of the polity where both circulators and local generalists were free of specific organizational duties, they maintained their previous work styles and modes of engagement with the economy. As a result, they developed two different approaches to economic reform and were gradually estranged from one another. This chapter explains how these two approaches coexisted and eventually collided and how this shaped the dynamics of reform in its first decade and beyond.

IDENTIFYING THE STRATEGISTS OF REFORM AND THEIR POLICY STANCES

In unsettled times, group initiatives often leap ahead of institutional changes. In the inaugural phase of China's economic reform, the bureaucracy at large was slow to reorient, but a core group of leading bureaucrats swiftly initiated an array of pioneering efforts, making an outsized impact on how reform started and proceeded. This group of economic reformers was composed of Deng's core allies, who shared in general his pragmatic way of thinking and his commitment to modernizing the Chinese economy. As soon as the major opponents to reform stepped aside, these economic reformers were appointed to commanding positions in the central government. I identified thirty-two officials who comprised Deng's strategy team. They headed agencies that were tasked with formulating the general direction of reform and addressing major problems that arose along the way. Such officials included the president, the premiers, the commissioners of the Finance and Economic Commission of the State Council, and the directors of the Central Finance and Economics Leading Group of the Chinese Community Party and the System Reform Commission.

All the leading officials identified here were incumbents, having served the socialist government for a minimum of two decades. Yet they differed in their career origins. In general, two broad career differences divide these Chinese officials: whether they served central or local government and whether they were specialists or generalists. The specialists are those who concentrated their careers in specific government functions and typically possessed specialized knowledge. Many in the specialist category were directors or commissioners in the ministries. The generalists had a much larger range of career experiences and thus had gathered general knowledge useful for a variety of matters and situations. In the context of the Chinese bureaucracy, generalists tended to be mayors, governors, and regional party leaders. Their work tasks involved mobilizing, managing, directing, or supervising. Cross-tabulating the two dimensions of difference yields four possible career types—central specialist, central generalist, local specialist, and local generalist—and I coded my protagonists into these four types. Table 2.1 shows the distribution across the four career types by their individual names and organizations. Table 2.2 tallies the number of officials in each category. Together the two tables show that elite reformers primarily clustered around two career types: central specialist and local generalist: twenty individuals fell into the former category and seven into the latter.

TABLE 2.1
Career types of reform elites in four strategy-making organizations/positions

Organizational affiliation	Central/special	Central/general	Local/special	Local/general
President and premiers	Bo Yibo, Yu Qiuli, Gu Mu, Chen Muhua, Qiao Shi, Kang Shien, Yao Yilin	Yang Shangkun	Li Peng, Tian Jiyun	Hu Yaobang, Zhao Ziyang, Wan Li, Yang Shuangkun
Finance and Economic Commission of the State Council	Chen Yun, Li Xiannian, Bo Yibo, Gu Mu, Chen Guodong, Kang Shien, Zhang Jinfu, Fang Yi			Wang Renzhong, Jin Ming
Central Finance and Economics Leading Group	Zhao Ziyang, Du Xingyuan, Yao Yilin, Zhang Jinfu, Gu Mu	Hu Qili		Zhao Ziyang, Wan Li, Xi Zhongxun
System Reform Commission	Liao Jili, Li Tieying, Zhou Taihe, An Zhiwen, Tao Li	Tong Dali		

TABLE 2.2
Number of elite reformers in the four career types

	Central	Local
Specialist	Central specialists	Local specialists
	N = 20	N = 2
Generalist	Central generalists	Local generalists
	N = 3	N = 7

My next analytical step was to find out where the elite reformers stood on key policies and whether there was an association between career type and policy outlook. While Chinese leaders did not leave easily traceable voting records on policy issues, they expressed their views on these policies, directly or indirectly and at the time or retrospectively, through other outlets such as speeches, policy papers, memoirs, and diaries. Sifting through this unsystematic yet valuable body of information revealed a pattern of transition from consensus to escalating disagreement between the central specialists and the local generalists.[1] Both groups concurred that market forces should be introduced to vitalize the Chinese economy and that the government should pivot from prioritizing heavy industry to developing light industries and the consumer sector. Yet as reform deepened and decisions shifted from whether reform should happen at all to how reform should be conducted, fissures opened between the two groups of officials.

As table 2.3 indicates, the central specialists and local generalists disagreed on a range of signature policies associated with the first decade of China's economic reform. These benchmark policies included allowing state-owned enterprises (SOEs) to retain profit realized through contracts with the state, setting up special economic zones (SEZs) to attract foreign investments, liberalizing prices across the economy, replacing for-profit contracting with taxes on enterprises, restraining government spending and investment, and fighting inflation. Local specialists such as Hu Yaobang, Zhao Ziyang, Wan Li, and Xi Zhongxun typically supported policies of decentralization and sought to give short-term incentives to producers (the first three policies in table 2.3).[2] Central specialists such as Chen Yun, Yao Yilin, Li Xiannian, Li Peng, Chen Muhua, and Tian Jiyun tended to support policies associated with centralization, rationalization, and macroeconomic prudence (the last three policies in table 2.3). There is a clear policy cleavage between the two groups of reformers.

TABLE 2.3
Stances of reform elites on major policies in the 1980s

	Profit contracting of SOEs	Special economic zone	Price liberalization	Tax on profit contracting	Fiscal austerity	Anti-inflation
Initiated or endorsed	Zhao Ziyang, Tian Jiyun, Wan Li, Hu Yaobang	Li Xiannian, Gu Mu, Xi Zhongxun, Yang Shangkun	Zhao Ziyang	Chen Yun, Tian Jiyun	Chen Yun, Yao Yilin, Li Xiannian, Li Peng, Liao Jili	Chen Yun, Yao Yilin, Li Xiannian, Chen Muhua
Objected	Li Xiannian, Wang Renzhong	Yao Yilin, Chen Yun, Li Peng	Chen Yun	Hu Yaobang	Hu Yaobang, Zhao Ziyang	Hu Yaobang, Zhao Ziyang
Undecided or wavering	Chen Yun			Zhao Ziyang		

Source: Compiled by the author.

The central specialists, upon closer examination, were concentrated in finance- and commerce-related agencies. Not surprisingly, they were included in the group of reformers identified in the previous chapter—the circulators, who had served in agencies such as the Ministry of Finance, the People's Bank of China, the Ministry of Commerce, and the Finance and Economic Commission of the party. To reiterate, the circulators became reformers because conducting finance- and commerce-related work allowed them to observe the economy through the flows and the interrelationships between sectors that were dismissed by traditional planners and advocates of heavy industry.[3] Through monitoring the socialist economy in terms of flows and interrelationships, the circulators discovered that there were built-in checks and balances among key macroeconomic indicators—say, budgets, credit, and price—to the extent that their mutual constraints were regulated by "inviolable economic laws."[4] According to the circulators, allowing markets to function enabled these economic laws to balance supply-demand relationships and better respond to the needs of the people.

The socialist past of the circulators directly predicts some of their policy choices but not all. The dynamics particular to the reform government kept shaping their evolving positions. Inflation in the reform era, for instance, generated experiences analogous to those that the circulators encountered in the 1940s as macroeconomic managers of the new regime, and this may have inspired their nearly knee-jerk aversion to it. Many other policy issues, as table 2.3 shows, spoke to relatively new challenges and initiatives that have to be analyzed in their own contexts. Many of these issues, such as those concerning the budget and the financial relationship between the SOEs and the state, had yet to acquire politicized meaning in the early reform context. Furthermore, there were notable inconsistencies in the circulators' approval patterns that demand explanation. For example, while approving some reformist proposals, the circulators vehemently criticized price liberalization and the establishment of SEZs, making them appear to be against reform. All of these apparent discrepancies and idiosyncrasies call for a nuanced investigation into the association between policy makers and the bureaucratic field in which they were embedded, paying particular attention to the circulators' coexistence with the local generalists and the possibility that this interrelationship altered or radicalized some of the circulators' preexisting inclinations. In other words, to understand why the circulators made the policy choices they did, we need to bring the local generalists into the picture and adopt a relational framework to assess the development of both groups' economic views.

MAKING LOCAL GENERALISTS INTO REFORMERS

Like the circulators, the local generalists were holdovers from the socialist era. Although their positions in the previous government were not as high ranking as those of the circulators, the local generalists represented a formidable force in the broader context of local governments across China and were quickly promoted to political primacy when Deng Xiaoping took the helm. They occupied a different location in the government bureaucracy and developed a different way to engage with the economy and its participants. Concretely speaking, the local generalists rose through the generalist career tracks, which typically culminated in positions as provincial governors or party secretaries. That is, they spent extensive amounts of time overseeing affairs in municipal or provincial jurisdictions prior to their ascendance to the central government as reform leaders. They disfavored centralized planning because it shifted power from local leaders to central ministries. Central planning, if strictly executed as outlined in China's First Five-Year Plan, would have relegated the local generalists to little more than cogs in the machine, stripping away their autonomy. As a result, they made a localist case against central planning and, more broadly, against centralized regulation and control.

The local generalists also differed from the circulators in their relationship with Maoist economic populism. As chapter 1 details, during the second half of the early history of the People's Republic of China, Mao urged the radicals to identify alternative pathways to productivity that relied on political campaigns. The circulators were sidelined for their belief in rationalized governance and their tolerance for market activities. The local generalists, however, were in a different position. They were deeply caught up in the radical style of economic policy making that promoted decentralization and "politics in command." They were at the forefront of the decentralization movement, which called for the mobilization of mass initiatives to generate economic output instead of relying on bureaucratic planning or private incentives.

One would think that the local generalists would have had ample reason to embrace the Maoist approach to the economy, since it decentralized resources and decision-making—and many local generalists did. A good proportion of the local party leaders sought to ally themselves with Mao to resist the central planners, even though this political choice simultaneously meant joining forces with the radicals in the central government, including the Gang of Four in the Cultural Revolution. But for one group of local generalists, this populist style of bureaucratic practice was more methodological than ideological. While their attitude toward the content of populist economic policy was ambivalent or even skeptical, local generalists subscribed to the work method associated with such policy, which made "going to the masses" an essential component of local governments' organizational routines.[5] For this particular group of local generalists, it was a method of discovery, allowing them to see the underbelly of the Chinese economy from which the radicals shied away. It paved the way for them to become reformers and to see both why economic reform was necessary *and* how to approach it.

Specifically, "going to the masses" gave the local generalists an awareness of and sympathy toward economic practices on the ground. In defiance of a ban on market activities and private productions, peasants and urbanites engaged in activities that either fell into gray areas or were simply illicit. Private production was kept alive on the side so long as it helped meet planned quotas. Collective lands were divided into small private plots to "rent" to households and individuals. Underground factories churned out products for small-scale urban and rural markets. The local generalists observed how these outlawed activities actually "worked" to the extent that they alleviated shortages, increased productivity, and met people's basic needs. Therefore, like the circulators, the local generalists realized the virtue of the market in a planned economy. The difference is that while the circulators saw the benefits of markets from the perspective of macroeconomic rationalization, the local generalists began with a much more intimate understanding of economic activities on the ground because of their local leadership positions. Recognizing the benefits of these prohibited activities, this group of local generalists either turned a blind eye to or secretly promoted this array of local initiatives to stimulate production.[6] In the end, they protected this type of underground subsistence economy.

Deng was periodically removed from high party and government posts by Maoist radicals, but when he was able to reclaim positions of power, this group of local generalists had brief periods in which they were able to claim the legality of these underground practices and even scale them up. Their policy moves during these windows of opportunity signaled to Deng their affinity with his views and their willingness to deviate from the Maoist doctrine. During his periods of political restoration, Deng promoted this group of generalists across China, creating a network of loyal and like-minded supporters. As the radicals receded from the political stage, the most trusted and capable of these supporters were summoned to Beijing. From there, the generalists had the opportunity to turn their set of local innovations and bottom-up initiatives into a nationwide push to relax Soviet-style planning and start the reform. For example, Premier Zhao Ziyang of the reform government served as the party boss in Sichuan and Guangdong Provinces in the Mao period. His inspection tours in these two provinces provided early inspirations for his strong support of decentralizing policies such as the household responsibility system and free trade zones. In 1962, Zhao traveled to a remote county in Guangdong and noticed that peasants were contracting out agricultural output to households. He later introduced this output contract system on a wider scale in Sichuan Province.[7] While serving in Guangdong, Zhao also learned about the locals' long-standing but now prohibited tradition of trading with Hong Kong and Macau. This observation planted the seeds for his open-door policies along the coastline.[8]

Local generalists' familiarity with local conditions also enabled them to claim social proximity to the producers on the ground, which became an important source of their policy authority. They maintained that their mobilization work, of going down to factories and farms, shortened the social distance between them and the local producers. In their encounters with real-life economic agents, they discovered that people had "insuppressible but hidden incentives."[9] Wan Li, the party secretary of Anhui Province, explained that working closely with agricultural regions allowed him to understand the wants and desires of the peasants. "Peasants felt happiest over getting two things," he posited, "material benefits and autonomy."[10] Wan later established the contracting-out system in agricultural liberalization. The local generalists believed that the suppression of material incentives resulted in a tremendous amount of underrealized potential in the Chinese economy. The purpose of reform, to the local generalists, was precisely to unleash the hidden incentives of the producers.

This is all to say that in the socialist period the circulators and the local generalists had already come to understand the economy in different terms, in spite of their shared economic outlook. The circulators tended to comprehend the big picture of the economy by analyzing statistics and the relationships among the economy's constitutive parts, including those between credit supply and demand and between the consumer sector and production. They observed the socialist economy using what we now generally understand as a macroeconomic framework. The local generalists focused on producers' incentives and engaged with the economy from a microeconomic perspective. Both types of bureaucrats defied the radicals' approach to the economy, but they did so in different ways. The circulators offered a macrocorrection to populist policy. They issued warnings about macroeconomic imbalance, and they regained power as experts in this area whenever an inflationary crisis arose. The local generalists staked out a microresistance to Maoist policy and tried to sustain bottom-up and private initiatives. The constituency of the local generalists was not an abstract conceptualization of "the economy" but rather "the people" in their jurisdictions. In this regard, references to "the people" were central to local generalists' claims of political and moral legitimacy, just as these references had been to the populists' claims. The difference is that to the populists, the people comprised an undifferentiated mass, a political collectivity to be mobilized and held up as an ideal. The local generalists, however, attempted to articulate a more authentic notion of the people—as individuals with needs and faculties. The circulators and the local generalists clashed with the Maoists on complementary but separate battlegrounds.

WORK STYLES AND THE STRUGGLE FOR DISTINCTION

The circulators and the local generalists were united in challenging the Maoist radicals. Despite their two different perspectives on the state bureaucracy, they were initially able to come together for the common cause of reform. Their union signaled that the consent to reform in the government was broadly based, drawn from both central technocratic and local political elements. Problems, however, arose in their attempts to actualize and govern the reform processes. Following the promotion of the local generalists to Beijing, they found they had to make decisions with the circulators. Close interaction between the two reinforced their different career identities and gave rise to mutual distrust. The political scientist Victor Shih in his book *Factions and Finance in China* also noted the fissure between the two groups of officials during this period and attributed it to differences in careers.[11] According to Shih, officials crafted policy in order to reward their power base of political supporters, so different career backgrounds meant different power bases and different rewards. I argue for a different mechanism by which career background translates into policy. Prior to the emergence of any explicit policy differences, discomfort and suspicion between local generalists and circulators already simmered on account of their differing work styles. *Work style* is an indigenous term for the bundles of bureaucratic practices that underpin one's approach to the subject of their work. Even when given the opportunity to transcend specialized duties and broaden their skill sets as overarching strategists, both groups of officials continued to adhere to their established ways of engaging with the economy, attesting to the "stickiness" of the bureaucratic practices with which they were familiar.

My examination of chronicles and news reports on the official activities that each group of strategists undertook points to two divergent types of practices.[12] Now working from Beijing, the local generalists had to adjust to the purview and rhythm of the central government. Yet they still spared time, more frequently than did the circulators, to go on inspection tours outside of the capital to scout out new incentives and new ideas for reform. Premier

Zhao Ziyang's decision to liberalize the price of agricultural food was made after conversations with vegetable growers in Guangzhou's suburbs.[13] President Hu Yaobang, another prominent generalist, set foot in every province across the nation and often trekked deep into the countryside despite his heart condition.[14] The circulators, in contrast, were accustomed to their technocratic mode of work, in which they collected information and monitored the economy. They continued to analyze data and hold meetings and were more likely to bolster their arguments by citing numbers and statistics than were the local generalists. Chen Yun's speeches and writings, for example, were always dense with numbers.[15] Such methodological exercises, the circulators emphasized, were geared toward analyzing the interrelationships among different sectors and between aggregate supply and demand,[16] all of which needed to be matched by a strong statistical capacity of the state.[17] Yao Yilin insisted that the collection of aggregate-level data could not fall behind the market reform because such data were the basis for policy strategies.[18] This is not to say that the circulators were uninterested in grasping what happened on the ground. Still, they considered the local generalists' ethnographic mode of gathering information less valuable as a source of data, inspiration, and legitimacy than sifting through the statistics. They were more comfortable as deskmen.

As both types of career bureaucrat now had to coordinate with one another on a regular basis to discuss policies, distinctions between them were articulated and dramatized with respect to their work styles. The conflict revolved largely around whose career credentials and work styles led to the more credible understanding of the economy—and thus authority in economic policy making. This type of competition was organized and animated in a different fashion than that of a naked competition based on the size of their respective power bases. Both groups had difficulties accepting and even comprehending one another's positions.[19] Mutual concerns started to flare up at meetings and in policy memos about five years into their new roles. The circulators were deeply suspicious of what they deemed the micromanagement style of the local generalists. Chen Yun wrote a letter to Zhao Ziyang suggesting that Zhao's group members "free [themselves] from daily work and find time to discuss big things and strengthen the regulation and control in macro-aspects."[20] Metaphorically, the circulators asked the local generalists to "speak 'Beijing dialect' from now on to be in tune with the central government."[21]

The response of local generalist Zhao Ziyang was characteristic of this tit-for-tat struggle over the question of which career experience imparted greater legitimacy.[22] While paying ritualistic respect to the circulators' expertise in public finance, local generalists defended their own advantages in economic policy making. Zhao highlighted the value of his source of knowledge: "Cadres in Beijing asked how I could do economic work since I only worked in localities; this is because I witnessed the excessive economic malpractice on the ground and the enormous prices people paid."[23] References to "the people" frequently appeared in local generalists' defensive arguments. The local generalist Ren Zhongyi also found Chen's desire to constrain demand in order to balance demand-supply relationships "incomprehensible" because "people's lives were already poor enough."[24]

TWO APPROACHES TO REFORM: GROWTH AND BALANCE

The first decade of China's economic reform is known for its experimentation and trial-and-error policy making. Some scholars argued that piecemeal reform allowed the economy to gradually "grow out of the plan"[25] and eased the pain of reform by creating winners without excessively punishing those who stood to lose their power and economic privilege.[26] The question as to how incrementalism impacted the reformers themselves is much less studied. I propose that incrementalism also led the bureaucracy to "grow out of the consensus," allowing ample time for the bureaucrats to recognize their internal differences, thereby gradually unraveling their coalition. The local generalists and the circulators agreed on the starting points of reform: downsizing central planning, allowing production for markets, introducing the contract responsibility system to rural areas, and liberalizing prices on a limited scale. This agreement did not guarantee a consensus on where the path should lead or where it might end. China's economic reform remained strategic in the sense that consistent oversight by strong leadership ensured that it proceeded at a controlled pace. Yet elite policy makers did not have the reform completely mapped out in detail. Instead, reformers solved problems as they arose without reversing course or shutting down the entire system. It was through the sequences of problem-solving strategies that systematic approaches to the economy took shape and career differences became paradigmatic.

In the decade under study, a set of interrelated issues associated with incremental reform commanded the reformers' immediate attention. Economic reform was feedback-loop heavy because it broadened the range of market participants and introduced new sources of incentives as well as conflicts. As more parts of the economy were pulled into the orbit of the market, new transmission mechanisms began to take effect and cause new macroeconomic spasms to ripple through the economy. Many of problems stemmed from the dual-track system that preserved the plan while unleashing market mechanisms. As the economy transitioned, gaps, loopholes, and mismatches between the plan and the market grew and created price discrepancies between the public and private sectors, which then generated risks of corruption and public resource stripping.[27] Thus, the pace and the measurement guidelines for a dual-track reform needed careful consideration. Many of the issues raised were not black-and-white, and answers were not readily available. Instead, these issues begged for nuanced approaches and were sensitive to slight differences in policy outlooks and methodologies. The growing difference between the circulators and the local generalists was magnified against this backdrop. Their career backgrounds and the policy practices they carried over drove their intuitive responses to emergent problems and informed their efforts to characterize those problems as they rose. In the course of identifying, explaining, and solving problems, the circulators and the local generalists ultimately developed two approaches to economic reform.

The local generalists developed a brand of market reform that focused on decentralization and growth. This approach was consistent with their sympathy for ground-up initiatives. With the household responsibility initiative succeeding in rural areas, the local generalists were eager to extend its underlying principle—decentralizing incentives—to the urban economy. They proposed policies to expand local autonomy and encourage local innovation. To do so, they worked to delegate policy authority and the right to allocate resources to lower-level governments. Under their aegis, localities were given new power to direct public investment, influence the disbursement of loans, trade directly with foreign countries, and even make monetary policies. Decentralization extended into the public sector. SOEs previously supervised by the central government and its ministries now fell under the jurisdiction of local governments. Together enterprises and governments formed local development coalitions that further eschewed central regulations. The local generalists were also adamant about setting up and expanding SEZs along China's coastline to attract foreign investments. The creation of SEZs was viewed as China's pathway to globalization; it was also an exemplary policy of decentralization. In these extraterritorial zones, enterprises enjoyed tax breaks and a favorable policy environment, and provincial and municipal authorities were given autonomy to approve foreign investment projects, retain foreign exchange income, and deal independently with foreign parties.[28]

The local generalists' push toward decentralization energized the local producers but planted the seeds of macroeconomic instability in the fledgling market economy. Local governments allied with the state banks, which now answered to local governments when extending loans rather than to their headquarters or financial regulators in Beijing. In this way, local governments acquired a de facto monetary authority to issue credit. The SOEs, already operating under soft budget constraints, were also pressured to invest liberally. The profits they generated were largely channeled into the coffers of local governments under the scheme of fiscal decentralization. All of this meant that a range of local actors had seized expansive control over policy levers on public investments. This newly formed array of power jeopardized the regulatory authority of the central government—most importantly, its ability to direct credit supplies and industrial investments—causing the economy to overheat periodically.[29] Buoyed by Deng Xiaoping's support, local generalists also lifted price controls on major commodities. This move turned out to be another catalyst that exacerbated price volatility.[30]

The eruption of illicit economic activities presented another category of unforeseen problems. Profiteering and corruption were by-products of the dual-track system, and decentralization only exacerbated them. Since economic reform was localized and largely uncoordinated by the central government, local developments were bound to exhibit variations in speed and magnitude. Regional price differentials added another dimension of discrepancies to those between controlled and marketized sectors. Profiteering space exploded between regions and sectors; state-controlled resources and privileged access tunneled their ways into markets, giving rise to lures for sizable profits. In addition, the SEZs provided fertile soil for corruption in the form of rampant smuggling activities along the coastline, feeding the growth of black markets around the nation. Corruption surged, eroding the government bureaucracy to an unprecedented degree.[31]

Even more revealing of the local generalists' disposition was their response to the malaise caused by decentralization. Undeterred by signs of overheating and bureaucratic wrongdoing, the local generalists insisted that these problems were only transitory and that decentralization remained the best means to achieve the core objective of economic reform—growth. Growth, they contended, was the ultimate solution to all the transitory problems.[32] The local generalists maintained that the project of correcting incentives and building up market agents was far from complete at this point. A market economy could not function without properly building its microfoundation. According to this logic, the problems that the transitioning economy faced, as a result of the local generalists' initiatives, were the necessary costs that China had to pay to jumpstart the economy and unlock its potential.

In their reaction to the marketizing economy and the rising problems associated with it, the circulators constructed their economic worldview around a different core idea—that of balance. Previously, the balance thinking developed by Chen Yun and extended by his fellow circulators in the 1950s highlighted the importance of creating a sound government budget and coordinating development between public finance and material planning. In the reform era, this group applied the argument for balance in assessing the ever-shifting relationship between planning and the expanding market. The circulators cautioned that any mismatch between the two could cause imbalance in the economy and thereby macroeconomic volatility. Their concern for imbalance also extended to intersectoral and interregional relationships, as they argued that excessive differences in the pace of marketization across sectors or localities yielded rent-seeking opportunities. Because of such risks, economic reform benefited from central coordination.[33] Song Ping and Yao Yilin, for example, stressed that each sector's reforms should proceed in concert with those of other sectors so that there would not be gaps or misalignments among them.[34] The circulators didn't deny the importance of growth. Yet they were convinced that balanced growth was a better kind of growth because it delivered quality and sustainability. Liao Jili emphasized that questions of proportional development should still be relevant to directing economic liberalization. A desire for high-powered growth should not displace the validity of these concerns.[35]

The circulators' preoccupation with balance grew out of their long-standing positions. It was an instinctual response to the local generalists' decentralization programs and their side effects during the course of reform. The circulators once again found themselves called to play the role of night watchmen of the Chinese economy, as they did in the socialist period, redressing any reckless pursuit of economic output. Their vigilance toward macroeconomic instability narrowed their concerns and cast them in a "conservative" light. The circulators, however, were unmoved by this negative characterization. To them, addressing macroeconomic instabilities and their underlying causes was more urgent than proposing new initiatives. From the standpoint of balance, the circulators argued that decentralization was taking a toll on the overall economy that outweighed its benefits. One of the most critical issues was that easy credit and a monetarized budget had indulged local governments' insatiable appetite for investment-fueled growth. Investment bursts led to sudden demands for raw materials and caused supply bottlenecks in the economy. This had become, according to the circulators, a chief source of overheating. The circulators were especially appalled at the delegation of monetary authority to local governments. They urged that this amounted to giving local officials the power to print money, a self-defeating inflationary policy. The circulators were also critical of SEZs because of the corruption and smuggling associated with them. While the local generalists paid frequent visits to the SEZs to encourage local morale and promise the enactment of favorable policies,[36] the circulators deemed the SEZs the quintessential embodiment of all the ills associated with decentralization and deficit-financed investments.[37] Chen symbolically refused to set foot in any of the SEZs, making clear his strong dislike of unregulated decentralization.

To be fair, before 1988, none of the problems of government deficits and rising prices triggered by decentralizing policies were severe enough to cause a major economic crisis.[38] Yet the circulators repeatedly framed these problems in crisis terms based on their long-standing sensitivity to macroeconomic fluctuations. Their technocratic work style only reinforced the significance of macroeconomic problems because macroeconomic trends were more likely to be detected and verified in statistical reports than in the testimonies of producers, who had a stake in ramping up investment and with whom the local generalists had closer affinities. By focusing on balance, the circulators also seized the opportunity to develop their balance thinking, based on their experience in the socialist period, into an ahistorical theory. This universalization of theory helped the circulators reinvent their authority in governing a marketized economy.[39] Balance thinking was not an analytically sophisticated theory; it lacked an econometric edifice and operated mainly by rule of thumb. Yet in an economic bureaucracy that was not known for theorization, the balance theory was one of the few theories that was formulated and promoted by bureaucrats (versus academics) and that was relatively coherent. In this regard, the circulators managed to maintain an intellectual edge over the local generalists.

THE CLASH OVER INFLATION

Elite reformers' economic outlooks were reflected in their routine approaches to market reforms. These outlooks also informed and were sharpened by their existential responses to imminent economic crises. Emergencies presented ideal opportunities for examining the unfiltered thinking of the policy elites, since emergencies touched off drastic action that exposed unpolished justifications. Critical situations also played a role in turning hidden conflicts into overt ones, forcing these conflicts increasingly into zero-sum situations. In this case, the uneasy coexistence of the two camps of bureaucrats gave way to an open clash over an exigent economic issue—an increasingly undeniable inflationary threat. The circulators stepped up their vigilance toward inflation, while local generalists remained indulgent. Their warring stances exposed the irreconcilability of their views and eventually resulted in the declaring of winners and losers.

As mentioned earlier, since the onset of reform, inflation had been a looming problem due to a confluence of factors related to overinvestment, loose credit control, and soft budget constraints. In the mid-1980s, inflation started to set in, reaching 10 percent in 1985 and peaking at 18 percent in 1988—levels unseen since the Great Leap Forward. Faced with the same symptoms, the two camps of reformers responded with different diagnoses. The circulators reemphasized that inflation was an unequivocal sign of imbalance. Yao Yilin warned that rising prices were symptomatic of a deteriorating economy.[40] To stem inflation, the circulators unambiguously called for retrenchment to rein in government spending and the monetary supply.[41] In contrast, the local generalists downplayed the severity of inflation and delayed any substantial action. At policy meetings that set growth targets, the local generalists remained committed to their vision. They tried to bargain with the circulators for a few more points in the growth rate. The disagreements over the speed of growth were so intractable that the National People's Congress could not pass the annual budget in 1988.[42] In meetings arranged to gauge the investment in coastal Guangdong and Fujian Provinces, Premier Zhao Ziyang perfunctorily admitted the importance of guarding against the danger of inflation only at the urging of the circulators. In practice, he was reluctant to impose austerity programs and aimed to keep firmly in place "special and flexible policies" for the SEZs. As circulators pressed further, he openly challenged the top-down method of achieving comprehensive balance and protested that a top-down approach should be combined with a bottom-up one.[43]

The local specialists' tolerance of inflation was not merely a gesture of self-defense in the wake of the circulators' challenge. Their growth-minded worldview conditioned them to interpret inflation in a different light. They had signed onto the view that inflation was not a threat but merely a symptom of a fast-growing economy, at most a growing pain of a transitioning economy.[44] To find examples of tolerance toward inflation, Zhao looked around the world for reassuring models. He sent his research team to Latin America, and the result was a rosy interpretation of inflation on that continent. Given that inflation was a worldwide problem affecting many countries in the late 1980s, the selection of country sites by Zhao's team was curious. The team's report stated that countries like Brazil had been accustomed to high levels of inflation during stages of high-speed development and its overall economy remained healthy.[45] This report further emboldened the local generalists. They were determined to go ahead with the comprehensive price reform of 1988 despite an inflationary environment and Chen Yun's now strong and personal opposition. Chen felt the necessity to admonish Zhao in the most direct fashion possible. He sent private letters to Zhao advising him that price liberalization was extremely dangerous, given the high level of currency issuance.[46] The subsequent economic history sided with the circulators' prediction. The inflation rate shot up shortly after the lifting of price controls on key commodities, triggering political instability across the country and setting the economic stage for the 1989 Tiananmen protest. In an unexpectedly abrupt way, this series of incidents ended the political lives of the local generalists and tarnished the reputation of their decentralization approach to economic reform.

This chapter continues to unpack the bureaucratic origin of China's economic reform by exploring the relationship between socialist careers and

the cultivation of reformers. It introduced the second group of reformers—
the local generalists who rose from the localities and also discovered the
market in the shadow of the socialist economy. The local generalists initially joined the cause of the circulators in support of Deng Xiaoping's
reform, but differences in career backgrounds that resulted in divergent
understandings of the economy ultimately tore this coalition apart. For the
circulators, the market was macro: it was reducible to price movements,
financial flows, and macroeconomic levers. For the local generalists, their
experience with "mobilizing the masses" shortened their social distance
from producers and economic practices on the ground. To them, the market was micro, and, therefore, incentivizing peasants and local enterprises
came to the fore. The difference in bureaucratic practices and methods of
discovery gave way to two distinct approaches to market reform. The circulators emphasized balanced development, while the local generalists were
preoccupied with decentralized growth. Their conflict eventually broke
into the open over an existential issue erupting in China's transitioning
economy: inflation. Economic overheating and its contribution to the 1989
political protests caused the decentralizing approach to lose its luster and
restored an aversion to macroeconomic imbalance to policy prominence
for decades to come. Yet as the next chapters show, the fall of the local
generalists in this particular era did not mean this type of career experience completely lost favor with the central economic bureaucracy. In fact,
economic bureaucrats continued to source staff from cohorts of local generalists. The difference is that in the new era of centralization, local origins
were no longer directly translated into a drive for decentralization and an
unchecked sympathy for localities. Instead, local experiences were tapped
and valued for state-building purposes.

The first decade of reform provides a unique opportunity to observe
the importance of career types as a resilient source of bureaucratic differences. While scholarship on this period contends that career bases repre-
sent bases of power and networks of political support, this chapter shows
that bureaucratic careers also produced dispositions that conditioned and
mediated bureaucratic power and the formation of policy outlooks. Even
after the elite reformers shed their prior organizational obligations and
ascended to leading positions in the economic bureaucracy, they fell back
on their previous organizational practices of observing the economy and
collecting what they considered to be data. In the first decade of reform, the
power of career dispositions was especially direct and unmediated because

institutional building lagged behind elite-pushed initiatives, thrusting the elite reformers to the forefront of history making. The economic bureaucracy, as an organization, stayed in the background and had yet to be used as means of change. Thus, elite actors' personal and collective charisma had a larger-than-usual impact on policy footprints. As the next chapter shows, as soon as elite actors realized the importance of harnessing bureaucratic institutions to accumulate power and advocate for policies, interelite competition and bureaucratic entrepreneurship acquired new levels of complexity and required an analysis that factors in the interaction of positions, dispositions, and organizations.

PART II
Consolidation

Chapter Three

THE RISE OF TECHNOCRATS

Market Rationalization and the
Macrocontrol Paradigm

In the early reform era, differences in the reformers' career trajectories were a source of disagreement over approaches to economic reform. As it turned out, this conflict ended rather abruptly. The local generalists had been willing to tolerate the Tiananmen movement and were forced out in the political turmoil that followed. At the same time, the circulators aged out of political power after having been recently vindicated. Yet the predictive effect of careers was hardly diminished as these cohorts of bureaucrats departed and new cohorts replaced them. A new group of technocrats rose, bound by their shared educational and career experiences and the ways in which these experiences impacted their outlooks. The technocrats championed a view of economics and politics different from that of the previous era's bureaucrats, and they initiated a paradigm shift in structuring state-market relations.

Unlike the circulators and the local generalists of the previous era, who coexisted in a competitive environment, the technocrats of the 1990s were able to achieve considerable hegemony over economic policy making and eventually made fundamental changes to the Chinese economic bureaucracy. In many ways, they scrambled the division between the circulators and the local generalists because they combined and intermingled both groups' traits and aspirations. They carried over the circulators' concern for regulatory authority and central coordination but also committed to growth and market dynamism like the local generalists. To be precise, they heralded a new era in the history of Chinese economic management in which both the market and the central state were significantly advanced. As a result, they used the construction of the central economic bureaucracy as a necessary means to build markets. And unlike their predecessors in the 1980s, this generation of technocrats was able to realize the fruits of their policies through the new institutions they created.

By tracing the rise of the technocrats, this chapter answers a number of long-standing questions associated with China's economic reform. Why did a regime crisis at the end of the 1980s result in a stronger commitment to market reform by the Chinese government, despite the anticipation of a prolonged retrenchment or even a reversal of economic reform? In retrospect, we know that the Jiang Zemin administration (1993–2003) oversaw a decade of double-digit growth with marketization proceeding at a much faster pace and on a larger scale than in the 1980s. Why did the technocrats, who had previously been deemed uncharismatic and politically weak, turn out to be a paradigm-changing force in Chinese elite politics and reset the course of economic reform? This chapter finds answers to these questions in the ways in which the technocrats constructed their basis of legitimacy and paved their routes to power. I argue that initiating the twin projects of state building and market building was instrumental in enabling the technocrats to obtain and consolidate their technocratic power. Developing market control through centralizing the fiscal, financial, and macroeconomic power of the state gave the technocrats a range of institutional powers and considerable policy authority.

FRAGMENTED AND NEGLECTED: THE ECONOMIC BUREAUCRACY IN THE 1980S

As chapter 1 explains, in order to bring about an end to populist politics, China's economic reform focused as much on restoring an effective central bureaucracy as on injecting new dynamism into the economy. In the first decade of reform, the reformers succeeded in the latter task but fell short on the former. They resumed the basic operation of the bureaucracy and upgraded its personnel, but they made no systematic efforts to significantly ramp up state capacity and put the state seriously to work. The economic bureaucracy in particular remained a patchwork of fragmented organizations until the end of the first decade of reform. Divisions of labor among the specialized industrial ministries[1] still reflected the material bias of the planned economy and could no longer be maintained as the command economy crumbled. Interagency coordination was another issue. It was often facilitated by personal connections rather than by stable channels of communication and command. As the veteran minister Yuan Baohua observed, "Jobs are created to accommodate people [*yinren sheshi*]" rather than the other way around. Interorganization coordination usually "relied on old acquaintances to get things done."[2] Vice Minister Zhang Yanning echoed Yuan when commenting on the "exceptional flexibility" of the economic bureaucracy. He noted that when directors or division managers from a ministry moved to a new agency, they often brought with them the entire division that they used to supervise, irrespective of that division's compatibility with the destination organization.[3] As a result, misalignments between functions and titles abounded and caused confusion.[4] In short, fragmentation and weak institutions largely characterized the economic bureaucracy in the first decade of reform.

To a large extent, the lack of attention to rebuilding the economic bureaucracy after the ruinous Cultural Revolution was a choice rather than a coincidence. As the previous chapter discusses, the local generalists' approach to reform was to decentralize the government and unleash private incentives. They perceived the economic bureaucracy as a holdover from the command economy and an obstacle rather than an aid to reform.[5] This deep-seated distrust of the central bureaucracy was reflected, quintessentially, in the way in which the leading local generalists, such as Premier Zhao Ziyang, organized their brain trusts. Zhao was formally in charge of running the country's day-to-day economic affairs, and, therefore, his relationship with the economic bureaucracy had a large impact on its status in the government. He did not rely on the economic bureaucracy to supply ideas or formulate groundbreaking policies. Instead, he surrounded himself with an array of consultative networks that consisted not of ministers but of economists and state think-tank researchers from the lower ranks of the bureaucracy whose views he largely shared.[6] These advisers were consulted on an ad hoc basis, with some of them incorporated into Zhao's task forces or secretaries' offices. The consultative style of economic policy making was not only a style of governance but also a mechanism for wielding power. Some authors argue that Zhao brought in the intellectuals and economists as his allies precisely to get around or even counter the economic bureaucracy.[7]

Local generalists lacked the basic motivation to rebuild the economic bureaucracy, and the circulators, despite their intentions, didn't have the capacity to follow through with this cause either. Naturally, the circulators would have preferred a strong central state that would exercise macroeconomic control, one of their chief policy goals. But their grip on the economic bureaucracy was weak at best. About a decade older than the local generalists, many of the circulators had already left formal roles in the bureaucracy and shaped policies only through residual connections and influence. In addition to lacking the resources, the circulators encountered their own limitations and were unable to imagine how a revamped bureaucracy might aid them. In fact, when called on to control inflation, the circulators frequently fell back on their old tool kit, using techniques such as credit planning, which did not require bureaucratic reconstruction. In any case, without the mediation of strong institutions, policy conflicts between the circulators and the local generalists took on factional characteristics. Scholars demonstrate that concerted efforts at state building often require a strong political will and a consensual and committed group of state builders who possess a decent amount of political control.[8] Disagreement over approaches to reform at a paradigmatic level was a clear manifestation of the lack of consensus among the leadership on how to organize state-market relations. Therefore, factionalist policy struggles further slowed the formalization of economic policy-making institutions and diminished the prospect of state building.

THE RISE OF TECHNOCRATS AND
THE DEMOBILIZATION OF POLITICS

The leadership of the post-Tiananmen administration arrived on a stage that had been abruptly emptied of the elite conflict typical of the previous era. This group of leaders had very different career profiles than those of its predecessors and was drawn from an ascending generation of officials who would be characterized as technocrats. As epitomized by President Jiang Zemin, Premier Li Peng, and Vice Premier Zhu Rongji, they were trained as engineers and spent a large proportion of their official careers in the central ministries. With a career portfolio that included an engineering degree, a specialist career, and central government experience, they

TABLE 3.1
Career profiles of Jiang Zemin, Li Peng, and Zhu Rongji

Name	College major	Years served in central ministries	Organization served the longest	Professional experience	Years served as a local generalist
Jiang Zemin	Electrical machinery	23	First Machinery Industry Ministry	Engineer in automotive manufacturing factory	4
Li Peng	Hydropower	4	Beijing Power Supply Bureau	Engineer in power plant	0
Zhu Rongji	Electrical machinery	30	State Planning Commission	Engineer in the Ministry of Petroleum Industry	4

Source: Compiled by the author from officials' CVs.

fit the basic definition of a technocrat: one who received technical education, was valued as an expert, and assumed high posts in the government.[9]
As table 3.1 shows, although both Jiang and Zhu had worked in local governments, the number of years they spent in central ministries as specialists greatly surpassed their brief time in the localities, mainly Shanghai,
as generalists. Li didn't spend much time in the central ministries, but he
nevertheless worked extensively in positions closely aligned with his expertise in electrical machinery and had little exposure to local governments.

Leaders were drawn from the pool of bureaucrats. Among those under
study, this continuity between leaders and bureaucrats is supported by shared
generational experiences that, in this case, united the technocrats. Generations are two to three decades in the making, although this is not to say that
there is necessarily a lag of approximately two to three decades between
when officials began their careers and when they assumed the highest positions. The Chinese Communist Revolution and government, compared to
those of the Soviet Union, were not known for practicing technocracy. As
chapter 1 discusses, waves of populist movements under the aegis of Mao
targeted technocraticism and those with cultural and educational capital.
Yet there was a brief period from 1949 to 1958 in which China did attempt
to follow the Soviets' "technocratic road"[10] to pursue socialist transformations.[11] It was in this period that Jiang, Zhu, and their contemporary peers

received their college education and spent the formative years of their official careers in the new government. There they blended early Communist activism with experiences in higher education, science, and centralized planning. Three decades later, in the wake of political chaos, they presented themselves as prime candidates to remake Chinese politics and the Chinese economy. The circumstances were ripe for their rapid ascent.

To explain the technocrats' rise, we need to analyze how their career origins prepared them for this thrust to the forefront. In particular, we need to explain to what extent their technocratic backgrounds played a role in their rise, focusing on how they translated these backgrounds into policy concepts as well as a strategy for gaining power. The first decade of reform ended with macroeconomic instability, political turmoil, and a military crackdown. Key leaders were removed for their inability to anticipate and effectively cope with the student movement. It was also believed that the economic reform had, through decentralization, contributed to the Tiananmen incident. Decentralization indulged inflation, lowered living standards, and paved the way for society-wide support of the student protests. Weakened central control, the result of decentralization policies, was also thought to have led to the explosion and unhindered expression of societal grievances. Decentralization as an economic program thus came under criticism due to its correlation with political instability and the fostering of centrifugal interests.

In their search for leaders to succeed the fallen Hu Yaobang and Zhao Ziyang, supreme regime gatekeepers like Deng Xiaoping and other "immortals" felt the need to look for alternative career experiences and governance styles. The technocrats presented themselves as worthy and prepared candidates, but the critical push for their ascendance stemmed from the expectations of the time. Seizing the authority to define the situation following Tiananmen, Deng declared that socialism could not afford another episode of political instability. "Stability should overwhelm everything [*wending Yadao yiqie*]," which would speak to the fundamental desire of the Chinese people, he declared.[12] Thinkers of the neoauthoritarian school within the Chinese Communist Party echoed Deng's message by drawing an analogy between the Cultural Revolution and the political climate in the 1980s. They argued that both periods saw an "explosion of political participation," breeding polarization and perpetuating crises. The dilemma between the need for mobilization and the threat of loss of control, according to this line of reasoning, was the fundamental baggage of authoritarian politics that China needed to overcome. In their eyes, the decade of the 1980s, though initially celebrated as an era of intellectual liberation, was a continuation of the era of the Cultural Revolution, encouraging a chorus of voices and popular engagement with national affairs and intellectual matters—that is, mass participation in politics.[13] The implicit call from the neoauthoritarian scholars was to mitigate or redirect popular interests in politics elsewhere in the interest of ensuring stability.

The arrival of the central technocrats on the political stage was an important part of the party's response to a dilemma often faced by authoritarian polities. Historically, technocracy has been one of the best methods for building authoritarian resilience. Technocrats were favored on the basis of their aversion to mass mobilization and political charisma. They were called on in this moment of crisis to bring their professional skills and their belief in technical rationality to reorder the Chinese economy. "Lack of charisma" was a common assessment of the new administration headed by Jiang Zemin.[14] It launched an era of "faceless bureaucrats" in China to the extent that some China scholars lamented that the study of Chinese elite politics would no longer exhibit the same drama and excitement as it had in prior decades.[15] The demobilization effect that the technocrats generated was precisely what was intended. Jiang had already impressed Beijing with his deft handling of student protests in Shanghai while he was the mayor in 1989: his emphasis on law and order and his ability to successfully deradicalize the students using nonviolent means contrasted sharply with what happened in Beijing.[16] Zhu's determination to forge Shanghai into China's financial center and his reputation as a no-nonsense leader attracted the attention of Deng, who stated that Zhu "knows about the economy [*dong jingji*]."[17] Li Peng, by no means a high-profile leader, was long considered an heir of the old generation of centralizers, and Chen Yun and Liu Lanbo, former minister of the electric power industry, allegedly favored promoting him.[18] A new road was paved for this next generation of leaders to revise the governance style and the political milieu of the 1980s.

TECHNOCRATS ON THE ROAD TO POWER

The Turn to the Central State

There is no doubt that the newly risen technocrats were also bureaucratic incumbents. Yet unlike their predecessors, they were relative newcomers to the pinnacle of the party-state. As a result, they didn't have wide webs of connections across the Chinese government and urgently needed to build their political bases and consolidate their power. The fact that they ascended during a time of crisis lent them some measure of exceptional power, but this simultaneously meant that they were promoted in a rather hasty fashion, and the question of power consolidation loomed large. Chinese officials did not assemble constituencies in the same way that elected politicians do in democracies, but they nevertheless needed to rely on proxy constituencies to build the vectors of their power. These constituencies could take a variety of forms: they could be instruments of governance, bases of political support, or jurisdictions for their policies. The central state, conveniently, could serve as the technocrats' constituency in all of these ways. To them, the state could be an instrument of power and a vehicle for policy effectiveness. Granted, a grip on the central bureaucracy was not the only route to power in Chinese politics. The local generalists of the 1980s had already shown that "playing to the provinces" was a viable political and economic strategy. The choice of where to locate one's key bases of power on the political map was as much a strategic calculation as a career habit. It is true that both Jiang Zemin and Zhu Rongji had worked in Shanghai as local generalists, but this four-year experience was rather transitory. In retrospect, the metropolitan location played more of a role by shielding them from the political turmoil taking place in Beijing and by showcasing their ability to develop Shanghai's economy. The central bureaucracy, on the other hand, where they spent many more years, was a more familiar habitat. Zhu, for example, frequently attributed the development of his economic acumen to his years at the State Planning Commission (SPC) and the State Economic Commission.[19] One of the officials in Zhu's administration whom I interviewed called Zhu "the last good planner," a planner who knew how to turn state control into market development.[20]

Intentions aside, the central bureaucracy remained too attractive to be underutilized as an instrument of power. One decade of decentralization had weakened the substantial power of the central bureaucracy, but the basic bureaucratic machinery was kept nearly intact. No major ministries were slashed. As a whole, the economic bureaucracy may have been ill coordinated, but through its constituent parts, it fulfilled a broad spectrum of functions, including planning, budgeting, credit dispersion, public investment, public-sector supervision, technology policy development, statistical analysis, and regulation of foreign trade. The question was now how to readapt and remold these functions to aid economic reform. To Chinese technocrats, a strong state was not a given. It was not a prior condition under which they rose to power. They rose *in spite of* a weak central state. For technocrats to wield power from the center, they would have to achieve a commanding position at the center of political power.

The Turn to International Learning

Aside from relying on the central bureaucracy, the technocrats turned to foreign development models to provide clarity and enhance their legitimacy. Scholars argue that in times of uncertainty, policy makers are more open to new ideas.[21] In the case of China, foreign ideas played an important role during this period but were still mediated by the local technocrats who selected them.

To the newcomer technocrats, uncertainty was a blessing more than a curse. It put them on an equal cognitive footing with the more experienced politicians—even Deng Xiaoping. In the midst of uncertainty, there emerged a paradigmatic inquiry into how to approach the relationship between markets and planning. This led to a rare spate of interest in theories, a conscious effort to search out generalizable rules and workable models, spurring an intense moment of social learning in the history of the People's Republic of China (PRC). As early as 1990, Deng spoke with "leading comrades" on the importance of "theoretically" grappling with the relationship between capitalism and socialism.[22] He encouraged the leadership to look into the experiences of the "economic take-off" in Japan and South Korea and the managerial philosophy of the Singaporean government.[23] Jiang Zemin and Li Peng argued for pausing the discussion of concrete policies and instead focusing on understanding the relationship between markets and planning in order to ask "theoretically and historically" informed questions.[24]

In October 1990, Jiang asked the System Reform Commission (SRC) to "sum up the essential experiences" where planning and markets were combined in an optimal fashion, drawing from the record of world history. Jiang was particularly interested in drawing lessons from the fact that, contrary to Karl Marx's prediction, capitalism was still alive and prospering.[25] The final report of the SRC started with Pareto's proposition that in order to achieve efficient allocation of resources, a perfect central planner and a fully competitive market were functionally equivalent. Unfortunately, as Friedrich Hayek pointed out, a perfectly planned economy is not feasible. The report went on to state that building on the legacy of the American New Deal and Keynesian economics, governments around the world had demonstrated a tendency to utilize "both the visible and invisible hands."[26] A letter from Henry Kissinger to Chinese officials was attached to the report. In it, Kissinger wrote that neither pure markets nor planned economies actually existed but that, in general, a market-based economy provided a more sustainable basis for growth.[27] Jiang had great respect for this grand but pithy report and urged the cadre of high-level officials to study it thoroughly. Li also cited this report when he met foreign experts from the World Economic Forum,[28] and he later instructed the drafting team of the Seventh Plenary Session of the Thirteenth Central Committee to review the conclusions of this report. Zhu Rongji, the newly promoted vice premier, went even further by making an explicit effort to bring China in line with international "best practices."[29] In 1993, in defense of the speed with which his scheme of financial reform was rolled out, Zhu stated that "there was nothing mysterious to it, as every country with an advanced market economy has done so. There are existing models we can turn to."[30]

The Turn to Market

With this turn to foreign models, the countries Chinese officials surveyed and the conclusions they drew from examining these countries mattered significantly to the direction of China's own economic reform. To assess this issue, I surveyed articles in *Internal Reference for Reform*—the party's second-largest internal reference publication—from 1986 to 1992. The journal's contents were classified in 1993, but its window of availability captures this process of rethinking China's economic reform and its changing locus of interests. My reading of all the articles on foreign countries shows a globalization of reference frameworks. Prior to 1989, economic reforms in Eastern European countries were of great interest to Chinese leaders and economic scholars alike. At the forefront, market socialism experiments in Hungary and workers' self-management in Yugoslavia alerted Chinese reformers to possible revisions of a rigid Stalinist economy.[31] Chinese policy makers welcomed the suggestions of

Eastern European experts because both groups had received similar kinds of training, spoke the same political economic language, and understood the common problems facing transitioning economies.[32] The collapse of Communism in Eastern Europe, however, led to a near disappearance of this set of common references. My results show that articles on Eastern and Central European countries took up 50 percent of all articles referencing foreign countries in 1987. This dropped to 19 percent in 1991 and to zero in 1992.

The fall of Communism in Eastern Europe forced Chinese elites to broaden their search for applicable case studies. With this shift, China's economic reform came to be viewed less as a case of socialist revision than one of structural reform. China's search for international examples was now no longer limited to the socialist bloc and expanded into the global capitalist wilderness. Policy elites were urged to broaden their views and "open their eyes to the whole outside world."[33] East Asian economies were the first bloc of countries to attract this new attention. In particular, South Korea's state-led development was considered successful and highly relevant to China. In *Internal Reference for Reform*, articles on South Korea surged from sporadic appearances in earlier years to a full one-third of all articles on foreign countries in 1990. Granted, Chinese policy elites had been interested in learning about East Asian economies in the 1980s, but the focus then had been technical proficiency, managerial methods, and corporate planning. After 1989, these elites took another look at South Korea—but now as a holistic model for development. To gain a deeper understanding of the South Korean experience, in December 1989, only six months after the June 4 protest at Tiananmen Square, a team of Chinese officials attended a UN-organized symposium in South Korea, even though the two countries did not have formal diplomatic relations. Chinese delegates were told that South Korea had scaled back state intervention because excessive state intervention had distorted Korea's economic structure and resource distribution. Instead, since 1979, the Korean state had focused on core tasks related to facilitating market competition, bridging income disparity, undertaking economic forecasting, and promoting macroeconomic stability. Chinese officials were convinced that this type of "indirect" state intervention was "more scientific and advanced."[34]

Beyond East Asia, countries with a tradition of strong state action vis-à-vis the economy also provided relevant examples. In this regard, the technocrats encouraged the expansion of official sampling to include many newly liberalizing economies (e.g., Vietnam) and established market economies that had sizable public sectors or that pursued policies of dirigisme (e.g., France, Italy, Thailand, and India).[35] The officials' visits, consultative meetings, and reports, involving a wide spectrum of countries and economic situations, resulted in two nearly unanimous conclusions: turning to markets to develop the national economy was both inevitable and desirable, and the state should play a role in facilitating marketization. The timing of China's international search for information surely contributed to the nature of the resulting conclusions. The early 1990s saw the blooming of a neoliberal era. What was happening in both the developed and the developing worlds was a synchronization of liberalizing policies across various forms of political economies. Traditionally planning-prone capitalist democracies, such as Japan, Korea, and France, were drifting toward fuller marketization, highlighting a sense of historical destiny for China, and in many ways, this provided clarity in a time of agonizing uncertainties.[36]

One could argue that in turning to marketization in this period, China had succumbed to the isomorphic pressures and mimetic desires that characterized the worldwide neoliberal turn in this period. Yet it is also essential to note that China's market building took into account peculiar domestic and international circumstances and dovetailed with the political aspirations of the technocrats. As the following sections show, the technocrats also didn't forgo the means of achieving market goals that were replete with "bureaucratic characteristics." Domestically, they projected themselves as historical agents bringing China in line with an inevitable trend in state-market restructuring. In the international community, China faced an acute problem of legitimacy following the crackdown on the student protests in 1989. The country's search for information in an international setting displayed an anxiety to fit in and served as a gesture of curiosity and openness toward the outside world. The learning tours, conferences, and meetings served unique diplomatic functions when formal ties broke down.[37] The conclusions this new generation of technocratic leaders drew sent out signals to the international community that China intended to continue to move toward international inclusion. The responses from the developed world were then expected to lend support to the technocratic government, which looked to quickly establish its authority amid political and economic insecurity.

ENGINEERS' NEW ASSIGNMENTS

Having decided to speed up the reform, the engineers-turned-technocrats were faced with an unprecedented task: building a market economy; it was one for which they were not well trained. This mission was far removed from what the Chinese engineers had been tapped to do for decades—central planning. Table 3.2 shows the distribution of college majors among elite economic bureaucrats across four generations of officials. Elite economic bureaucrats are defined as those with an administrative ranking of vice minister or above in an economic policy-making agency. Those officials in the first generation were born in the first two decades of the 1900s and assumed leading positions in the economic bureaucracy in the 1980s. Those in the second generation were born in the late 1920s and 1930s and rose to primacy in the Jiang/Zhu administration in the 1990s. The first and second generations resembled one another in that engineering dominated their educational backgrounds. In the first generation, 36.4 percent of the economic officials who attended college or technical secondary school were trained in engineering. Among the second generation, 33.3 percent were engineers. The slight drop in the percentage of engineering degrees from the first to second generation is less analytically significant if we consider the rest of their majors. Among the first generation, the percentage of economics degree holders trailed closely the percentage of engineering majors. Among the second generation, engineering majors claimed unchallenged dominance. This is because officials in this generation were mostly schooled after the establishment of the PRC, in a period when "bourgeois" economics courses were removed from the national curriculum. The primacy of engineers in the second generation was even more pronounced

TABLE 3.2
Distribution of college majors for the four generations of elite economic bureaucrats

	Engineering (%)	Economics (%)	Political economy (%)	Finance (%)
Generation 1	36	21.2	9.1	9.1
Generation 2	33.3	6.7	15.6	11.1
Generation 3	9.7	24.3	6.1	14.6
Generation 4	15	32.5	2.5	5

Source: Compiled and calculated by the author from elite economic bureaucrats' CVs.

when compared to the sharp decline in engineering degrees among the third-generation officials, as economics quickly climbed to become the hegemonic discipline.

This cross-generational comparison puts in perspective the historical position that the second-generation engineers occupied at the crossroads of China's economic reform. Unlike their first-generation counterparts, who were mostly planners, the second-generation engineers were expected to be market builders. Unlike the third-generation economics majors, who appeared to be a more natural fit for directing market reform, the second-generation engineers faced a task of self-transformation. The following analysis explains how they lived up to this task and what approaches they took to achieve their goals. In their journey to transform the Chinese economy and themselves, their engineering background had a palpable impact on their policy styles, ideologies, and practical choices.

PROBLEM SOLVING AND THE MAKING
OF A NEW POLICY PARADIGM

As soon as it was clear that reform would continue, the engineers-turned-technocrats swiftly began their state-building project. They did so by solving a series of interrelated problems—an effort that lent itself to the creation of an overarching policy paradigm for managing the economy through what they called *macrocontrol*. They singled out two issues to tackle—the fiscal weakness of the central state and inflation. In the course of solving these "problems," they nudged the parameters of economic policy closer toward perceived market standards and at the same time mobilized whatever technical, administrative, and political means were available to achieve them. The problem-solving approach to policy reflected a pattern of pragmatic behavior, which many claimed stemmed from the methodology and epistemics of engineering.[38] The flexible means they used to solve these problems also brought about a new bureaucratic way of making economic policy in the state, which would mold many subsequent ministries.

Strengthening the Fiscal Sinew of the Central State

The technocrats identified the declining influence of the central state over the economy as one of the most urgent issues facing the new administration.

The lack of fiscal means would certainly derail the technocratic project of state building. The technocrats pointed to evidence showing a weakened grip by the political center: plummeting government revenues, especially those of central government, were glaringly at odds with the growing economy. Government revenue as a percentage of GDP, already low to start with, dropped from 23 percent in 1984 to 13 percent in 1992. This situation boded ill for any attempt to direct and discipline powerful local fiefdoms into following the policies of the central government. Building national markets, as the technocrats sought to do, required a strong state capacity in place, breaking off "the independent kingdoms"—the provinces.

By foregrounding the issue of declining central tax revenues, the technocrats sought to arrest a long-term trend of decentralization fostered by the previous administration. When presenting issues to the rest of the government, they also adopted an alarmist vision and argued that the imbalance was an imminent crisis that justified immediate action. In reality, no one had designated a clear threshold of central government revenue as a percentage of GDP beyond which the state would collapse. Emboldened by Premier Zhu Rongji's direction, Ministry of Finance (MOF) officials canceled their visit to Yugoslavia in 1987 after having attributed the collapse of its government to a diminished government revenue/GDP ratio, which had fallen to 11 percent. They argued that China's fiscal revenues, after years of erosion, were also "on the edge of the cliff" and "would fall at any time into an abyss if tipped over."[39] At stake was the central government's authority and credibility vis-à-vis local governments. Tax officials revealed that the central government, in more than one instance, had to "borrow" revenues from the local governments and, worse still, was not even able to pay them back.[40] Zhu vividly described this situation: "With no grain at hand, even the chickens would not come when you call upon them."[41] For the first time, the loss of central authority in relation to the local governments was explicitly discussed and presented as a crisis of the state.

With the problem identified, the reconstruction of China's fiscal institutions exemplified a technocratic pursuit of rationalization based on existing models. In 1994, the new administration introduced tax assignment reform and officially cast the arbitrary fiscal contracting system of the 1980s into the dustbin of history. The tax reform standardized and simplified tax categories and unified the tax rates for state-owned and privately owned enterprises in order to level the playing field. Tax revenues were divided between the central and local governments based on what the two entities were entitled to collect in accordance with their respective functions.[42] Value-added taxes were introduced as a gradual replacement for sales taxes in order to reduce double taxation and facilitate the circulation of goods across regional markets. The tax reform was modeled on the established tax categories and the division of fiscal rights and duties across different levels of governments used in "mature market economies."[43] Vice Minister of Finance Xiang Huaicheng explained that the "tax sharing system was not invented by us. It has existed for a long time. It is widely implemented in countries around the world."[44] To better learn from international experiences, China obtained a $6 million loan from the World Bank to invite foreign experts to China for dozens of intensive consulting sessions it hosted. Beijing also dispatched Chinese fiscal officials to Australia, Germany, Japan, and other countries that were considered "standard bearers" of tax-sharing systems.[45] As intended, the reassignment of taxes allowed the central government to claim a larger share of government revenues. In fact, the impact of reform was immediately reflected in the state coffers the following year. Central government revenue more than doubled, with its share of all tax revenues climbing from 21 percent in 1993 to 52 percent in 1995. This percentage has been stable around the same level up to 2022, attesting to the enduring efficacy of this institutional redesign.

Even the most compelling technocratic justification for tax assignment reform, however, would not sway the local governments. After all, claims on tax revenues are at the heart of any government's interests. Local governments would not capitulate to tax reform without a fight. In the worst-case scenario, as the central officials were aware, provincial governments would talk to each other and form a united front against the central government.[46] If this were to occur, what had begun as an institutional shake-up would indeed escalate into a political earthquake. A technocratic reform in the name of technical rationality, public utility, or national interests might have given the central government some justification for making such a substantial change. But it was clear that with so many interests at stake, political arm-twisting was also anticipated to combat resistance.

The ways in which the central technocrats sought consent from local power holders reflected a combination of their pragmatism, political acumen, and negotiation skills. Characteristic of a technocrat, Zhu Rongji refrained from using any campaign-style persuasion and mobilization. He explicitly admonished fiscal officials not to ideologize tax reform and not to present it as an attempt to correct the historical wrongs of the previous administration. He suggested that they explain the problem-solving rationale behind the fiscal reform: the central government was strapped for cash and was not able to do its job on behalf of the whole country.[47] Operating under this desensitizing framing, Zhu led a team of sixty fiscal officials to seventeen provinces in 1993 to persuade and negotiate with them one by one. Zhu's team started the tour with the rich coastal provinces, which were set to face a deeper cut in their tax revenues and were also expected to show stronger resistance. Guangdong was the first province to break. As expected, provincial officials expressed outspoken opposition. The central officials walked them through the impeccable math they had prepared, showing that the cut of local revenues would not be as large as local officials anticipated, in that all government revenues would rise following the tax-sharing reform, and also conceded that the central government was willing to give Guangdong special treatment in sales tax retention. To push for Guangdong's final assent, Zhu and the tax officials made a major compromise with regard to tax refunds from the central to provincial governments, putting Guangdong's dissent to rest. Guangdong's acceptance modeled to the rest of the nation the capitulation that the technocrats hoped to achieve. At other stops, Zhu's team applied a similarly mixed method of technical reasoning, moral pressures, arm-twisting, and, at times, individually tailored offers. This divide-and-rule strategy proved successful in preempting a possible concerted resistance. The way in which the technocrats pushed through difficult policy decisions and negotiated with local power holders showcased their political skills and demonstrated pragmatism in action. This process of centralizing the fiscal power of the state was the first triumphant victory in the battle to establish the authority of the technocratic government.

Inflation Control and the Restoration of Financial Order

Inflation and the lack of financial discipline became another acute problem the new administration identified and tackled. Inflation control in this period marked the third instance in the history of PRC that inflation was associated with the consolidation of central technocratic power. In the first instance, economic specialists of the new Communist regime established their reputation by stemming hyperinflation in late Republican China and centralized the monetary regime in the late 1940s. In the second instance, following periods of inflation in the 1980s, the circulators clawed back the authority over economic policy they had lost to local generalists. The first half of the 1990s presented another opportunity for the technocrats to make a similar bid. The inflation rate shot up from 6.3 percent in 1992 to 14.6 percent in 1993 and reached a record high of 24.26 percent in 1994, a level unseen in the history of the PRC. This happened because the restarted economy encountered two obstacles simultaneously: shortages of basic materials and a troublesome financial exuberance. The exact threshold for a threatening inflation rate was a matter of interpretation. In any case, the technocrats seized the inflationary macroeconomic environment to present themselves as new "money doctors," vowing to rein in government spending and public investment.

To the technocrats in this period, inflation control acquired an additional purpose—centralization. This was possible because inflation at the time was associated with a concern for regulating local public investments. In the early 1990s, a local investment frenzy made a dangerous comeback following the official resumption of economic reform. Local governments interpreted Deng Xiaoping's southern tour and the articulation of an intent to build a "socialist market economy" as another call for "markets without administration."[48] The local interpretation of the official policy indeed conveyed a profound cognitive dissonance between the local leaders and the central technocrats at this juncture. "Reassured" by this misinterpretation, local capital investments soared. Real estate development boomed, and banks extended loans to local enterprises. Bank-affiliated trust and investment companies proliferated around the nation and poured funds into the already overheating financial and real estate markets. All of these investment activities received a green light from local governments, many of which actively participated by using local branches of state banks as vehicles to disburse funds. Against this background, the technocrats felt the need to send a clearer message across China on the financial front.

Zhu Rongji's commitment to revamping China's financial system began with reassessing the role of China's central bank. The issue with the People's Bank of China (PBOC) was articulated simply and clearly: the bank did not behave like a central bank and should be made into a "real" one.[49] As it was, many of the PBOC's strictures prevented it from taking a commanding position in the monetary system. For starters, the PBOC was still a vehicle for public investment, disbursing funds budgeted for state projects through its local branches. In an increasingly marketized environment, this meant that a large proportion of such activities were profitable. What exacerbated the danger was that the local branches of the PBOC were funded by a system of profit retention rather than formal government budgets. With one foot in the waters of the market, the bank was unable to conduct neutral central-banking functions. The PBOC's organizational and command structures were also decentralized. Local branches were more beholden to local governments than to bank headquarters in Beijing. Local branches of the PBOC received funding from local governments, giving them control over the bank's personnel. As a result, these local bank branches were de facto growth partners of local governments.

With these problems diagnosed, the new administration worked to strip the PBOC of its commercial and investment functions, centralize its operations, and replenish its personnel. The early success of tax assignment reform had boosted the morale and authority of the central government and set the tone for recentralization. As a result, central banking reform met much less resistance from local governments than fiscal reform did. Again, the technocrats referred to existing approaches for building central banking autonomy. Modeled on the U.S. Federal Reserve, they established nine superprovincial banks to replace the province-based branches and boost independence.[50] The technocrats also updated the PBOC's personnel, aligning their skills and visions with the expectations of their new roles. Zhu demanded that the backbone cadre of China's central bank be those "familiar with the macro-economy": that is, those who were attuned to and knew how to be responsive to macroeconomic conditions at the national level rather than to local economic growth.[51]

With its infrastructure revamped, the PBOC then needed to learn how to "behave" like a central bank. This meant equipping it with modern monetary tools and enabling it to influence the parameters of economic activities. In the second half of the 1980s, a group of reform-minded PBOC officials and researchers had experimented with the use of such monetary tools as required reserve ratios and interest rate adjustments.[52] Yet these measures were not effective primarily because the Chinese state banks, under soft budget constraints, didn't respond to these instruments. Zhu and his technocrats understood that for the PBOC to act like a central bank in a market economy, a market-like economy should be in place to respond to monetary signals. Thus, the technocratic bureaucracy needed to engineer the kind of environment in which state interventions would be effective. To this end, the state banks had to be nudged toward being market actors. Starting in 1993, policy functions of the state banks were gradually removed for the purpose of "commercializing" the banks. A range of policy banks were established to take over the management of policy loans earmarked for development goals, leaving the four major state banks to focus on profit-oriented business. In the meantime, the PBOC hurried to craft a "modern" monetary policy framework, shifting the nature of its tool kit from direct to indirect interventions. Credit plans were gradually replaced by a growing list of monetary instruments, revolving around open market operations, deposit reserve ratios, and interest rate structures.[53]

The administration also attempted to craft a regulatory framework for the financial system. Regulatory commissions were assembled to oversee the banking, insurance, and securities industries.[54] In addition to governmental regulation, Zhu showed tremendous interest in adopting Western tools for industrial self-regulation, opening government doors to foreign central bankers, investment bank managers, and treasury officials and seeking their advice. In this period, it was commonplace to see the premier going to great lengths to praise the accounting and auditing standards of Western financial industries. He emphasized the need to build an equivalent system with the help of repatriated Chinese students who had studied finance and accounting abroad. "We are not going to make a word-to-word copy [of what they do], but we need to use them for references and to borrow [some of their measures]," Zhu explained. "After all, the West had engaged in market economies for hundreds of years."[55]

ECONOMIC POLICY THROUGH MACROCONTROL

While modernizing China's financial system to address the underlying causes of inflation, Zhu Rongji's cabinet also engaged in a broad range of administrative measures to rein in inflation and its immediate causes. The unapologetic deployment of heavy-handed measures speaks to an important aspect of their engineering-inspired pragmatism: long-term institutional development should be always accompanied by short-term adjustments and the mobilization of existing administrative means to address exigent problems.

This administrative pragmatism was expressed in a barrage of measures known as the *sixteen points*, a concerted attempt to stamp out potential triggers for inflation. Table 3.3 lists the sixteen measures and their purported objectives. It also characterizes the policies in terms of whether they mainly appealed to administrative methods, market levers, or both. Eleven of the sixteen items addressed administrative measures, which came in different colors and shapes. Some of them used stop-and-go methods for behavioral control (items 2, 4, 6, 8, 10, 11, 12, 14, and 15), while others appealed to outright rationing (items 5, 9, and 13). Still other measures involved administrative judgments (items 8, 12, 14, and 16) on the kind of purchasing or investment activities that were still worth pursuing in an overheated economic environment. Executive action was accompanied by legal and prosecutorial action (items 4 and 13), and law enforcement was dispatched to stamp out illicit activities that had previously been tolerated (items 2, 10, and 11). The sixteen points even harnessed anticorruption measures as a form of regulation to close macroeconomic loopholes and penalize those who resisted (item 13).

Why did the market-friendly technocrats resort to aggressive administrative means to control inflation? One could argue that because of their immersion in the socialist central bureaucracy for two decades, the technocrats could not shed their controlling instinct when it came to economic regulation. The past still weighed heavily on them, but here I argue that the situation mandated that the technocrats take a more tactical approach in order to cope with the bureaucratic environment and achieve their goals: a connection of disposition to entrepreneurship that any paradigm-building bureaucrats must make. The mobilization of ad hoc and drastic administrative measures had an attractive feature: it could "bluff" and shock the local governments and the banks into submission in part because policies that relied on unambiguous bans or blunt demands for immediate results helped "perform" the urgency of the situation and signal to the offenders the seriousness of the matter.[56] The implementation of the sixteen points exemplified such dramatic and performative action. In controlling the money supply (item 1), for example, commercial banks were asked to literally recall cash that was already in circulation.[57] In demanding the banks reclaim their long-term loans (item 2), only one month of notice was given, an extremely harsh deadline and a tall order. Although these measures could be draconian, Zhu believed that "if you do not go one size fits all, your words

TABLE 3.3
The sixteen points for controlling inflation (1993)

			Characteristics of policy measures		
Point	Item title	Policy specification	Administrative methods	Market levers	Mixed
1	Controlling money supply	Controlling base currency issuance and restricting cash circulation			✓
2	Prohibiting illegal capital raising	Forbidding banks to receive short-term deposits at high interest rates to finance long-term loans used in real estate development	✓		
3	Actively leveraging the interest rate	Raising interest rates		✓	
4	Prohibiting "chaotic" raising of capital	Forbidding nonbanking companies to conduct deposit-taking business	✓		
5	Controlling lending	Subjecting bank loans to quotas	✓		
6	Paying back depositors	Asking banks to return funds to depositors seeking withdrawals without delays and excuses	✓		
7	Strengthening financial reform	Turning the PBOC into a central bank			✓
8	Reforming the investment and financing structure	Stopping irrational and redundant investment			✓
9	Issuing national debt	Issuing national bonds and assigning quotas for purchase by government organizations and state-owned enterprises			✓
10	Refining the management of issuing and trading shares	Stamping out illegal issuing and trading of stock certificates by enterprises	✓		
11	Restructuring the foreign exchange market	Cracking down on black market foreign exchange and recalling foreign exchange certificates	✓		
12	Strengthening control over the real estate market	Stopping the appropriation of state land or collective farmland for luxury property schemes	✓		
13	Tightening tax loopholes	Assigning tax quotas to tax collectors to punish those who collected appropriable fees rather than taxes	✓		
14	Stopping construction projects	Assigning categories of importance to construction projects and stopping the "unimportant" ones	✓		
15	Controlling prices	Controlling prices in key sectors that might stimulate inflation	✓		
16	Controlling purchasing power	Tightening spending by government-owned entities	✓		

Source: Compiled by the author from "Opinions of the Central Committee of the Communist Party of China and the State Council on the Current Economic Situation and Strengthening Macro-control" [Zhonggongzhongyang guowuyuan guanyu dangqian jingji qingkuang he jiaqiang hongguantiaokong de yijian], no. 6, 1993, issued by the State Council.

do not count."[58] Equally importantly, the extensive use of administrative measures gave the technocrats a source of self-invented urgency and thus power when their formal authority was yet to be established.

The sixteen points were a patchwork of rapid-fire measures aimed at addressing disparate issues, but together they constituted the first attempt by the central government to manage the economy in a coordinated fashion at the macro level. In fact, following the success of the sixteen points, *macrocontrol* (*hongguan tiaokong*) became the official term for a growing set of activities in the economic bureaucracy.[59] Note that *macrocontrol* is different from *macroeconomic policy* in the Chinese context. While macroeconomic policy encompassed "distant" policies that influenced the economy on the aggregate level, macrocontrol refers to a much larger umbrella of targeted and direct measures. In this regard, the sixteen points set a precedent for what macrocontrol could look like, showcasing its comprehensive breadth. While each policy in the sixteen points may appear to be contingent, their accumulative implementation produced durable institutional consequences. First, the sixteen-point program fostered the establishment of new task forces, such as the National Leading Group for Clearing Triangle Debts, with some of their functions later incorporated into the regular operations of the ministries. Second, it allowed existing agencies to flex their previously underused muscles and turn them into routine methods of control. The effect on the economy was felt almost immediately. Peaking in 1994 at 24.26 percent, the inflation rate fell to 16.8 percent in 1995, 8.3 percent in 1996, and 2.8 percent in 1997. It quickly plunged below zero in 1998 and 1999. Although the 1997 Asian financial crisis may have played a role, some critics argued that Zhu's anti-inflation policy contributed to the drastic reversal of macroeconomic conditions and unnecessarily slowed down the growth rate.[60]

Regardless of the technical causes of deflation, what is important to note is that the administration responded to this new reality with similar macrocontrol policies, transforming this response into an all-weather policy paradigm. Acting on signs of deflation and a dip in the growth rate, the central government choreographed a wide range of macrocontrol policies that were now geared toward steering the economy in the other direction. The monetary supply was loosened, construction projects were resumed and encouraged, rounds of national bonds were issued to finance infrastructure development and capital formation, and engines of growth,

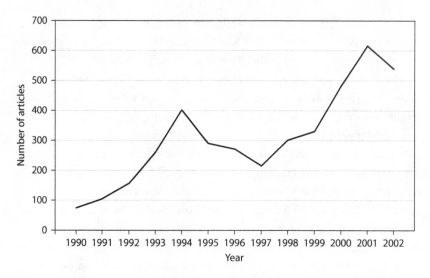

FIGURE 3.1. Number of government documents on macrocontrol issue from 1990 to 2002. *Source*: Compiled by the author from "China Laws & Regulations Database" at "Wanfang Data Knowledge Service Platform" [Wanfang shuju zhishi fuwu pingtai], https://c.wanfangdata.com.cn/claw.

centered around urban expansion and real estate development, were reignited. On the surface, antideflation policies were a stark reversal from the sixteen points: quantitative levers were now ratcheting up in the opposite direction, with sectors that had been explicitly discouraged now promoted. That is, in times of both hardship and exuberance, the central bureaucracy consistently used activist management and control. This is reflected in the number of government documents (laws, bylaws, directives, briefs, and so on) issued throughout Zhu's economic administration related to macrocontrol. As figure 3.1 shows, while overall the number of documents trends upward, there are peaks closely associated with intensified episodes of macrocontrol from 1993 to 1995. The first wave clearly overlapped with the antiinflation episode. The second wave, from 1998 to 2002, was even stronger, indicating aggressive use of macrocontrol measures in the deflation period.

MINISTRIES JUMPING ON THE BANDWAGON OF MACROCONTROL

Originally used for inflation management, macrocontrol could serve as an overarching framework for managing the economy because of its wide-ranging applicability. The capacious agenda of macrocontrol attracted the rest of the economic bureaucracy like a magnet. It provided a historic opportunity for them to transform their relationships with planning and acquire new projects that would be more compatible with the mixed socialist market economy. As noted previously, early efforts toward state building had already had profound effects on the economic bureaucracy. Macrocontrol sent even wider ripples throughout the economic bureaucracy, for it affected not only those agencies that would thrive in a marketized economy such as the PBOC but also those that would otherwise lose their functions in this new environment. The State Economic and Trade Commission (SETC) was a prime example. The SETC was responsible for drafting annual plans in the command economy. With the withering of the planned economy, it was left with a fairly narrow agenda—updating the technologies of state-owned plants. It was macrocontrol that cast the agency in a new light. Now the SETC could harness technological upgrading as an important tool of public investment with its allocation of funds expanding and contracting in tune with macroeconomic conditions.

The rising importance of macrocontrol altered the pecking order among the ministries based on their relevance to this new mission. The specialized industrial ministries were among those that suffered most. They were slashed because their narrow-minded focus on sectoral investment was perceived to be a macroeconomic liability in an environment of overheating. The MOF, in contrast, emerged as a winner in the new regulatory landscape. It had allegedly become "the most important comprehensive agency for macro-control"[61] because of its expanded role in tax policies and fiscal management. This potential reordering of bureaucratic power pushed individual agencies into soul-searching and self-induced conversions. Cognizant of the revitalizing power of macrocontrol, individual agencies proactively transformed themselves into macrocontrol arms of the state. In this regard, the elephant in the room was clearly the SPC. The soaring status of the MOF was a slap in the face of the SPC, a stark inversion of its role as a fiscal arm of the SPC in the era of the command economy. Zhu Rongji showed no mercy. He argued that the SPC was less important because it did not have useful tools and because the meaning of planning had changed. *Planning* now referred to an ability to use fiscal and financial tools flexibly to manage the economy.[62] This imminent threat to the once dominant SPC was a wake-up call. Led by Zeng Peiyan, another engineer-turned-technocrat in the same generation as Zhu, the SPC vowed to remake itself into a "macro-control department" and "an excellent aid to central economic policy." Seizing the moment of antideflation management, the SPC proposed that it could play a role by speeding up fiscal activism, channeling it through the commission's long-standing strength in deploying and supervising large construction projects, thus reequipping it with an ability to stimulate the economy in a short time frame. To this end, the SPC obtained approval rights over large public investments, regained importance, and successfully remade itself into an indispensable pillar of fiscal management.[63]

THE TECHNOCRATIC REMAKING OF THE ECONOMIC BUREAUCRACY

The technocratic project of this decade had a considerable impact on the institutional configuration of the economic bureaucracy. It is worth going into detail about this impact because this array of changes reset the bureaucratic environment in which future generations of economic bureaucrats would have to operate.

Differentiation as Structuration

The first major observation is that centralization enhanced the degree of specialization across the ministries. Professionalizing the PBOC and separating the monetary and investment functions of the state sharpened the division of labor between the PBOC and the MOF. If financial rationalization was an imported source of specialization, macrocontrol served as an indigenous source of bureaucratic differentiation. On the crowded bandwagon of macrocontrol, various ministries learned to differentiate themselves. They played up their existing endowments, reinvented tool kits, and carved out and divided policy jurisdictions. Macrocontrol shaped the bureaucracy into what Pierre Bourdieu calls a social "field,"[64] in which ministries developed a stake in their mutual orientations and engaged in policy distinctions.[65]

As a result of specialization, agency boundaries hardened. Ministries became delimited units containing institutions, professional knowledge, and policy tools. An increased degree of specialization was reflected in

TABLE 3.4

Cross-organizational turnover for the four generations of elite economic bureaucrats

Generation	Organizations served	Years served in each organization
1	5.01	9.49
2	5.31	8.55
3	5.35	8.56
4	4.71	11.51

Source: Calculated by the author from elite economic bureaucrats' CVs.

the slowing of personnel movement across organizations, as specialization placed a premium on transferring knowledge and skills. Table 3.4 captures the trend in personnel movement. The point of interest here is the fourth generation of officials. These bureaucrats started their careers in the late 1980s or early 1990s and matured throughout the Jiang/Zhu administration. While largely unaffected by the bureaucratic logic of the 1980s, this generation was influenced by emergent patterns in the bureaucracy in the 1990s and later. As we can see, those in the fourth generation exhibited a sudden decline in cross-organizational turnover, measured by the number of organizations they served and the average number of years they worked in each organization.

This does not mean that Chinese economic bureaucrats had shifted toward becoming narrow technical experts. As Cheng Li, a longtime observer of Chinese elite politics, pointed out, unlike technocrats in Western democracies, who tend to be technical and nonpolitical, Chinese technocrats always stand out for their political identity—their loyalty to the Communist Party above all else.[66] This means they were equipped, by default, with a basic understanding of administrative operations and access to the powerful tools of the Leninist state. As this chapter shows, Chinese technocrats' array of political knowledge and access, when used effectively, could still compensate for their lack of wide connections or charisma. And their political engagement would always sustain their broad-based vision and prevent them from becoming too technical and narrow.

That being said, declining career mobility and increased specialization did change the relationship between individuals and organizations. The old relationship between free-floating individuals and rigid ministries observed in the 1980s was reversed, creating better correlations between the skill sets of individuals and the expectations of the ministries. The ministries became powerful entities in their own right. More than before, they thrived on specialized bodies of knowledge and organizational resources. Their officials learned to be more patient in acquiring these skills and resources and in using the ministries as necessary vehicles to advance their power and policy visions. As part III of this book shows, while Chinese bureaucrats did continue to move across agencies, organizational specialization nevertheless increased the overall technocratic character of the economic bureaucracy and shaped the kind of strategies bureaucrats deployed to get ahead.

Agenda Setting and the Symbolic Power of the Central State

Following the technocratic reform, the standing of the central economic bureaucracy vis-à-vis the localities improved significantly. Some of this newly accrued central power was material and tangible. The central state had enhanced its fiscal standing, and this served as the most fundamental condition for other forms of state power to fall into place. Organizational centralization shifted the loyalties of local branches of central ministries away from local governments and toward their headquarters in Beijing. This round of vertical streamlining took place across a wide range of policy domains, including central banking, tax collection, market competition, product quality, land and other resources, and customs. These changes greatly reduced local governments' interference in the regulatory functions of the state.[67]

Another dimension of power that the central state newly obtained was symbolic. The expansion of its symbolic power was most vividly expressed in the ability of the central state to define policy agendas for the localities. Existing literature on central-local relations in China does not pay sufficient attention to this strand of power: the ability of the central government to define crises and set development agendas for the localities. The purpose of resorting to macrocontrol was precisely to lend the central bureaucracy the power to declare and manage crises. Central bureaucrats as macroeconomic managers came to define when a crisis should be announced and what its nature was (inflationary or deflationary). They then determined the desirable level of aggregate investment and the policy instruments to be used to achieve the macroeconomic targets. As bureaucrats worked to smooth macroeconomic cycles, anticipate their fluctuations, and deploy forward-looking monetary guidelines, crisis management became a routine function of the economic bureaucracy. In this process, their power to set the state's agenda during periods of inflation derived from the state's designation of what was an irregular financial institution or a redundant construction: that is, the determination of who had overstepped the boundaries and which projects would have their funding slashed to cool down overall investment. Agenda-setting power expanded even more aggressively in deflational moments, as economic bureaucrats mulled over what sectors to support and what development initiatives to prioritize. Since a low-inflation environment has consistently characterized the period from 1996 to the present, macrocontrol has remained focused on deflation management for a long period.

Co-opting the Local: Shifting Central-Local Relations

As intended, technocratic reform in the Zhu Rongji era altered the relationship between the central economic bureaucracy and local governments. Here I want to clarify that it did so not by suppressing the development needs of local governments but by co-opting and absorbing them into the orbit of central economic policies. Therefore, the powers that the central economic bureaucracy gained were those of authority, not coercion. Tax assignment reform, for example, did change the formula of revenue distribution in favor of the central government. Yet by design, the reform also required the central government to rebate a proportion of the taxes back to local governments, enhancing the scheme of fiscal transfers from rich to poor provinces through central allocations. From 1993 to 2008, the percentage of local government spending funded by tax refunds and transfer payments from the central government grew from 14.6 percent to 38 percent.[68] Therefore, local governments benefited from central revenue growth to a certain degree. But to receive fiscal transfers, they were subject to terms set by the central government.

The agenda-setting power acquired by the central bureaucracy compelled the local governments to attune themselves to the bureaucracy's policy signals. An incorrect reading of "tight" or "loose" macroeconomic policy could result in the launch of new projects that would later be halted by the central authorities. In contrast, an informed interpretation of the development priorities, such as those set in five-year plans and other urban or sectoral development plans, would put local governments in a good position to adjust local development proposals to central expectations and receive financial support from the central government. The reorientation to the center affected the ability of the central ministries not only to dole out public investments but also to determine how public investment funds were disbursed. Ministries invited local governments to apply for centrally managed and earmarked grants, used to sponsor local development projects that the central government identified as its priorities. As some scholars have observed, this system of "management through projects" had become a fixture of China's fiscal institutions and a mode of economic governance in its own right. In effect, it increased the power of the ministries and, by extension, the role of central technocrats in shaping local development agendas.[69] A similar earmarking function was built into the tax transfer scheme. In fact, one-third of the tax refunds from the central to the local governments was designated for specific policy areas.[70] Altogether these schemes of specialized funding and public investment allowed the central government to pull the strings of local development and herd localities toward the national priorities delineated by the central government.

Institutional development through absorbing the local into the central was also evident in the rising share of local generalists who were attracted to jobs in the economic bureaucracy. To measure change in the career backgrounds of the elite economic bureaucrats (vice ministers and higher), I calculated the proportion of time they spent in different policy areas across four generations. Figure 3.2 lists the top four functional areas that consumed the most time during their official tenures. As the figure shows, the second generation of economic officials, the subjects of this chapter, had an increased presence in banking and local generalist positions compared to the previous generation. These changes were largely sustained through the latest generation. The expanded representation of banking experience among the second-generation officials is not surprising. The need to revamp the financial system under Zhu Rongji demanded bureaucrats who had experience in central banking and commercial banking. In comparison, the increased percentage of local generalists requires more explanation.

On the surface, a larger presence of local generalists in the economic bureaucracy seems to contradict the trend of bureaucratic centralization; in effect, it showed the ability of the central bureaucracy to present itself as an attractive career destination for local generalists. As chapter 2 shows,

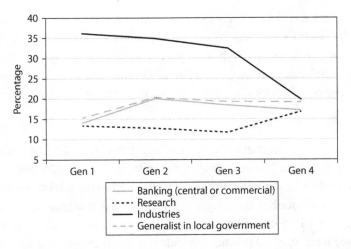

FIGURE 3.2. Percentage of careers spent in major policy areas for four generations of elite economic bureaucrats. *Source:* Compiled by the author from elite economic bureaucrats' CVs.

local generalists could constitute a conflicting force in the central economic bureaucracy. The lifelong local generalists in the 1980s—represented by President Hu Yaobang and Premier Zhao Ziyang—embraced a career identity and policy outlook that differed from those of the central bureaucrats. They saw the central bureaucracy as a roadblock to advancing their prolocality policies and looked elsewhere for political allies. In the Zhu administration, the local generalists and the central economic bureaucracy had a different relationship. The economic bureaucracy attracted local generalists who might otherwise have followed through on a generalist career. Destination matters. Those who worked for the local governments with an eye toward Beijing may not have considered the localities as the ultimate source of their accrued power. Instead, they may have worked on turning their local backgrounds into assets useful to the central government. As figure 3.2 shows, since the 1990s, the central economic bureaucracy has continued to promote officials with local generalist backgrounds. Yet the number of such local generalists never reached the point where they formed a cluster of powerful interests in their own right and started to systematically undermine the central government. The local-generalists-turned-economic-bureaucrats, in this case, were not infiltrators into the central bureaucracy. What they translated from their local generalist experiences was not precisely local "interest" but a form of locally sensitive knowledge and skills, which could prove useful in dealing with localities or making policies to which local governments were receptive. The next chapter showcases such a group of locally grown state managers who used ideas sourced from local experiences to reform the country's public sector.

The Zhu Rongji era marked a decisive departure from the first decade of economic reform. The economic bureaucrats nudged the rules and organization of the Chinese economy closer to those found in market economies. They also introduced an indigenous *macrocontrol* framework to manage the economy in both inflationary and deflationary times. All of the policy changes were pursued through centralizing and reengineering the central economic bureaucracy. In sum, this era saw the advancement of both the state and the market and reset central-local relations for decades to come. The leaders of this paradigmatic transformation were the technocrats. They entered the bureaucracy in the early period of the PRC, when the country was attempting to follow the Soviet Union's "technocratic road" to socialism. The technocrats of this generation were mostly trained as engineers and entrusted with rationalizing the planned economy. Three decades later, following a major economic and political crisis in 1989, they rose to political primacy as presidents, premiers, and elite bureaucrats and aimed to steer the country out of the mode of political mobilization and toward economic efficiency. This chapter has focused on this group. It accounts for their historical origins, the economic and political circumstances of their ascendance, and the strategies they used to consolidate their power.

This chapter finds an intrinsic relationship between the backgrounds of the technocrats and their pathways to power. Three aspects stand out as the technocrats took on the task of reforming the economic bureaucracy. First, the rise of the technocrats was associated with their fitness for governing in a particular historical moment marked by uncertainty and a yearning for discipline and order. The technocrats dispensed with uncertainty by bringing clarity and rationality to an upended political economy and putting China back on the track of growth and stability.

Second, the technocrats' long-time immersion in the central bureaucracy led them to utilize the state to conduct market reform. After strengthening the economic administration, they used it to integrate national markets, install market discipline, and enforce market rules. Market building was done emphatically through state building.

Third, these officials' technocratic proclivity affected the content of their economic programs. A technocratic pursuit of efficiency and rationality led to some degree of openness to borrowing from foreign models, particularly in the areas of central banking, taxation, and finance where widely accepted standards were considered available and well established. The technocrats also had another side, one associated with their engineering background, which fostered their pragmatic vision of economic reform as a form of problem solving. The twin pursuits of legitimacy and pragmatism were reflected in the ways in which they managed China's macroeconomy, using whatever means were available—whether market levers or administrative fiats.

In sum, in this period the technocrats reorganized state-market relations and "technocraticized" China's economic bureaucracy overall. In the decade following this technocratic turn in the economic bureaucracy, other subtypes of technocrats with different backgrounds began to emerge. They would go on to make the expertise of the state more central and often would harness it for market-building purposes.

Chapter Four

NATIONAL CHAMPIONS AND THE ORGANIZATIONAL APPROACH TO ENTERPRISES AND MARKETS

As chapter 3 shows, the state rebuilding of the 1990s enhanced the bargaining power of the central bureaucracy vis-à-vis local governments and reversed the decade-long decentralization approach to China's economic reform. Leaders of this movement—the central technocrats—had less tolerance for the development of local "kingdoms." The new administration, however, absorbed local leaders into the central economic bureaucracy, turning them into central state managers and central bureaucrats and making sure that their economic outlook closely aligned with the centralist technocratic agenda of the new era.

This chapter uses state-owned enterprise (SOE) reform to illustrate this career movement. In the second half of the 1990s, it became clear that economic reform could not make breakthroughs without addressing the heart of the socialist economy—the SOEs. Competition from the booming private sector and foreign capital squeezed the profit space of the SOEs, and the state sector was increasingly perceived as a burden to the economy, not a security. Yet unlike the fiscal and financial reform that proceeded unhesitatingly during this technocratic era, public-sector restructuring lacked obvious models to follow and could not be rationalized in a similar way. As a result, public-sector restructuring beginning in the mid-1990s became a pioneering effort, in which new ideas, faces, and initiatives were tested out. It was from this effort that a new group of bureaucrats emerged, having successfully experimented with SOE reform in their local jurisdictions. Their ascendance to the central bureaucracy epitomizes one of the pathways by which locally grown bureaucratic and managerial expertise was enlisted to aid centralization and national market integration.

I also focus on SOE reform here because the peculiarity of China's public-sector reform, one of its understudied aspects, illustrates the central theme of this book: that the backgrounds of policy makers have tremendous influence on policy products, channeled through career advancements and collective leadership. SOE reform worldwide was understood as a movement of privatization. Make no mistake, China's SOE reform at the end of the 1990s followed unequivocally a trend of liberalization, privatization, and deregulation. The net outcome of this trend was a dramatically downsized role for SOEs in the Chinese economic structure. Once an absolute monopoly, SOEs in 2018 comprised less than 5 percent of China's enterprises, 10 percent of its total employment, and 40 percent of its assets.[1] What also accompanied liberalization, however, was the reorganization of the state sectors, revolving around the restructuring of interenterprise relations. This process grouped SOEs into economic unions, essentially making them more interconnected and larger than they otherwise would have been. This chapter shows that this linking-up method precipitated the famous construction of the national champions in the 2000s and was associated with a ground-up bureaucratic movement in the state from the Mao era to the 1990s. Thus, it also helps explain why a liberalizing reform ended up producing state enterprises that were more powerful and colossal than even those in the socialist era: a result not at all predetermined by state structures or central political wills.

In summary, this chapter shows that a particular breed of bureaucrat sharing similar career trajectories was instrumental in pushing forward the enterprise grouping strategy for restructuring the public sector. These bureaucrats shared a career background that began with managing local SOEs, led to supervising regional industries, and ended in leading the State Economic and Trade Commission (SETC) in the central government. Deviating from an intention to preserve the dominance of the state sector, these managers-turned-bureaucrats built interenterprise linkages in order to build markets and overcome the problem of bureaucratic departmentalism, which they had experienced firsthand as both SOE managers and regional industrial supervisors. Their subsequent efforts to build a national team of central SOEs elevated such market integration strategies to the national level and also expanded this organizational approach to managing enterprises into an approach that could manage the entire economy.

UNCERTAINTY AND DELEGATION IN
CHINA'S ENTERPRISE REFORM

In the universe of economic policy, some areas have garnered more consensus among the professional communities than others. As chapter 3 shows, Zhu Rongji's technocratic administration pushed through reform in policy domains where agreement on best practices had been reached. These areas included central bank independence, value-added taxes, and regulations for forging competitive and fair markets. Other policy areas, however, were much less settled, and public-sector restructuring was one of these. It lacked a shared confidence in what the most desirable approach to restructuring might be, whether state enterprises should exist at all, and whether they should be subjected to different standards than private enterprises. Only a small number of countries with state sectors the size of China's were able to overhaul them in such a short time frame, and it was unclear whether these limited examples generated any readily transferable and widely accepted formulas. Surely, enterprise reforms in both the Communist and post-Communist countries provided the most relevant reference points for China. Yet they yielded at best mixed results, with more cautionary tales than inspiring examples. As part of the shock-therapy approach to reform, rapid and large-scale privatization had damaging consequences for the economy that became apparent only three or four years into its implementation. That is, even in a period marked by a high motivation to learn from abroad, the technocratic government found no good models in the area of SOE reform.[2]

The administration partly tackled the problem of the absence of best practices by delegating initiatives to local economic managers. Central guidance on SOE reform was kept vague and provided more information on what not to do than on what to do. It called for an end to approaches associated with the decentralization strategy of reform, primarily the contracting-out system implemented in the 1980s. The technocrats and their intellectual allies widely believed this system to be a primitive and inadequate measure for establishing enterprise autonomy. The central government also gave a vague nod to changes involving ownership structure and corporate control but did not specify, for instance, how ownership reform should be tackled or what efficiency standards should be used.[3] From the outset, the central technocrats refrained from micromanaging reform. After all, they had spent most of their careers in the central ministries and were more comfortable managing the macroeconomy than weighing in on microissues of enterprise efficiency. Hence, state-sector restructuring was one of the areas where Premier Zhu and central technocrats like him were willing to consider local ideas and to promote local industrial managers to national leadership positions.

THE SHARED CAREER SEQUENCES OF SOE REFORMERS

As it turned out, the group of bureaucrats who eventually emerged to oversee public-sector reform had extensive experience in managing SOEs and local industries, experience that the central technocrats didn't possess. Like protagonists portrayed in other chapters, this group of officials shared traits in their career backgrounds. Their career tracks had a higher degree of isomorphism than did the career tracks of the bureaucrats analyzed in other chapters: not only did the SOE reformers share similar experiences, but also their career trajectories followed the same sequence. Each sequence can be divided into three steps, with transitions between steps occurring roughly around the same time. The SOE reformers spent the first segment of their careers at local state-owned factories from the 1950s to the 1970s, followed by time in local government positions overseeing regional industries in the 1980s. Their careers peaked in the final stage when key figures among them were promoted and assumed leadership positions in the SETC throughout the 1990s and early 2000s. It was at the SETC that this group of bureaucrats eventually claimed the principal authority for enterprise reform. As table 4.1 shows, although the SETC directors served different organizations and regions, they held structurally equivalent positions within a generic pattern.

Careers are sequences of individual choices made in a historical context, and early career moves circumscribe the possibilities available later on. In this sense, the factory manager—local generalist—central bureaucrat sequence was by no means a Markov chain–like "random walk." Each step in the sequence can be properly contextualized in history. Indeed, this particular sequence was so common that many officials belonging to this generation followed it. After sorting the career sequences of all elite bureaucrats

TABLE 4.1
Career trajectories of SETC directors

Name	First leg of career	Second leg of career	Third leg of career
Li Rongrong	Wuxi Oil Pump Factory, Wuxi, Jiangsu (1968–1986)	Jiangsu provincial government (1986–1992)	SETC (1993–1998)
Jiang Qiangui	Beijing Organic Chemical Factory, Beijing (1974–1978)	Beijing municipal government (1979–1991)	SETC (1992–2003)
Xu Penghang	Daye Steel Factory, Daye, Hubei (1964–1983)	Hubei provincial government (1983–1992)	SETC (1992–1996)
Yang Changji	Shenyang Northeastern Pharmaceutical Factory, Shenyang, Liaoning (1964–1981)	Henan provincial government (1981–1989)	SETC (1992–1996)
Zhang Zhigang	Ningxia Agricultural Machine Building Factory, Zhongwei, Ningxia (1966–1979)	Ningxia provincial government (1980–1992)	SETC (1992–2002)
Zhang Wule	Lanzhou Steel Factory, Lanzhou, Ningxia (1971–1985)	Gansu provincial government (1985–1996)	SETC (1996–1997)
Wang Zhongyu	Jilin Paper Mill, Jilin, Jilin (1953–1980)	Jilin provincial government (1982–1992)	SETC (1992–1998)

Source: Compiled by the author from directors' CVs.

in the same administration as the SOE reformers, I found that 15 percent of them followed this three-step sequence. Having been born into the late 1930s and early 1940s meant that by the time they joined the workforce in the 1950s, the country was engaged in socialist industrialization aimed at catching up with the West. Thus, it was not surprising to see that the industrial sectors absorbed a large volume of urban employment and attracted talent and devotion. In my data set, 47 percent of all second-generation economic bureaucratic elites had their first jobs in the industrial sectors. In addition to the supply-demand logic of the labor market, the socialist moral principle championed egalitarianism and honored manual labor. These principles, when translated into work practice, instilled patience in the youth through immersion in industrial production on the shop floor. This practice resulted in a prolonged period on the shop floor before promotion to management positions. As a consequence, as illustrated in table 4.1, the bureaucrats of this generation began their careers in exceedingly humble circumstances, a phenomenon unseen in other generations.

According to scholarship on organizations and careers, first jobs often have a formative and lasting impact on subsequent careers.[4] Lengthy exposure to industrial production had far-reaching effects on the economic views formed by the SOE reformers. First, it socialized the SOE reformers in the views of producers. A productionist bias was hardly unexpected, given the socialist economy's plant-based makeup and its disregard for the role of consumption, markets, and finance in evaluating enterprise success. Due to this socialization effect, managers, as we see later, continued to carry this view into the market economy even when alternative schemes for evaluating corporate efficiency became available. Second, long-standing experience on the ground afforded the SOE reformers practical knowledge that would help them recognize what worked and what didn't work in the enterprises of "actually existing socialism" in China. This knowledge was especially valuable in an era when the five-year plan as it existed on paper disguised how it was actually implemented or avoided.

The second transition in their careers from state factories to local government coincided with the onset of China's economic reform. The local governments turned to their own managerial expertise to run the economy. After all, at the dawn of the reform, the Chinese economy remained synonymous with the SOEs. Those who had proven records in running SOEs were called to assume local government positions and charged with overseeing regional industrial production and developing local economies.

The third transition to the SETC invoked a more centralized mechanism of personnel selection. Ministry-level promotion is inevitably subject to intervention by the top leaders. Even here, idiosyncratic promotions were limited by the availability and the makeup of the rising pool of bureaucrats from which trusted officials could be drawn.

Overall, the career sequences of SOE reformers carried the heavy imprint of the historical circumstances that shaped the allocation of job opportunities and candidate pools. Patterned careers, as seen among the SOE reformers, encoded distinctive generational experiences that shaped the particular ways in which these bureaucrats were involved in the Chinese economy.

BUILDING INTERENTERPRISE LINKAGES TO SURVIVE THE IMPERFECTION OF PLANNING

While career locations are shaped by state structures and historical circumstances, the specific experiences that actors gain from their careers are important in their own right. It goes without saying that not all officials occupying similar positions advanced to the next levels and to similar destinations. We need to analyze, within each leg of their careers, what these reformers did at each official position, how they accumulated authority, and what possible connections linked their career phases and positional experiences. This information allows us to trace how actors progressed through their sequence by coping with changing mandates and advancing their policy positions, something the following section discusses in detail.

Notably, the SOE reformers were also socialist incumbents. They were promoted from previous positions running wholly state-owned factories in the environment of a planned economy. Standard accounts of enterprise reform in China take it for granted that enterprise reform was a reform-era idea and had existed only since 1978.[5] In fact, SOE managers in the socialist period had long tinkered with the system and deviated from the official scripts. In fact, similar to what chapter 1 discusses, many of the ideas used to restructure the area of enterprise management were labeled "reforms" but were, in effect, long-time practices that had been helping enterprises survive hardship and evade constraints since the Mao period. One of these ideas was the linking-up method of organizing interenterprise relations. As early as the late 1960s and 1970s, factory managers engaged in the practice of building economic ties with fellow enterprises in the shadow of the command economy.

Linking up was not so much a conscious effort to create markets as a pragmatic response to the imperfections of planning. Chinese central planning trailed far behind that of the Soviet Union in its precision and scope. Ideally, material supplies should have flowed downward vertically from the central planners, beginning with the industrial ministries and moving to local factories within each ministerial jurisdiction. In return, revenues and material reserves should have made their way back to the center for redistribution. The reality on the ground, however, was very different. The range of planned goods within the orbit of central planning in China was far narrower than that of its Soviet counterpart. Miscalculation, miscoordination, and mismatches abounded in allocating materials and striving for intersectoral balances. This suboptimal state of affairs was a function of both the weak administrative capacity of the Chinese state and a deep-rooted ideological resistance to top-down impositions. Evidence of the latter was forcefully articulated in major political movements, authorized by Mao, denouncing bureaucratic controls and celebrating mass initiatives in economic production. These interruptions further eroded the power of central planning.

In this context, state factories fell through the cracks between the malfunctioning planned economy and the forbidden market. Nominally, SOEs remained attached to government organs; they were affiliated with either ministries or local governments and were supposed to look to these supervising government agencies to obtain supplies. Yet failures in vertical allocation turned a privilege into a liability. Hierarchical affiliations thwarted alternative relationships that state factories could otherwise have had with one another. To a large extent, state factories' artificial separation from one another mirrored bureaucratic departmentalism in the government.

In the absence of either hierarchy or markets to allocate resources, SOEs turned to a network approach to find resources by horizontally connecting with other enterprises in the same region. They signed interenterprise production agreements and exchanged a variety of goods and resources, including raw materials, processing capabilities, information, equipment, and technologies. The success of linking up hinged on the ability of SOEs to find good matches and secure local supply chains. In doing so, factory managers were pushed to the forefront to liaise with other managers and connect with brokers—sometimes those in the government—who had access to stopgap resources. In this way, networks and linkages emerged among local factories; these dyadic exchanges crosscut and overlapped with one another, percolating into localized circuits of network exchange and, not uncommonly, were conducted and maintained in the form of barter. As the Cultural Revolution smashed technocratic control and instigated aggressive decentralization, it forced local economies to improvise in order to survive. Renewed commerce and exchange between towns and villages, built onto age-old commercial routes and interpersonal relationships, kept local economies going.

Economic reform did not initiate this behavior but came to accept it after it was already widespread. The official start of reform though did allow the managers a form of entrepreneurship they were keen to pursue. The SOE managers I interviewed told me that in the late 1970s and early 1980s, many of them began to escalate the erstwhile semiclandestine behavior to actively "get around hierarchy" and connect horizontally. They scaled up their survival tool kits and referred to them as "reforms." Policy documents issued by the central government approved "building horizontal linkages" among enterprises and passed this directive back to local economic leaders. By 1986, it was estimated that more than five thousand of these "co-operational agreements" had mushroomed nationwide to connect enterprises and that approximately two-thirds of participating enterprises had formed "economic unions" that were more binding than those among other enterprises.[6]

The positive impact of building these linkages on the careers of the SOE reformers was considerable. The most obvious benefit was that these linkages left a traceable track record of good performance and earned the SOE reformers credentials following the institutionalization of the linking-up method. Of course, building horizontal linkages was not the only reform that tackled SOE inefficiency. Yet it was distinctive from other enterprise reform measures because it was the only practice that concerned the issue of inter-enterprise relationships and was thus not reducible to the prevailing decentralizing measures that revolved around fostering the contractual autonomy of the enterprises. As the post-Tiananmen administration declared decentralization an inadvisable policy approach, the linking-up method survived the political change and even thrived in the new wave of enthusiasm for integrating the national economy spurred by the new administration. The less obvious impact was that this method generated new skill sets for managers who implemented it. Managers had to venture out of their comfort zones to make friends and partners. One manager described how this was not at all natural to those like him who "only know about technical matters and don't know how to conduct [themselves]."[7] Under this new mandate, SOE managers honed a wider portfolio of social skills and connections than if their enterprises had remained production units of the planning machine. Those who excelled at such self-transformation were recognized and rewarded, pushing their careers to the next stage in the reform era.

MERGING ENTERPRISES, MERGING MARKETS: A PROVINCIAL PROJECT

Beyond providing credentials and skills, the formative years the SOE reformers spent in enterprises shaped how they conceived problems and devised solutions. Concretely speaking, this array of experiences exposed reformers to certain types of solutions that then shaped their identification and framing of problems in other settings. This is not to say that this group of factory managers was inherently dogmatic or kept imagining fictional problems into existence. Early ways of doing things, when proven effective, did lead the SOE managers to apply established interpretations to subsequent comparable situations. They tended to identify similar problems or frame problems in ways they were personally well equipped to solve. This is how the second career leg of SOE reformers connects back to the first.

By the early 1980s, the SOE reformers had left the state factories, which had consumed nearly their entire youth, and made their way into local governments. Some of them moved directly to provincial governments, while others spent time in city-level government before being promoted. The SOE-managers-turned-regional-industrial-managers contended that the problem of bureaucratic departmentalism appeared even more acute when viewed from the perspective of a region. From this elevated vantage point, unnecessary fault lines and disconnections were more apparent. The regional industrial managers argued that a web of production and technical linkages could have been developed to connect dozens, if not hundreds, of enterprises within their jurisdictions. Had the local bureaucrats not had the experience of industrial production, they may not have been able to conceive how enterprises were connected.

To the regional industrial managers, building horizontal linkages was meant to reestablish the natural and organic relationships among enterprises. These linkages were intrinsic to industrial production, but the socialist bureaucracy had obstructed them, defying economic gravity. For example, Xu Penghang, the key SOE reformer who later directed the SETC, expressed his outrage at seeing the existence of five levels of ore mines from his position as the supervisor of Huangshi's industries. Each of the ore mines was affiliated with a different part of the government: the central industrial ministries, provincial governments, municipal governments, prefecture governments, or township governments. Each of these enterprises sought to be self-sufficient. While a small city like Huangshi certainly had many enterprises in proximity to one another, viable economic ties were absent.[8] As Xu described the paralyzing situation: "One mine has a tail without a head, another having a head without a tail." Using this biological metaphor, Xu decried the violation of natural law by bureaucratic departmentalism.[9] Across China from the mid-1980s to the early 1990s, regional industrial managers who had previously been SOE managers were making similar diagnoses and entertaining similar solutions.[10] Building horizontal linkages went beyond the original purview as corporate strategy and became regional developmental policy.

In spite of the resemblance, it would be a mistake to treat the second phase of the SOE reformers' careers as a mere repetition of the first phase. Enabled by their newfound administrative power as regional industrial managers, the scope and depth of their linking-up activities expanded. Above all, mergers and acquisitions (M&A) came to be widely used as a more assertive method for linking up enterprises. In 1988 alone, 2,856 enterprises merged 3,424 enterprises into their existence.[11] Certainly, enterprises had acted on their own initiative, but the provincial governments were also eager to play the roles of initiator and matchmaker. In addition, provincial M&A was a substantive step forward because linking up in the first phase was based on exchange and collaboration and did not touch the issue of ownership. Provincial M&A aimed to build tighter ties among participating enterprises. Furthermore, mergers grew into a larger scheme to build what reformers called enterprise groups (qiye jituan). As a result, Chinese enterprise groups joined associations of enterprises that bound subsidiaries to the central coordination of parent enterprises via a wide variety of close or loose ties, ranging from shareholding relationships, influence over investment, management, and personnel, to relationships of suppliers/customers and technological cooperation. Thus, in this phase, the landscape of state industries underwent substantive reorganization.

It would be a mistake to think that interenterprise restructuring was conducted only for efficiency purposes. Granted, forging industrial groups was considered a useful organizational strategy that enabled the "optimal allocation of resources" and also a forceful antidote to the problem of bureaucratic barriers.[12] However, the original purpose of efficiency was undercut by varying motivations and capacities on the ground. For example, the degree of internal integration varied considerably across the newly assembled enterprise groups. The efficiency argument was also complicated by the fact that some provinces used the opportunity as a disguise to incorporate and bail out failing enterprises.[13] Yet the overall impact of this consolidation on the organization of Chinese enterprises remains profound. It is reported that managerial coordination by the parent company generally induced a deeper division of labor between plants and between investment and production functions. Chinese enterprise groups increasingly resembled operationally diversified conglomerates.[14]

Through their roles in administratively led mergers, the regional industrial managers continued to grow and expand their skill sets. From their new vantage points, they became unsympathetic toward lower-level government protectionism. To them, intervention by higher government authority in mergers was unavoidable thanks to the market and the political realities on the ground. Chinese markets at that time were too underdeveloped to provide an impetus for performance. Local governments were not willing to give away their corporate offspring for the sake of larger-scale efficiency either. Wang Zhongyu, however, explicitly argued that provincial governments, filled with experienced former SOE managers like himself, should consciously accelerate the formation of enterprise groups and markets in "a more organized and planned fashion."[15] In pushing through merger deals, regional industrial managers served as brokers, coordinators, and arbitrators. They learned to work and negotiate with all affected parties to hammer out schemes for evaluating enterprises and compensating the major stakeholders.

Corporate mergers in the public sector, even in present-day China, are far from pure market transactions. In the very first merger wave in the 1980s, the conspicuous absence of developed capital markets and associated rating and consulting industries made it nearly impossible to evaluate state assets using price mechanisms. Instead, mergers answered to a moral economy that valued relationships and externalities. In this context, the regional industrial managers conducted evaluations and negotiated the compensation to local governments that stood to lose their enterprises and thereby their revenue sources.[16] In many cases, mergers and consolidations did not involve any financial transactions. It was up to the administrative negotiators to devise a formula for dividing ownership among state entities. The transaction cost that the regional industrial managers needed to address therefore required a balancing of intergovernment relations, like those between provincial and county governments.[17] Furthermore, even if proxy market-based calculations of some sort could be introduced to evaluate the assets involved and project future revenue streams, government coordinators still needed to take into consideration a wide range of externalities affecting local employment and social stability. It was too complex to put a price tag on these public and political goods. Regional industrial managers thus engaged in a delicate dance among the social, the political, and the economic spheres, feeling out the rules of commensuration

implicit across domains. In this process, resources that provincial governments controlled were not readily monetarized. Policy favors or promises
of future state investments, for instance, were frequently used to appease
local governments that would otherwise obstruct the mergers. This array
of experiences accorded the regional industrial managers a distinctive set
of coordinating skills and evaluative knowledge, which later proved to be
valuable in leading consolidation at the national level.

Building interenterprise linkages was also different in the second phase
than in the first because in the second phase it took on a territorial dimension and aimed for market integration. The goal was to rebuild territorial markets that had been separated by geographical and institutional
boundaries. Lamenting the rural-urban divide as similarly unnatural
and counterproductive, regional industrial managers encouraged urban
enterprises to link up with rural counterparts so that rural manufacturing
by the booming town- and village-owned enterprises and the expanding
rural consumer base could be pulled into the orbit of the urban economy.
They hoped that a truly integrated "regional" economy would emerge to
facilitate the circulation of materials, capital, labor, and goods.[18] Another
way to integrate regional economies was to link raw material–producing
regions with manufacturing regions. In still other cases, regional industrial
managers worked to provide the infrastructure, transportation, information, and services needed to facilitate the connection of local economies.
This new strand of activities involved a wider range of resources and
policy tools than would have been required by enterprise-based consolidation. Territorial consolidation fulfilled the role that the SOE managers had originally played, perhaps in spite of themselves, in forming and
building markets.

As a large number of provinces led by this generation of regional industrial managers converged on similar development strategies, competitive
pressure between provinces mounted. Referencing what fellow provinces
had done to integrate regional supply chains and build large enterprise
groups became common. These references allowed provincial leaders to
justify similar actions within their own jurisdictions. External pressure lent
support to the use of the powerful mandates needed to seek compliance
from unwilling enterprises.[19] By the end of 1988, more than twenty-seven
provinces and cities were involved in building enterprise groups. Notably,
less than 7 percent of the mergers involved cross-provincial transactions,

highlighting the province-based focus in this wave of mergers.[20] Subnationalism was also reflected in the pride provincial leaders took in venturing out to other provinces, annexing extraprovincial resources, and in this way making inroads into national markets.[21] Effectively, Chinese provinces became the new sites for imagining the virtues of market development, industrial competitiveness, and economic modernization.

MARKET COORDINATION AND NEW-STYLE MACROECONOMIC MANAGEMENT: THE RISE OF THE STATE ECONOMIC AND TRADE COMMISSION

In the first and second phases of the SOE reformers' careers, the convergence in their career patterns was uncoordinated. In the third phase, regional industrial managers from around the nation were promoted in 1992 to a newly established ministry—the State Economic and Trade Commission. After this point, they acted in concert, and their actions were inseparable from the initiatives of the new agency. Invariably, establishing a new ministry was as much a political project as one driven by functional necessity. Zhu Rongji, the premier-elect, saw the SETC as a site for developing his own expert base and sought to align it with his policy visions. The memoir of Zhu's aide Zhao Weichen offers a peek into crucial personnel decisions of the sort that were usually conducted behind closed doors. From the outset, the premier viewed the provinces as a source of fresh talent for staffing the SETC. In explaining why this particular group of provincial leaders was chosen, Zhao explained that the premier valued their "enterprise management experience and comprehensive leadership capabilities."[22] That means their selection was based neither on a generalized evaluation of competency nor on their personal relationship with Zhu. Instead, Zhu valued their biographical traits. Both their professional competence *and* their political coordination skills were in line with his technocratic administration.

That being said, individual leaders' roles in directing bureaucratic behavior should not be overestimated. The SOE reformers were not mere agents of the premier or vehicles for implementing his ideas. For one thing, Zhu's personnel decisions should not be interpreted as his endorsement of specific enterprise reform measures. In his otherwise detailed description of how the SETC leadership was assembled, Zhao did not mention any specific measures for SOE restructuring. Zhu's appreciation of the SOE reformers' experience in the state sector was palpable, but at this point, the central government remained agnostic about what specific approach should be undertaken to restructure the state sector. Second, even with the premier's blessing, the SETC was not automatically granted resources and control. After all, ministries' jurisdictions were not obvious or predetermined. Instead, the SETC was thrown into an already crowded economic bureaucracy dominated by powerful incumbent players. The State Planning Commission (SPC) and the System Reform Commission (SRC) already shared broad economic policy mandates similar to those of the SETC. The People's Bank of China and the Ministry of Finance were also on the rise, with their power and reach extended beyond restoring the financial order. The SETC was a newcomer, vaguely charged with safeguarding production and commerce and lacking clear policy mandates or associated resources.

The mission uncertainty felt by the SETC spoke to the intrinsic nature of ministerial work. Sponsorship by top patrons could get you only so far; to establish policy authority, a ministry needed to find its own footing. In its essence, ministerial work differed greatly from the work of local governments. In the provinces, government authority was easy to delimit: it extended to the territory governed. Ministries, however, had to invent their own jurisdiction, building on a complex and shifting landscape of budgets, policy tools, specializations, charisma, collective commitment, political backing, and so on. Moreover, each ministry was embedded in the "field" of central bureaucracy and competed with fellow ministries for overlapping jurisdictions and uncharted policy domains. In the case of SOE reform, for example, many ministries—charged with general missions such as planning, reform, or production—had the potential to articulate their relevance. But no ministry in the central government was able to claim dominant authority over SOE reform just yet. Although the SETC directors had direct experience managing and restructuring state enterprises, they could not dominate without first establishing generalized authority of some sort. Making aggressive moves to seize policy areas in which other ministries also had a stake would surely ruffle feathers and invite a backlash against the fledgling agency.

In an address to his staff, Wang Zhongyu, the SETC director, revealed the delicate enterprise of building authority in the crowded bureaucratic field:

We need to work at a high level. I won't compete with you for the work that you are already doing. I can do the work that you are not able to do. *Jingmaowei* [SETC] does coordination work in comprehensive policy and comprehensive planning. Its work will overlap [with that of other agencies] and we will learn to work in crosscutting areas. We cannot go about without any policy tools, but just having policy tools does not work either. We need to set our focus at a high level. If we cannot deliver decent work on major issues, we are not playing the role of general staff and assistant [to the central leadership].[23]

On the one hand, the director recognized the importance of acquiring forceful policy tools and working with others in crosscutting jurisdictions. On the other, he suggested that in order to build a sustainable basis of effectiveness in the long run, the SETC needed to turn technical and coercive power into broad-based authority at a higher level. This meant that the SETC needed to construct a type of expertise that differed from existing modes of economic management so that it could minimize head-to-head competition with other agencies.

After a period of fumbling along and acting as a firefighter for the economy wherever emergencies arose, the SETC discovered a yet-to-be-occupied role that it could assume—market coordinator. At first glance, the combination of *market* and *coordination* is an oxymoron. In theory, the market itself is a mechanism of coordination that allocates resources based on price information. For a transitioning economy filled with yawning gaps between inchoate markets and the residue of the planned economy, however, the need for coordination was real. Symptomatic of such institutional incongruities were the broken connections between sites of production and channels of distribution; market information did not flow smoothly among sectors and localities or across the urban-rural divide. To a large extent, an economy in transition embodied the dark sides of both the market and the plan. As administrative boundaries collapsed with market boundaries, this caused overinvestment in some segments of the economy and underinvestment in others—and eventually a structural mismatch between supply and demand. To address these sources of instability, classical macroeconomic policy could not come to the rescue. Macroeconomic levers commonly used in advanced market economies did not always function as intended because Chinese economic actors responded to a far more complex set of incentives than simple price signals. To defend against recurrent microshocks, Chinese enterprises adopted drastic measures ranging from frequently stopping production to building excessive inventories, which further reinforced production cycles.[24] This narrative constitutes the SETC's interpretation of the ongoing high inflation in this period, which, as chapter 3 details, had spurred a panoply of policies to macrocontrol the economy.

Just as many other agencies embraced the macrocontrol frenzy, the SETC bureaucrats made their own pitch from the perspective of market coordination. They argued that their expertise in enterprise management could help with this effort. Specifically, they proposed to play a role by transmitting information, closing gaps between segmented markets, reorganizing interenterprise relationships, alleviating strangleholds and smoothing shocks in supply chains, and correcting supply-demand mismatches.[25] To the SETC bureaucrats who had experience in enterprise management and production, this set of tasks was not foreign. Centering their identity on "enterprise work," SETC bureaucrats claimed they were accustomed to tying together "thousands of strands and loose ends," given that the nature of enterprise work was coordination. The SETC had coordinated (*xietiao*) among a heterogeneous mass of parties, including a wide range of government entities that possessed regulatory power and influence over enterprise investments.[26]

To this end, the SETC immediately dispatched its bureaucrats to conduct "comprehensive coordination of market operations" (*jingji yunxing zonghe xietiao*) and branded their efforts as "new-style macroeconomic management."[27] The SETC's activity list in this regard was long, detailed, and unapologetically micromanagerial. It induced enterprises to limit production and reduce inventories, build reserves of key products, remove bottlenecks in material supply chains, disentangle interenterprise debt chains, and smooth out their cash flows; it also helped enterprises connect with far-flung markets and linked up landlocked and coastal provinces.[28] In justifying this microapproach, SETC bureaucrats explained that because "planning does not reflect markets, markets do not allocate resources efficiently [either]. We can only strengthen comprehensive coordination in economic operations with persistent micro-adjustments, and thereby safeguard the normal operation of our economy."[29] At a deeper level, microadjustments (*weitiao*) were adopted because the SETC believed that "market problems are fundamentally structural in nature."[30] To the SETC directors, markets were not ruled by supply-and-demand relationships in the abstract; rather, they were constituted of parts, interrelationships, and flows that were subject to decisions made by enterprises and government actors alike. This articulation profoundly spoke to the economic worldview of the SETC bureaucrats, a way of thinking attributable to their production-centered economic experience and early work in integrating regional markets. In principle, what SETC directors did in coordinating economic operations was not vastly different from what they had done as regional industrial managers battling bureaucratic departmentalism and consolidated markets. In both periods, they sought to administratively approximate the effect of markets in places where market institutions were yet to be built or had failed to function.

The SETC's comprehensive market coordination was successful in three senses. First, it "worked"—as far as its goal of short-term macroeconomic management was concerned. Microadjustment smoothed out economic cycles and addressed short-term mismatches between supply and demand, which helped bring down inflation. The immediate efficacy of the SETC's unconventional macroeconomic regulation helped the agency swiftly establish its reputation.

Second, viewed from the perspective of the agency, this new-style macroeconomic management succeeded in carving out a unique niche for the SETC in the space of Chinese economic policies. Table 4.2 lays out the space of different policy "genres," defined by two axes—structural/universal and central/local. Structural approaches are those policies that purport to change the economic structure and the relationships between different parts of the economy, such as sectors or regions. Universal approaches are across-the-board economic policies that seek to affect economic activities indiscriminately within certain jurisdictions. The central-local dimension alludes to a difference in epistemology, whether policies were formulated and issued at arm's length by the central bureaucracy or were developed locally and closely tailored to local conditions. The SETC did not engage in direct competition with other agencies, in that it occupied a quadrant of its own, as shown in table 4.2. The powerful SPC was kept at bay, since its bureaucrats largely took comfort in sitting at their desks, processing project applications, and formulating sectoral development priorities. This epistemic division of labor resulted in different ways of experiencing work for Chinese economic policy makers. While SPC

TABLE 4.2
Policy genres and the SETC's niche location in the economic policy field

	Central	**Local**
Structural	Industrial policy, project approvals (State Planning Commission)	New-style macroeconomic management (SETC)
Universal	Macroeconomic policies (People's Bank of China)	Local economic regulations (Local governments)

officials described their overload as having an excessive number of "gunny sacks of documents," SETC officials identified the nature of their work as "a lot of phone calls" with local officials and state enterprise managers because "enterprises are at localities, and you have to communicate with them diligently, so that problems can be discovered locally and solved locally."[31] In describing the qualifications needed for the task of micro-managing China's macroeconomy, SETC directors said that one needed "a body as strong as steel, a mind as clear as a computer, and a belly as large as Buddha's."[32]

Third, the success of the SETC was reflected in the reorganization of its relationship with other ministries. In arguing for the need to coordinate markets, the SETC "coordinated" other agencies into its orbit in spite of resource constraints. A considerable source of power for addressing macro-economic imbalance was the power to define microlevel emergencies, and the SETC's identification of an emerging situation put pressure on other agencies to comply and cooperate with its efforts to coordinate a response. In explaining what the SETC's "coordination work" meant, Director Wang revealed how the role of coordinator could turn into the power to leverage other organizations' resources:

Some of our comrades contend that *jingmaowei* [SETC] has so many tasks, but since it has neither policy tools nor a penny, how can it conduct work? Although we don't have a penny, the things we deal with involve tens of billions of yuan. After we submit the questions we coordinated and researched to the State Council, tens of billions are settled like that. . . . Following our coordination, work is assigned to all [relevant agencies]. When it involves money, the banks will go implement it. When it involves planning, the State Planning Commission will go carry it out. When it is about inventory, the factories will go trim it back.[33]

Thus, while not possessing sufficient policy resources of its own, the SETC had considerable cognitive authority, enlisting other agencies to buy into its definition of the situation and turning them into vehicles to fulfill its own organizational goals. To better monitor macroeconomic situations and identify shortfalls, the SETC mandated that other agencies submit economic information from their respective sources to the SETC, thus situating the agency at a hub of information sharing and interagency cooperation, a position that even the most powerful agency—the SPC—was not able to claim. With its success established in the three senses described here, the SETC quickly gained a strong footing in the bureaucracy, paving the way for its engagement in enterprise reform.

BEYOND THE NATIONAL TEAM: A NATIONAL MOVEMENT OF MERGERS AND MARKET INTEGRATION

After building up its organizational profile, the SETC was poised to make headway in enterprise reform. Previously, SOE reform was decentralized, with local experiments and ways of doing things flourishing. Around 1995, however, the road was clear for the central bureaucracy to play a more authoritative role in enterprise reform. A crucial turning point came that year when the deteriorating performance of SOEs slipped to a historical low point: 33.53 percent of SOEs were experiencing losses, with the return on assets across the public sector dropping to a meager 3 percent. The abysmal situation compelled the central leadership to overhaul the public sector; calling for a breakthrough in enterprise reform, the central leadership turned to its ministerial arms for ideas.

Against this backdrop, the SETC put forward a strategy of "grasping the large and letting go of the small." This proposition, by offering a dual-track approach, satisfied the need to reduce the burden on the state while also rejecting across-the-board privatization. "Letting go of the small" applied to the small- and medium-sized enterprises, which tended to be found in light and consumer industries where competition from cooperative and private enterprises was the steepest. In spite of the pain of "giving away biological sons," it was agreed that the Chinese state was left with no option but to liquidate or privatize small SOEs showing losses in order to avoid long-term pain.[34] Large SOEs, however, were in a different category. They tended to be in capital-intensive and technology-heavy sectors. SETC officials argued that liquidation would risk leaving gaping holes in the economy.[35] Russia's shock-therapy approach served as a cautionary tale. Its public-sector restructuring decimated many industries, some of which never recovered.[36] Additionally, large SOEs performed less poorly than small SOEs by virtue of the lack of competition in their sectors and the skilled workforces they employed. Therefore, these enterprises remained key contributors of government revenues and were less likely to be targeted.

To better seize the large SOEs and improve their performance, the SETC rolled out a familiar proposal—tightening inter-SOE linkages. In line with their previous approach to restructuring enterprises in provinces, the SETC bureaucrats suggested forging national-level enterprise groups. Creating enterprise groups was considered an organizational approach that would extract greater potential from large SOEs when privatization was no longer an option. This proposal was solidified in 1997, in a directive calling for "strategic restructuring [*zhanluexing gaizu*] of State-owned Enterprises" and establishing 120 trial national enterprise groups.[37] To the SETC bureaucrats, the task of integrating national markets, when viewed from the perspective of interenterprise linkages, was far from completed. Ironically, province-level enterprise grouping, led by the SETC officials themselves, had contributed to a national-level fragmentation along provincial lines. In addition, sectors were another dimension of division that separated the SOEs. Enterprises with products spanning sectoral boundaries were rare, if not nonexistent. Therefore, the SETC bureaucrats, again driven to achieve the goal of market integration, led a national movement of mergers and takeover activities focusing on bridging provincial- and ministerial-based fragmentation. Adding momentum for enterprise grouping was a heightened concern for the competitiveness of domestic companies in the face of China's prospective entry into the World Trade Organization, scheduled for 2001.[38] The playing field for consolidated Chinese enterprises was now envisioned to be international in nature. Regardless of how the scale of competition was conceived, the underlying conviction held by SETC officials remained the same: the more integrated enterprises were, the more competitive they would be. Viewed from this perspective, national restructuring was a logical extension of provincial consolidation.

Forging enterprise groups was certainly not an idea monopolized by the SETC. Notably, key policy makers in other central agencies had also been involved in enterprise grouping. Yet a comparison of their profiles with those of SETC bureaucrats reveals a number of unrivaled advantages that the latter held. I will use Chen Jinhua, director of the SRC, another key economic agency, as a point of comparison. Just like the SETC bureaucrats and many officials in this generation, Chen had rich managerial experiences in SOEs. He was the manager of China Petroleum & Chemical Corporation (Sinopec) for seven years before relocating to the central economic bureaucracy. Chen himself had actually played a crucial part in assembling Sinopec as an enterprise group.[39] He had Premier Zhu Rongji's trust, a broad web of political connections, and a nonministerial background that kept him away from entrenched interministerial struggles. These advantages would all come in handy for directing central government–led mergers, especially those involving the industrial ministries, as was the case with Sinopec. Yet Chen's portfolio lacked a crucial component: experience overseeing regional industries and economies. It was this strand of experience that essentially equipped SETC officials with the skills necessary for coordinating a wide range of government actors and for aggregating knowledge beyond individual merger cases. Chen may have been a first-rate manager, but his training remained managerial and not industrial.

In contrast, SETC officials were equipped with a supply-chain perspective thanks to their role as regional industrial managers, giving them an understanding of the makeup of the various sectors and the relationships among them. This allowed the SETC bureaucrats to grasp interenterprise relationships from a higher vantage point, which was particularly useful in assessing mergers that spanned sectors. In addition, in spite of Chen's leadership position in an important ministry at the same ranking as the SETC, he did not have a corps of bureaucrats on his side who shared similar career experiences and policy views. Therefore, as charismatic and politically savvy as Chen was, he was not able to build a collective momentum at his SRC to seize enterprise reform. As a result, although the SRC expressed strong interest in leading enterprise reform and the "grasping the large" initiative, its chance of success quickly faded as SETC officials rolled out a series of concrete measures and impressed the leadership with their qualifications and preparedness.[40]

With the SETC's leading status in enterprise reform established, the agency's bureaucrats gathered a growing array of policy tools and financial resources to ensure that they could follow through on implementation. Restructuring SOEs in a country that remained theoretically committed to socialism inevitably involved recommitting to state investment and compensating losers. The SETC channeled state capital to retained SOEs but also compensated affected parties when SOEs were cut loose. For these purposes, the SETC was granted control over 30 billion yuan to be used for debt-to-equity swaps, a popular method for refinancing and recapitalizing indebted but salvageable SOEs.[41] To compensate the SOEs that were "let go" and cover the costs associated with layoffs and downsized benefits, the SETC asked for resources to establish a bankruptcy fund.[42] As a result, substantial resources started to flow in after this young agency successfully seized jurisdictions over SOE reform.

Yet ministerial power was never merely monetary. The SETC's structuralist conceptualization of markets essentially led to a pick-and-choose approach to SOE reform. A lot of the SETC's power involved selecting, classifying, and evaluating enterprises based on their potential and worthiness, requiring an array of cognitive powers that surely carried tremendous implications for resource allocation. Mergers between enterprises were authorized mostly on a case-by-case basis. Selective targeting was applied not only to enterprises but also to cities. The SETC granted cities "pilot" status in order to fast-track their public-sector restructuring. This status came with policy favors and financial support from the central government. Beginning in 1994, applications for pilot city designations started to trickle in to the agency. By 1997, 111 pilot cities were considered ready to launch the SETC's reform measures. The cities with pilot status enjoyed a wide range of supporting measures, including SOE debt cancellation, refinancing opportunities, and cash flow injections from the central government.[43] In addition, the SETC had a say in recommending restructured SOEs to the State Security Commission for public listing.[44] To be sure, such recommendations remained suggestive, as the commission had no obligation to honor the SETC's recommendations. Nevertheless, the SETC's opinions were treated as both a vote of administrative confidence and an informed endorsement from bureaucrats who had the industrial expertise to evaluate the worthiness of a particular SOE, a body of knowledge the financial experts at the State Security Commission did not have. Therefore, the SETC played a role typically reserved for specialized consultants in advanced liberal economies in the run-up to public offering.

Taken together, all the policy tools that the SETC had recently acquired, both material and symbolic, were vehicles for executing the SETC's policies and institutionalizing its organizational power. It is worth emphasizing that the SETC obtained policy tools *after* its successful efforts to establish a broad-based authority in economic management. This causal order challenges the conventional view that bureaucratic agencies had to have tangible resources to develop authority. This description of how the SETC obtained authority points to the importance of career experiences and organization-level entrepreneurship, which has been central to my analysis.

The SETC-led enterprise reform generated immediate results. Two years into the policy of forging enterprise groups to "grasp the large," trial enterprise groups saw a 21 percent increase in their profits, higher productivity, and increased investment in R&D. Internally, enterprise groups also reported increasingly active managerial functions on the part of parent companies.[45] With these results in place, the SETC immediately declared its strategy an initial success.

The national consolidation movement, in return, stimulated an unprecedented wave of regional M&As, with many of these mediated by the SETC. This wave took place on a larger scale than the consolidation instituted by the regional industrial managers in the 1980s. Also, while the regional industrial managers of the 1980s directed consolidation within their jurisdictions largely on their own, the SETC was brought in to arbitrate and facilitate cases that would otherwise have aborted in this new wave of consolidation. During the heyday of national restructuring, the number of provincial enterprise groups increased by 1,474 in 1997 to 2,155 in 1999, a 46 percent increase in just three years. In fact, provincial-level restructuring proceeded at an even faster pace than the reorganization of national enterprises. From 1997 to 1999, the percentage of provincial enterprise groups among all enterprise groups increased from 62.2 percent to 78.2 percent.[46] Data are lacking in order to assess what proportion of local mergers was subject to intervention by the central ministry. Inferring from a number of documented high-profile cases, it is safe to say that without ministerial assistance and pressure, the number of completed local mergers would have been lower. In the documented cases, we see that it was often the provincial government that sought help from the SETC to restart halted negotiations and mediate conflicts with recalcitrant prefectural governments or powerful SOEs.[47] Not uncommonly, the SETC had to reach into its own pocket, as well as its policy tool kit, to offer refinancing options or the opportunity to go public in order to persuade the reluctant parties.

Furthermore, it goes without saying that in merger cases that involved outer-province enterprises, the SETC's participation was often decisive and indispensable.[48] As a result of the SETC's coordination at both the national and the provincial levels, Chinese state enterprises grew in size and deepened their interconnections.

CREATING MONOPOLIES OR MARKETS?

To be sure, the SETC-led enterprise restructuring relied heavily on administrative tools and government fiats. Yet consideration for the market remained central to explaining the motivation and content of the SETC's enterprise policies. The SETC bureaucrats did not see a fundamental tension between their organizational approach to the economy and market principles. To the Chinese practitioners, organizational intervention was a necessary means to construct markets. This section discusses in detail how the SETC bureaucrats attempted to engineer markets and their constitutive elements—actors, outcomes, and principles—by shaping the design of the enterprise grouping.

First, the SETC intended to select trial enterprises and cities to operate more fully as market actors. This practice, which appeared to "pick winners," could have been more accurately described as an effort to "pick risk takers" in China's fledging markets. The goal was to grant "policy dividends" for those enterprises that were willing to wean themselves off government-controlled resources and plunge into market competition. This strategy of selecting market actors fit well with the SETC's initial modesty as an agency without resources. Using the "trial" designation, the SETC granted enterprises market-based rights and removed government constraints on a wide range of corporate activities involving management, investment, trade, and financing. Trial enterprises could now make decisions that were previously considered sensitive, including managing and trading state assets, attracting nonstate investors, issuing bonds, and obtaining semisovereign status when engaging with foreign parties.[49] In the face of complaints from a minority of trial enterprises that didn't recognize the full value of the "trial" designation, SETC Director Wang Zhongyu encouraged them to dispense with the old mode of dependence thinking: "The word 'trial' itself was an enormous invisible asset. Whatever you do—importing, joint ventures, or foreign negotiations, you go in with higher status. More importantly, when you wear the hat of a 'trial enterprise,' you can make larger strides in reform. All bodies of institutions will show you more understanding and support, and they will meddle less. Otherwise, you cannot move anything, go anywhere."[50]

Wang's tirade reflected the real obstacles that SOEs faced from obstructive government actors who were reluctant to give up their control over enterprises—so much so that simply removing their obstruction, at the urge of SETC, would yield institutional dividends to the system. The SETC also expected trial enterprises to adopt higher-risk corporate strategies than had been the norm in the pretrial period. In a regulatory regime where large and risky undertakings by SOEs were subject to approval by various government organs, the SETC urged its peers to turn on green lights so trial enterprises could foster their ambition and inculcate a competitive spirit, preparing them for global market competition.[51] Therefore, by loosening up control and giving away some enterprises to markets, the SETC actually accrued more authority as a deregulator.

Second, SETC-led restructuring attempted to engineer a nationally integrated market that could be characterized as one filled with oligopolistic competition. Unlike a monopoly, with a single seller that faces no competition, an oligopoly consists of a number of sellers, all of which have large shares of the market but which still need to compete with each other in the same market. Prior to restructuring, state enterprises, although more numerous, tended to monopolize protected local markets, taking comfort in their position as big fish in small pools. The SETC officials consciously pursued their goal of oligopolistic competition by directing mergers, restructuring large SOEs in sectors where the entry barrier was high, and using other means of reorganization such as repartition to break up large enterprises and reallocate their market shares. Following restructuring and consolidation, there were fewer SOEs, but they had grown larger in size, and their corporate structures were more centralized. And now these restructured central SOEs had to compete with one another in much more integrated national markets. As the dust from restructuring national enterprises settled around 2003, nearly every sector—from petroleum, telecommunications, civil aviation, and finance to even defense—had at minimum two or three large SOEs ready to compete in overlapping geographical areas, in similar product markets, or for the same consumer base. Some sectors saw even more competitors than in the prerestructuring period.

Large steel enterprises, for instance, increased from four to eight competitors, autos from three to six, chemicals from four to seven, and electronics from three to seven.[52]

Intriguingly, SETC officials engineered this oligopolistically competitive environment to resemble the organization of advanced economies. The Japanese *keiretsu* system once served as one of the important reference cases for SETC bureaucrats in forging China's own enterprise groups. Following the 1997 Asian financial crisis, however, Japanese industrial organization became a negative example of overconcentration, which reminded the Chinese policy makers of the importance of instilling mechanisms for competition in the public sector.[53] With regard to how much competition was optimal, the SETC analyzed the state of market concentrations in major industries in the U.S. economy. It noted that the heat wave of mergers and acquisitions had dramatically consolidated the American markets and cut down the number of top players in key sectors. Chinese policy makers interpreted this outcome as a natural outgrowth of decades of competition and consolidation, an optimal balance achieved between economies of scale and market efficiency. They believed China should emulate and approximate similar outcomes.[54] The explicit reference to advanced economies and the way in which they were taken as positive or negative "lessons" underlined the SETC bureaucrats' desire to take shortcuts to arrive at similar states of market composition.

Third, consideration for the market can be seen in the SETC bureaucrats' tolerance of closures, liquidation, and bankruptcy. The SETC stipulated early on that bankruptcy was a necessary means for restructuring the state sector. Local officials had shunned bankruptcies due to employment concerns and frequently used enterprise grouping in the hope of breathing new life into SOEs that were incurring losses. In contrast, the SETC, with remedial funds at hand and a rationalizing motivation, was more prepared to authorize bankruptcies and liquidation as part of restructuring. In fact, one of the benefits associated with the "pilot" status the SETC assigned was greater freedom to deploy bankruptcy with central assistance.[55] The SETC's steadfast support of a nationwide bankruptcy wave proceeded to a point where, in the face of simmering social tension and criticisms of state asset loss, Premier Zhu Rongji ordered the State Council to halt the massive bankruptcies in 1997.[56] The SETC officials reluctantly obeyed but resumed their insistence on "letting market forces operate" to shut down underperforming enterprises.[57] The SETC's relaxed approach to public-sector bankruptcy underscored its desire to assert a ministry-level rationale for market efficiency that also governed other aspects of its restructuring policies and that transcended the concerns of local politicians and top leaders.

This chapter analyzes a defining period in China's enterprise reform that came to significantly shape the organization of China's public sector and its industrial landscape. It shows that this reform movement was led by bureaucrats in the SETC, who proposed a strategy of merging SOEs in order to forge large enterprise groups. I argue that this national movement of enterprise grouping, culminating in the creation of a national team of central SOEs, was not based on an impetus to create monopolies so much as on the need to construct and integrate markets through industrial reorganization. This chapter uncovers this little-researched motivation by tracing the career trajectories of the SETC bureaucrats and their previous experiences with linking up enterprises to survive a planned economy and with building regional markets in the reform period. In a policy environment of delegation and uncertainty around how to approach SOE reform, these reformers were able to stand out by drawing on their shared career experiences to develop an organizational strategy for the SETC, where they were concentrated. Under their leadership, the SETC, a young agency without resources, was able to seize authority over SOE reform and turn its market coordination activities into portfolios for managing the macroeconomy.

Through the lens of Chinese enterprise reform, this chapter reveals another unconventional route to market creation taken by Chinese economic policy makers who understood and imagined markets through the lens of their bureaucratic careers. Like the previous chapter, this chapter illustrates a pattern of state centralization under the aegis of the post-Tiananmen technocratic government, in which managerial control over the public sector moved upward through the administrative layers and local reformers were effectively incorporated into the central bureaucracy. The SOEs had once been embedded in local ecologies. Following waves of mergers and consolidations, they were organized according to their internal rationalities, their management was centralized, and they were detached from local communities. This chapter shows that the conglomeration movement in

China had a bureaucratic logic built into it. It unfolded together with the ascending trajectories of the SOE reformers, who turned locally grown ideas and policies into projects they believed would help integrate markets and the national economy.

This chapter features the SOE reformers but also captures the rise of a new paradigm for managing the Chinese economy, which I call an organizational approach. This approach, which the SETC bureaucrats practiced at various points in their careers, was consistently based on the idea that the government could manage the economy by reorganizing interenterprise relationships and actively coordinating relevant economic actors and regions. This organizational approach achieved paradigm status, as it was used not only to overcome local protectionism and achieve economies of scale in the public sector but also to change the economic structure, manage supply-demand relations, and integrate markets in the entire economy. The SETC provided a platform to systematically advance this organizational approach to the economy. With this approach, the SOE reformers were able to build the SETC into an agency with an exceedingly wide-reaching portfolio that also included inflation control and macroeconomic management.

PART III

Effervescence

THE REMAKING OF PUBLIC FINANCE IN CHINA AND THE FINANCIAL APPROACH TO ECONOMIC CONTROL

As part II of the book shows, the marriage between technocracy and state centralization changed the position of central bureaucrats in the Chinese state. The new era obviated the battle between the central bureaucrats and the local generalists that had dominated the political scene since founding of the People's Republic of China (PRC). Instead, in the 1990s, as we see in chapter 4, the local generalists' work experience was absorbed into the central bureaucracy and repurposed to forge a new generation of state managers who thought locally but reigned nationally. After the 1990s, the central economic bureaucracy no longer had to fight decentralizing forces. Different breeds of central economic bureaucrat with divergent career trajectories emerged, guided by distinctive understandings of the economy that sometimes conflicted. As the central economic bureaucracy became crowded, ministries served as the power centers of this area and as the means through which bureaucrats could amass organizational resources and build constituencies.

This chapter depicts one such bureaucratic movement that brought a new generation of financial bureaucrats into power, analyzing their advocacy for recasting state-market relations in financial terms. This movement started with two independently developing intellectual circles on the periphery of the Chinese state. These two forces were able to coalesce and capitalize on the centralization calls of the Zhu Rongji era to advance their "state + market" formula for developing financial markets and expanding public investments. As a result, in a span of only two decades, China nearly reversed the parameters of its public finance from a fiscal practice that celebrated balanced budgets to one that liberally levered its sovereign power to borrow. This approach escaped budget constraints and channeled public investments through the development of financial markets. The financial reformers' economic ideas also carried tremendous institutional consequences, as they refashioned old government agencies and created new ones through which they could implement a financialized way of conducting public finance. This chapter charts a road to bureaucratic power repeatedly observed in this book: bureaucrats' solutions became institutionalized in a paradigmatic way to reorganize the economy, which, in return, increased the authority of the original advocates.

THE BALANCERS AND THE NARROW TREATMENT OF PUBLIC FINANCE

Fiscal solvency was an important component of national sovereignty in the Mao period. Self-reliance was a geopolitical stance that also extended to the financial realm, culminating in the idea of a debt-free government. The aversion to debt was both domestically and externally applicable and morally charged. Borrowing from the international financial markets or from the great powers was viewed as risking China's exposure to a financial form of imperialism. The first generation of reformers still remembered when the Soviet Union mounted tremendous pressure on China to repay its loans in the 1960s in spite of China's struggling economy.[1] Internal debt was also politically undesirable. Borrowing from the people undercut government creditworthiness, as the socialist state was supposed to allocate and provide, not borrow. Being free of debt obligations was therefore associated with political prudence, moral virtue, and socialist abundance. Casting indebtedness in this light, Premier Zhou Enlai announced to the National People's Congress in 1975 with great pride that China was a country with a balanced budget and no external or internal debt.[2]

This sterilized conceptualization of debt in the Mao period would have been easier to shed if it had not been backed up by the balance theory, an influential and deep-rooted theory widely circulated in the bureaucracy. It consisted of a set of macroeconomic principles with influences lasting into the first decade of economic reform. As chapters 1 and 2 have elaborated, the creation of the balance theory was associated with one particular strand of first-generation reformers—the *circulators*— who understood the socialist economy from the perspective of flows of resources and saw fundamental flaws in an accumulation perspective on a socialist economy that was preoccupied with heavy-industry investment at the expense of the overall fiscal and credit balance of the economy. The circulators survived the Mao period and advocated for market reform. They saw the introduction of market mechanisms into the planned economy as a promising way to correct investment overheating in industries and discipline public investments. In the reform era, they became the *balancers*, adapting the balance theory to the new environment and relentlessly emphasizing the importance of fiscal prudence, credit soundness, and the prevention of inflation at any cost. Therefore, despite smacking of neoliberal-style austerity, this macroeconomic management had an indigenous and socialist origin.

To impose financial discipline, the balancers resorted to pulling the traditional strings of the economy through the use of financial planning. The problem with this method was that with economic reform, credit markets began to grow outside of the orbit of public finance. To rein in local bank lending, for example, the balancers fell back on restoring the authority of the Credit Plan and the Fiscal Plan: that is, the use of credit rationing and fiscal allocations to regulate the movement of material resources and their supply-demand relations. This set of methods was increasingly untenable because financial planning worked best when the full apparatus of a planned economy—price control, material supply allocation, and production plans—was in place so a priori credits and budgets could be matched with demand. As the Chinese economy grew out of the plan, the effectiveness of this strategy declined. Turning to the method of planning was also politically costly. It placed the balancers on the "conservative" side of the political aisle, in spite of themselves. As chapter 2 notes, it cost them credibility in their authority struggle with the local generalists, who were more growth-driven and appeared to be bold reformers.

The balancers' strange indifference to the expanding credit markets was likely due to repertoire constraints. An examination of their writings and speeches in the early reform era reveals that they had little to say about financial markets—and even less about how to engage with them. What limited the imagination and eventually the power of the balancers was their narrow conceptualization of public finance. To them, budget planning was the main financial lever that the state possessed vis-à-vis the economy. Placing budgeting at the center of the state's financial life reflected the lasting materialist bias of the Chinese economy. Fiscal money was a thing just as tangible as other goods and did not tolerate the separation of possession and consumption. Government revenues had to be raised and put into the coffers in order to be spent. As a result, the business of public finance was to allocate and redistribute—that is, budgeting. Li Xiannian, one of the key balancers, famously commented on the distributive nature of public finance, saying it was a way to move money from one pocket to another, not to create new pockets.[3] In other words, this substantialist view of public finance saw real substance in fiscal money that has to be "earned" in order to support spending. A failure to see fiscal power as a claim to money-creation authority of the state ended up drawing a stark line between the fiscal and the financial domains, blinding the balancers to their interconnections.

The lack of leverage over credit markets was a lost opportunity not only for the balancers but also for the central state. As markets expanded and the plan receded, national wealth began to accrue to Chinese society without going through central distribution. This trend was reflected in the rapid expansion of accounts of local enterprises, small producers, and private households. Deposits grew by 16.6 times and loans by 6.6 times from 1981 to 1990.[4] There was much to be celebrated about the societalization of wealth. Whether this had to happen at the expense of basic central state capacity was debatable. Local branches of the state banks amassed deposits from these new wealth holders and harnessed them to meet local developmental needs, which did not necessarily align with central government goals. Three years into the reform, thirty thousand new branches of state banks emerged, reaching their tentacles into cities, towns, and the countryside around the nation. These local branches of state banks acted more as part of locally integrated credit circuits than as subordinates to their headquarters.[5] Locally sourced funds reinforced the decentralization of the banking system and further undermined the authority of the central bureaucracy. In terms of national wealth distribution, the growing deposits in local state banks were accompanied by the deteriorating fiscal health of the central government. The share of central government revenue plummeted from 40 percent of total government revenues in 1984 to 20 percent in 1992. For the first time in the PRC's history, it was the semiautonomous local banks, not the central state, that served as the largest reservoir of national wealth and made critical decisions on how to allocate it.

It was clear to any financial bureaucrats who were interested in restoring the financial authority of the bureaucracy that they needed to engage with growing financial markets and accumulated household savings. They needed to incorporate both the state and the market into the policy formula and develop new ties between them so the state could harness forces of the financial market to develop the economy. Under the influence of the fiscal/financial dualism at the time, the Ministry of Finance (MOF) and the People's Bank of China (PBOC) fell short of meeting this forward-looking mandate. They responded to the growing might of local banks by introducing a debate premised on a zero-sum understanding of fiscal and financial money. They dwelled on the question of whether China should have big public finance and small banks (*dacaizheng xiaoyinhang*) or small public finance and big banks (*xiaoyinhang dacaizheng*):[6] that is, whether the central state should centralize national income through tax collection and revenue redistribution or allow the banks to channel societal savings to public investment and business. The debate thus pitted the fiscal against the financial, perceiving them as two disparate ways of mobilizing and distributing financial resources with no viable linkages between them. This understanding further disengaged the MOF from the banks and, by extension, from China's growing credit markets and pools of household savings. Immersed in the balance tradition, the MOF warned that the deposits held by the banks were a "tiger in a cage" that, once unleashed through investment, would become a potential source of inflation.[7] Conventional explanations for the weakness of the central state in the 1980s focused on its eroded tax base.[8] While government revenue was foundational, my account also delves into how the old generation of financial bureaucrats limited their own power through their understanding of public finance. As the following sections demonstrate, the power of the new generation of financial bureaucrats stemmed precisely from their ability to more imaginatively construct the state-finance nexus and devise the mechanisms by which the central state could leverage growing societal wealth.

THE WUDAOKOU SCHOOL AND THE MARKET-BASED
ATTEMPT TO BUILD CENTRAL BANK AUTHORITY

As the balancers' perspective on public finance continued to dominate in the early reform period, two political and intellectual forces were forming on the margin of the bureaucracy that provoked a rethinking of public finance and the role of the central state in China's expanding credit markets. One force was the PBOC's own graduate school—the Wudaokou School of Finance, sponsored by Liu Hongru, one of the vice directors of the PBOC. The other was an intellectual network that emerged across state think tanks and self-identified as the Comprehensive Reform School. Both shared a view on how best to approach economic reform and what the correct order of steps was to achieve it. While these intrabureaucracy movements were distinctively intellectual in origin, both forces owed their existence to some form of state sponsorship. From early on, these networks served as more than just intellectual forums for learning and discussion. As institutions spun off of the bureaucracy, they had privileged access to state-controlled information and occasionally to key political figures. Eventually, they produced not only ideas but also bureaucratic careers. This and the next two sections discuss the formation of each group in turn and also examine how they worked together to make fundamental changes to the configuration of China's public finance.

To put the founding of the Wudaokou School in context, it is necessary to include a discussion on the PBOC's struggle to become China's central bank in the reform era. Although the real call for restructuring the PBOC came as part of the central technocrats' plan to restore financial order in the 1990s (see chapter 3), there were some vague attempts to turn the PBOC into China's central bank as early as 1983, when the State Council announced that the PBOC would be China's central bank. Yet characteristic of many aspirational policies in this period, this decision was not followed by substantial institutional efforts. The council didn't specify what the organizational structure of China's central bank should look like or even what a central bank should and could do. Unsurprisingly, the PBOC met substantial obstacles translating this State Council decree into real authority. The PBOC attempted to establish a council, headed by PBOC officials, to hold regular meetings with the relevant ministries—most importantly, the MOF, the State Planning Commission (SPC), the State Economic and

Trade Commission, and the state banks. To its chagrin, the PBOC was not even able to bring other ministerial stakeholders to the table. The state banks were especially recalcitrant; they viewed the PBOC as, at most, having the same administrative ranking that they did and therefore as lacking the authority to command them.[9] Without executive power, the PBOC fell back on the credit plan to control the money supply, with very limited effectiveness. Moreover, although the credit plan entailed instruments for controlling aggregate money supply and credit rationing, it was, after all, an appendix to the physical plan rather than a response to the real change in the base money. Thus, by honoring the credit plan, the PBOC relegated itself to a position secondary to that of the SPC, with the latter retaining the ultimate say in the formulation of broad targets for output growth, investment, and inflation.[10] Under this scheme, there was hardly any room for developing central bank autonomy.

With the uncooperative state banks and the powerful planning commission blocking the PBOC's effort to assert monetary authority, Liu turned his attention away from the bureaucratic turf war to appeal to the developing financial markets in an effort to build the PBOC's constituencies. In order to engage with the cutting edge of the financial markets, they first needed to be studied. In this regard, financial practice had already leaped ahead of public knowledge about finance. From the early 1980s, seminal forms of financial products and innovations were already surfacing in the shadow of the plan. Local governments, often unacknowledged by the central government, were developing their own financial levers; going far beyond merely exploiting local bank deposits, they issued bonds, sourced extra-budgetary revenues, and established trust companies, raising funds from unconventional sources to meet the insatiable needs of local development. As early as 1984, some Chinese enterprises started to issue stocks publicly or semipublicly, adding more new experiments to the mix. In academia, however, finance courses were conspicuously absent from university curricula. Although general Western economics courses had appeared in colleges, finance was still considered the frontier of capitalism, a low priority on the agenda of curriculum modernization. In the government, regulatory knowledge of modern finance was even more scarce. Even Liu, allegedly among the best informed and most reform-minded of the central bankers, had exposure to capitalist banking only through political economy courses he took during his graduate study in the Soviet Union in the 1950s. Since the beginning of the reform, he and his colleagues scrambled to fill the gaps in their knowledge through private study and tours of foreign countries, which, according to Liu, were inefficient and unsystematic.[11] This pedagogical underdevelopment was also due to political sensitivity attached to financial reform. Financial liberalization remained a taboo for Chinese economic reform.[12] This can be seen in the fact that wherever the phrase *capital market* (*ziben shichang*) needed to appear in an official document, it was replaced by the phrase *fund market* (*zijin shichang*) to avoid using the word *capital*.[13]

Against this background, Liu's idea of establishing an in-house training school for a new generation of central bankers was meant to reduce publicity and add a layer of official protection for a closed-door learning environment. As was the case with many economic ideas in the early reform period, state sponsorship paradoxically provided intellectual privilege, informational advantage, and a larger degree of freedom of discussion than would otherwise have been possible. The location and naming of the school spoke to the intention of its founders to keep it inconspicuous. The PBOC's graduate school of finance was created in and named after its modest location in the neighborhood of Wudaokou, a then underdeveloped area still dotted with rice fields and villagers' houses, on the outskirts of Beijing.

Wudaokou designed a curriculum exclusively to keep these future central bankers informed of on-the-ground innovation. Precisely because the intention to train the next generation of central bankers was explicit, its educational mission was to engage students with policies and government agencies, not just to produce ideas in ivory towers. In terms of curriculum, Wudaokou set stringent requirements: students had to master econometrics and English on top of basic theories of finance, which, according to Liu, would prepare them with the tools needed to communicate with foreign central bankers and experts in the international financial community. In addition to rigorous training, Wudaokou students enjoyed real-time access to the *process* of financial policy making in the central government. They were able to obtain an insider look into the policy challenges revolving around financial reforms and even had opportunities to convey their suggestions to policy makers. Liu used his connections to invite frontline bureau-level policy makers of the PBOC as well as private practitioners to give lectures. Impressed by the students' passion for and knowledge of financial reform, guests quickly turned their lectures into consultative sessions, inviting suggestions from students on a variety of topical issues, including the development of monetary tools, financial liberalization, and the possibility of using direct financing in China.[14] Seating themselves in the front row of China's financial reform, the Wudaokou students were found to be "as informed as the ministers."[15] Second- and third-year students were already invited to do policy research at the PBOC. From 1981 to 2010, Wudaokou graduated 1,700 students. As table 5.1 illustrates, many of these graduates became China's most prominent financial regulators and managers in the central bureaucracy. Outstanding graduates joined the PBOC immediately after they matriculated. Liu's plan for speeding up the personnel turnover of the PBOC succeeded. Many other graduates assumed positions in financial regulatory agencies, and still others started their own firms in the private sector. As the fund industry blossomed in the late 1990s, Wudaokou alumni managed nearly half of China's private and public assets. In a sense, Wudaokou supplied the field of finance itself.

The flow of new blood into the PBOC changed the positioning of the bank vis-à-vis China's fledgling financial markets. While the older generation of financial bureaucrats saw the newly emerging financial institutions as threats to the mission of enforcing macroeconomic discipline, Liu and his students perceived them as compatible with building central-bank effectiveness. Granted, as the Chinese economy was increasingly monetized, modern monetary policy overall gained relevance in economic

TABLE 5.1
Wudaokou graduates in the financial bureaucracy

Name	Position	Nature of position
Wu Xiaoling	Vice governor, PBOC	Central banker
Hu Xiaolian	Vice governor, PBOC	Central banker
Du Jinfu	Vice governor, PBOC	Central banker
Sun Guofeng	Director, Monetary Policy Bureau, PBOC	Central banker
Wei Yingning	Vice chair, China Insurance Regulatory Commission	Financial regulator
Zhu Congjiu	Vice chair, China Securities Regulatory Commission	State financial regulator
Peng Chun	CEO, Central Huijin Co.	State financial manager
Li Hong	China International Capital Corporation Limited	State financial manager
Zhang Yujin	General manager, Shanghai Stock Exchange	State financial manager

Source: Compiled by the author from officials' CVs.

management thanks to a gradual process of financial deepening. Yet monetary policy still had to pass through the four big banks that controlled 87 percent of national savings and 97 percent of loans in 1985. The new central bank officials experimented with a range of indirect monetary instruments, including reserve requirements, lending facilities, and interest rates, with limited success. The state banks were simply not responsive to minor adjustments in these facilities, as the borrowing cost for the bulk of their loans was already low in a system of financial repression.

Cognizant of the difficulty of transforming the entrenched banking sector, Liu led the renewed PBOC in staking out a strategy he called "encircling the cities from the countryside," in which an array of financial institutions was set up outside of the framework of state-owned banks.[16] The encircling metaphor invoked the military tactic that the Chinese Communist Party used in the 1930s to take over regions previously controlled by the Nationalist Party. It is indicative of the unfavorable circumstances in which the reformist PBOC officials found themselves as they sought to build a responsive constituency for their monetary policy. Shenzhen, a special economic zone with a permissive policy environment, was well suited for the establishment of experimental banking institutions. Under the sponsorship of the PBOC, the first joint stock bank, Shenzhen Development Bank, was created and started to issue stock to the public. Soon thereafter, the first bank without a single state-owned share, China Merchants Bank, debuted in Shenzhen. The Nanyang Commercial Bank, the first foreign-owned bank to set up a branch in China, was followed by a few others. With early success in Shenzhen, this commercial banking wave spread to Beijing, Shanghai, Guangdong, Fujian, and other parts of China. The Bank of Communication in Shanghai was explicitly tasked, as the first "comprehensive bank," with bridging the sectoral and regional segregations created by the state banks and with assisting in the integration of China's fragmented financial markets. In searching for qualified managers for this new breed of institution, Liu again tapped into the Wudaokou alumni network. He called in graduates who had started their financial careers as fund managers to draft charters and assume managerial positions for the newly created joint stock banks.[17]

As a result, the central bankers and the private bankers, bound by their school ties, coordinated to create an array of new market actors that aimed to introduce competition and apply pressure to the state banks. Not only did they offer more attractive rates to solicit deposits, but also they raised funds directly by issuing stocks, integrating them into the financial market to a far greater degree than were the state banks. Beyond directly investing in building financial markets from scratch, the PBOC gave a green light to China's booming trust industry, which hosted two thousand trust companies with financial assets of more than 600 billion yuan. Residing in a legal gray zone, trust companies acted as shadow banks, taking deposits and making loans at more competitive interest rates.[18] They also expanded widely into a variety of financial sectors, ranging from stocks and real estate to asset management. Trusts set up by local governments were "window companies" that allowed those governments to borrow money and issue bonds domestically or even internationally. While the State Council raised concerns about trusts as a threat to the credit plan, the PBOC's public response was visibly ambiguous. Liu believed that the development of multitiered financial markets was a more efficient way for the Chinese state to make use of household savings.[19] By the end of the 1980s, as a function of these new developments, the PBOC's credit outlook had gone beyond the scope of the credit plan to include credit to nonbanking financial institutions, direct financing of enterprises, and credit to the comprehensive banks.[20] Liu did not shy away from celebrating how this strategy had facilitated the formation of transmitting mechanisms that had allowed monetary policies to become more effective.[21]

COMPREHENSIVE REFORMERS AND THEIR MARKET VIA THE STATE FORMULA

While the Wudaokou model represented a concentrated effort to change the flows of ideas and personnel of the central bank from within, the Comprehensive Reform School emerged from an interorganizational network that began with no claim to power but that eventually permeated the financial bureaucracy on a wider scale than the Wudaokou movement.

Similar to the birth of Wudaokou, the Comprehensive Reform School was initially associated with a central figure and an intellectual movement. In the latter case, the economist Wu Jinglian led the team. In the early 1980s, Wu worked in the Chinese Academy of Social Sciences (CASS), China's largest state think tank, and the Development Research Center housed at the State Council. At CASS, Wu trained a close-knit group of his students, coauthoring papers with them and passing along his way of thinking. At the Development Research Center, he had the ear of officials on the State Council. To further increase his influence over policies, Wu made a pivotal move by reaching out to Zhou Xiaochuan, a young bureaucrat at the SRC who was the son of Zhou Jiannan, the PRC's first minister of the machinery industry.[22] Zhou Xiaochuan graduated from Qinghua University with an engineering degree but found that his real interest lay in reforming the Chinese economy, not automating machines. With a princeling background and a degree from Qinghua, Zhou had the "red and expert" qualities of an official. He enjoyed protections and freedoms similar to those enjoyed by Liu's Wudaokou graduates. At the age of thirty-six, Zhou was already leading a reformist state think tank, the Economic System Reform Research Institute at the State Commission for Restructuring the Economic System, and had the attention of Premier Zhao Ziyang. An intellectual force in his own right, Zhou accepted Wu's invitation and formed a strong partnership with his group because they shared similar views on the necessity of across-the-board market reform.

A network of like-minded think-tank researchers and bureaucrats formed around the Wu-Zhou nexus. To obtain a sense of the cohesion of this intellectual network, I used network analysis to map the pattern of coauthorship among the comprehensive reformers. Figure 5.1 visualizes the result. We see an abundance of crosscutting collaborative relationships, which define the general cohesion of the network. The Wu-Zhou nexus not only constituted one of the busiest intellectual pathways but also held the network together, as each of them also collaborated with other core members of the network. The cohesion sustained among the Comprehensive Reform School members through coauthorship networks marks a difference from the Wudaokou reformers. While ideas were also central products of the Wudaokou graduates, those reformers were deeply enmeshed in governing practices early on and didn't develop prominent intellectual personalities to the same extent that the comprehensive reformers did. The early policy authority of the latter was directly derived from their ideas and their intellectual cohesion.

In a crowded opinion market like the one marking the early reform period, the members of the Comprehensive Reform School stood out for unapologetically championing integrated and systematic approaches to market reform.[23] In their "comprehensive" package of reform, many

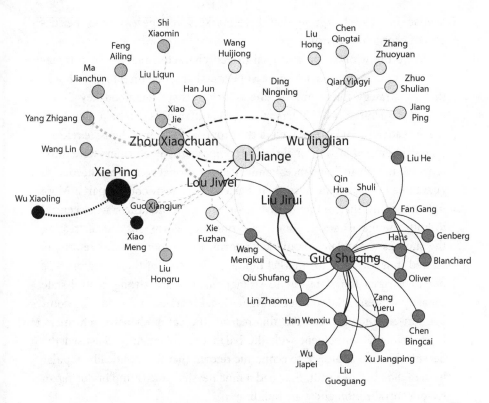

FIGURE 5.1. Coauthorship network of the Comprehensive Reform School. *Source*: Compiled by the author from Duxiu Database of Publications, "Duxiu Academic Search," https://www.duxiu.com/.

policy areas—including finance, tax, trade, and price—were intrinsically interconnected and had to be reformed in tandem with one another. Because of their emphasis on interdependence, they saw that the boundary between the fiscal and the financial was artificial. They advocated for the implementation of a tax-sharing system between the central and local governments while simultaneously developing financial markets, with an overall goal of constructing a competition-enhancing macroeconomic environment that could level the playing field and make efficient use of capital resources.[24] To the comprehensive reformers, both the reordering of public finance and the fostering of financial markets were key steps in the construction of a market environment. In particular, they attached greater importance to the development of financial markets than did the

Wudaokou School, arguing that these markets were necessary to the success of economic reform.

While the wide scope and goal-driven characteristics of the comprehensive reform approach bore a superficial resemblance to the shock-therapy strategy for economic liberalization, there remained key differences between the two. Understanding the differences will help illuminate the bureaucratic stakes involved in the proposal for comprehensive reform. As self-identified institutionalists, the comprehensive reformers were more sensitive to reform "sequences" and the institutional conditions needed to guarantee success than were their Eastern European counterparts. More fundamentally, the comprehensive reformers identified the state as central to both the means and the ends of economic reform. Instead of treating the state as a problem for market reform, the comprehensive reformers viewed it as a vehicle for market building. The goal of their program was not to weaken the state but to strengthen it, since strong central-state capacity was essential to integrating national markets and enforcing competition-enhancing rules. For this reason, the comprehensive reformers, in coincidental agreement with the balancers, vehemently chastised the decentralization approach to economic reform that was politically popular in the 1980s.[25] As a result, they had a much easier time fitting in during an era of centralization and state building.

Their opposition to decentralization allowed the comprehensive reformers to present themselves as "modern" reformers. In particular, they abhorred the contracting-out system (*chengbaozhi*), which allowed local governments to bargain over their tax revenues with the central government and enabled state enterprises to retain profits after submitting ex ante negotiated dues to the state. This form of decentralization through contracts, as the comprehensive reformers lamented, was equivalent to "tax farming in feudal times" and would not aid in the development of a modern economy for China.[26] Instead, the comprehensive reformers' plan purported to replace tax contracting with tax-sharing schemes that could strengthen the fiscal standing of the central government in relation to that of the local governments. Similar to Liu Hongru and his Wudaokou graduates, the comprehensive reformers felt an urgency to centralize monetary authority within the PBOC. They also perceived that the construction of interbank markets and other financial markets was conducive to establishing across-the-board monetary regulations and, in this way, permanently dispensing with the use of particularistic credit rationing.[27]

The difference in the comprehensive reformers' perspective as compared to that of the Wudaokou School was also clear from the outset. Though they took similar positions on the questions of central banking and financial markets, the comprehensive reformers nevertheless saw a bigger picture of the economy and had a particular concern with the issue of state capacity. Their positions at state think tanks freed them from administrative tasks and narrow organizational standpoints. With no particular organizational affiliation, the comprehensive reformers appeared to be less self-interested than were the central bankers. From their vantage point at the state think tanks, they were able to collect a wide range of information, providing a bird's-eye view of different parts of the state apparatus, which allowed them to postulate how those parts fit together and could be reassembled to further the cause of reform. Their career origins thus provide important clues as to why their subsequent careers proved to be more organizationally versatile than did those of the Wudaokou graduates. Before we delve into this question, however, we will examine how these burgeoning intellectual forces in the Chinese state banded together in order to gain influence.

WUDAOKOU GRADUATES AND COMPREHENSIVE REFORMERS JOINING FORCES

The lack of bold financial reform in the Hu Yaobang/Zhao Ziyang administration made for an environment that constrained the financial reformers. On the one hand, as mentioned earlier, balance thinking had yet to exhaust its influence in the Chinese government. On the other, the administration considered financial reform a low priority on what was already a lengthy to-do list. Administration leaders understood "playing to the provinces" to be the political engine of economic reform and balked at the prospect of pursuing financial statecraft.[28] The knowledge basis of the administration, defined mostly by local generalists, was far removed from matters of financial expertise. The generalists' lack of preparation in this area was manifest in the 1984 "Decision of the CPC Central Committee on Economic System Reform," which had only one vague sentence relating to financial reform: a statement of the need "to reform China's financial system."[29] One State Council official explained why details had not been more forthcoming:

"Fiscal revenue is akin to a transparent teacup. You can tell how much water is in there. Banking is an opaque teacup. You have no idea what is going on inside."[30] This comment captured an old-fashioned understanding of public finance similar to that of the balancers in the upper stratum of the bureaucracy. It also highlighted the general dearth of understanding of what financial reform would entail.

Lacking a fast track for advancing their ideas publicly, the comprehensive reformers and the Wudaokou graduates put together a research partnership backstage in the 1980s that proved to be generative in the decades to come. In 1984, Liu Hongru, then the PBOC's vice governor, preached to Zhao on the importance of upgrading China's financial system to satisfy increasingly diversified financing needs without driving the monetary supply out of control. In spite of a lackluster response, Zhao was willing to look into the matter and assembled a research team, led by Liu, which brought together the Wudaokou graduates and the comprehensive reformers.[31] Through this task force partnership, the two groups commenced what would become a long-standing tradition of collaboration, sharpening and consolidating their shared vision in the process. For example, Wu Xiaoling, an outstanding Wudaokou graduate, collaborated with multiple members of the Comprehensive Reform School, including Li Jiange, Lou Jiwei, Wu Jianlian, and Lou Jiwei. They coauthored internal policy suggestions, organized academic conferences, and attended policy sessions. This all occurred during Wu's gradual ascendance through the ranks of the PBOC. When the core comprehensive reformer Zhou Xiaochuan joined the PBOC as its new governor in 2002, Wu Xiaoling was the vice governor. Together, the two eventually acquired a formal venue in which to advance their proposals. We know that their partnership dated back to the mid-1980s, but the 1984 task force marked the beginning of their joint influence. At the conclusion of its work, the task force drafted a memo calling for the development of a central bank that had a firmer grip on monetary control and for the crafting of a financial system that featured multiple types of financial institutions and "multiple forms of credit and financing" beyond bank credit.[32] Because of the weak leadership commitment and resistance from those who benefited from decentralization, this proposal, together with another attempt at financial reform in 1986, did not get off the ground. Yet participating in efforts to design China's financial reform, with direct access to top leadership, gave the task force members a type of "reform capital." It broadcast to the rest of the bureaucracy their special access and status, given their unrivaled expertise in matters of finance despite their humble administrative ranking, keeping them relevant until new opportunities could arise. Early collaboration provided this group with sources of cohesion and trust that served as mechanisms of coordination even after individual members dispersed along divergent career paths.

TECHNOCRATIC CENTRALISM AND THE ROAD TO FINANCIAL BUREAUCRATS

As chapter 3 explains, the post-Tiananmen era marked the rise of a technocratic government in China. The Jiang Zemin/Li Peng (later Zhu Rongji) administration, consisting mostly of engineers, governed using a policy paradigm of state centralization and market expansion. This stance of the new government complemented the comprehensive reformers' longstanding positions. Even more curiously, some of the key reforms the new administration put in place upon assuming power—including tax-sharing reform and liberalization of the exchange rate regime—were precisely what the comprehensive reformers suggested in the 1980s. It is doubtful that the comprehensive reformers were the only group of bureaucrats who had this idea or that the top leaders simply hadn't consulted other sources of advice. What explains the convergence was likely their shared receptiveness to Western institutional practice, a pragmatic attitude toward the role of the central state, and a belief in the efficiency of markets. Not surprisingly, it was during Zhu's premiership that the comprehensive reformers, together with the Wudaokou graduates, found themselves promoted swiftly up through the ranks toward ministry-level positions in the economic bureaucracy. A career path from state think tank to ministerial post had been uncommon in the Chinese government. The Chinese bureaucracy has overwhelmingly preferred practical to theoretical knowledge, valuing the former for its utility in governance. However, the technocrats' patience with models and theories, as chapter 3 describes in detail, opened doors to a nerdier strand of bureaucrats, allowing them to transform their intellectual achievements into political power. While in the grand scheme of things the rise of the comprehensive reformers makes sense in this era, there is still something puzzling about their career outcomes. As table 5.2 shows, after leaving think tanks, the comprehensive reformers spent the

TABLE 5.2
Comprehensive reformers in the financial bureaucracy

Name	First leadership position in a financial agency	Highest leadership position in a financial agency	All financial agencies served	Percentage of official tenure spent in financial agencies (%)
Zhou Xiaochuan	1991, PBOC	Governor, PBOC (2002–2013)	Bank of China, State Administration of Foreign Exchange, China Construction Bank, Securities Regulatory Commission, PBOC	81.8
Guo Shuqing	2001, PBOC	Vice governor, PBOC (2001–2005)	System Reform Commission, PBOC, State Administration of Foreign Exchange, China Construction Bank, Securities Regulatory Commission, Banking Regulatory Commission	58.6
Lou Jiwei	1998, MOF	Minister, MOF (2013–2016)	CASS, MOF, China Investment Corporation, National Council for Social Security Fund	64.7
Li Jiange	1994, Securities Regulatory Commission	Vice chair, Securities Regulatory Commission (1994–1998)	Securities Regulatory Commission, Central Huijin Co., China International Capital Corporation Limited, Shenyin Wanguo Securities	67.7
Xie Ping	2003, Central Huijin Co.	CEO, Central Huijin Co. (2005–2010)	PBOC, Central Huijin Co., China Investment Corporation	100
Xiao Jie	2001, MOF	Minister, MOF (2016–2018)	MOF	81.1

Source: Compiled by the author.

majority of their official careers in financial agencies. The concentration in financial leadership clearly defies the "comprehensiveness" of their erstwhile policy interests and raises the question of how the comprehensive reformers became exclusively financial bureaucrats.

As chapter 3 shows, financial reform was a linchpin in the central technocrats' push for centralization and market efficiency. Inflation in the early 1990s provided its immediate impetus, but there was also a determination to address the root cause of inflation, restore the monetary authority of the central government, curb the local government investment frenzy, and reduce the debts of the state-owned enterprises (SOEs). Vowing to clean up the financial chaos, the engineers-turned-technocrats approached these problems with an engineering mind-set, and as a result, they solved old problems and created new ones. This round of anti-inflation efforts, when administered in a micromanagerial fashion, risked throwing the baby out with the bathwater. In 1994 alone, more than six hundred trust, insurance, and financial leasing companies were ordered to close.[33] Administrative interventions alleviated the liquidity crisis with immediate results, but simply shutting down small and nonbanking financial institutions suppressed lending and proved counterproductive. Obviously, this also suffocated the secondary markets that were then budding across China.[34] Indeed, this wave of inflation management planted the seeds for the credit crunch and underinvestment that would create problems in the years to come. This outcome led to a recognition of the importance of delegating financial work to experts who knew how to work with the market, not against it. Expert bureaucrats who could solve problems *and* provide long-term institutional solutions were needed.

In spite of a general openness to outside ideas in this era, drawing talent from outside the state bureaucracy to fill financial leadership roles in the central government remained a nonstarter.[35] For the insiders, the comprehensive reformers were the closest palatable alternative. Equipped with expertise matching that of their Western counterparts, they also had "royal" status because they had connections to the state and had never held career positions outside of it. Although they showed a wide-ranging interest in economic reform, their knowledge of public finance and the financial sector was robust and even appeared to be unrivaled in the bureaucracy. As a result, the comprehensive reformers were ideal candidates to be groomed as the next generation of China's financial bureaucrats.

By this point, the comprehensive reformers had already accumulated a stock of political capital waiting to be cashed out. They had served as advisers on the new administration's technocratic reform and had communicated directly with Premier Zhu, an amount of access disproportionate to their humble positions at state think tanks. In this regard, Lou Jiwei, a key figure in the Comprehensive Reform School, played an indispensable role. Lou impressed Zhu with his straightforward character and fresh suggestions on tax-sharing reform and macroeconomic management while working at the Research Office of the State Council.[36] Handpicked by Zhu as his secretary, Lou followed him to Shanghai from 1988 to 1992 and then back to Beijing when Zhu became vice premier. Through Lou, the comprehensive reformers found a patron in the top leadership. In step with Zhu's ascendance to the position of "economic czar" from 1994 to 2003, the comprehensive reformers quickly transitioned themselves out of the state think tanks and into the ministries.

After the comprehensive reformers got a foot in the official door, they ascended rapidly because they were able to offer solutions to economic problems that could meet the mandates of the situation while also preparing the ground for developing China's financial markets in the long run. That is, the solutions they formulated were tailored toward the specific needs of the problems at hand and, when viewed collectively, constituted what I call an array of *paradigmatic solutions*, which saw the economy and conceptualized its problems in a certain light. This was all in line with an intention to marry the state with the market. Expressed in terms of finance, this meant developing financial markets while also strengthening the ability of the state to leverage those markets. This combined formula had long eluded the balancers and the old generation of financial regulators. In the new era, it promised to meet the new administration's aspiration to modernize the financial architecture of the Chinese economy while also attending to China's constant need for massive capital accumulation. Gradually, the accumulation of paradigmatic solutions created institutions themselves. They altered the roles of the PBOC and the MOF in the Chinese economy and profoundly transformed the scope and meaning of public finance for the Chinese state in general. Eventually, a new paradigm of state-finance relationships came into being. The following sections highlight two areas in which the financial reformers provided distinctive diagnoses of and prescriptions for a series of economic problems.

UNDERINVESTMENT AND THE PROPOSAL
FOR BUILDING A NATIONAL BOND MARKET

Following five years of inflation, the Chinese economy quickly dived into a phase of deflation and underinvestment around 1996. Previous methods of inflation control were effective as far as the immediate goal was concerned, but their drastic and draconian characteristics also tended to backfire. Centralization of credit control and policy retrenchment slowed down investment nationwide. Raw material production and infrastructure construction took particularly hard hits and dragged down the entire economy. The traditional array of public investors was sluggish in its response and could not rise to the occasion. SOEs were too heavily indebted to take their own initiative. The state banks, as they became increasingly rational, grew increasingly risk averse and scaled back their lending. Local governments had always shown little interest in investing in infrastructure even when they had more credit power. Soon the drop in investment was reflected in the growth rate. GDP growth dropped to a single-digit rate in 1996 for the first time since the new administration had assumed office. The timing of the 1997 Asian financial crisis certainly didn't help by further depressing growth. Beijing's promise not to devalue the yuan gave China a positive reputation in the international financial community but rendered an export-led stimulus unviable as an option to revive the economy. Instead, China had to explore mechanisms of internal expansion to stimulate the economy.[37]

One way to encourage this endogenous growth, according to the comprehensive reformers, was to increase the government's ability to borrow. As early as 1994, Lou Jiwei had suggested developing China's bond markets to build the central bank's monetary tools.[38] In the face of slow growth and deflation, he put forward this suggestion again in the new context—and now with a sense of urgency and purpose. The MOF was considered the ideal candidate to issue bonds. The SPC was also considered but was rejected due to its excessive focus on growth, which impaired its creditworthiness as a bond issuer. In comparison, the MOF was more detached from the immediate performance of the economy and would more likely act as an unbiased representative of the sovereign, which boded well for its ability to maintain purchasers' confidence.[39] In other words, the MOF's ostensible neutrality allowed it to exercise fiscal activism. This financial scheme cast

TABLE 5.3
Issuance of long-term construction national bonds (1998–2002)

Year	Amount (in billions of RMB)	Purpose
1998	100	Infrastructure construction
1999	110	Infrastructure construction, SOE technological upgrading
2000	150	Infrastructure construction, SOE technological upgrading, development of West China, ecological environment construction
2001	150	Ongoing construction projects, development of West China
2002	150	Ongoing construction projects, development of West China

Source: Huachuang Securities, "Special Times, Special National Bonds" [Tebie de shihou, tebie de guozhai], research report, June 6, 2019, http://pdf.dfcfw.com/pdf/H3_AP201906061333935053_1.pdf.

the MOF in a new light and in a role different from its historical role as a conservative fiscal disciplinarian and budgetary gatekeeper.

As table 5.3 shows, beginning in 1998 the MOF rolled out a multiyear scheme to issue national bonds earmarked for infrastructure construction and other capital projects. It was not coincidental that 1998 was the year in which Lou ended his brief tenure as vice governor of Guizhou Province and was appointed the vice minister of the MOF. Under Lou's supervision, the MOF issued 660 billion yuan in special purpose national bonds between 1998 and 2002, equivalent to two-thirds of the tax revenues of the entire country in 1998. These bonds were expected to be purchased by the commercial banks and, in this way, channel state investment to projects around the nation. This ordinary bond-based Keynesian measure, when put in its historical context, was rather extraordinary. The balance thinking that defined the tenor of China's public finance had long regarded Keynesianism as a reckless idea that ran counter to the need to discipline the budget. The hesitancy to issue national bonds was reflected in the fact that before 1998 special purpose bonds were counted as deficits on the government balance sheet. The 1998 issue, however, spearheaded a new accounting practice where long-term national bonds for construction purposes showed up under the category of "Central Government Funds," thus flipping their status from a form of liability to an asset.

Underpinning this new categorization was a general optimism in the economic bureaucracy that linked state investment to the growth potential of the economy. Financial instrumentality was considered indispensable to building a bridge between the two. The comprehensive reformers served as this bridge. As Premier Zhu Rongji explained to the public, "Before 1993, we used financial overdrafts to make up for deficits. . . . Now our method was to use state investment. The Ministry of Finance issued national bonds to the banks. This would use the money that the banks could not lend out on their own. With regard to risk, the improvement of SOEs would take care of it."[40] Zhu was right that issuing national bonds created liquidity, not money. By moving money out of household and corporate accounts, the central government was also able to tap into the vast pool of national deposits without printing more money and raising concerns about inflation. That is, by lubricating the circulation of financial flows in the economy, this solution avoided reviving the trauma of inflation, which was not so remote in the bureaucratic memory.

This first wave of national bond issuance stimulated growth through the reworking of public finance; its far-reaching significance also lay in altering and greatly expanding the role of the MOF in managing the national economy. For the first time, the MOF became an indispensable macroeconomic policy maker thanks to its use of demand management and its capacity to borrow as a sovereign entity. Fiscal policy now took on an expanded meaning beyond budgeting to include managing short-term economic cycles and enhancing growth prospects when needed. The comprehensive reformers explicitly welcomed this macroeconomic turn of China's fiscal policy, calling it a step toward modernizing the macroeconomic framework of China's economic policy and a mode of fiscal expansion superior to that of decentralizing tax revenues and credit implemented in the 1980s.

In addition, through national debt issuance and management, the MOF found its own entry into financial markets, making the agency a key market builder in its own right. This newfound role was associated with the changing mode of bond issuance, which increasingly relied on markets and the cultivation of institutional investors. In the 1980s, the selling of national bonds was minuscule and unmediated by bond markets. Employees and households were mobilized as "patriotic individuals" to purchase a limited range of bond products. The MOF also negotiated quotas with local governments and other governmental parties and pressured them to purchase their share. Not only was the administrative cost of these methods high, but also the MOF ran the perpetual risk of failing to meet the issuing targets, as the long maturity and illiquid nature of government bonds made them unattractive to individual buyers and defiant local governments.[41] In 1990, the National Bond Bureau of the MOF, led by Gao Jian, explored taking the first steps to marketize bond issuance. The problem then was that the markets and market actors to buy and sell the bonds didn't exist. The National Bond Bureau had to assemble and legalize a range of trust and security companies in order to create a batch of primary dealers that could purchase its bond products. In 1991, transferring bond products was made legal, and secondary marketplaces started to develop. In 1995, the MOF used tender offers to issue bonds for the first time. Still, the bond market remained small, and the bond yield curve could not form.

Against this backdrop, aggressive bond issuance after 1998 was monumental; building on this momentum, it rapidly cultivated the development of the bond market and the secondary markets. The scope of dealers and underwriters expanded to include insurance companies and asset management firms. Interbank bond markets took shape quickly as well. Diversified product structures with various interest rates and maturities made the formation of a yield curve both possible and credible, and it then became an important benchmark of the success of the financial market in general.[42] With the deeper entanglement of national bonds with the financial markets, the MOF needed to manage its risks in relation to the capital market and thus cried out for more in-house experts with the relevant specialist knowledge. National bonds became an increasingly professionalized domain of economic management in the MOF's growing portfolio. Under the direction of the Comprehensive Reform School veterans, the MOF became the critical link between the financial markets and public investments. It made substantial decisions on when and what bonds should be issued and in what volume, decisions concerning the scope and timing of public investment that previously were made almost exclusively by the State Council and the planning agencies.[43]

CORPORATE CONTROL AND THE EVALUATION OF STATE ASSETS THROUGH FINANCIAL MARKETS

Treasury bonds and fiscal activism alleviated the liquidity crunch and bumped up demand in the economy, but they did not solve the financial system's underlying problem: the indebtedness of the SOEs and their lackluster performance. SOE reform was a policy area where there were no obvious best practices to adopt. Diverse local conditions and sectoral differences made the leadership hesitant to impose any top-down resolutions. Indeed, the otherwise confident leaders of the Jiang/Zhu administration offered no concrete plans. Instead, they delegated authority to ministries and localities, which were to develop their own initiatives. As chapter 4 details, this delegation allowed the emergence of managers-turned-industrial-bureaucrats and their conglomeration approach to SOE reform. This model used cross-region mergers as an effective way to integrate national markets. Precisely because of the robust action taken on behalf of the leadership, the comprehensive reformers, who otherwise had little experience with industries, also felt that they could claim SOE reform as one of their intellectual jurisdictions if they reconceptualized enterprises in ways that were closer to their expertise. In the end, they defined the essence of Chinese SOEs in financial terms and made connections between SOEs' debt problems and China's developing financial reforms.

Since a financial understanding of enterprises was rather new, the comprehensive reformers felt the need first to improve financial literacy among the officialdom. The Jinglun conference was such an occasion, as foreign intellectual allies were enlisted to promulgate financial knowledge. Around 1994, the comprehensive reformers teamed up with the institutional economists from the United States to introduce the idea of corporate control to the Chinese government, making the argument that it was relevant to China's financial market reform. The Jinglun conference, sponsored by the Ford Foundation and hosted in Beijing, allowed the comprehensive reformers to bring together American economists and Chinese bureaucrats to exchange ideas about how to improve corporate efficiency. The conference was even able to attract Premier Zhu Rongji's attention; he sent his aides to take careful notes of the proceedings, and following the conference, he met the foreign delegates.

Translating theories of corporate control into the Chinese context, the comprehensive reformers proposed that Chinese SOEs suffered from their own share of insider-control problems, which boiled down to the inability of the state owners to control their corporations. To address this problem, China could introduce mechanisms of corporate governance to correct the SOEs' poor performance. Concretely speaking, in the Chinese case, the vast amount of state investment in SOEs did not translate into power to their owner—the Chinese state. As a result, state investment remained invisible to the market. That is, the state was the nominal owner of all SOEs but could not exercise its rights as an active shareholder. The lack of a financial market that could properly evaluate and circulate state assets was another issue. Because of the lack of ownership activism and proper market pricing, opportunistic pricing remained rampant and risked undervaluing state assets. Stakeholders who had insider information, such as managers and local governments, could hijack corporate agendas in ways contrary to the interests of the real owners. Employees could also pressure managers to divert profits from reinvesting to bettering salaries and working conditions. To exercise shareholder rights, the comprehensive reformers suggested setting up shareholding agencies to personalize and professionalize state ownership. These shareholding agencies would have strong financial expertise and a robust financial perspective on corporate performance.[44] This reform scheme, if implemented, would further remove the ties of the SOEs to communities and local stakeholders and make them answer to their ultimate owner—the state.

With the implementation of shareholding reform and the development of financial markets, the debt issue of the SOEs resurfaced and acquired new significance. SOE debts negatively impacted the financial markets in two ways: SOE debts at the state banks were clearly toxic to China's banking sector, and state assets in the form of bad loans were highly illiquid, constraining the SOEs' ability to participate in and benefit from the expansion of China's capital markets. To address this debt issue, the comprehensive reformers floated the idea of debt-for-equity swaps. The idea was that the banks would convert SOE debts into shares or set up asset management firms to purchase bad loans from the banks and become shareholders in the SOEs. In either case, this maneuvering introduced shareholders on behalf of the Chinese state, shareholders who could claim a stake in SOE performance and also collect dividends.[45]

The insider-control discourse didn't immediately prompt policy action, but it started to change the terms in which the privatization of SOEs was discussed by the state and by the public. Previously, officials and managers around China proceeded with SOE privatization with a sense of inevitability. With the arrival of the shareholding model, privatization attracted greater attention from the public and the media as potentially immoral and unjust. This was somewhat unexpected and potentially unfathomable to observers in capitalist economies, as the shareholding revolution had invariably enhanced private property regimes in their economies. While the shareholding reform in China similarly shifted stakeholder participation practiced in the socialist period, it came with a twist—the preservation of state ownership. As China began to examine state ownership, manager-directed selling and buying, which had been the prevailing method used to privatize SOEs, became highly problematized. Seizing on societal attention to this trend, the comprehensive reformers offered a definition of this prevailing practice that framed it precisely as a regrettable instance of insider control and state asset loss and called for the introduction of markets to correctly value state assets.[46] The heightened attention to state asset loss politicized the discussion of SOE reform and alarmed the leaders in Beijing, who had been waiting to see how the situation progressed. They closed down many decentralization experiments, shifting the locus of SOE reform decisively away from various forms of privatization and toward the state + market formula.

BANK RECAPITALIZATION AND THE PROLIFERATION OF STATE SHAREHOLDERS

While Chinese policy makers grew increasingly receptive to the shareholding model for restructuring the state sector, they could not proceed until the SOEs' non-performing loans (NPLs) at the state banks were addressed. Because of their enormous magnitude, public-sector debts so deeply affected the health of the banking sector that systemically reorganizing these debts would mean restructuring the state banks in their entirety. Until then, financial reform had more or less underestimated and avoided this issue. What finalized the government's resolve to come to terms with bank restructuring was the 1997 Asian financial crisis. Interpretations of the causes of the crisis varied considerably within the Chinese government. Some argued that the integration of Asian economies into the global financial market led to exposure to financial speculation. Others thought the opposite, contending that it occurred because the East Asian economies were not sufficiently liberalized and globalized.[47] The official assessment of the crisis and its implications for China turned out to be typical of what a technocratic government in this era would do: it stepped around the ideological question of whether China needed more or less liberalization and drew a lesson as technical and concrete as possible, focusing solely on the issue of the vulnerability of state banks. The assessment argued that if nothing was done, the Chinese state-owned commercial banks would not be resilient enough to weather a crisis. They were burdened with weak capitalization, NPLs, and a lack of market discipline. Zhu Rongji portrayed the NPL issue as life-threatening to China's financial system and called for major surgery.[48]

Regardless of how the financial crisis was interpreted, what happened afterward in the Chinese government, as in many other places, was that the crisis promoted the authority of financial experts. Zhu delegated the initiative to devise specific programs to restructure the banking sector to the comprehensive reformers and, not surprisingly, to PBOC officials. While remaking the state banks into real corporations was the ultimate goal, the urgent task at hand was to remove the SOEs' debts from the balance sheets so the state banks could be recapitalized. In doing so, this coalition of reformers creatively invented, leveraged, and moved around the financial resources of the state in order to remake market actors.

Zhou Xiaochuan, the leader of the Comprehensive Reform School, was entrusted with overhauling the state banks, a mission as unprecedented as it was complex. As a first step, China Construction Bank, one of the "big four" state banks, was chosen to be the model case for recapitalization. In 1998, Zhou was transferred from his post as vice governor of the PBOC to head the China Construction Bank so he could personally lead the effort. A range of financial and accounting maneuvers was then taken. Using the American government's efforts to clean up bad debts during the savings and loan crisis as a model, in 1999 Zhou and his colleagues proposed a "bad banks, good banks" strategy to take over the bad loans from the state banks. Four asset management corporations (AMCs) were created in 1999 and capitalized by issuing 40 billion yuan in special AMC bonds to the MOF and 858 billion yuan in ten-year bonds to the other state banks. In 2000, Zhou moved to run one of the AMCs, Cinda, and showcased to the rest how the acquisition of NPL portfolios should be done. Drawing funding from more bond issues and a credit extension of 634 billion yuan by the PBOC, the AMCs transferred NPLs worth 1.4 trillion yuan from the banks to their accounts.

Even with the NPLs removed from their books, the state banks still had weak capital bases. Initially, the MOF had issued 270 billion yuan in special purpose treasury bonds to lend to the banks as capital, but this was not at all sufficient to make up for the capital shortage. In 2002, Zhou had just started his eleven-year tenure as governor of the PBOC, while Wu Xiaoling, a Wudaokou graduate, became the director of the State Administration of Foreign Exchange. Note that two leading figures of the Comprehensive Reform School and the Wudaokou school—Zhou and Wu—who had an intellectual partnership dating back to the 1980s, had now assumed the most important positions in public finance and could coordinate in a formal fashion. Together, they proposed to use foreign exchange reserves that the PBOC controlled to set up a financial holding company, Central Huijin, to invest in the state banks. In addition, the PBOC issued another 567 billion yuan in compulsory special bills to inject more funds into three of the big four. The financial technocrats kept both rounds of recapitalization away from the national budget to avoid having to go through approval by the National People's Congress, which would slow down the process. Quickly learning to deploy the power of sovereign promises, the MOF, as the ultimate steward of public finance, ramped up its own scheme to recapitalize the banks and establish shareholding. In 2005, the MOF transferred an NPL portfolio of 246 billion yuan from the Industrial and Commercial Bank of China (ICBC) and the Agricultural Bank of China (ABC) to an account comanaged by these two banks. In its place, the two banks received an MOF IOU, which was to be paid from future streams of tax and cash dividends the MOF was set to receive from the banks on account of the ministry's twin roles as tax collector and shareholder of the banks.[49] In 2006, with strengthened capital bases and external corporate control, the government felt ready to float shares of the state banks on capital markets to attract strategic and retail investors.

With bad loans removed and good assets injected, only one step remained to institute corporate control in the state banks—shareholder professionalization. The new role that the MOF and the PBOC assumed vis-à-vis the state banks did personalize the state shares, but these two administrative bodies were not professional financial investors and had divided attention. Inspired by the PBOC's move to establish Central Huijin, the MOF issued bonds to create its own shareholding entity, the Chinese Investment Corporation (CIC), to professionalize its asset management. The comprehensive reformer Lou Jiwei, its first chairman of the board, invited Wall Street veteran Gao Xiqing to be its CEO. Shortly thereafter, the PBOC followed up by creating another financial entity, Huida, to make more space for financializing its debt obligations.[50] The competition to hold shares of the state's financial assets was intense.[51]

Once created, these state holding companies acquired professional lives of their own. The CIC morphed into more than a shareholder of the state banks, eventually becoming a sovereign wealth fund and an institutional investor of the Chinese state, directly reporting to the State Council. The CIC took over Huijin and expanded its shareholding portfolio to seize majority shares of the big four, China Development Bank, and dozens of other joint stock banks, securities firms, and insurance companies, with total assets of 4.75 trillion yuan and profits of 492 billion yuan in 2018. The earliest batch of AMCs, created to clean up the NPL portfolios, were all scheduled to close down after ten years, but this didn't happen, and they only grew larger in terms of their assets and the types of business licenses they held.[52] This organizational growth called into existence a new profession within the state—the state asset manager. State holding corporations and asset management firms were new career outlets for the comprehensive reformers and for young graduates and financial talent. In general, as parastatal organizations, they also created new routes and posts through which bureaucrats could circulate within the state, further blurring the line between the administrative state and the financial sector.

Financial shareholding fundamentally changed the relationship of the financial bureaucracy with the banking sector. Initially, the Wudaokou graduates adopted an encircling strategy to indirectly pressure the state banks by encouraging the birth of competing financial institutions. Now the financial reformers at the MOF and the PBOC fully recognized the strategic importance of the state banks and attempted to grapple with their issues head-on—most importantly, the banks' historical baggage and inefficiency. The MOF and the PBOC created formal institutional linkages with the state banks, structured in corporate and semicorporate arrangements, in the hope that the state banks would behave more like market actors. They built market infrastructure around the banks and introduced some elements of competition, mechanisms of corporate control, and new evaluative standards of corporate efficiency revolving around return on assets. Through building markets and their actors, the Chinese state also changed its own identity and governance style via both the *process* of recapitalization and its intended *outcome*. The role of the MOF was remarkably transformed, as was the meaning of public finance. What public finance entailed shifted from the era of the balancers, where budgeting and vehicles of public investment were what mattered, to a new perspective that encompassed a sprawling range of functions, including shareholding, macroeconomic regulation, state asset management, and financial investment. Underpinning the change was a financialized understanding of the economy and the role of sovereign power in creating financial leverage and solving (or delaying) historical economic problems in entirely new ways.

Like advanced liberal economies, the Chinese economy has become increasingly financialized and debt-ridden in the past two decades. This trend has not taken place independent of government but has been deeply tied to a movement in the economic bureaucracy that aimed to alter the parameters of public finance so that the focus was on capitalizing on the state's sovereign capacity to borrow, not maintaining fiscal balance. This chapter traces the biographical origin of this movement in the confluence of central bankers trained at the Wudaokou School of the PBOC and the Comprehensive Reform School, a network of like-minded state think-tank researchers. Through a series of advising activities that proposed financialized solutions to problems such as SOE debt and shortages of capital needed for development, these financial thinkers coalesced, gradually amassed authority in the bureaucratic field, and eventually assumed important posts across finance-related agencies (the PBOC, MOF, state banks, and AMCs). Their concerted ascendance eventually consolidated ad hoc solutions into a paradigm of economic development centered on sovereign borrowing and debt-driven development, influencing a wide range of policy domains, including SOE restructuring, the development of financial markets, and macroeconomic management.

While uncovering the bureaucratic intention behind China's financialization movement, this chapter simultaneously uncovers the state origin of the development of financial markets in China, which, in retrospect, has closely followed a classic Polanyian plotline—national expansion and development of markets dis-embedded them from local ecologies. In the 1980s, it was the local circuits—local state banks, governments, and societies—that mobilized finance. Markets were fragmented and developed without central administration, and financial flows escaped central control. The development of national financial markets—through the centralization of the banking system, the circulation of state assets in the financial markets, and the cultivation of institutional investors by the state—was immensely useful in breaking up local financial communities and allowed the central state to greatly improve the legibility of conditions on the ground. The development of financial markets did not undermine the sovereign power of the state but rather enhanced and leveraged it. Through this centralized but highly leveraged financial system, the Chinese state was able to bypass the local system to extract money and raise capital to support national development projects and sustain the large capital formation necessary for that development stage of the Chinese economy.

Chapter Six

THE ASCENT OF THE INDUSTRIAL VIEW

Industrial Policy for Making a
Manufacturing Superpower

Beginning in the late 2000s, a new policy paradigm dedicated to improving China's industrial competitiveness gained traction within the Chinese government and society. It culminated in the birth of the widely known *Made in China 2025* initiative, which was intended to strengthen China's indigenous innovation and improve its international competitiveness. This policy wave notably departed from the previous approach to industrial development, which for decades had stressed the comparative advantage theory and focused on developing labor-intensive industries. The aspiration to transform China from the "world's factory" into a manufacturing superpower spurred a paradigmatic rethinking of development in general. It reminded the policy makers that China's industrialization was yet to be finished, deindustrialization was premature, and industrial competitiveness defined the quality of development. The contrast of this message to that of the financialization approach to growth, as discussed in the previous chapter, could not be clearer. Though the industrial reformers emerged later than the financial reformers, the two approaches overlapped and created tension in the bureaucracy. They constituted two poles in the bureaucratic field, greatly broadening the spectrum of China's economic policy making.

Attributing the rise of this industrial program to China's state capacity or central political will is tempting, but this chapter shows that the rise of the competitiveness-oriented industrial policy was tied to collective movements slowly taking place in China's economic bureaucracy. This chapter draws the full arc in which industrial policy as a new policy domain of the Chinese state surfaced, subsided, and reemerged. In this process, it compares the previous three periods to this more recent one to explain why a competitiveness-driven industrial agenda didn't arise earlier. In the first period (mid-1980s to late 1980s), the State Planning Commission (SPC) sought to develop cross-sectoral policies despite the fact that it lacked the organizational capacity to institute them. In the second period (early 1990s to 2003), industrial policy was largely subordinated to the macrocontrol policy paradigm and did not have autonomy or tools of its own. In the third phase (2003 to 2008), industrial policy makers lacked the specialized backgrounds needed to make industrial policy into a sophisticated and far-sighted vision for development. It is only in the fourth period (2008 to present) that we see a range of conditions that make techno-industrial policy possible. These conditions include a group of committed bureaucrats who possess the intentions and skill sets needed to formulate new industrial policy, a new and entrepreneurial ministry capable and autonomous enough to execute the program, and a growing constituency sympathetic and receptive to the competitiveness agenda.

While these conditions took a decade to converge, a decisive shift occurred following the birth of the Ministry of Industry and Information Technology (MIIT) and its attempt to become the most important industrial policy maker in the Chinese state. The MIIT, led by a team of engineers-turned-industrial-technocrats, undertook a series of initiatives to construct an alarming economic reality and match it with an ambitious set of self-reliant and innovation-driven programs. This pattern of policy formation and power consolidation then followed a radiating path from the MIIT to a coalition of central agencies, from the central government to local economies, and from the bureaucracy to the general public. This chapter documents this process and uncovers the rarely acknowledged bureaucratic origin of China's industrial policy, which appeared long before it gained the geopolitical importance it has today.

BUREAUCRATIC FRAGMENTATION WEAKENS INDUSTRIAL POLICY

Industrial policy concerns the strategic efforts by the government to promote the development of particular industries and the structural transformation of the economy.[1] To a certain degree, central planning is an extreme version of industrial policy. Still, in the lexicon of the policy world, industrial policy is considered less totalizing and interventionist than central planning and, in general, presupposes a market economy as the landscape for intervention. Nevertheless, the similarity between planning and industrial policy is clear. During China's transition toward a more marketized economy, this kinship between planning and industrial policy made the latter an attractive career possibility for Chinese planners who wanted to shift their roles without having to entirely move away from their previous expertise. As early as the 1980s, the idea of industrial policy had already gained traction. Thus, the SPC and industrial ministries entertained the possibility of advancing industrial policy to renew their relevance to market reform. Since the beginning of the economic reform, the SPC, previously the most powerful ministry, had been looking to reverse its declining status. In the second half of the 1980s, the SPC, unprompted by any central direction, discovered that industrial policy might help it to reclaim its position.

Initially lacking formal industrial policy expertise within its ranks, the SPC formed partnerships with a number of research institutes in the central government that had also been attracted to the idea of structural management as central to planning. In 1987, the SPC teamed up with the Industrial Policy Research Group (IPR) at the Development Research Center of the State Council to produce a series of high-profile reports on "adjusting the industrial structures of the Chinese economy." Though a small agency, the IPR occupied a nodal position in the chain of bureaucratic approval for large industrial and construction projects.[2] From this vantage point, the IPR adopted a structural mode of thinking and focused on the spillover effects of major industrial undertakings on regional economies and other related sectors. Compared to the specialized ministries, which limited their focus to particular sectors, the IPR had an integrated view of industries that better positioned it to grasp the larger ramifications.[3] Trained in science and engineering, the IPR researchers borrowed from system engineering theory in science and harnessed its "system" epistemology to analyze Chinese industries as an interconnected whole.[4] This way of thinking provided intellectual justification for the SPC to formulate its own industrial policy.[5]

The SPC attempted to establish an industrial policy wing under its own roof by drawing industrial policy researchers from the IPR to staff its new offices. Liu He, for example, who turned out to be the key architect of China's earliest industrial policy programs, made a formative move in his career from the Development Research Center to the SPC in 1987. Yang Weimin, who studied industrial economics at Renmin University and industrial policy theory at Hitotsubashi University of Japan, joined the SPC in 1989. To host this new array of personnel, the SPC created the Industrial Policy Bureau. This bureau went on to recruit graduates from the Department of Industrial Economics at Renmin University, which was known for its ties with Japanese industrial policy circles.[6]

Equipped with this new set of capabilities, the SPC rolled out China's first industrial policy program in 1989—the "Current Decision on the Key Points of Industrial Policy." In spite of being China's first such program, its vision of what China's own industrial policy could look like was both broad and comprehensive. It started out by mapping the structure of Chinese industries and their internal linkages and then meticulously showcased how to calculate the correlative degrees between industrial sectors/products based on technological and production connections. From these calculations, the program derived a priority sequence for developing particular industries. It targeted the development of industries that were projected to generate large market demands, sustain deep linkages with other industries, and hopefully advance technologies and accumulate foreign reserves.

In spite of this laudable vision, the SPC's program encountered difficulty with execution. Industrial policy initially surfaced in China because of a bureaucratic impetus. Its failure also came about for a bureaucratic reason: the fragmentation of the Chinese bureaucracy in this period prevented industrial policy from becoming a legitimate and actionable policy domain. As central planning fell apart and the SPC lost its commanding position in the Chinese economy, the Chinese bureaucracy around it also cracked along existing fault lines, particularly between the central ministries and local governments. The decentralization approach to economic reform implemented in this period exacerbated the fragmentation. It was the local governments that assumed authority over state-owned enterprises and industrial investments. They were their own industrial policy makers and tailored their sectoral priorities to regional needs and local bureaucratic thinking. This array of local actors was not impressed with the SPC's national vision and continued to be attracted to processing and light industries because these industries generated large short-term demands and had low entry barriers. Driven by local initiatives, production bases for color

TVs, fans, refrigerators, and plastic products mushroomed throughout the country. In the wake of the light-industry bias in the local investment frenzy, the SPC's industrial policy had little power to steer investment toward the sectors that the agency aimed to promote.

Aside from government decentralization, the economic bureaucracy fractured along ministerial lines. There was a strict sector-based division of labor among China's specialized industrial ministries. One can easily appreciate these divisions from their ministerial names—the Ministry of Electric Industry, the Ministry of Electronics Industry, the Ministry of Coal, and the Ministry of Metallurgy, to give a few examples. These divisions, which were a residue of the centrally planned economy, paradoxically grew wider in the early reform era because the SPC lost its ability to coordinate the industrial ministries through central planning. Theoretically, the industrial ministries could have served as avenues for industrial policy based on sectoral targeting. In reality, however, sector-based jurisdictional struggles often turned into aggressive squabbling between ministries over government funding and policy favors. In this process, which sectors received preference for state investments was determined not so much by a structural and holistic view of Chinese industries as by interministerial power balance.

The heavy toll that a fragmented bureaucracy took on industrial policy was apparent in China's attempts during the 1980s to upgrade Chinese industries through technological importation. The mechanical industry adequately illustrates the resultant inefficacy. Ministry- and locality-controlled enterprises, answering to their own bureaucratic masters, all attempted to build their own mechanical systems from scratch and thereby remain self-sufficient. As it turned out, few of them were able to maintain high standards.[7] Rarely were capabilities and knowledge consolidated or connected across regions, sectors, or even enterprises. The drawbacks of this system thwarted national-level attempts to import foreign technology and equipment to jump-start China's productivity. Instead, to maximize their own self-sufficiency, ministries and local governments vied for investment grants and import quotas. Each entity preferred importing complete sets of technological equipment with little regard for their actual needs and their capacity to absorb and indigenize these technologies. State-level internal coordination —in the form of, for instance, collective negotiations with foreign export parties—was scanty. As a result, problems such as overpaying and bringing in "blind and redundant imports" abounded, resulting in excessive waste of the limited fiscal resources and foreign reserves that China had at that time. Chen Jinhua, the former director of the SPC, called the phenomenon "unprecedented in the world history of importing technological equipment" and attributed it to the "institutional problem" of bureaucratic fragmentation.[8]

INDUSTRIAL POLICY IN THE SHADOW OF
THE MACROCONTROL PARADIGM

In the 1990s, industrial policy regained attention due to its usefulness in macroeconomic management, pushing it to the forefront of economic policy making. Yet the imperative of managing the fluctuation of supply-demand relations relegated industrial policy to little more than a tool for achieving short-term objectives. As chapter 3 details, the macroeconomic preoccupation was bureaucratically constructed; it was not precisely the case that the Chinese macroeconomy was undergoing such wild swings that it demanded absolutely undivided attention. Macrocontrol arose as an analytical paradigm used to both define and solve problems. It had become an instrument used by the newly assembled technocratic government to assume wide-ranging and unfettered authority to reshape the Chinese economy. In this environment, it was nearly impossible for a rigorous industrial policy agenda, such as that concerning technological competitiveness, to emerge on its own terms. The macrocontrol paradigm authorized the rise of more-expedient kinds of industrial adjustments, such as developing industries to alleviate supply shortages. All of these prevented the development of industrial policy into an autonomous policy domain.

The SPC was once again at the forefront of harnessing industrial policy in the 1990s, but by then, its vision had shifted. The agency tried to use industrial policy to support its ascendance as an indispensable macro-control arm of the state. Specifically, the SPC first used sectoral industrial policy as a means to control overheating. Industrial policy was believed to excel at alleviating structural causes of inflation—particularly overinvestment in processing industries by the local governments. Local investments had driven up demand for basic industries (raw materials, energy, construction, and infrastructure) and caused a cluster of large bottlenecks in the economy.[9] In this context, the SPC confidently reintroduced the idea of "pillar industries" in 1994.[10] It ranked the pillar industries according to importance—but this time based on their usefulness in relieving bottle-necks, not on their cross-industry importance.

Deflation in the second half of the 1990s provided even a stronger impetus to enlist sectoral targeting as a strategy for regulating public investment. Around 1996–1997, the Chinese economy reversed from overheating to what was recognized as a slump, slipping below what had previously been a double-digit growth trajectory. To reverse this trend, the administration furnished the macrocontrol framework with a panoply of activist policy tools. Looking to identify new engines of growth, the SPC rediscovered many more of its earlier industrial policy proposals, repurposing them as road maps to identify avenues for public investments.[11] With the aid of bonds issued by the Ministry of Finance, the SPC put itself in a financially favorable and politically legitimate position, regaining its authority to direct industrial investments. In the process, the need to manage deflation pegged industrial policy even more closely to a narrowly defined growth-oriented agenda.

While effective in the short term to facilitate fiscal activism, the use of industrial policy came at a cost. It significantly watered down the original intent to improve sector-specific competitiveness. With an excessively inclusive and often inconsistent scope, this collection of sectoral plans bore a greater resemblance to an across-the-board stimulus package than to a meaningful and focused program for targeting specific industrial sectors. Rather than emphasizing sector-specific competitiveness, the macroeconomically oriented sectoral plans concerned themselves with expanding production capacity and market concentration.[12] The plan for developing the automobile industry, for instance, was preoccupied with forecasting future market demands and installing the right kind of product structures to meet these demands. The theme of indigenous innovation was mentioned only ceremonially and in passing, and there was never any follow-up to establish rigorous definitions or set standards, not to mention any substantial measures to achieve it. The development of China's automobile industry in this period largely carried out the fundamental intention of growth-oriented industrial policy and has often been cited as a failed case of industrial policy per se.[13] In spite of an initial desire to improve technological capabilities in China's automobile industries, industrial policies for this sector were nearly completely oblivious to this original concern. Instead, they helped a host of Chinese state-owned automakers establish joint ventures with notable foreign automakers with a goal of lowering domestic sales prices, improving economies of scale, and driving up domestic markets. Under this scheme, no advanced technology was transferred, and China continued to lag behind in components and parts manufacturing.

As this particular kind of industrial policy expanded in the shadow of macrocontrol, a more subtle problem was developing in the Chinese state that hampered its ability to develop technologically sensitive industrial policy. This problem came about because of the changing knowledge structure across the board in the economic bureaucracy, caused by the massive exit of sectoral specialists from the central government. This brain drain was caused in part by an ambitious government reform plan that in 1998 abolished the ten industrial ministries in order to decisively transition the Chinese government away from a planned economy and toward a market economy. The few remaining specialized industrial ministries were incorporated as bureau-level units into a generalist economic agency—the State Economic and Trade Commission (SETC), an agency that also jumped on the bandwagon of macroeconomic management. Other functions were spun off to new nongovernmental industrial associations. The elimination of industrial ministers was welcomed as a positive move toward rooting out industrial patronage. The implication for industrial policy making was that this caused the loss of a critical cluster of experts who embraced sector-specific perspectives on the economy and possessed knowledge of sector-specific technologies and thus who could have advocated for more professionally minded industrial policy. The removal of industrial specialists from the economic bureaucracy shifted its knowledge structure in a generalist direction, suitable for making general economic policies such as those concerned with across-the-board growth and macroeconomic stability. These developments did not bode well for the hope of devising policies to drive innovation, as such policies required a minimal understanding of industrial technologies.

A GENERALIST AGENCY AND ITS INDUSTRIAL POLICY OF EXCESS CAPACITY MANAGEMENT

So far, we have examined two periods in which industrial policy was brought to the forefront of economic policy and seen why a more rigorous and focused industrial policy was not developed in these periods. As

TABLE 6.1
The evolution of industrial policy making prior to the rise of the competitiveness agenda

Agency	Relevant career backgrounds	Autonomy of industrial policy	Jurisdiction of industrial policy
SPC 1.0	Yes	Yes	No
SPC 2.0	Yes	No	Yes
NDRC	No	No	Yes

table 6.1 summarizes, in the first phase, industrial policy makers at the SPC had pertinent training and career backgrounds for industrial policy making, and they articulated industrial policy as a distinctive policy domain. Yet the SPC in this period lacked levers and influences on enterprises and local governments—the jurisdictions that would execute its industrial policy. In the second phase, the SPC regained its power and sought to use sectorally selective interventions to manage the macroeconomy. As far as industrial policy was concerned, it was not autonomous but secondary to the purpose of macroeconomic management. This section introduces a third episode of industrial policy development to serve as a historical and comparative case. In this phase, a newly assembled ministry, the National Development and Reform Commission (NDRC), was the main industrial policy maker. The NDRC, however, fell short on another front: the career backgrounds of its policy makers were not relevant to industrial management. For this reason, industrial policy again turned away from what was originally envisioned.

The NDRC was born out of a merger between the SPC and the SETC. When the macrocontrol paradigm governed the economy, the competition between the SPC and the SETC in macromanaging the economy had become intense. Cognizant of this rivalry, the new Hu Jintao/Wen Jiabao administration combined the two agencies into a new superministry to reduce interministerial friction. The broad portfolio passed down from the two generalist predecessors allowed the NDRC to grow into an exceedingly powerful ministry. One might suppose that under such a broad tent, industrial policy would receive even less focused attention.

There was a difference between the NDRC and its precursors, however, that had far-reaching implications for the evolution of industrial policy. Unlike the SPC and SETC, the NDRC kept its doors wide open to local generalists. The career portfolios of NDRC directors illustrate this trend.

On average, NDRC directors spent only 1.43 years working in industrial ministries compared with 10.9 years working in local governments as mayors, governors, or party secretaries supervising regional development. In comparison, the SPC commissioners spent only 3.3 years on average as local generalists in their official careers. The unusual tolerance of nonspecialists was seen in the appointment of Zhang Ping as NDRC director. Before joining the NDRC, Zhang had never worked in an economic policy–related agency and was unquestionably a local generalist. In terms of educational background, he received his highest degree from a technical secondary school, which made him unusual among his ministerial peers. Yet this profile didn't prevent Zhang from having a particularly long tenure at the NDRC, overseeing the agency for eight years (from 2005 to 2013). The turn to nonspecialists was characteristic of the bureaucratic and generational shifts then under way. The departure of the industrial specialists from the administrative state was a function of previous government reform. More broadly, the deemphasis on industrial development in China's reform strategies to that point was also reflected in the changing backgrounds of the economic bureaucrats as a whole in this period. Engineers in Zhu Rongji's generation were phased out of the state without being replaced. This all happened at the time when the economic bureaucracy was growing more powerful vis-à-vis the localities and, as chapter 3 mentions, was able to attract local generalists to serve in national regulatory roles.

The discussion of the backgrounds of the NDRC bureaucrats is useful because, as observed in other parts of the state, the career portfolio of an agency has strong influences on the kind of policy it advances. The NDRC settled on a narrowly construed industrial policy agenda focused on slashing excess capacity, which didn't require specialist industrial backgrounds. According to the NDRC, a number of key industries, such as energy and construction materials, were suffering from overproduction and "destructive competition" as a result of previous rounds of economic stimulation.[14] To correct this overcapacity the NDRC used sectoral targeting. Yet the way it executed this policy was administrative, simplistic, and heavily interventionist. The agency aggressively targeted the steel industry, which, according to its calculations, had produced far more than was needed.[15] It mobilized the "widest range of the most concentrated and strict measures since the beginning of economic reform," including controlling credit, limiting land supply, delicensing, and issuing administrative orders to call off projects. The agency was even able to sign administrative contracts, "letters of intent," with local governments to secure their pledges to reduce production. The localities that didn't meet targets for bringing down excess capacity would face punitive consequences.[16]

Overcapacity management in the steel industry generated immediate results. Optimism led the NDRC to extend its policy to a growing list of "excess" products: electrolytic aluminum, cement, calcium carbide, and automobiles. Albeit narrow in its focus, overcapacity management turned out to be one of the agency's most widely used tools because of its expediency, quantifiable objectives, and compatibility with other regulatory tools at its disposal, all used in the service of achieving short-term results. In my interviews with NDRC officials, they explicitly defended setting numerical targets to cut down production capacity. One of the officials confessed, "If you don't have a number, people won't take you seriously. Having a number allows different layers of the government to break down the target and hold the lower-level government accountable."[17]

To some extent, their experience supervising local development equipped the local generalists with an operative understanding of how local governments functioned. This body of knowledge facilitated the successful implementation of central policies. However, the lack of industrial experience placed a cap on the degree of technicality involved in policy programs and limited the ways in which industrial efficiency was conceived. Considered together, a local generalist background had an effective affinity with overcapacity management. Further, a lack of specialist knowledge proved to be less of a burden to overcapacity management because quantitative production control did not require background knowledge in the technological makeup of sectors or intersectoral linkages. That is, excess capacity management was palatable to a generalist mind, and the role of local knowledge in aiding its implementation only highlighted its desirability.

THE COMPARATIVE ADVANTAGE APPROACH PREVAILS

Before diving into the fourth period, we will pause and examine the social and intellectual environments that conditioned the thinking behind the industrial development in the earlier periods. An unsympathetic environment made it difficult to advance the competitiveness agenda and could have impeded it entirely. This lack of sympathy can be traced back to the very impetus of economic reform. The reform came about as a corrective to the obsession with heavy industry in the Mao period. Reform was meant to rectify previous policy errors—in particular, the single-minded promotion of heavy industries at the expense of agriculture and consumption. Shifting investment to light industries, agriculture, and the consumer sector was considered an important step to "normalize" the economy.

In the intellectual realm, skepticism about developing heavy industry was gaining ground along with the rising popularity of Third Wave ideas among the leadership and policy circles. The Third Wave perspective, which claimed there was no need to industrialize along traditional paths, arrived in China just as the country opened its doors to foreign economic ideas and policy fads. The celebration of the information technology revolution and the promises of deindustrialization in the developed world fascinated Chinese officials, who also looked to turn away from Soviet-style industrialization. Alvin Toffler's book *The Third Wave* sold over thirty thousand copies in its first Chinese edition. This best-seller charmed Premier Zhao Ziyang to the extent that he designated it an official must-read for all those in the Chinese government at the bureau level and higher. When meeting with the American economist Walt Whitman Rostow, Zhao referred to the Third Wave and communicated his optimism that China could skip the phase of developing traditional industries and directly reap the fruit of the new technological revolution.[18] The leadership also invited another futurist, John Naisbitt, to visit China to educate high-level officials and drive home the ideas that manufacturing was a sunset enterprise and that tertiary industry represented the future.[19] This line of assessment provided intellectual justifications for heated investment in light industries and consumer products by local entrepreneurs across China, who were attracted by their low entry barriers. Tall-order industrial policy, as originally offered by the SPC in the first phase, did not receive warm support from central leaders and certainly met with resistance from local governments.

Moving on to the technocratic era in the 1990s, the project of building central state capacity by the Jiang/Zhu administration was largely intended to rationalize markets and build regulatory efficacy. On the industrial front, it was the comparative advantage theory that informed China's approach to manufacturing in the 1990s. Largely compatible with the framework of markets and free trade, the comparative advantage theory gained popularity in the early 1990s, a time when China looked to improve its legitimacy in the international community and deepen its connections with the global economy. The pursuit of the comparative approach to industrial development required the top leadership to make a conscious choice to do so and explicitly reject a more self-reliant approach at key historical junctures. Around 1991, shortly after an economic and political crisis that shocked the world and paused economic reform, the new administration decided to proceed with marketization to build a socialist market economy. From October to November 1991, President Jiang Zemin held eleven intensive meetings with top economic bureaucrats, economic scholars, and area specialists to work out the details.[20] Industrial development was on the agenda. Wang Huijiong and Lin Yifu, two of Jiang's twenty-one advisers, were expected to have a particular impact on industrial policy. Wang, a student of Ma Hong and a core researcher at the Development Research Center of the State Council, was a key adviser to the early industrial policy program chartered by the SPC in the first phase. He had studied engineering together with President Jiang at Jiaotong University back in the 1940s, and he reminded his former classmate that technological progress had allowed advanced economies to claim disproportionate amounts of technological rents from the global economic surplus. To join this club, China also needed to engage in value-added production.

Lin, a younger and less established researcher, argued for the opposite of Wang's proposal. Lin was a researcher at the Research Center for Agricultural Development of the State Council and held a PhD in economics from the University of Chicago. He was brought in by Zhou Xiaochuan, then vice governor of the Central Bank, to coach the leadership in the comparative advantage theory, which Zhou also endorsed.[21] Speaking the language of resource allocation and factor endowments, Lin advised against focusing on capital-intensive development and advocated taking advantage of China's cheap labor supply to "produce for the world." Curiously, both Wang and Lin referred to the East Asian model of industrialization but drew from it opposing lessons. Lin attributed the East Asian success to early engagement with labor-intensive industries and the promotion of export-led development, which, according to Lin, contrasted with the failing import substitution industrialization adopted by Latin American countries to promote capital-intensive sectors. In contrast, Wang emphasized the relentless attempts by the East Asian countries to protect domestic industries and strategically use industrial policy to boost their positions on value chains.

Based on the comparative advantage theory, Lin offered a light-touch industrial policy recipe—if it could even be counted as industrial policy at all. This approach cleared the obstacles for both Chinese local economies and foreign companies to invest in process industries and labor-intensive manufacturing in China. Expressing immediate interest in and agreement with Lin's assessment, Jiang added his own caveat: an abundant supply of labor could not replace the role of precision machinery in manufacturing. He therefore proposed that China continue to import foreign technologies and equipment to upgrade its technology.[22] Note that Jiang's response was not contradictory but rather complementary to Lin's proposal, for it did not propose to improve China's indigenous capacity to develop technology.

As it turned out, the leadership's endorsement of the comparative advantage theory set China on a path of labor-intensive production and export-driven development that it followed for a decade and that dovetailed with the rise of global outsourcing and value chains in the 1990s. Retrospectively, capitalizing on China's "advantage," a cheap and disciplined labor force, provided the country with tremendous growth benefits and global opportunities. Its social and environmental costs have been thoroughly discussed but its impact on industrial policy much less so. The hegemonic status of the comparative advantage theory squeezed out alternative perspectives that might have led industrialization in another direction. Instead, the comparative advantage approach to manufacturing set off a ripple effect across the economic bureaucracy that resulted in a lax attitude toward technological advancement. The implicated policies included those regarding industrial processing zones, labor law and practice, foreign direct investment (FDI), trade liberalization, technology and R&D policies, and government procurement. China's particularly favorable treatment of FDI was markedly different from the protectionist approach of East Asian economies. The general absence of protective measures and the low entry barriers to Chinese industries indicated a trusting attitude toward global integration. Government procurement and technology imports serve as additional examples. Until 2008, government procurement of heavy equipment for large projects had no local sourcing requirements and consistently favored foreign products.[23]

A widespread optimism supported the massive import of technologies as a way to upgrade Chinese industries, premised on the assumption that technology, like any other productive factor, would cross national borders according to the principle of supply-demand relations and the logic of profit. In contrast, the development of domestic high-tech industries was marked by low-quality growth. R&D contributed only 4.8 percent to the final value added to high-tech products. These products were also internationally uncompetitive; they made up only 1.8 percent of all Chinese exports.[24] Equally revealing, the domestic high-tech industry was classified in national accounts as a "tertiary industry."[25] This categorization for accounting purposes was not trivial, as the development of high-tech industries was then counted as the expansion of the service sector rather than as the integration of advanced technologies to assist industrialization. This fact exposes the mental framework that Chinese policy makers adopted to sever the development of the high-tech sector from manufacturing, which discouraged the exploration of their interlinkages.

INDUSTRIAL COMPETITIVENESS AND THE BIRTH OF THE MIIT

I identify the emergence of techno-industrial policy with the birth, in 2008, of the Ministry of Industry and Information Technology. There was a rising awareness of the importance of developing high-tech industries several years before this ministry came into existence, but the labor-intensive and export-led growth model had yet to run out of steam. In 2005, the yuan-dollar exchange rate started to decline after a decade of devaluing the Chinese currency, undercutting the price competitiveness of Chinese exports. This change led to a sense of uneasiness among the policy makers and prompted them to rethink the sustainability of this model. Toward the very end of the Jiang Zemin administration, the rhetoric shifted regarding industrial development, encapsulated in the official proposal for new-style industrialization (*xinxing gongyehua*). In 2002, at the Sixteenth National Congress of the Communist Party of China, President Jiang went to some length to call for the pursuit of "industrialization featuring high scientific and technological content, good economic returns, low resources consumption, and little environmental pollution." He acknowledged the need to develop "high-technology industries as a leading force" and "basic and manufacturing industries as the linchpin of China's industrialization."[26] Jiang also mentioned advancing information technology to transform old-line industries. The Hu Jintao administration continued to build on this agenda and was even serious about executing it. To be sure, none of the content in the new-style industrialization was entirely new. Still, it was unprecedented that this aspiration for high-quality industrialization was elevated to the heights of central party policy. The direct impetus behind the proposition was not fully transparent. Multiple sources of mine mentioned the role of the 1995 Third Industrial Census, which showed dire results and pointed to a worryingly low level of productivity among Chinese industrial enterprises.[27] The census prompted reflection among those individuals in the bureaucracy who were trained to be sympathetic to the cause of industrialization. Wei Liqun was one of the bureaucrats who was deeply alarmed by the census. He was an SPC veteran and the director of the Research Office of the State Council at the time. Going against the grain of the policy fads at that time, Wei was a long-time observer of how China fared on the *quality* of its industrial development. He allegedly penned part of Hu's speech on taking the high road of industrialization.[28]

The quiet surfacing of figures like Wei reveals the simmering energy building for this agenda. Yet for any economic idea to take hold in the government, it needs bureaucratic soil that can receive and cultivate it. Often this means having a critical mass of like-minded officials and an organizational home where the new agenda can be formulated and executed. Therefore, in the case of promoting industrial competitiveness, even with official recognition the odds were against it. This was because agencies and personnel that might have been sympathetic were scattered around the economic bureaucracy. The Ministry of Information, the sole survivor of the 1998 government reform that abolished the industrial ministries, was notably weak. Its regulatory power was limited to a few sectoral enclaves—chiefly telecommunications and aerospace. The Ministry of Science and Technology was another candidate. It housed a sizable group of scientists-turned-bureaucrats and had a clearly designated mission to stimulate R&D in advanced technologies in a range of scientific fields. Yet the ministry was close to universities and research institutions and remained largely detached from industries except for a few high-profile megaprojects, such as the development of high-speed rail and domestic manufacturing for China's own commercial aircraft.[29] The distance between precommercial technological development and industrial applications set severe limits on the influence the Ministry of Science and Technology could have on industrial policy. Another potential enthusiast for integrating information technology with industry was the State Information Center.

The center consistently collected economic information and monitored industrial development from the perspective of "informationizing" the Chinese economy and society. It was not coincidental that Liu He, a pioneering industrial policy maker who had formerly directed the Industrial Policy Bureau at the SPC, saw the State Information Center as the next logical step to extend his career. Yet the influence of the center was largely confined to research and statistics. Taken together, existing agencies pertinent to this mission were too weak or too narrowly sectoral or they lacked the industrial jurisdiction needed to take on the imperative of a full-scale technological upgrade across Chinese industries.

Against this backdrop, the birth of the MIIT was promising in two ways. First, it was precisely this agency that rounded up scattered facilities and agencies and tasked them explicitly with the mission of integrating information technology with industries. Agencies including the former Ministry of Information, the State Information Center, and the Commission for Science, Technology, and Industry for National Defense were formally incorporated into the MIIT, as were the functions related to industrial management and planning at the NDRC. The State Council sent its blessing by actively promoting and promulgating across the government the rationale behind its founding, explaining why China needed an agency like the MIIT. The fragmentation of expertise in industrial management in the Chinese government had been acknowledged as an indication that coordinating the development of industries and technologies would be difficult.[30] The MIIT was expected to unite these disparate elements.

The career backgrounds of the bureaucrats at the MIIT showed that it was better positioned than previous ministries to develop more specialized industrial programs. An examination of the career backgrounds of the MIIT directors reveals a clear contrast with those of the commissioners of the existing industrial policy-making body—the NDRC. The MIIT's bureaucrats stood out for the technical proficiency evident in their career portfolios. Table 6.2 compares this characteristic in the SPC, NDRC, and MIIT. Of the three agencies, the MIIT ministers spent the least time on average working as local generalists, 2.78 years, and the most time working in industrial factories, 5.83 years. Notably, the MIIT officials had on average nearly four years of exposure to the specialized industrial ministries. This was rather unusual because the agency was founded ten years after the industrial ministries were abolished and five years after the founding

TABLE 6.2
Average number of years spent in three major career areas by SPC, NDRC, and MIIT ministers

	Local generalist	Industrial factory	Industrial ministry
SPC	3.35	3.18	8.97
NDRC	10.92	4.25	1.43
MIIT	2.78	5.83	3.94

Source: Calculated by the author from elite economic bureaucrats' CVs.

TABLE 6.3
Disciplinary focus of highest degree earned by SPC, NDRC, and MIIT ministers

	Engineering (%)	Economics (%)	Science (%)
SPC	53	32	11
NDRC	60	35	0
MIIT	77	0	5

Source: Calculated by the author from elite economic bureaucrats' CVs.

of the NDRC. However, industrial ministry experience was preserved in other parts of the bureaucracy and made its way into the MIIT. As table 6.3 shows, the educational backgrounds of the MIIT leadership tell a similar story. The agency hosted the largest percentage of engineering *and* science majors across the three agencies: 77 percent of MIIT ministers took their highest degree in engineering and 15 percent in science. This, again, was highly unexpected because even the SPC, which operated during a time when these majors reached their greatest popularity, didn't have such a high concentration of officials with science and technology training. The glaring absence of economics majors at the MIIT was also noteworthy. The steady increase in economics majors among Chinese officials during the reform period is reflected in the fact that 35 percent of the NDRC directors majored in economics. In comparison, the MIIT turned out to be a huge outlier in this regard, in spite of the fact that it was the youngest agency among the three. Altogether, the highly unexpected concentration of expertise regarding industries and technologies predisposed the MIIT to make a novel kind of industrial policy, one that would be unlike what had previously been attempted.

In spite of its endowments, the MIIT was not automatically equipped with the power and policy tools needed to formulate groundbreaking programs. As has been shown in other chapters, economic policy is often born as much out of a need for self-invention as structural necessity. Seldom were the contents of policies hardwired into the system or completely dictated by the mandates of the environment. Also, even with official blessings, ministerial power was not given but had to be developed in the context of the bureaucratic field and its fluid jurisdictional boundaries. The conditions were often unfavorable for new ministries. The MIIT's initial standing was undetermined precisely for these reasons. Its stated function of industrial management was poorly specified, and it was even unclear which industries fell into its jurisdiction in the first place. The MIIT, like many other new agencies portrayed in this book, was left to its own devices to delineate its exact duties.

Predictably, from the outset, the MIIT faced a formidable rival in industrial policy, the NDRC, which was the most powerful economic ministry at that time. A superagency nicknamed "the little state council,"[31] the NDRC was in charge of formulating "long-term and medium-term development strategies" and developing "yearly [guidance] plans" to "optimize economic structures," all of which had implications for industrial policy. In addition, the NDRC enjoyed superior political standing, a metric often proxied in the Chinese government by the political rankings of its individual ministers. From 2003 to 2008, 36 percent of NDRC ministers and vice ministers were ranked at the ministry level (*zheng buji*). This proportion dropped to 27 percent from 2008 to 2012 and soared to 63 percent in 2013. Even at its lowest point, the NDRC was ahead of any ministry in the economic bureaucracy in terms of the political weight of its leadership. This high political profile granted NDRC officials both formal and informal bargaining power over other state agencies.[32]

FINDING A NICHE IN CHAINS AND PARTS

Learning to survive and thrive in the shadow of the NDRC required bureaucratic entrepreneurship on the part of the MIIT. In the first three to four years of the MIIT's existence, the NDRC was clearly dominant and was able to impose its own scheme for a division of labor with the MIIT. Reluctant to give away its regulatory power over industrial sectors, the NDRC handed over only unimportant sectors to the MIIT, such as dairy products, pesticides, textiles, mechanical parts, and home appliances. In addition, the NDRC wished to incorporate the MIIT into its own industrial policy agenda and assign it simply to implement programs to reduce excess capacity.

Instead of engaging in a sector-by-sector turf war with the NDRC, the MIIT started by constructing an epistemic front and turning its way of seeing the economy into an advantage. It analyzed Chinese industries in a brand-new way: by dissecting industrial structures from the perspective of *chains*. That is, instead of looking *into* each industry, MIIT-sponsored research and policy work looked *across* sectors to conceive their interconnections based on interindustry spillover effects and technological linkages. This cross-sectoral intervention allowed the MIIT to occupy an unclaimed epistemic location in the space of industrial policy, foregrounding issues of technological competitiveness that transcended sectors. As table 6.4 shows, the MIIT was the first policy maker to combine a cross-sectoral perspective with a concern for competitiveness. Previous industrial policy makers— the NDRC, SPC, and industrial ministries—remained sectorally minded, regardless of whether they were guided by the macroeconomic or the competitiveness rationale. The Ministry of Finance and the People's Bank of China were cross-sectoral, but they were mainly macroeconomic agencies. Taken as a whole, the MIIT's policy perspective was unique.

Utilizing this chain perspective, MIIT officials attached vital importance to general-purpose technologies (*gongxing jishu*), the research and commercialization of which would benefit a wide range of related products and industries. Previously, it was the industrial ministries that assumed the role of facilitating research on shared technologies, and even then, they did so only within a sector. With the industrial ministries abolished, this task was delegated downward to state-owned conglomerates. This was unfortunate, according to the MIIT bureaucrats, because

TABLE 6.4
Epistemic perspectives of various ministries on industrial policy

	Macroeconomic rationale	Competitiveness rationale
Sectoral perspective	National Development and Reform Commission, State Planning Commission	Industrial ministries
Cross-sectoral perspective	Ministry of Finance, People's Bank of China	Ministry of Industry and Information Technology

individual enterprises had neither the research capacity nor the incentives to pay for researching prototype technologies that required large capital outlays, long maturation periods, and tolerance for high risks. The MIIT officials declared that the agency had an undeniable duty to stimulate the provision of what it considered an important array of "public goods" of Chinese industries.[33]

In addition to rendering industrial structures as chains, the agency broke down industrial products into parts and components. The MIIT lamented that China was good at assembling things but lacked the capacity to manufacture its own foundational equipment and machinery at a sufficiently high quality.[34] According to the MIIT, the production of high-grade basic parts and components was the linchpin of manufacturing success; these parts and components were essential for upgrading China's basic and material industries. Arguing in this vein, the agency also indirectly faulted China's previous approach to technological importation and its underlying belief that capability could be built by importing equipment without understanding that equipment's constituent parts. Similar to the advancement of the chain perspective, the focus on parts and components spoke to an attempt to articulate new frameworks for parsing China's industrial reality.

Following a number of years of marginalization, the MIIT put its ideas to the test. It formulated a set of technological policies in equipment manufacturing and identified several lines of key general-purpose technologies to promote. The MIIT did not shy away from filling its programs with technical terms and detailed technological standards. For instance, the MIIT's initiative inviting research and manufacturing for high-end computer numerical control machine tools was sixty-eight pages long, setting meticulous technical benchmarks and local content requirements.[35] In fact, the MIIT's unapologetic commitment to technicality was a crucial way for the agency to distinguish itself from the NDRC, whose programs remained broad-stroke guidelines for improving individual sectors that lacked technical criteria.

To further its programmatic initiatives, the MIIT promoted the catchy idea of *intelligent manufacturing* and turned this into a flagship program. To make manufacturing smart meant integrating digital network technology—such as the internet of things, big data, cloud computing, and artificial intelligence—into every step of the manufacturing process.[36] Of course, the MIIT bureaucrats were not the first in the world to invoke this idea. The frequent references to Germany's Industry 4.0 in its programs indicated the source of the inspiration.[37] The adoption of the intelligent manufacturing initiative provided much-needed justification for this young organization to expand its jurisdiction. Consistent with earlier efforts to promote industrial policy in general-purpose technologies and key parts and components, the push for intelligent manufacturing was a cross-sectoral reform that promised positive sector-specific outcomes. By applying the initiative to making a sector more "intelligent," the MIIT made itself relevant to the development of many industries that previously fell outside of its jurisdiction.

As the intelligent manufacturing program gained traction, the MIIT was able to join the NDRC as a fellow industrial policy maker. In some cases, it even seized sectors that had been traditionally under the supervision of the NDRC. For instance, since 2010 the NDRC had been responsible for promoting strategic emerging industries, as listed in table 6.5. The same table shows that, as of 2016, the MIIT had become an equal partner to the NDRC in co-overseeing almost all industries identified as strategic emerging industries. Notably, even equipment manufacturing had become the

TABLE 6.5
Ministerial division of labor in the supervision of strategic emerging industries

Industry	NDRC	MIIT	MSC
Equipment manufacturing		√	
Software	√	√	
Integrated circuits	√	√	
Internet+	√	√	
New materials	√	√	
Photovoltaics			
Aerospace	√	√	
Big data	√	√	
Satellites	√	√	√
Biomedicine	√	√	√
AI	√	√	√

Source: Compiled by the author from "Division of Labor for the 13th Five-Year Plan of the State Council for Emerging Strategic Industries" [Guowuyuan shisanwu xinxing zhanluexing chanye guihua zhongdian renwu fengong fangan], Beijing, 2016, and sectoral policy programs of major agencies.

sole responsibility of the MIIT. Apparently, not all industries were neatly categorized with clear boundaries and regulators. The photovoltaic industry, for instance, was a rapidly rising industry that answered to no leading regulators. A number of agencies, such as the NDRC, the National Energy Administration, and the Ministry of Land and Resources, had issued policies related to technical standards, electricity prices, and land use for this industry. In such cases, the MIIT's mission added clarity, enhancing its own advantage. The MIIT contended that the development of the photovoltaic industry was an opportunity for promoting innovation and the green economy. It then appointed itself the principal guardian of this sunrise industry under its intelligent manufacturing framework.[38]

After several rounds of bureaucratic initiatives, the MIIT began to realize substantial bureaucratic payoffs. One crucial benefit pertained to the budget. As explained earlier, previous industrial policies were pegged to macroeconomic regulations and rose and fell according to macroeconomic imperatives. By detaching industrial policy from macroeconomic policy, the MIIT's agenda of technological competitiveness allowed it to obtain a favorable budgetary position. It earned the agency more regularized budgeting power than had previously been the case. Investment in R&D, for instance, was less subject to the whims of macroeconomic factors than to the incremental logic of technological advancement. With its programs gathering steam, the budget of the MIIT increased steadily by 12 percent per year from 2012 to 2018. One of the big-ticket items earmarked as "expense for science and technology" increased by 15.6 percent per year and stood around 27 billion yuan in 2018.[39] This item took up 43.4 percent of the entire ministerial budget. It essentially covered two types of activities: first, it was used for the MIIT's in-house laboratories, research projects, and institutes; second, it was allocated by the agency to enterprises participating in the MIIT's programs. In comparison, the NDRC's funds for science and technology took up only 23 percent of its total budget and had remained consistently small, partially because the NDRC did not have research facilities of its own. The NDRC's annual budget, as a whole, fluctuated to a larger extent than did that of the MIIT. The budget associated with the NDRC's key function—strategy and planning—was closely tied to development initiatives and large projects that had life cycles of their own, with many of them expanding and contracting in accordance with macroeconomic needs.[40]

ALLIES AND NETWORKS: THE MIIT ON THE ROAD TO POWER

After securing a footing in industrial policy making vis-à-vis the NDRC, the MIIT extended its bureaucratic entrepreneurship to building partnerships with other agencies. At this point, the MIIT's vision had percolated into other parts of the bureaucracy through collaboration with various forces in the central bureaucracy that were equipped with technological research capabilities. The MIIT and the Ministry of Science and Technology (MST) were logical allies. Their coalition sponsored the combination of technology policy and industrial policy. As it turned out, 13.2 percent of all industrial policies issued by the MIIT were coauthored with the MST. In comparison, collaborations between the NDRC and MST were tenuous, accounting for only 5 percent of all NDRC-led industrial policy programs. The MIIT-MST partnership engaged in activities that ranged from issuing cross-industry guidelines and formulating enterprise-based technological innovation programs to promoting specific high-tech products such as environment-protection equipment and batteries for electric vehicles.[41] The MIIT also worked to link MST-affiliated research institutes and universities with industrial enterprises that participated in its programs. This coalition fostered the commercialization of basic science capabilities and essentially marked the end of the separation of upstream technological research and industrial development, which had been a long-standing weakness in China's national innovation system.

Beyond formal interministerial collaborations, the MIIT's agenda continued to act like a magnet, attracting disparate policy resources. From its position as a nodal agency, it connected technological research institutes, academies, former bureaucrats from industrial ministries, and representatives from industrial associations into a variety of policy networks. Previously marginalized researchers and bureaucrats were valued again and were given an outlet and an organizational sponsor to materialize their projects. In the "expert consultation committee for intelligent manufacturing" that the MIIT assembled, nineteen of the thirty-five experts were drawn from universities and research institutes, ten from industrial associations, and six from industrial enterprises.[42] Among these three types of advisers, the participation of the industrial associations was particularly novel. Previously, industrial associations served as employment reservoirs to absorb former bureau chiefs and engineers from abolished industrial ministries and were for the most part inactive. Through consultative policy making, the MIIT recycled these lines of expertise back into the policy realm.[43] Industrial associations bridged bureaucracy and business and disseminated industry-wide information and technological standards to a wider circle of enterprises than the MIIT could reach on its own. As each party brought to the table indispensable sets of resources, the decision-making structure of these policy networks tended to be flatter than was typical for efforts led by a central ministry. Therefore, the MIIT's initiatives also introduced into the Chinese economic bureaucracy a refreshing decision-making style, contrasting notably with the NDRC's proclivity for dominating its policy constituencies with one-sided power.

THE ORIGIN OF MADE IN CHINA 2025

The ascendance of the kind of industrial policy that the MIIT had championed culminated in 2015 in the birth of *Made in China 2025*, a multistage initiative to transform China from the world's factory into a manufacturing and technological superpower. This plan, once released, took the world by surprise and stirred considerable controversy regarding China's bid for global dominance. The birth of this plan has often been attributed to a grand strategy plotted long ago by the central leadership.[44] Previous discussion in this chapter, however, sheds light on a series of bureaucratic developments that led up to Made in China 2025. By investigating exactly how this initiative was formulated and by whom, this section reveals its ministerial authorship. I find that the emergence of this long-range plan was inseparable from the entrepreneurial efforts of the MIIT to consolidate its policy authority in the central government and across China.

When making policies, few ministries in the central government are constantly mindful of how those policies affect China's standing in the world. The MIIT was exceptional in this regard. To a large extent, a global vision was intrinsically embedded in the competitiveness agenda. But the MIIT carried this comparative reasoning to its fullest extent, repeatedly justifying its policies by pointing to gaps between China and advanced economies and presenting itself as a guardian of Chinese industries. The comparative exercise allowed the agency to present itself as an indispensable observer of the field of international technological development, and its comparisons served to apply pressure to other parts of the bureaucracy, prodding them to acceptance.

Made in China 2025 was a product of this comparative reasoning. Starting in 2013 and continuing into 2014, the Bureau of Development Planning of the MIIT sought to partner with the Chinese Academy of Engineering; the General Administration of Quality Supervision, Inspection, and Quarantine; and various industrial associations and private research institutes to assemble a team consisting of 150 experts who were to systematically assess the status of China's manufacturing. The project picked the United States, Germany, Japan, Korea, France, England, India, and Brazil—the world's eight most advanced manufacturers according to the MIIT's standards—as benchmarks. While the comparative dimension was always integral to the MIIT's competitiveness agenda, this research project represented the agency's largest and most quantitatively rigorous effort to rank major industrialized economies and identify gaps where China did not measure up. These investigations subjected China to a comprehensive range of comparisons, including indicators related to value added, productivity, and informatization, to name a few. The result ranked China as the world's fourth manufacturing power but showed that this position was shored up mainly by sheer volumes and quantities, not quality or competitiveness.[45] China lagged behind the United States, Germany, and Japan in crucial aspects related to product quality, sustainability, and industrial structure optimization. Following this assessment, the MIIT-led team proposed three ten-year plans to improve China's scores on this evaluation scheme.[46]

In January 2014, the MIIT team had an opportunity to brief Vice Premier Ma Kai about their report, allegedly impressing him with the thoroughness of the study and alarming him with the unfavorable results. Immediately, Ma appointed the MIIT to be the lead agency to "turn consultation into action."[47] Made in China 2025 was the first of the three ten-year plans. In the course of elaborating the plan to the point it could be executed, the previous bureau-level effort was elevated to a ministerial course of action. Ministry-wide policy networks were further mobilized to refine the plan. Therefore, while Made in China 2025 appeared to be a paradigm-changing shock to outsiders, this book shows that this program was a logical extension of what the MIIT had long advocated in its own path to achieve bureaucratic authority. It is understandable that the strong sense of national consciousness contained in Made in China 2025 led observers to believe it was the result of a national strategy. This both was and was not the case. The MIIT's appeal to national consciousness was an organizational strategy to project urgency and provide moral justification, with the intent of enhancing its organizational authority in the competitive field of industrial policy making. As it turned out, the birth of Made in China 2025 secured the triumph of the MIIT's policy agenda over that of its bureaucratic rivals.

SOCIETALIZING INDUSTRIAL POLICY

As the MIIT was stepping up its efforts on the bureaucratic front, public support was shifting in favor of the cause of indigenous innovation. In many ways, the two developments mutually reinforced one another. One early source of public support was from intellectuals anchored in academic institutions. They were public-facing social scientists in public policy, political science, and economics departments who knew how to respond to the public's curiosity with an accessible narrative that contextualized industrial development in institutions. Two political economists in the School of Government at Beijing University, Lu Feng and Feng Kaidong, initiated a wave of research by publishing empirical case studies in accessible outlets and attracting followers outside the academy. By comparing the failure of the automobile sector with the success of the high-speed rail and large commercial aircraft industries, their studies conveyed the importance of extending the state's commitment to investing in capital-intensive industries and insisted on the synergy that could be fostered between state investment and enterprise-level innovation. Sifting through China's track record in importing and indigenizing technology, this group of scholars informed their readers that China should shed the illusion that technology was a public good that could be bought and transferred in the market. They went one step further than the MIIT officials in articulating that this was because developed countries, through a range of legal, economic, and political devices, would not allow developing countries to obtain leading technologies or build broad-based industrial systems. Besides, technological know-how was tacit knowledge and could be learned and preserved only within organizations. China had to innovate on its own.[48]

The field of economics also created opportunities to provide theoretical justifications for competitiveness-based industrial policy. Evolutionary economics emerged on the margin of the professional field around 2003 and made its way into the policy world. This nonmainstream economical thinking was an obvious protest against the hegemonic dominance of neoclassical economics, which extended to a significant segment of China's government and academia. Evolutionary economics treated the economy as an open and dynamic system in which the nonlinear development of technology and institutional behavior, not market expansion, provided the impetus to economic development. Leading voices such as Jia Genliang, a Renmin University economist, played an important role in popularizing its tenets and explicitly challenging the comparative advantage theory. According to evolutionary economists, the comparative advantage theory, in essence, followed neoclassical economic doctrines, as it was based on the idea of efficient resource allocation and market-conforming policies. Evolutionary economics, instead, sought a more rigorous role for industrial policy. Chinese evolutionary economists pointed to the windows of opportunity that the ongoing third industrial revolution provided to late developers. In the early stage of this revolution, late developers could leapfrog by engaging in high value-added production. To this end, the state should help enterprises expand their capabilities and push them to move to higher value-added segments of global value chains. To create an environment in which this would happen, China needed to protect its domestic markets, eschew FDI, and avoid being trapped in labor-intensive production. Although it was unlikely that the policy ideas of MIIT officials originated from a systematic study of evolutionary economics, these officials enlisted it as an intellectual source to rationalize their thinking. Citations to evolutionary economists such as Geoffrey Hodgson began to appear in publications by MIIT researchers and officials.[49] Even in the absence of mutual referencing, the discursive convergence between the reasoning of the MIIT officials and the writings of evolutionary economists was apparent. Both operated on the premise that postindustrial society was a myth, as human societies continued to live through waves of industrial revolutions, with economies constantly undergoing structural changes that were nonlinear, dynamic, and institutionally determined.[50]

Societal support for indigenous innovation was not limited to public opinion leaders in academic positions. For the first time in the history of China's economic reform, a societalization of support for building industrial competitiveness emerged and expressed itself in internet-based popular movements. The Industrial Party (Gongye dang), which first surfaced in 2011 and 2012, was one of the movements that supported competitiveness-based industrial policy. Predicated on intellectual reasoning similar to that of evolutionary economics, the discourse of the "industrial party" added a nationalist bent to its arguments. It attributed the colonized status of modern China to technological stagnation and rediscovered the virtue of the Mao period for laying the groundwork for a broad-based industrial system that influenced China's subsequent development. According to the "industrial party," the Mao period in Chinese economic development, often disparaged, was instrumental in setting China apart from many other industrialization aspirants that struggled to build basic manufacturing capacity. Going forward, it called for China to completely abandon the free-market illusion and revive the goal of self-reliance promoted in the Mao period.

The Industrial Party and the MIIT echoed one another in normalizing support in Chinese society for the competitiveness-based industrial policy. In addition to engaging in policy discussions, the "industrial party" encouraged its followers to embrace an industrial temperament (*gongye qizhi*) in their daily lives. This referred not only to the development of industrial literacy but also to the adoption of a set of lifestyle choices, cultural values, and aesthetics that celebrated the progressive role that advanced industrial and technological products played in improving human lives and experiences with modernity. This promotion of industrial temperament paved the way for the MIIT's advocacy for the construction of an industrial culture beyond the Chinese government. This soft initiative aimed to enhance sensitivity to and appreciation of the role that industrialization played in Chinese people's lives, past and present. A host of programs worked to preserve historical industrial sites, build industrial museums, and sponsor businesses that fused art, culture, and industry. Such efforts animated a robust demographic base in Chinese society that consisted of young to middle-aged graduates working in the technical or skill-intensive fields of science, technology, engineering, and mathematics.[51] Note that the forms of societal participation in the techno-industrial policy paradigm were different from those seen in financialization. Financialization in China and elsewhere saw the rise of investment societies, in which ordinary citizens claimed their membership by investing in financial assets (in China, these were mostly real estate, stock, and wealth management products). Thus, the motivation for societal participation during financialization was more material than ideological. In the case of industrial policy, the opposite was true. Promoting ideological commitment to high-tech industrialization left more room for state bureaucrats to exercise moral leadership in the name of the nation.

SINKING DOWN TO LOCALITIES: EMBEDDEDNESS AND THE TERRITORIAL DIMENSION OF INDUSTRIAL POLICY

As the social climate became overwhelmingly receptive to the MIIT's platforms, the agency achieved a level of power that was reflected in its ability to penetrate local governments and economies. This is manifest in the territorial turn that many of its industrial programs have taken since 2015. In fact, the ability of the MIIT's policies to sink down to local economies is another indicator that the competitiveness agenda has achieved a paradigmatic status. Localization of central industrial policy was what the SPC dreamed about but could never achieve in the 1980s. As table 6.6 shows, from 2015 to 2018 the MIIT initiated far more territorial programs than did the NDRC. Its four major programs aimed at setting up centers, model bases, or pilot programs in selected regions and cities that were considered to be well prepared and equipped to upgrade local manufacturing. Model status allowed local governments to access MIIT-administered grants, research assistance, information, technical support for their regions, and assistance to local industries to develop their own flagship products. Otherwise defiant local governments actually cooperated with the political center in this case—a telling sign that a critical array of constituencies was in place for the MIIT's programs. From the perspective of local governments, industrial upgrading changed the course of local development and demanded more patience as

TABLE 6.6
National territorial programs of key industrial policy-making agencies

Year	Agency	Programmatic content
2000 (renewed in 2013)	MST	Torch development centers for high-tech industries
2003	NDRC	National high-tech industrial bases
2009	MIIT	National model bases of new industrialization
2015	MIIT	Pilot and model programs for intelligent manufacturing
2016	MIIT	National entrepreneurship and innovation model bases for micro and small enterprises
2016	MIIT	Innovation centers for manufacturing industry
2018	MIIT	Pilot and model programs for big data industries

Source: Compiled by the author from Wanfang Legal Database, China Laws and Regulations Database in Wanfang Data Knowledge Service Platform [Wanfang shuju zhishi fuwu pingtai], https://c.wanfangdata.com .cn/claw.

many of the traditional manufacturing bases across China looked to transition in the new economic environment. This upgrading arrested a previous tendency among many manufacturing-heavy provinces and cities, particularly in the coastal areas, to expel old-line industries and woo investments in skill-intensive and high-tech sectors instead of upgrading existing manufacturing capabilities. This wave was led by Guangdong Province and was articulated by its party secretary Wang Yang in 2008 as an effort to "empty the cage to welcome the new birds [*tenglong huanniao*]." It gained traction in other provinces such as Zhejiang and Jiangsu that faced similar challenges associated with rising labor costs.[52] The MIIT's call to revamp manufacturing instead of dismantling it altered local development strategies, focusing them on a continuous process of industrialization.

The MIIT was certainly not the only industrial policy maker able to build local constituencies. As discussed earlier, the NDRC had its own unique advantage in disciplining and incentivizing local governments. Still, the MIIT's approach to industrial policy gave rise to a type of localization of bureaucratic power that differed from that of the NDRC. A comparison of two similarly intended programs—the NDRC's "Guidelines from the High-Tech Industry Development Bureau of the National Development Planning Commission for National High-Tech Industrial Bases" (2003) and the MIIT's "Special Action to Establish Pilot and Model Programs for Intelligent Manufacturing" (2016)—illustrates this point. Both were territorial programs intended to advance technological development, but they differed markedly in the kinds of policy tools deployed and the actors invited to participate. Specifically, the chief policy tool that the NDRC used was state investment in selected industrial bases. Under this scheme, the agency was little more than a vehicle for financing. This type of assistance reflected a long-standing conviction of the NDRC that there was a direct association between capital investment as input and technologies as output.[53] Generally speaking, the NDRC's program was a growth strategy.

The MIIT's program utilized a shrewder form of power and mobilized a wider range of policy tools to steer local development. It prioritized specific products and technologies deemed to have large spillover effects. It then nudged the development of such products so they would meet the high technical standards that the agency set as a precondition for obtaining state investment. These standards could be related to research cycles, operational costs, and energy efficiency. More importantly, after early-stage funding, the

2016 program followed up with a plethora of institutional supports, such as sponsoring basic and applied research related to local specialty industries, constructing online platforms for sharing information and diffusing technology across factories and localities, liaising with foreign experts and manufacturers, facilitating interenterprise collaboration within industrial bases, promoting proven cases and successful models, and connecting local industries with national industrial associations.[54] In other words, when localizing and verticalizing its policy reach, the MIIT also harnessed horizontal resources from its policy networks in the central bureaucracy to construct a grid of coordination up and down the government. Situated at the hub of this grid, the MIIT was an indispensable broker, pooling an unprecedented array of resources to meet and direct local developmental needs. While the effects of these programs are still being felt, their impact on the MIIT's standing in the Chinese government was almost immediate. Local governments quickly reoriented themselves to keep abreast of activity by the new authority, with many of them setting up local departments specifically to communicate and engage with the MIIT.

Industrial policy has a discernible affinity with planning. During the reform era, Chinese policy makers had long attempted to use industrial policy to shift away from central planning and revamp the role of the state in economic management. Yet industrial policy did not acquire paradigmatic characteristics until 2008. Conditions for a policy paradigm to rise were not met in the previous phases of reform. The SPC's industrial policy programs in the 1980s appealed to the idea of sectoral targeting, but the agency lacked the capacity for execution. In the 1990s and beyond, a different type of problem arose. Industrial policy would benefit from the enhanced state capacity of the Jiang Zemin/Zhu Rongji era, but the gravity of economic ideas prevailing in the economic bureaucracy pulled it into the orbit of the macrocontrol policy paradigm, which called for macroeconomic stability and short-term economic growth. Manufacturing sectors did develop but were largely directed by the dominant comparative advantage theory, which promoted labor-intensive and light industries for export and eschewed the questions of indigenous innovation and technological competitiveness.

In contrast, the period from 2008 to the present saw the confluence of several favorable elements that essentially advanced a focused, highly motivated, and technologically savvy industrial policy agenda that was not reducible to other policy goals. These elements included a concentration of industrial policy makers with industrial managerial backgrounds, receptive local governments that could serve as constituencies, a policy mission that was not easily co-opted by others, and a public sympathetic to the competitiveness agenda. All of these elements could not have been activated in concert without an entrepreneurial ministry. The MIIT was able to combine these elements to create synergy, developing them in ways that were also sensitive to power struggles in the bureaucratic field. Through building allies, constructing policy networks across state boundaries, and pushing its policies down to localities, the MIIT significantly expanded its competitiveness-based version of industrial policy from a ministry function to a national development strategy.

To a large extent, the rise of techno-industrial policy was the rise of a new policy paradigm of economic management. This policy paradigm called for a more detached stance toward short-term growth and the macroeconomic exigencies that had preoccupied China's economic policy for two decades. It unapologetically defined the country's economic success as the result of its manufacturing and technological competitiveness, which also gave economic policy an unprecedented nationalist appeal. The industrial policy approach to development could not be more distinct from the financialization approach to economic management that was also taking place in earnest and that offered an opposing vision of development. While the financial approach focused on financial markets and real estate, the industrial approach focused on the "real economy" and manufacturing. Aside from different industry focuses, the two approaches provided divergent conceptualizations of how resources were constituted and moved through an economy. To the financial reformers, resources needed to flow as extensively as possible across units of the economy to facilitate their efficient allocation. To the industrial reformers, resources and skills were developed in organizations and had a tacit nature. These reformers considered it more efficient for these resources to stay put as "patient" capital aimed at developing long-term capabilities.

With a global race for technological superiority among the great powers, the importance of China's industrial policy to the world will only grow. Indeed, political sensitivity and geopolitical considerations accumulated around this domain to the extent that China's industrial policy could no longer exist as a ministry-level responsibility; instead, it required top-level direction and whole nation (*juguo*) mobilization. With these escalation mechanisms piled on top of one another, it is easy to overlook the fact that this wave of industrial ambition was initially cultivated through evolution-ary movements located in the economic bureaucracy. This chapter, along with others, reminds us that to locate the origins of new policy paradigms, it remains vital to focus on the ministries, departments, and bureaus, where careers, ideas, and resources combine to give rise to change.

CONCLUSION

China's economic reform is known for its incremental and experimental characteristics. Both the official discourse in China and the scholarly observations abroad have posited that China's economic reform "crossed the river by feeling the stones." This method has allegedly allowed China to escape the shock-therapy approach to economic liberalization implemented in Eastern and Central Europe and is the hallmark of China's economic reform. This book shows that the ad hoc nature of China's reform is exaggerated. Focusing on the central economic bureaucracy, where the majority of the economic programs were formulated, it demonstrates that China's economic policy making was not simply cobbling together decentralized experiments. Instead, the course of reform was governed by several distinct overarching strategies and policy paradigms. That is, it is more accurate to say that reformers created waves and currents that carried China across the river and determined the speed and direction of China's economic development. Further, these systemic approaches to managing the Chinese economy emanated from the heart of the state bureaucracy and were closely tied to bureaucratic careers that developed in the Chinese state. The first contribution of this book is to identify the major paradigms that shaped the investment of state resources and attention and that changed how the economy was understood and approached in China's economic and development policies.

Paradigms are not technical or ad hoc changes. They are approaches to the economy and to state-market relations in general. Paradigms, as identified in this book, can have humble origins—associated, for instance, with practical solutions to economic problems, unconventional ideas emerging on the margins, or new career paths developing unnoticed. These initial efforts can nevertheless grow and expand into policy movements that involve a significant amount of collective action, organizational resources, and authority struggles. Eventually and at their essence, paradigms shape the terms in which the economy is represented and the ways in which economic problems are framed, and the connections that are conceived between issues redraw jurisdictional domains.

The first shift in economic policy paradigms was the inception of economic reform itself. Starting at the end of the 1970s, reform relaxed central planning and introduced market forces into the Chinese economy. The second paradigm emerged in the early 1990s and was no less significant than the first. It reversed the decentralization approach to economic reform and used the central state to speed up market development.

Under the aegis of a more centralized state, a multitude of approaches to managing a growing economy emerged. From the mid-1990s, an organizational approach to the economy gained traction. This approach attempted to influence the parameters of the economy by managing enterprises and their interrelationships. Originating in public-sector reform, this approach sought to achieve economies of scale by consolidating interfirm linkages and building Chinese conglomerates. Soon this structural method expanded into the realm of macroeconomic management, using enterprise management as a means to calibrate supply and demand. Closely following the organizational approach was the financial approach to reform, which also matured in this period of recentralization, with its influence lasting into the present. In its essence, the financial approach systematically used credit and public debt management to solve problems related to budget constraints and diminished growth. Around the mid-2000s, yet another approach to economic development took center stage, revolving around the rise of techno-industrial policy. This paradigm attached importance to manufacturing competitiveness in defining China's economic success and promoted technological leapfrogging and self-reliance. In spite of their shared reliance on a centralized state, as table C.1 shows, the three approaches are defined by their variant views on the economy, which

TABLE C.1
Different policy movements and their paradigmatic views on the economy

Policy movement	View of the economy	View of industries	Engines of growth	Macroeconomic policy	Enterprises
Conglomeration	Organizational	Sectors	Economies of scale	Structural methods	Interenterprise linkages
Financialization	Financial	Intersectoral	Financial markets, debt-driven growth	Market levers	Corporate control
Industrial competitiveness	Industrial	Intersectoral	Technology, manufacturing	N/A	Technological chains

Source: Compiled by the author.

generated different conceptions of its basic constitutive elements and affected multiple policy domains related to the industries, the enterprises, and the macroeconomy. The coexistence and apparent contradictions of these paradigms speak to the unexpected incoherence of China's economic development strategies. This book thus hints at the potential reasons why the China model is difficult to pin down.

How do we explain the emergence of economic policy paradigms? Examined internally, the development of paradigms does not appear to have followed any obvious logic. For instance, their evolution defies the notion that reform has been a linear progression toward liberalization. As we have seen, recentralization followed a period of decentralization and didn't completely turn away from the idea of planning. Industrial policy didn't emerge immediately following the unraveling of the planned economy but lay in wait until decades of marketization were complete. While one is tempted to rush to conclude that the return to state control is now the order of the day, we also see the breathtaking pace of growth in the financial markets, which is traditionally associated with an advanced phase of capitalism.[1] These ostensible reversals and parallel developments scramble any teleological scheme for development or transitions. If China's economic policy does contain a systematic nature, it does not appear to be driven by innate tendencies in the development of markets or polities. Nor, as this book shows, is it a direct reflection of top leaders' goals and interventions at any given point in time. Instead, I argue that reform began in the middle, working its way out from second-tier economic bureaucrats who turned ideas into solutions and solutions into systemic approaches to transforming the economy.

Underpinning each shift in paradigms was a group of bureaucrats who pushed for change to the extent that their career advancement was dependent on the successful escalation of their policy views. The basis of grouping bureaucrats varied. In some cases, the bureaucratic group was the dominant social type among a generation of economic bureaucrats. In other cases, it was made up of rather marginal subtypes of bureaucrats, niche occupants, or voluntary networks and social circles. Despite the varying size and prominence of the bureaucratic groups, what marks each as distinct is the same characteristic: career experiences. This book identifies the key bureaucratic groups and the distinctive career experiences that wove each one together. Economic reform, for instance, was initiated by a coalition of the local generalists and a group of central bureaucrats who worked in the financial arms of the socialist state. The shift to recentralization was engineered by a generation of technocrats who came of age and assumed political influence in the early 1990s. The organizational approach to managing the Chinese economy was engineered by factory-managers-turned-industrial-bureaucrats who directed the conglomeration movement, first at the local and then at the national level. The rise of the financial approach was attributed to a joint force of central bankers and think-tank researchers who ascended at the margins of the state and eventually seized critical posts at financial agencies and beyond. Behind the rise of techno-industrial policy was a concentration of engineers-turned-bureaucrats in a new ministry—the Ministry of Industry and Information Technology (MIIT)—and their efforts to vest the agency with a new mission to claim a footing in industrial policy. As bureaucrats moved across the terrains of the bureaucracy and built their careers, they recycled experiences from their past and retooled them for new struggles to obtain authority. The formations and transformations of bureaucratic career trajectories are vital social forces emerging within the state that melt "hard" structures in the bureaucracy and cause it to change.

As the bureaucracy has evolved, so has the Chinese economy. To be more precise, the Chinese economy has evolved with heavy bureaucratic imprints. Markets were designed by bureaucrats, the macroeconomy was managed using the tools available in the bureaucracy, and Chinese companies were cultivated and nudged by bureaucratic intentions. Yet I do not agree with those who argue that state ownership and control have turned the whole economy into China Inc. Nor do I focus on the bureaucratic intervention into specific high-profile companies such as Huawei. My subject of analysis is policies and their paradigmatic influence on the economy, many aspects of which have not been pieced together by other observers. This book demonstrates that policies were not whims of the leadership or simply reflections of gravitational forces intrinsic to the Chinese economy. It points out, for instance, that the export-led growth approach to development, which appeared to be a response to objective changes in the global economy and China's existing "endowment," was a function of policy deliberation. Chapter 6 shows that as a new policy paradigm took hold, this approach was immediately scaled back, if not completely reversed. As the Chinese economy slows down and a "new normal" sets in, the intensifying competition over what kind of development China needs will ultimately take place at the level of policy paradigms. Regardless of what the uncertain future holds, this book shows that as long as bureaucratic decision-making remains important in Chinese politics, we cannot understand what is happening in the Chinese economy without grasping what is happening in the bureaucratic state. Examining how bureaucrats construct the economy and build markets in their image gives clarity to what otherwise would appear to be irregularities in the shift of economic policy paradigms. As the Chinese bureaucracy and the economy coevolved, policy changes were regularly tied to the rhythm of bureaucratic movements, coming in waves.

A STATE REMADE

As bureaucrats made policies, they also remade the Chinese state. Organizations change the people who inhabit them; people also change the organizations where they work—it is invariably a recursive process. The Weberian account of the bureaucracy tends to aggrandize the complex and immutable structure of the state bureaucracy and lose sight of how bureaucrats have agency. This book seeks to do justice to this aspect of personnel-organization interactions. To the Chinese bureaucrats, the state was a vehicle of policy change that they could mobilize to pursue their agenda. Since the aspiration to advance their policies was motivated in part by intrabureaucratic competition for authority, the forms and outcomes of such intrabureaucratic struggles also had an impact on the bureaucratic organizations.

The trajectory of China's economic governance bears out this point. When the central state was seen by some as an obstacle to reform in the 1980s, intrabureaucratic competition was factionalist and beholden to strong personalities, further fragmenting the economic bureaucracy. Technocrats in the 1990s, however, incorporated the state into the stimulation of market development and, for this purpose, recentralized the Chinese state. To this end, the central bureaucracy increased its sway over local governments and absorbed local generalists, together with their interests and local knowledge. With a new range of tool kits and personnel, the state became a more effective regulator and macroeconomic manager. Following recentralization, the Chinese state was stronger and allegedly more "modern," according to the designers of this technocratic movement, thereby offering more opportunities, resources, and stakes in the struggle over bureaucratic authority. The question of development had decisively changed from whether China needed the central bureaucracy to develop its economy to what kinds of state intervention were desirable. As a result, intrabureaucratic competition since the late 1990s has been channeled into varied projects of state building. Because the state was the venue of bureaucratic competition, such competition was formalized and manifested through jurisdictional claims and interministry rivalries. Bureaucrats with different career trajectories attempted to seize posts in the upper echelons of the bureaucracy and influence the reorganization of the state in their favor. These lines of development over the last two decades produced a paradoxical outcome in the evolution of the Chinese state: an increasingly powerful and autonomous central economic bureaucracy was also becoming crowded, competitive, and internally incoherent. This phenomenon raises questions about the relationship between state autonomy and cohesion, which are too often assumed to develop in tandem with one another. The Chinese case, however, shows that empowerment of the bureaucracy can also lead to its internal fragmentation.

The relationship between the state and state actors described in this book compels a rethinking of the concept of state capacity and the question of what causes it to change. State capacity is defined as the ability of a government to accomplish policy goals.[2] The formation of state capacity, as this book shows, is a much more dynamic process than this definition implies. In the short course of China's economic reform, we see that the Chinese state has traveled through stages of unraveling, reassembling, and multiplying. This happened in a country with a strong bureaucratic tradition and under the stewardship of an authoritarian party, both of which would be expected to reinforce bureaucratic power. Yet state capacity changed in conjunction with the transformation of state policies in the sense that state policies also changed the state. In setting goals, policy makers determined the kind of state capacities required to achieve those goals. That is, it was through the *process* of pursuing policy goals that the capacity of the state was altered. How policy goals were set, who set them, and how they were pursued were endogenous to the formation of state structures and goals; the state cannot be treated as an objective and unchanging precondition to policy making.[3] Instead, state capacities, in large measure, were forcefully and artfully created and engineered by bureaucrats in the process of developing and expanding policy paradigms across the nation and in localities. This book showcases an analysis of state capacity by viewing the state not as a preexisting and unitary actor but as a venue in which state actors jostled, innovated, and sometimes failed at their attempts to amass power. In this process, the state was frequently mobilized as an object of change and a vector of transformative policies.

MARKETS WITH BUREAUCRATIC CHARACTERISTICS

This book tells the story of the rising power of Chinese economic bureaucrats. Because of the period in Chinese history being considered, this is inevitably also a story about the rise of a market economy. China's market reform didn't displace or undercut the power of central economic bureaucrats. In fact, one could argue that their net power has significantly expanded in terms of strengthened central state capacity, the range of tools available to intervene in the economy, the variety of new constituencies built, and the intellectual directorship they wielded in the field of economic thinking. How is it that a market reform that was supposed to target the bureaucracy ended up empowering it? Granted, the scholarship on state-market relations has long argued that market expansion does not necessarily come at the cost of the administrative state. Even neoliberal policies need a state to execute them.[4] This book, too, confirms the proposition that the state and the market coevolved and the pivot to marketization required institutional work to bring it about—that is, statecraft. Yet the existing scholarship does leave a gap: it devotes much more attention to analyzing how the state served the purposes of the market than the other way around.

This book shows that market expansion also served the purposes of the state. In this way, it revisits a less discussed theme in Karl Polanyi's account of the rise of market societies: that national market formation also enhances the sovereign power of the state.[5] I argue that in the Chinese case, market expansion was achieved through a specific mechanism—bureaucratic decision-making. What bureaucrats thought about markets and what they intended to do with them mattered for the kind of economic reform they instituted. In China, no official would now deny the legitimated role of the market in organizing people's economic lives. Market-based reform remains the official line and, surprisingly, the politically progressive and correct thing to say. Yet it makes a vital difference whether Chinese policy makers think markets are sacred or profane and whether they approach them ideologically or instrumentally. This book offers an opportunity to investigate how the incentives and dispositions of the policy makers played into their thinking about the usefulness of the market. Overall, this book finds that economic bureaucrats largely treated markets as means to larger ends rather than as ends in themselves. They used markets to expand bureaucratic power and solve bureaucratic problems. This is not to say that bureaucratic motivation directed all of market expansion. Markets certainly can take on a life of their own, thriving on the profit-seeking incentives of myriads of individuals and firms that participate in it. China is no exception. Bureaucratic considerations matter, however, at the stage of policy formulation—before incentives unleashed by these policies fall into place.

Specifically, the chapters in this book show at least three modes of instrumental engagement with markets by economic bureaucrats. First, central bureaucrats aimed to use markets to integrate national territories and overcome bureaucratic fragmentation at the local level. Chinese local governments tended toward operating like independent kingdoms during periods when the central state was enfeebled. Central economic bureaucrats repeatedly resorted to the market to break regional barriers. In the socialist period, this was manifested in the decision to allow markets to develop alongside the planned economy in order to alleviate bureaucratic fragmentation exacerbated by a top-down command economy. Central bureaucrats went out of their way to preserve market exchanges, traditional trading patterns, and the age-old craft economy in an attempt to enact linkages across regions that had been artificially divided by administrative boundaries. This pragmatic view of harnessing markets to assist nation-state building was apparent as early as the first years of the socialist period and was foundational to forming the identity of the first generation of reformers and their germinal understanding of the political utility of the market. In the reform period, an argument for speeding up the integration of national markets resurfaced. In this case, central technocrats sought to end the decentralizing approach to economic reform and crack down on the rampant local protectionism associated with it. Building national markets and linking enterprises in different local jurisdictions were considered progressive efforts that would modernize the Chinese economy. The central bureaucrats, in these cases, presented themselves as lofty thinkers above the fray who were able to act on behalf of the whole country. In effect, territorial integration by way of market building paved the way for boosting central state power and lending authority to the central bureaucrats.

Second, economic bureaucrats fostered the development of markets to build their constituencies. Markets could be turned into constituencies for policy makers because market expansion creates new bases of support and new forms of policy engagement. Thus, support for market expansion proved to be crucial for reform-minded bureaucrats who aimed to sideline the old-guard planners and carve out a regulatory space and a new object of management of their own. For instance, the financial reformers in the 1980s championed the development of China's financial markets in the cracks of the state banking system in order to build a constituency responsive to the application of modern macroeconomic tools. This effort suited their aspiration to become a new generation of central bankers who knew how to apply the indirect levers used in macroeconomic management. Economic bureaucrats in these cases applied pressures from outside back into the bureaucracy and (re)invented their relevance for governing the prospective markets.

Third, central bureaucrats attempted to use markets—in particular, the financial markets—to manage state assets. This was considered a reform attempt as well, as it aimed to instill financial discipline in the public sector by subjecting state enterprises to rules of corporate control. The financial way of exercising corporate control and state ownership required that abstract state ownership be replaced by active owners and shareholders. To this end, a swath of positions was created in the economic bureaucracy to embody this state ownership. This new form of statecraft aroused new rounds of competition among ministries and agencies that were attempting to seize the right to manage China's massive state assets, with the Ministry of Finance and the People's Bank of China being the key contenders. This case epitomizes how even the latest stage of capitalist development, financialization, when coupled with bureaucratic motives, can take on a different meaning and play to the advantage of the bureaucracy. Overall, resorting to markets in this case created bureaucratic positions and enhanced bureaucratic power.

All three modes of engagement with the market reveal that the Chinese bureaucrats played a more active role in shaping the development of the market than a regulatory state framework allows. It could be argued that in these three senses China's market reform engaged China in a form of *bureaucratic capitalism*. The traditional conception of bureaucratic capitalism is a capitalist property arrangement hijacked by bureaucratic control through, for example, massive corruption. What I intend by invoking this term is to highlight that bureaucrats viewed the market through bureaucratic lenses and developed tremendous stakes in market expansion. This resulted in a pragmatic attitude toward market development and, to outsiders, a paradoxical embracing of markets without adhering to their underlying principles. The view of the market by Chinese bureaucrats is a recurring theme throughout the book. To keep this theme alive, it shows that these bureaucrats' approach to markets is a central pillar that supports the larger universe of their policy ideas. It reveals a critical way in which bureaucratic practice participated in and shaped the production of economic ideas.

CHINESE BUREAUCRACY AND GLOBALIZATION

Even if I have been able to substantiate that Chinese policy makers didn't simply follow the lead of capitalist drives and market incentives, one could still question whether China's economic reform was a mere footnote in the story of globalization. Undeniably, China has been an active participant in and beneficiary of globalization. China's integration into global trade and investment has defined the very content of its reform. China's rise in the past four decades paralleled the heyday of globalization and the full-scale formation of global value chains, in which China is now a linchpin. Despite the current geopolitical push to deglobalize, China's commitment to global economic exchanges seems unwavering, revealing the extent to which China's development has benefited from globalization and the belief that such benefits will likely be extended into the foreseeable future. The question then comes down to how China's integration into the global world squares with the endogenous explanation of policy change offered in this book. Specifically, as much as this book seeks to explain the formation of policy ideas, it needs to address the question as to whether global forces also played an important role in shaping the formulation of economic policy.

This book shows that global economic ideas have made inroads into the Chinese polity but that the economic bureaucracy remains a powerful filter of global influence. Bureaucrats did learn from international best practices and foreign models, but such international learning was highly selective and almost always combined with an attempt to translate foreign referents to fit domestic situations. Specifically, Chinese bureaucrats were committed to molding the state to fit the formula of market development and ensuring that its programmatic policies, in the long run and in aggregation, did not undercut bureaucratic power. To do so, the Chinese economic policy makers had to be vested with a considerable measure of autonomy from international actors. The absence of coercion from international financial institutions such as the IMF and from hegemonic countries alike was indeed unusual among developing countries. The reasons why this was the case warrant a discussion beyond the scope of this book. It suffices here to mention that the size of the Chinese economy and its particular forms of entry into globalization played a part. China's alluringly large domestic markets served as a counterweight to foreign intervention. Foreign capital was injected into the Chinese economy largely through foreign direct investment (FDI) instead of international commercial lending, relieving China of the stringent conditions often attached to such lending to developing economies. Additionally, China was already implementing, without being pressured, some core elements of the Washington Consensus that had been promoted to the developing world. China's historical sensitivity to macroeconomic prudence, privatization of the public sector, and embrace of FDI were among the key examples.

In the absence of explicit coercion, the impetus of international social learning in the Chinese case tended to be normative and mimetic—but it is important to note that such normative and mimetic interests in foreign referents were largely applied at the programmatic and technical levels of policy making. Norm subscription or norm borrowing at the paradigmatic level was rare. If anything, bureaucrats in different parts of the state system learned from different parts of the world, following a selective pattern of pairing between bureaucratic groups and foreign ideas. In addition, bureaucrats incorporated learned foreign models as ingredients for making their own paradigms. For instance, the financial reformers ascending at the turn of the twenty-first century harnessed the shareholder model of corporate control prevalent in Anglo-Saxon countries to modernize China's public sector and manage its massive state assets. MIIT technocrats referred to Germany's Industry 4.0 when setting the technological benchmarks for Made in China 2025 but localized it with a much wider range of state support. In other words, foreign ideas were used in a highly specific fashion and had to obtain entry into the Chinese state and relate to bureaucratic stakes in the proper way to gain traction.

As noted, international learning varied by bureaucratic location, but it also varied across periods. The 1990s, for instance, were marked by a concerted effort to learn from the West, especially in the areas of finance, corporate governance, and central banking. This decade was characterized as a rosy period in China's relationship with the West, leading up to China's accession to the World Trade Organization in 2001.[6] Yet even in this honeymoon period, learning remained instrumental and pragmatic. Chinese technocrats applied the methods they learned as disciplinary techniques to make the Chinese government more efficient. The generous references to foreign practices also served a domestic political purpose. Central technocrats used them to make a case for centralizing the Chinese state, which at that time was weak in terms of its authority over local governments. Appealing to international best practices lent normative power to the central state and boosted its status as a bearer of technocratic rationality and efficiency. As soon as the power of the central state was secure, learning was more decentralized: individual agencies ceased to be as coordinated in their efforts and fought among themselves for authority by appealing to different economic lessons that privileged their particular agencies. In sum, the changing dynamics of the bureaucracy explain how international economic learning varied among periods.

CONCLUSION

THE RISE OF POWERFUL POLITICAL CHARISMA

When President Xi Jinping took the helm of the party in 2012, he embarked on a path toward tightening political control and centralizing personal authority, a direction that had been out of fashion since the end of the Mao era. In the realm of economics, Xi broke with institutional precedents by establishing and personally overseeing several high-profile economic policy-making bodies within the party, attempting to use them to project his influence over the national economy. These moves were poised to sideline the State Council, and the state bureaucracy appeared to be in jeopardy.

In spite of the president's hovering attention, the situation on the administrative ground defies an easy characterization as a deviation from the existing course of economic policy. Xi's economic policies have been filled with baffling contradictions. Liberalization of financial markets proceeded apace and even picked up momentum, welcoming even more foreign investment and shareholding. Despite spasms of regulatory crackdown on the finance sectors, financial markets, and the highly leveraged real estate sector, these continue to be an important part of the growth engine. Debt-driven development shows no signs of slowing down. On the other hand, techno-industrial policy has also gained steam. The drive for technological supremacy and self-reliance has reached a white-heat frenzy in the five years since 2019, spurring a spending spree across the nation and down to the localities in the hope of developing high-tech industries and key technologies. These latest lines of policy development, while self-contradictory, fit the classical pattern of the coexistence of financialization and industrialization described in this book.

On the personnel front, to say that the bureaucracy has been displaced is hardly accurate. There has not been a massive turnover in the economic bureaucracy under Xi's presidency. In fact, his administration inherited more than half of the ministers and vice ministers from the last administration, the highest retention rate compared to all previous administrations. At Xi's side, his handpicked right-hand men were not foreign to the bureaucratic establishment but rather were drawn from the heart of it. Wang Qishan was a financial reformer in the central government in the 1980s and 1990s. Liu He, portrayed in chapter 6, was a planner-turned-industrial-policymaker who built his career firmly in the economic bureaucracy. Taken together, how do we make sense of an ambitious leader's relationship with the economic bureaucracy? Does Xi's rise subvert the thesis of the book?

I argue the opposite. Not only does the thesis presented in this book not falter in the wake of recent political developments in China, but also it helps us to decipher the new political moves. Xi was clearly motivated to undercut the authority of the economic bureaucracy. But the reason he felt the need to do so was related to what has been argued in this book. Xi's hallmark political project has been to uproot the centrifugal power centers that have allegedly festered within the party-state and have threatened regime integration and officials' undivided loyalty to the party, and the economic bureaucracy was perceived to have become part of this concern. As this book shows, the course of economic reform has seen the rising power of the ministries, and the economic bureaucracy as a whole has become a crowded and competitive place as each ministry attempts to outcompete others for organizational fiefdoms, resources, and domination. These scenes were too unruly and disorganized for controlling political leaders to accept. Certainly, the problems of an overbearing economic bureaucracy are not the same as those of political factionalism and patronage. Informal politics thrives on gathering informal resources built around personalities. Bureaucratic power is collectively wielded, and its beneficiaries are bureaucratic collectives and formal organizations. Yet bureaucratic overcrowding, albeit by way of legitimate means of growth, apparently has constituted its own source of paralysis to the extent that it is believed to have impaired party unity and affected the party's capacity to govern and therefore to warrant an external intervention. The mobilization of small leading groups within the party, directly led by Xi, is precisely intended to overlay and override the economic bureaucracy, creating a center of command, coordination, and information within the party to rein in the decentralized competition in the state.

Intentions aside, actual policies that the administration instituted have yet to come close to bringing about any revolutionary changes to the parameters of economic governance. Previous bureaucracy-originated policy threads didn't recede but were kept alive and well; they have even developed further in the new administration. The previously mentioned coexistence of efforts to industrialize and financialize is one example among many. After all, the accumulation of policy programs, in the course of their elevation to paradigms, had cultivated established circuits of knowledge, secured organizational resources, tightened policy networks, and fostered vested interests in their reproduction. If this book offers any insights into how to address the problem of the bureaucracy, it indicates that the surgical correction has to start right at the center of the bureaucracy, where ideas, power, and interests are deeply attached to bureaucratic interests and careers. Any imposition of drastic change requires scrambling the bureaucratic field and rewiring the career trajectories to open up alternative pathways for ideas and constituencies. Yet career trajectories, unlike organizations, cannot be washed away like sandcastles by political waves. As we see in the book, following the demise of organizations, bureaucrats continued to circulate within the state, finding their own ways to coalesce and rise. Career paths and paradigms transpire at an evolutionary, not a revolutionary, pace. The ways in which the Chinese bureaucracy is enclosed and organized allow it to both support regime continuity and resist external intervention.

Xi's ascendance invokes the classic sociological debate over the relationship between charisma and bureaucracy. In a typical Weberian analysis, charisma is dynamic and the bureaucracy static. Charisma is bestowed with a magical power in the ascendant stage that allows its possessor to effectively and often dramatically take over bureaucratic institutions. Xi's ability to do so, aided by an authoritarian context, is more or less expected, given this understanding of charismatic power. This book prompts us to rethink this proposition by raising challenges to the assumption of bureaucratic stasis. It asks to what extent the characterization of the bureaucracy as a grouping of routinized, rationalized, and institutionalized organizations was wrongheaded in the first place.

Bureaucracy does not have to be corrupt to be political, self-serving, or entrepreneurial. It can be a dynamo of careers, activism, knowledge, and self-interests. Around the world, populist leaders claim to have smashed bureaucratic machines while railing against the "deep state." An array of evidence has shown that populist regimes have done some damage to bureaucracy, but the long-term effect is uncertain, and the populist rhetoric is often overblown.[7] The ability (and also the willingness) of politicians to transform the bureaucracy when they are in power has been grossly exaggerated. The challenge is logistical as much as political. Positions to be held by political appointees often go unfilled many months or even years into a new presidency. It turns out that assembling the right kind of persona, together with the mix of resources, information, and expertise they embody, which can take generations to build, in a short time is extremely difficult. If the challenge is daunting even for government bureaucracies built to welcome shifting partisan influence, it is even more so where Chinese political leaders rely on a system of career bureaucrats to govern and where career bureaucrats leave employment largely on biologically determined retirement schedules. Historically, Mao attempted to redo or even undo the bureaucracy by mobilizing a mass attack on the government. But history tells us that resorting to a Cultural Revolution–style siege of the bureaucracy comes at a huge cost: it invites a legitimacy crisis for the regime because the bureaucracy has become such an important part of how Chinese government and society are organized, embodying the Chinese version of elitism as well as serving as a bastion of stability and continuity and sometimes as a symbolic force of rationality in Chinese society.

THE CHINESE ECONOMIC BUREAUCRACY
IN THE CHANGING WORLD

As I conclude this book, the world has become a different place from the one in which China found itself throughout most of its economic reform. Populist and nationalist movements have vowed to implement xenophobic policies and scrutinize all aspects of a country's foreign engagements. The rising tension between the United States and China disrupts one of the world's busiest corridors of economic exchange and destabilizes the global environment for all. A pandemic swept the globe and effectively put the brakes on the globalization of value chains, which were already being rewired after 2008. All the forces converged in the same direction to compel countries to look inward and rethink their development strategies at home. Large economies, such as the United States and China, revamped laws and policies to seek economic security and self-reliance. Both countries have favorable national conditions in which to push through such transitions. China, for instance, has a relatively broad industrial base, a large domestic market, and well-rounded domestic supply chains. With signs of delinking looming, the country has sought to rebalance the economy by making it walk on two legs—production *and* consumption—and pegging the stimulation of the service economy to the development of domestic markets. As this book shows, the economic bureaucracy is not a stranger to diversification. China's evolving economic bureaucracy has already facilitated the wide expansion of the economy, unintentionally preparing China for the current moment of deglobalization. The bureaucracy's historical legacies and its engagement with compressed development stimulated the production of contradictory policy strategies, which, when added up, fostered a well-rounded economy with mixed constituent sectors, markets, technologies, and organizational forms.

How will the economic bureaucracy fare in periods of global delinking? This book provides a basis for projecting that its power will likely increase, as global delinking furthers the advantage of state insiders whose legitimacy does not rest on dealing with foreign constituencies. The economic bureaucrats are already one group of this kind. The preservation and circulation of tacit knowledge within the administrative state will be protected and reinforced by hardening boundaries. With the delegitimation of external input, the economic bureaucracy is poised to enhance its status as a national hub of economic ideas, information, and authority. As it currently stands, China's preparation for a deglobalized world, articulated in the concept of *dual circulation*, includes a desire to extract a homegrown momentum for growth and claim institutional dividends by further integrating national markets and tearing down local protectionism. National-level market integration, as this book has shown, is a familiar element in the template of bureaucrats' strategies to expand central power. Hence, the turn to domestic markets will likely benefit, again, the national designers who decide how the integration process should proceed and be rationalized.

A deglobalized economy is certainly not an economy free of risk. In transitioning to a more self-sufficient economy, growth may slow, unemployment may rise, and macroeconomic indicators may jitter. The rise of these new sets of economic problems, some ballooning into crises here and there, will likely sustain the power of the bureaucrats and technocrats alike and may temporarily hold off ambitious attempts by nonspecialist political leaders to seize decision-making power over the economy. The need to expand market frontiers (if a market economy is to be upheld) and search for new sources of growth will likely disfavor excessive centralization of economic policy making and support the continued tolerance of bureaucratic competition over ideas and programs. This book provides insights into how the past and present of the Chinese bureaucracy will determine its future. The Chinese economic bureaucracy has demonstrated a considerable degree of agility and plasticity, allowing it to adapt to changing circumstances. Yet the evolutionary speed at which such adaptation has happened may also serve as a stabilizing, albeit suboptimal, force against rapidly changing political winds and shifting global policy fads. Nevertheless, as this book shows, the ability of Chinese economic bureaucrats to look to the past to solve future problems has grave limitations and may eventually compromise the Chinese economy's dynamism as the Chinese government further diminishes its international learning. Allowing a bureaucratic capture of political power also risks replacing the dynamism and initiatives that could potentially spring from society itself. How far the economic bureaucracy can expand before it meets major pushback remains to be seen.

LIST OF ABBREVIATIONS

AMC:	Asset Management Corporation
CASS:	Chinese Academy of Social Sciences
CCP:	Chinese Communist Party
CIC:	Chinese Investment Corporation
CIRC:	China Insurance Regulatory Commission
CR:	Cultural Revolution
CSRC:	China Securities Regulatory Commission
FTOSC:	Finance and Trade Office of the State Council
GLF:	Great Leap Forward
MFTEC:	Ministry of Foreign Economic Relations and Trade
MIIT:	Ministry of Industry and Information Technology
MOF:	Ministry of Finance
MST:	Ministry of Science and Technology
NDRC:	National Development and Reform Commission
PBOC:	People's Bank of China
SETC:	State Economic and Trade Commission
SOE:	State-Owned Enterprise
SPC:	State Planning Commission
SRC:	System Reform Commission

ACKNOWLEDGMENTS

Writing a book has been a profound journey, full of academic challenges and personal growth. The completion of this work has been made possible by the generosity, wisdom, and support of many incredible individuals. I am grateful to all of you who have contributed to the life of this book and for this opportunity to express my gratitude and appreciation.

First and foremost, I would like to thank my mentors at Yale University. My greatest debt is owed to Julia Adams, who has been my intellectual and spiritual beacon, guiding me through the highs and lows of my journey in a new country and discipline. It is Julia who taught me to transcend physical and mental boundaries in intellectual pursuits and to face pressure with grace and humor. Her spirit of optimism, boundless generosity, and faith in agency—both sociological and personal—are present on every page of this book.

Philip Gorski's blend of philosophical thinking and precise analytical execution has done much to both shape and improve my scholarly approach. He encouraged me to probe further and nurture my fledgling ideas with insights and questions until they were ready for publication. Emily Erikson introduced me to a whole new world of network analysis and provided fresh perspectives on thinking about bureaucratic organizations. Her sharp advice was instrumental in keeping me on track at critical junctures. Deborah Davis has been tremendously supportive with her time, reading every draft that has come across her desk and offering valuable insights from her expert knowledge of China. Ivan Szelenyi's influence extends far beyond our two overlapping years at Yale. He encouraged me to ask big questions and helped me contextualize my observations within the comparative perspectives of post-communist transitions. I am also grateful to Jonathan Wyrtzen, Rene Almeling, Peter Stamatov, James Scott, Peter Purdue, and Steven Pincus for sharing their ideas and expertise with me. My friends and fellow graduate students at Yale created a rich intellectual environment for this project. I want to thank Xiaohong Xu, Kristen Plys, Esther Kim, Wei Luo, Yu Liu, Gulay Turkmen-Dervisoglu, Rui Gao, Thomas Crosbie, Alison Gerber, Andrew Junker, Jensen Sass, Seongsoo Choi, Ted Fertik, and Christopher Miller, among many others, who supported me in various ways. Regular attendance at the Comparative Research Workshop, The Transition to Modernity Colloquium, Political Theory Workshop, and James Scott's breakfast group exposed me to new ideas and friends, making my graduate studies fulfilling and stimulating.

At Brown University, the Watson Institute for International and Public Affairs enriched my thinking about states and governance, providing a vibrant community of scholars and policy makers along with a great synergy of interdisciplinary scholarship of which I could never have imagined being a part. Andrew Shrank, Nitsan Chorev, and Patrick Heller were generous with their time, offering invigorating comments and suggestions that helped me better grapple with the puzzles of this book. Stimulating conversations with Mark Blyth, Michael Kennedy, Edward Steinfeld, Josh Pacewicz, Chas Freeman, Richard Boucher, and Paget Henry helped broaden the scope of my inquiry. An amazing group of postdoctoral fellows, including Julia Chuang, Jonas Nahm, Rajesh Veeraraghavan, and Atul Pokharel provided abundant collegiality and emotional support, leaving me with great memories along with their intellectual imprints.

I feel fortunate to have discovered an academic home in the Sociology Department at the University of Virginia (UVA), where I am surrounded by wonderful colleagues who have supported me through the process of writing and rewriting the chapters in this book. Simone is an unfailing source of innovative ideas and warmth. He meticulously read and commented on every single chapter of this book and helped me dispel self-inflicted confusion and achieve clarity. Adam Slez made sure that the logic of my chapters added up and that my Chinese case could serve as a general model for understanding how bureaucracy works. Jennifer Bair helped me conceive linkages between states and global value chains. She also went above and beyond by offering to substitute teach my classes despite her busy schedule when I was overwhelmed by a high-risk pregnancy. Isaac Reed, Krishan Kumar, and Elizabeth Gorman shared their invaluable insights in comments and conversations. Josipa Roksa and Ekaterina Makarova have nourished my years at UVA with their intellects and hospitality.

In addition, I would like to thank many people for their feedback on earlier drafts of the book. Special thanks go to Joel Andreas and Bai Gao for their advice at my book workshop. Joel Andreas reminded me to spell out the details of histographies and to give my protagonists equal weight in archival investigations. Bai Gao helped me stabilize the assumptions of my investigation, allowing me to rule out alternative explanations with more confidence. Others provided useful comments on subsequent drafts, including John Padgett, Miguel Centeno, John W. Mohr, Orlando Patterson, Johanna Bockman, Tianbiao Zhu, John Fisher, Xiaohong Xu, Le Lin, Nicholas Wilson, Balazs Vedres, Yang Zhang, and Muyang Zhou. Between 2012 and 2014, I presented earlier versions of this work at the East Asia Workshop of Politics, Economy and Society at the University of Chicago, the Workshop in History, Culture, and Society at Harvard University, the Comparative Research Workshop at Yale University, the Socialism and Post-Socialism summer workshop at Central European University, and the Graduate Workshop of the Tobin Project in Cambridge, Massachusetts. I extend my gratitude to the participants at these events for providing stimulating feedback at opportune times.

At Columbia University Press, my heartfelt thanks go to Eric Schwartz for his enthusiastic support of this book. His expert shepherding throughout the entire publication process made the experience immeasurably better. Lowell Frye and Zachary Friedman, part of a stellar production team, provided invaluable editorial assistance. I am also grateful for the Middle Range series editors, Peter S. Bearman, Emily Erikson, Christopher Muller, and Catherine Turco, who saw the initial potential in my book manuscript. Three anonymous reviewers provided encouraging and perceptive feedback on the manuscript, helping me connect my ideas and findings with a broader audience.

This project would not have been possible without unwavering support and nourishment from my family. My deepest thanks go to them. Above all, I thank Yusong Huang for his understanding and intelligence. Not only did Yusong offer his sharp intellectual engagement, when our children arrived and time for intellectual debates became scarce, he continued to provide steadfast emotional and logistical support that made the completion of this book possible. My two children, Paxson and Ellory, brought new perspectives to my world and added new meaning to who I am and what I do. Special thanks to my extended family in China who inspire me with their warmth, entrepreneurship, and faith in a better future. I am grateful to my parents-in-law, Bingbing Wang and Qian Huang, for their help with our family when it was most needed. Finally, I owe everything to my mother, Meiqing He, and father, Jiangang Wang. They nurtured me with unconditional love, much-needed reminders, and encouragement to pursue my dreams. My mother's resilience, optimism, and endless curiosity are unfailing sources of light, illuminating my paths through adventure and uncertainty. My father's bottomless kindness, dry humor, and philosophical inclination teach me to balance my commitments to communities and my desire to ask unconventional questions. To them and to their love, this book is dedicated.

NOTES

INTRODUCTION

1. Karl Polanyi, *The Great Transformation: The Political and Economic Origins of Our Time* (Boston: Beacon, 2001).
2. Thomas S. Kuhn, *The Structure of Scientific Revolutions* (Chicago: University of Chicago Press, 2012).
3. Gil Eyal, Ivan Szelenyi, and Eleanor R. Townsley show in their book *Making Capitalism Without Capitalists: The New Ruling Elites in Eastern Europe* (London: Verso, 1999) that Eastern Europe attempted to liberalize the economy in the socialist period from a similar starting point—marketization without a capitalist class.
4. Bruce J. Dickson, *Red Capitalists in China: The Party, Private Entrepreneurs, and Prospects for Political Change* (Cambridge: Cambridge University Press, 2003); Yongshun Cai, "China's Moderate Middle Class," *Asian Survey* 45, no. 5 (September/October 2005): 777–99; Chris Smith, "Living at Work: Management Control and the Dormitory Labour System in China," *Asia Pacific Journal of Management* 20, no. 3 (September 2003): 333–58.
5. Ivan Szelenyi and Eric Kostello, "The Market Transition Debate: Toward a Synthesis?," *American Journal of Sociology* 101, no. 4 (January 1996): 1082–96.
6. Chalmers A. Johnson, *MITI and the Japanese Miracle: The Growth of Industrial Policy, 1925–1975* (Stanford, CA: Stanford University Press, 1982); Peter B. Evans, *Embedded Autonomy* (Princeton, NJ: Princeton University Press, 1995); Alice H. Amsden, *Asia's Next Giant: South Korea and Late Industrialization* (Oxford: Oxford University Press, 1989); Meredith Woo-Cumings, ed., *The Developmental State* (Ithaca, NY: Cornell University Press, 1999); Robert Wade, *Governing the Market: Economic Theory and the Role of Government in East Asian Industrialization* (Princeton, NJ: Princeton University Press, 2003); Atul Kohli, *State-Directed Development: Political*

Power and Industrialization in the Global Periphery (Cambridge: Cambridge University Press, 2012); Stephan Haggard, *Developmental States* (Cambridge: Cambridge University Press, 2018).

7. Kenneth G. Lieberthal and David M. Lampton, eds., *Bureaucracy, Politics, and Decision Making in Post-Mao China* (Berkeley: University of California Press, 2018).

8. Tobias ten Brink, *China's Capitalism: A Paradoxical Route to Economic Prosperity*, trans. Carla Welch (Philadelphia: University of Pennsylvania Press, 2019); Yeling Tan and James Conran, "China's Growth Model in Comparative and Historical Perspectives," in *Diminishing Returns: The New Politics of Growth and Stagnation*, ed. Mark Blyth, Jonas Pontusson, and Lucio Baccaro (New York: Oxford University Press, 2022), 143–66.

9. Josh Pacewicz, *Partisans and Partners: The Politics of the Post-Keynesian Society* (Chicago: University of Chicago Press, 2016).

10. Marion Fourcade-Gourinchas and Sarah L. Babb, "The Rebirth of the Liberal Creed: Paths to Neoliberalism in Four Countries," *American Journal of Sociology* 108, no. 3 (November 2002): 533–79.

11. Max Weber, *Economy and Society: An Outline of Interpretive Sociology*, ed. Guenther Roth and Claus Wittich (Berkeley: University of California Press, 1978).

12. Erin Metz McDonnell, "Patchwork Leviathan: How Pockets of Bureaucratic Governance Flourish Within Institutionally Diverse Developing States," *American Sociological Review* 82, no. 3 (June 2017): 490.

13. James C. Scott, *Seeing Like a State: How Certain Schemes to Improve the Human Condition Have Failed* (New Haven, CT: Yale University Press, 1999).

14. Tim Hallett and Marc J. Ventresca, "Inhabited Institutions: Social Interactions and Organizational Forms in Gouldner's 'Patterns of Industrial Bureaucracy,'" *Theory and Society* 35, no. 2 (April 2006): 213–36. Scholars also insist that the formations of bureaucratic structures and ethos have social origins and are interactive with social conditions that shape the state bureaucracy. See Bernard S. Silberman, *Cages of Reason: The Rise of the Rational State in France, Japan, the United States, and Great Britain* (Chicago: University of Chicago Press, 1993); Philip S. Gorski, *The Disciplinary Revolution: Calvinism and the Rise of the State in Early Modern Europe* (Chicago: University of Chicago Press, 2003).

15. Ben Ross Schneider, *Politics Within the State: Elite Bureaucrats and Industrial Policy in Authoritarian Brazil* (Pittsburgh, PA: University of Pittsburgh Press, 1992), 9.

16. Josh Pacewicz, "Tax Increment Financing, Economic Development Professionals and the Financialization of Urban Politics," *Socio-Economic Review* 11, no. 3 (July 2013): 413–40. Sarah Babb, in her book *Managing Mexico*, shows that the young generation of technocrats has a stake in instituting neoliberal policies to better utilize their expertise in economics and win the epistemic battle with the old generation of bureaucrats made up of lawyers. Sarah Babb, *Managing Mexico: Economists from Nationalism to Neoliberalism* (Princeton, NJ: Princeton University Press, 2001).

17. Calculated by the author from officials' CVs.

18. This fact invites a departure from existing treatment of Chinese elite politics in which only top leaders are worthy of biographical attention. The artificial separation between top political elites and faceless bureaucrats makes it impossible to determine how top leaders form their ideas and ambitions and to what extent leaders' individual idiosyncrasies may reflect the collective characteristics of the pool from which they were drawn.

19. Joel Andreas, "The Structure of Charismatic Mobilization: A Case Study of Rebellion During the Chinese Cultural Revolution," *American Sociological Review* 72, no. 3 (June 2007): 434–58; Bo Rothstein, "The Chinese Paradox of High Growth and Low Quality of Government: The Cadre Organization Meets Max Weber," *Governance* 28, no. 4 (November 2015): 533–48; Xueguang Zhou, *The Logic of Governance in China* (Cambridge: Cambridge University Press, 2022).

20. Yuen Yuen Ang's work considers systematically and explains the seemingly Janus-faced character of China's economic development: corruption on one hand and high growth and bureaucratic entrepreneurship on the other. See Yuen Yuen Ang, *China's Gilded Age* (Cambridge: Cambridge University Press, 2021), *How China Escaped the Poverty Trap* (Ithaca, NY: Cornell University Press, 2016), and "Beyond Weber: Conceptualizing an Alternative Ideal Type of Bureaucracy in Developing Contexts," *Regulation & Governance* 11, no. 3 (August 2017): 282–98.

21. Scholars have shown that patrimonial politics is crucial to the construction of modern states in both the incipient and the developed stages of the state. See Julia Adams, *The Familial State: Ruling Families and Merchant Capitalism in Early Modern Europe* (Ithaca, NY: Cornell University Press, 2005); Julia Adams and Mounira Maya Charrad, eds., *Patrimonial Power in the Modern World* (Los Angeles: SAGE, 2011).

22. Xueguang Zhou, *The Logic of Governance in China*; Ho-fung Hung, "Grandpa State Instead of Bourgeois State: Patrimonial Politics in China's Age of Commerce, 1644–1839," in *Patrimonial Capitalism and Empire*, ed. Mounira M. Charrad and Julia Adams, Political Power and Social Theory, vol. 28 (Bingley, UK: Emerald, 2015).

23. Wen-Hsuan Tsai and Chien-Wen Kou, "The Party's Disciples: CCP Reserve Cadres and the Perpetuation of a Resilient Authoritarian Regime," *China Quarterly* 221 (March 2015): 1–20.

24. Max Weber, in his essay *Politics as a Vocation*, defines politics as the pursuit for a portion of power or for influence over the division of power. Max Weber, *Politics as a Vocation* (Melbourne: Hassell Street, 2021).

25. Wu Xiaoling, "Practices and Explorations for Establishing Financial Market Order" [Chuangjian jinrong shichang zhixu de tansuo], in *Witness Major Reform Decisions: An Oral History of Reformers* [Jianzheng zhongda gaige juece: gaige qinlizhe zishu], ed. China Society of Economic Reform (Beijing: Social Sciences Literature, 2018), 571–84.

26. Lieberthal and Lampton, *Bureaucracy, Politics, and Decision Making*, 15.

27. Fu Mingxian and Zhang Huaiping, *Market Economy and Government Functions and Institutional Setup* [Shichang jingji yu zhengfu zhineng ji jigou shezhi] (Wuhan: Hubei People's, 1997), 47.

28. Interview with Chinese official, Beijing, June 15, 2014.

29. For an exemplary study of the coercive power of the Chinese state, see Wang Yuhua, "Coercive Capacity and the Durability of the Chinese Communist State," *Communist and Post-Communist Studies* 47, no. 1 (March 2014): 13–25.

30. Patrick Wilson, *Second-Hand Knowledge: An Inquiry Into Cognitive Authority* (Westport, CT: Greenwood, 1983); Leonard Seabrooke, "Epistemic Arbitrage: Transnational Professional Knowledge in Action," *Journal of Professions and Organization* 1, no. 1 (March 2014): 49–64.

31. For an excellent account of the neoliberal/economics turns of leftist parties in Europe and the United States, see Stephanie L. Mudge, *Leftism Reinvented: Western Parties*

from Socialism to Neoliberalism (Cambridge, MA: Harvard University Press, 2018); and Elizabeth Popp Berman, *Thinking Like an Economist: How Efficiency Replaced Equality in U.S. Public Policy* (Princeton, NJ: Princeton University Press, 2022). For a general account of the depoliticization of politics and the advancement of economics in public life, see David Harvey, *A Brief History of Neoliberalism* (Oxford: Oxford University Press, 2007); Xiaohong Xu, "The Great Separation: The Cultural Revolution and the Political Origins of Ordoeconomism in China" (paper presented at the annual meeting of the Association for Asian Studies, Honolulu, HI, March 2022); and Hui Wang and Christopher Connery, "Depoliticized Politics, Multiple Components of Hegemony, and the Eclipse of the Sixties," *Inter-Asia Cultural Studies* 7, no. 4 (December 2006): 683–700.

32. I use *generations* to divide the reform era into smaller periods in order to better present the data and track the change. Generations can be approximated by administration effect. An official belongs to generation 1 if their career reached elite level, defined as a vice ministerial ranking or above, in the Hu Yaobang/Zhao Ziyang administration (1981–1989); to generation 2 if elite in the Jiang Zemin/Zhu Rongji administration (1992–2002); to generation 3 if elite in the Hu Jintao/Wen Jibao administration (2002–2012); and to generation 4 if elite in the Xi Jinping/Li Keqiang administration (2012–2022).

33. Calculated by the author from officials' CVs.

34. Mark Blyth, *Great Transformations: Economic Ideas and Institutional Change in the Twentieth Century* (New York: Cambridge University Press, 2002), 11.

35. Bureaucracy that deals with nonuniform events is subject to increased levels of conflict. See Eugene Litwak, "Models of Bureaucracy Which Permit Conflict," *American Journal of Sociology* 67, no. 2 (September 1961): 177–84.

36. Zhou Xiaochuan, "Financial Reform Should Allow Trial and Error" [Jinrong gaige yinggai yunxu shicuo], *Securities Times* [Zhengquan shibao], November 19, 2012, http://money.sohu.com/20121119/n357973071.shtml.

37. Hugh D. Whittaker, Timothy Sturgeon, Toshie Okita, and Tianbiao Zhu, *Compressed Development: Time and Timing in Economic and Social Development* (Oxford: Oxford University Press, 2012).

38. On a corporate scale, Neil Fligstein also shows that managers with different career backgrounds advance different conceptions of corporate control. See Neil Fligstein, *The Transformation of Corporate Control* (Cambridge, MA: Harvard University Press, 1993).

39. See chapters 3 and 4.

40. Kimberly J. Morgan and Ann Shola Orloff, eds., *The Many Hands of the State: Theorizing Political Authority and Social Control* (New York: Cambridge University Press, 2017).

41. Pierre Bourdieu, *On the State: Lectures at the Collège de France, 1989–1992* (Cambridge: Polity, 2015); Loïc Wacquant, "Crafting the Neoliberal State: Workfare, Prisonfare, and Social Insecurity," *Sociological Forum* 25, no. 2 (June 2010): 197–220.

42. For examples of factionalist accounts of Chinese politics, see Andrew J. Nathan and Kellee S. Tsai, "Factionalism: A New Institutionalist Restatement," *China Journal* 34 (July 1995): 157–92; Lowell Dittmer and Yu-Shan Wu, "The Modernization of Factionalism in Chinese Politics," *World Politics* 47, no. 4 (July 1995): 467–94; and Tsou Tang, "Chinese Politics at the Top: Factionalism or Informal Politics? Balance-of-Power Politics or a Game to Win All?," *China Journal* 34 (July 1995): 95–156.

Fragmented bureaucracy and history can also preserve and give rise to islands of effectiveness in unlikely environments. For those in patrimonial and predatory states, see McDonnell, *Patchwork Leviathan*; and Michael Roll, ed., *The Politics of Public Sector Performance: Pockets of Effectiveness in Developing Countries* (London: Routledge, 2013).

43. In sociology, *social location* is a key concept for understanding how one's position in society influences their identity and view of the world. In this book, I use the idea of location to characterize the process of economic knowledge formation in terms of how one's social, institutional, and network positions shape one's economic ideas. For scholarship in a similar line of inquiry, see Emily Erikson, *Trade and Nation: How Companies and Politics Reshaped Economic Thought* (New York: Columbia University Press, 2021); Marion Fourcade, *Economists and Societies: Discipline and Profession in the United States, Britain, and France, 1890s to 1990s* (Princeton, NJ: Princeton University Press, 2010); and Simone Polillo, *The Ascent of Market Efficiency: Finance That Cannot Be Proven* (Ithaca, NY: Cornell University Press, 2020).

44. Kuhn, *The Structure of Scientific Revolutions*; Peter A. Hall, "Policy Paradigms, Social Learning, and the State: The Case of Economic Policymaking in Britain," *Comparative Politics* 25, no. 3 (April 1993): 275–96.

45. This phrase is part of the official discourse on how China's economic reform started and proceeded. See Dayang Wang, "The Origin of Crossing the River by Feeling for the Stones" [Mozhe shitou guohe de laili], *Study Times*, April 11, 2018, http://cpc .people.com.cn/n1/2018/0412/c69113-29921565.html.

46. Hall, "Policy Paradigms, Social Learning, and the State"; Peter A. Hall, *Governing the Economy: The Politics of State Intervention in Britain and France* (Cambridge: Blackwell, 1986).

47. Scott Frickel and Neil Gross argue that institutional formations that were not traditionally characterized as social movements, such as scientific/intellectual movements, are similar in many respects to social movements and are constituted through organized collective action. I make similar observations in this book in characterizing bureaucratic movements. See Scott Frickel and Neil Gross, "A General Theory of Scientific/Intellectual Movements," *American Sociological Review* 70, no. 2 (April 2015): 204–32.

48. For a comprehensive account of the kinds of structural opportunities and constraints China faced in the reform era, refer to Ho-fung Hung, *The China Boom: Why China Will Not Rule the World* (New York: Columbia University Press, 2015).

49. Richard Kraus and Reeve D. Vanneman, "Bureaucrats Versus the State in Capitalist and Socialist Regimes," *Comparative Studies in Society and History* 27, no. 1 (January 1985): 111–22.

1. THE SOCIALIST CIRCULATORS AND THE BUREAUCRATIC ORIGIN OF CHINA'S ECONOMIC REFORM

1. Calculated by the author from ministers' and vice ministers' CVs.

2. Lawrence King and Ivan Szelenyi, "Post-Communist Economic Systems," in *The Handbook of Economic Sociology*, ed. Neil J. Smelser and Richard Swedberg (Princeton, NJ: Princeton University Press, 2005), 205–32.

3. Susan L. Shirk, *The Political Logic of Economic Reform in China* (Berkeley: University of California Press, 1993); Raviprasad Narayanan, "The Politics of Reform in China: Deng, Jiang and Hu," *Strategic Analysis* 30, no. 2 (April 2006): 329–53; Tang Tsou, "Chinese Politics at the Top: Factionalism or Informal Politics? Balance-of-Power Politics or a Game to Win All?," *China Journal* 34 (July 1995): 95–156.

4. Barry Naughton, *Growing Out of the Plan: Chinese Economic Reform, 1978–1993* (Cambridge: Cambridge University Press, 1995); Justin Yifu Lin, *Demystifying the Chinese Economy* (Cambridge: Cambridge University Press, 2011); Bill Brugger, "Underdeveloped Socialism and Intensive Development," in *Chinese Marxism in Flux 1978–84: Essays on Epistemology, Ideology and Political Economy*, ed. Bill Brugger (London: Routledge, 2019).

5. Naughton, *Growing Out of the Plan*, 38–46.

6. Sebastian Heilmann and Elizabeth J. Perry, *Mao's Invisible Hand: The Political Foundations of Adaptive Governance in China* (Cambridge, MA: Harvard University Asia Center, 2011).

7. Xue Muqiao, *Memories of Xue Muqiao* [Xue muqiao huiyilu] (Tianjin: Tianjin People's Press, 2006).

8. National Archives Administration of China, *The Central Committee of the Communist Party of China in Xibaipo* [Zhonggong Zhongyang zai xibaipo] (Shenzhen: Haitian Publisher, 1998), 938.

9. Yao Jin, *100-Day Interviews of Yao Yilin* (Beijing: History of Chinese Communist Party Publishing, 2008), 185–86; Xue, *Memories of Xue Muqiao*, 132–33.

10. Xu Shan, "Xue Muqiao: The Red Currency Struggle" [Xue Muqiao: Hongse huobi zhanzheng], in *Oriental Outlook* [Dongfang liaowang zhoukan], August 24, 2009.

11. Chen Yun's Former Residence and Qingpu Revolution History Memorial Hall, eds., *Getting Close to Chen Yun: Oral History Museum Collection Catalog* [Zoujin Chenyun: koushu lishi guancang ziliao jilu] (Beijing: Central Literature Publishing, 2008), 117.

12. Zhang Zheng, Zhang Dasheng, and Wang Xiaokuan, eds., *Full Record of the Economic Development of the People's Republic of China* [Zhonghua renmin gongheguo jingji fazhan quanjilu], vol. 1 (Beijing: China Society Publishing, 2010), 273.

13. Examples include Yao, *100-Day Interviews of Yao Yilin* and Xue, *Memories of Xue Muqiao*.

14. David M. Bachman, *Chen Yun and the Chinese Political System* (Berkeley, CA: Institute of East Asian Studies, 1985), 36.

15. Bachman, *Chen Yun and the Chinese Political System*, 33.

16. Central Party Literature Press, *Biography of Li Xiannian (1949–1992)* [Lixiannian zhuan] (Beijing: Central Party Literature Press, 2009), 544.

17. Zou Huiqin, *The Study of Economic Thoughts of Li Xiannian* [Lixiannian jingji sixiang yanjiu] (Xining: Qinghai People's Press, 1993), 129–30; Xue, *Memories of Xue Muqiao*, 160.

18. Li Xiannian, "Activating Rural Markets" [Huoyue nongcun shichang], in *Li Xiannian on Public Finance, Banking, and Trade: 1950–1991* [Li Xiannian lun caizheng jinrong maoyi], vol. 2 (Beijing: China Financial & Economic Publishing, 1992), 143–47.

19. Bachman, *Chen Yun and the Chinese Political System*, 41. For example, as soon as the State Planning Commission was created in 1952, many of the ministries formally under the jurisdiction of the Central Finance and Economy Commission that Chen Yun headed were transferred to the commission.

20. For a thorough description of the features of China's mixed economy, see Tobias ten Brink, *China's Capitalism: A Paradoxical Route to Economic Prosperity*, trans. Carla Welch (Philadelphia: University of Pennsylvania Press, 2019).

21. Yao Yilin, "On the Work of Commerce (1957)" [Guanyu shangye gongzuo wenti], in *Selected Documents of Commerce and Economic Work* [Shangye jingji ziliao xuanbian], ed. Department of Management of Hangzhou School of Commerce (Hangzhou: Hangzhou College of Commerce Press, 1982), 21–22.

22. Central Party Literature Press, *Biography of Li Xiannian*, 535.

23. Jia Kang, Shi Wei, and Liu Cuiwei, "Li Xiannian's Thoughts on Comprehensive Balance" [Li Xiannian de zonghe pingheng caizheng sixiang], in *The History of Ideas on Public Finance in China* [Zhongguo caizheng sixiang shi] (Shanghai: Lixin Accounting Publishing, 2018), 74–86; Guan Mengjue, *The Economic Thoughts of Chen Yun* [Chenyun tongzhi de jingji sixiang] (Beijing: World Affair, 1984); Yuanxiu Pei, "The Formation and Development of the Comprehensive Balance Theory" [Zonghe pingheng lilun de xingcheng he fazhan], *Frontline* [Qianxian] 3 (1981): 54–57.

24. Li Xiannian, "Current Financial Situation and the Work of Banking, 1954" [Dangqian caizheng zhuangkuang he yinhang de gongzuo renwu], in *Li Xiannian on Public Finance, Banking, and Trade: 1950–1991* [Li Xiannian lun caizheng jinrong maoyi], vol. 2 (Beijing: China Financial & Economic Publishing, 1992), 33–42.

25. Li, "Activating Rural Markets."

26. Barry J. Naughton, *The Chinese Economy: Adaptation and Growth*, 2nd ed. (Cambridge, MA: MIT Press, 2018), 72.

27. Yao, "On the Work of Commerce," 22.

28. Li, "Current Financial Situation and the Work of Banking," 33–42.

29. Li, "Current Financial Situation and the Work of Banking."

30. Zhao Ziyang, *Prisoner of the State: The Secret Journal of Premier Zhao Ziyang*, ed. Bao Pu, Renee Chiang, and Adi Ignatius (New York: Simon & Schuster, 2010), 22.

31. Chen Lixu, "Chen Yun and Li Xiannian" [Chenyun yu lixiannian], *Century Elegance* [Shiji Fengcai] 3 (2014): 14–20.

32. Ivan Szelenyi and Eric Kostello, "The Market Transition Debate: Toward a Synthesis?," *American Journal of Sociology* 101, no. 4 (January 1996): 1084.

33. Bo Yibo, *A Memoir of Major Decisions and Events* [Ruogan zhongda juece yu shijian de huigu] (Beijing: History of Chinese Communist Party Publishing, 1991), 549–50.

34. Bachman, *Chen Yun and the Chinese Political System*, 43.

35. Dwight H. Perkins, "China's Economic Policy and Performance," in *The Cambridge History of China*, vol. 15, *The People's Republic*, part 2, *Revolutions Within the Chinese Revolution, 1966–1982*, ed. Roderick MacFarquhar and John K. Fairbank (Cambridge: Cambridge University Press, 1991), 478.

36. Bo, *A Memoir of Major Decisions and Events*, 489.

37. Bo, *A Memoir of Major Decisions and Events*, 78.

38. Li Jie and Yu Jundao, *Records of Mao Zedong (1945–1957)* [Shilu maozedong], vol. 3 (Beijing: Beijing Lianhe Publishing, 2018), 515.

39. There had been sober reflections by party elites on the suitability of the Soviet model for the Chinese reality. The possibility of decentralizing the allocation of resources and economic decision-making had been entertained even within the central economic bureaucracy. Now recast in the political radicalism of the GLF, decentralization was rolled out in an accelerated and uncoordinated fashion and blended

with other antiauthority elements. The deterioration of China's relationship with the Soviet Union played an important role in precipitating populist counterattacks. Because the end of Soviet assistance and the exodus of its experts from China made the previous plan to emulate Soviet planning even less feasible, Mao and his local allies explicitly suggested rejecting bureaucratic rigidity and central regulation and instead tapping into China's indigenous tradition of "walking the mass line" as a key resource and distinctive edge that China had for stimulating economic growth and catching up with the Soviet Union.

40. Bo, *A Memoir of Major Decisions and Events*, 465.

41. Harry Harding, *Organizing China: The Problem of Bureaucracy, 1949–1976* (Stanford, CA: Stanford University Press, 1968), 146.

42. Victor D. Lippit, "The Great Leap Forward Reconsidered," *Modern China* 1, no. 1 (January 1975): 92–115; Carl Riskin, *China's Political Economy: The Quest for Development Since 1949* (Oxford: Oxford University Press, 1987), 142.

43. The GLF also caused a severe subsistence crisis for great numbers of Chinese people, especially those in the countryside.

44. Gu Mu, *A Memoir of Gu Mu* [Gumu huiyil] (Beijing: Central Party Literature Press, 2009), 382.

45. Riskin, *China's Political Economy*, 201–18.

46. He Yaowu and Wu Li, *Documenting Sixty Years of State Affairs* [Liushinian guoshi jiyao] (Hunan: Hunan People's Press, 2009), 125.

47. At first, key industrial projects were shielded from the radicals' control. As Mao's health deteriorated and the radicals' struggle for power intensified, however, their reach extended beyond culture and ideology and made inroads in industrial sectors. Their intervention threatened the previously protected large industrial undertakings authorized by Mao himself, causing production and transportation to halt in the mid-1970s. See Gu, *A Memoir of Gu Mu*, 272–73.

48. Arunabh Ghosh, *Making It Count: Statistics and Statecraft in the Early People's Republic of China* (Princeton, NJ: Princeton University Press, 2020).

49. The national movement of "learning from Dazhai in agriculture" in the 1960s was a prime case in point. This campaign urged people from various regions across China to emulate the farmers of Dazhai village in Shanxi, inspiring them to embrace self-sacrifice and engage in principled political endeavors.

50. The fact that those who fell from power amid factional struggles in Mao's China were rarely killed speaks to another key difference between Stalin's Soviet Union and Mao's China. Chinese political losers were mostly sidelined and reeducated, often with their original political ranking preserved. Retrospectively, we know that this way of preserving the elites made possible China's incumbent-led economic reform. Yet the preceding analysis shows that a reversed causality may also be true: that cyclical economic crises reserved a role for the circulators, who established their initial authority in economic policy precisely because they were able to stem inflation and restore macroeconomic stability. By rationalizing and retrenching the economy, the circulators were able to claw back some of their lost authority or, at a minimum, to prove their remaining worth in moments of exception—with the populists' grudging acknowledgment.

51. Naughton, *The Chinese Economy*, 83.

52. Gu, *A Memoir of Gu Mu*, 229, 232.

53. Naughton, *The Chinese Economy*, 69.

54. Yu Qiuli, director of the State Planning Commission (1975–1980), had a background in heavy industries and openly clashed with Gu Mu and Li Xiannian on the need to scale down investment and readjust the economy. See Central Party Literature Press, *Biography of Li Xiannian*, 1086.

55. "Li Xiannian's Speech in Chicago" [Lixiannian zai zhijiage de yanjiang], *People's Daily* [Renmin ribao], July 27, 1985; Christopher Marquis and Kunyuan Qiao, in their book *Mao and Markets: The Communist Roots of Chinese Enterprises* (New Haven, CT: Yale University Press, 2022), find yet another connection between the socialist era and the reform era economies: Maoist ideology was imprinted on the careers and worldviews of the private entrepreneurs as well.

56. Bachman, *Chen Yun and the Chinese Political System*, 130; for example, since 1957 Li Xiannian had played a role of publicizing Chen's three balance theory and also had added his own extensions.

57. J. M. Montias, "Planning with Material Balances in Soviet-Type Economies," *American Economic Review* 49, no. 5 (December 1959): 963–85.

58. Perkins, "China's Economic Policy and Performance," 490.

59. Brugger, "Underdeveloped Socialism and Intensive Development."

60. The circulators avoided becoming merely the implementing force for their Soviet masters, protecting themselves from losing their autonomy.

61. Chen Yun, "Several Explanations of the First Five Year Plan (06/30/1954)" [Guanyu diyige wunianjihua de jidian shuoming], in *Selected Manuscripts of Chen Yun (1949–1956)* [Chenyun wengao xuanbian] (Hubei: Renmin, 1982).

62. Central Party Literature Press, *Biography of Li Xiannian*, 530.

63. Cao Yingwang, *Founding Commander-in-Chief of Economics and Finance Chen Yun* [Kaiguo jingji tongshuia chenyun] (Beijing: China Translation and Publishing, 2015), 245.

64. Bo, *A Memoir of Major Decisions and Events*, 155.

2. BALANCED DEVELOPMENT OR DECENTRALIZED GROWTH?
ELITE REFORMERS IN THE 1980S

1. The availability of public materials on elite reformers' economic views impacted the design of this study in two ways: first, not all officials commented on economic issues to the same degree; second, they discussed economic policy with varying specificities. As a result, information of elite reformers' positions on certain policies is simply not obtainable. Even if officials do convey opinions on policies, some supported them with detailed reasoning, while others didn't. Yet this inevitable limitation is less of a problem if the volume of the available materials on certain officials matches their importance in economic debates and if those who had large stakes in the direction of economic reform were also more expressive and explanatory. The fact that figures such as Zhao Ziyang and Chen Yun left behind voluminous writings on economic issues, for example, largely confirms this. In other words, those who wrote and talked more were also those who had greater influence on reform policies.

2. The fact that the group of local generalists was led by the president and the premier did not automatically guarantee their victory in battle with the central specialists.

Centralists Chen Yun, Li Xiannian, and Bo Yibo were founding revolutionaries of the People's Republic of China and enjoyed supreme political status in the party, on par with the newly selected president and premiers.

3. David M. Bachman, *Chen Yun and the Chinese Political System* (Berkeley, CA: Institute of East Asian Studies, 1985); Chen Yun, *Selected Works of Chen Yun* [Chen Yun Wenxuan] (Beijing: People's Press, 1995); Zhang Jincai, "Chen Yun and the Transformation of Central Leading Organizations on Economics and Finance" [Chenyun yu Zhongyang caijing lingdao jigou de bianqian], *Beijing Party History* 1 (2013): 24–28; Central Party Literature Press, *Biography of Li Xiannian (1949–1992)* [Lixiannian zhuan] (Beijing: Central Party Literature Press, 2009); Zou Huiqin, *The Study of Economic Thoughts of Li Xiannian* [Lixiannian jingji sixiang yanjiu] (Xining: Qinghai People's Press, 1993); Yao Jin, *100-Day Interviews of Yao Yilin* (Beijing: History of Chinese Communist Party Publishing, 2008).

4. Xue Muqiao, *Memoirs of Xue Muqiao* [Xuemuqiao huiyilu] (Tianjin: Tianjin People's Press, 2006), 186.

5. Franz Schurmann, *Ideology and Organization in Communist China* (Berkeley: University of California Press, 1969).

6. Gu Mu, *A Memoir of Gu Mu* [Gumu huiyil] (Beijing: Central Party Literature Press, 2009), 170.

7. Cheng Zhongxuan, "My Years of Serving as a Secretary at the Guangdong Provincial Party Committee," *China Through the Ages* 4 (2013): 15–21.

8. Zhao Ziyang, *The Course of Reform* (Hong Kong: Century Publisher, 2009), 113.

9. Wan Li, "Further Develop New Agriculture," news release of Xinhua Press no. 4712, 1982.

10. Wan, "Further Develop New Agriculture."

11. Victor Shih, *Factions and Finance in China: Elite Conflict and Inflation* (Cambridge: Cambridge University Press, 2009).

12. I chose those materials that documented official activities as exhaustively as possible, including newspaper reports (e.g., *People's Daily*) and chronicles (e.g., *Chronicles of Chen Yun*).

13. Zhao Ziyang, *Collected Works of Zhao Ziyang* [Zhao Ziyang wenxuan], vol. 1 (Hong Kong: Chinese University of Hong Kong Press, 2016), 253.

14. Tian Jiyun, "Hu Yaobang in Our Hearts" [Women xinzhong de Hu Yaobang], *China Through the Ages* 11 (2015): 13–14.

15. Wu Guoyou, "To Look at the Practical Characteristics of Chen Yun's Idea of 'Seek Truth from Facts' from an Economic Perspective" [Cong jingji shijiao kan Chen Yun shishiqiushi sixiang de shijian tedian], in *Chen Yun and Contemporary China* [Chenyun yu dangdai zhongguo], ed. Zhu Jiamu (Beijing: Contemporary China Publishing, 2010), 360.

16. Yang Mingwei, *Late Years of Chen Yun* [Chen yun wannian suiyue] (Beijing: People's Press, 2005), 115–16.

17. Yuan Baohua, "Industrial Census Is an Important Part of Four Modernizations" [Gongye pucha shi sihuajianshe de yixiang zhongyao jichu gongzuo], in *Economic Works of Yuan Baohua* [Yuan Baohua Jingji Wenji] (Beijing: China Economic Press, 1991).

18. Yao Yilin, "Statistics Is the Basis for Making Policies" [Tongji shi zhiding zhengce de zhuyao yiju], *Jingjixue Wenzhai* 4 (1984): 54–55.

19. Liu Hong, *The 1980s: The Glories and Dreams of Chinese Economists* [Bashi niandai zhongguo jingjixueren de guangrong yu mengxiang] (Nanning: Guangxi Normal University Press, 2010), 60.
20. Chen, *Selected Works of Chen Yun*, 337.
21. Yang, *Late Years of Chen Yun*, 151.
22. In terms of political power and professional authority, they were at least on par with the president and premier. In addition, Deng was well-known for his leadership style, which involved "robust action"; he also balanced competing views and refrained from issuing premature verdicts. See Ezra F. Vogel, *Deng Xiaoping and the Transformation of China* (Cambridge, MA: Belknap Press of Harvard University Press, 2013); John F. Padgett, "The Politics of Communist Economic Reform: Soviet Union and China," in *The Emergence of Organizations and Markets*, ed. John F. Padgett and Walter W. Powell (Princeton, NJ: Princeton University Press, 2012), 271–315.
23. Zhao, *Collected Works of Zhao Ziyang*, 253.
24. Guan Shan, "Ren Zhongyi on Deng Xiaoping and Guangdong's Reform and Open Up," *China Through the Ages* 8 (2004): 8–17.
25. Barry Naughton, *Growing Out of the Plan: Chinese Economic Reform, 1978–1993* (Cambridge: Cambridge University Press, 1996).
26. Lawrence Lau, Yingyi Qian, and Gerald Roland, "Reform Without Losers: An Interpretation of China's Dual-Track Approach to Transition," *Journal of Political Economy* 108, no. 1 (February 2000): 120–43.
27. Wu Jinglian and Ma Guochuan, "The Role of the 'Dual-Track' System and Its Consequences," in *Whither China? Restarting the Reform Agenda*, trans. Xiaofeng Hua and Nancy Hearst (New York: Oxford University Press, 2016), 120–34.
28. Yingyi Qian, "The Process of China's Market Transition: The Evolutionary, Historical, and Comparative Perspectives," in *China's Deep Reform: Domestic Politics in Transition*, ed. Lowell Dittmer and Guoli Liu (Lanham, MD: Rowman & Littlefield, 2006), 233.
29. Naughton, *Growing Out of the Plan*; Qian, "The Process of China's Market Transition."
30. Lowell Dittmer, "China in 1988: The Continuing Dilemma of Socialist Reform," *Asian Survey* 29, no. 1 (January 1989): 12–28.
31. James T. Myers, "China: Modernization and 'Unhealthy Tendencies,'" *Comparative Politics* 21, no. 2 (January 1989): 193–213.
32. Hu Deping, *Why Did China Need to Reform? In Memory of My Father Hu Yaobang* [Zhongguo weishenme xuyao gaige: siyi fuqin Hu Yaobang] (Beijing: People's Press, 2011), 41–42.
33. Chen Yun, "On the Relationship Between Planning and Market" [Jihua yu shichang wenti], *Macroeconomic Research* [Hongguan jingji yanjiu] 32 (1982): 2–4.
34. Song Ping, "The Speech of Comrade Song Ping on the Opening Ceremony of the National Conference of Macroeconomic Management" [Songping tongzhi zai quanguo hongguan jingji guanli wenti yantaohui kaimushi shang de jianghua], *Planned Economy Research* [Jihua jingji yanjiu] 9 (1986): 3–7; Yao Yilin, *One-Hundred Nights Conversation with Yao Yilin* [Yao Yilin baixitan] (Beijing: History of Chinese Communist Party Publishing, 1988), 466.
35. Liao Jili, "On the Question of Efficiency, Proportion and Speed" [Tantan xiaoyi bili he sudu wenti], *National Economic Planning and Management* [Guomin jingji jihua yu guanli] 7 (1983): 17–23.

36. Shih, *Factions and Finance in China*, 115; Zhao, *The Course of Reform*, 152; Tian Jiyun, *The Great Practice of Reform and Open-Up* (Beijing: Xinhua, 2009), 335–39.

37. Ezra F. Vogel, *One Step Ahead in China: Guangdong Under Reform* (Cambridge, MA: Harvard University Press, 1990), 1712.

38. Justin Yifu Lin, Tao Ran, and Liu Mingxing, "Decentralization and Local Governance in China's Economic Transition" (paper prepared for the conference "The Rise of Local Governments in Developing Countries," London School of Economics, May 2003).

39. A search in the Duxiu Database of Publications yielded 163 articles that applied the circulators' balance theory from 1981 to 1989, reflecting its broad influence on economic thinking in this period.

40. Isabella M. Weber, *How China Escaped Shock Therapy* (Abingdon, UK: Routledge, 2021), 240.

41. Party Documents Research of the Central Committee of CCP, "Around the Breakthrough of Price Liberalization in 1988," *China Through the Ages* 10 (2005): 22–25. Chen Yun and Li Xianian had retired from their formal positions, but they exerted influence through informal channels. See Weber, *How China Escaped Shock Therapy*, 230.

42. Vogel, *Deng Xiaoping and the Transformation of China*, 451.

43. Central Committee of the Chinese Communist Party, "A Summary of the Guangdong, Fujian Provincial Discussion Meeting" [Guangdong, Fujian liangsheng zuotanhui jiyao], in *Compilation of Important Documents Since the Third Plenum of the 11th Central Committee* [San Zhong Quanhui Yilai ZhongyaoWenxian xuanibian], ed. Document Research Center of CCP CC, vol. 3 (Beijing: People's Publisher [Renmin chubanshe], 1986), 1169–83.

44. Zhao Ziyang, *Prisoner of the State: The Secret Journal of Zhao Ziyang*, ed. Bao Pu, Renee Chiang, and Adi Ignatius (New York: Simon & Schuster, 2009), 98, 146; Hu, *Why Did China Need to Reform?*, 42.

45. Wu, "To Look at the Practical Characteristics of Chen Yun's Idea," 144.

46. Zhu Jiamu, *A Biographical Chronicle of Chen Yun* [Chen Yun nianpu] (Beijing: Central Party Literature Press, 2000), 342.

3. THE RISE OF TECHNOCRATS: MARKET RATIONALIZATION AND THE MACROCONTROL PARADIGM

1. These include the Ministry of Metallurgical Industry, the Ministry of Chemical Industry, and the Ministry of Petroleum Industry, among a dozen others.

2. Chen Jinhua, *Memories of the Eventful Years* [Guoshi yishu] (Beijing: History of Chinese Communist Party Publishing, 2005), 328.

3. Zhang Yanning gave the example of the merger of the Machinery Commission into the System Reform Commission (which oversaw nonindustrial matters), which took place simply because the commissioner of the former agency received a new job assignment in the latter. See Zhang Yanning, "Experience of the Decision-Making Process of State-Owned Enterprise Reform" [Qinli guoyou qiye gaige de juece guocheng], in *Witness Major Reform Decisions: An Oral History of Reformers* [Jianzheng zhongda gaige juece: gaige qinlizhe zishu], ed. China Society of Economic Reform (Beijing: Social Sciences Academic, 2018), 241–51.

4. People-based coordination was not an optimal substitute for institutional coordination. It was said that factional struggles and interpersonal grudges stemming from the ten-year Cultural Revolution left a "social minefield" in the bureaucracy, where officials had relationships of gratitude or enmity with one another depending on how they were treated by the same people in the years of political turmoil. See Yuan Baohua, *A Memoir of Yuan Baohua* (Beijing: People's University Press, 2008), 328.

5. Joseph Fewsmith, *Dilemmas of Reform in China: Political Conflict and Economic Debate* (Armonk, NY: Routledge, 1994), 15.

6. Julian Gewirtz, *Unlikely Partners: Chinese Reformers, Western Economists, and the Making of Global China* (Cambridge, MA: Harvard University Press, 2017).

7. See, for example, Carol Lee Hamrin, *China and the Challenge of the Future: Changing Political Patterns* (New York: Routledge, 2019), 7.

8. Miguel Centeno, *Democracy Within Reason: Technocratic Revolution in Mexico* (University Park: Pennsylvania State University Press, 1997), 36.

9. Li Cheng and Lynn White, "The Fifteenth Central Committee of the Chinese Communist Party: Full-Fledged Technocratic Leadership with Partial Control by Jiang Zemin," *Asian Survey* 38, no. 3 (March 1998): 231–64.

10. Joel Andreas, *Rise of the Red Engineers: The Cultural Revolution and the Origins of China's New Class* (Stanford, CA: Stanford University Press, 2009).

11. Li Cheng, *China's Leaders: The New Generation* (Lanham, MD: Rowman & Littlefield, 2001), 9.

12. Deng Xiaoping, "The Urgent Task Facing the Third Generation of Leadership" [Disandai lingdao jiti de dangwuzhiji], in *Selected Works of Deng Xiaoping* [Deng Xiaoping Wenxuan], vol. 3 (Beijing: People's Press, 1994), 309–14.

13. Xiao Gongqin, "China's Changing of the Guard: The Rise of the Technocrats," *Journal of Democracy* 14, no. 1 (January 2003): 60–65.

14. David Shambaugh, "The Dynamics of Elite Politics During the Jiang Era," *China Journal* 45 (January 2001): 101–11.

15. David Bachman, "The Paradox of Analyzing Elite Politics Under Jiang," *China Journal* 45 (January 2001): 95–100.

16. Robert Lawrence Kuhn, *The Man Who Changed China: The Life and Legacy of Jiang Zemin* (Shanghai: Shanghai Translation Publishing, 2004).

17. Yu Yiqing, "How Deng Xiaoping Resisted Oppositions and Promoted 'Dark Horse' Zhu Rongji" [Deng Xiaoping Ruhe Lipai Zhongyi Fuzhi Heima Zhu Rongji], 2015, http://politics.people.com.cn/n/2014/1121/c1001-26067334.html. See also Laurence J. Brahm, *Zhu Rongji and the Transformation of Modern China* (Singapore: Wiley, 2003), xxix.

18. Li Peng, *Memories of Li Peng* [Lipeng huiyilu] (Beijing: China Electric Power, 2014); Victor Shih, *Factions and Finance in China: Elite Conflict and Inflation* (Cambridge: Cambridge University Press, 2009), 68, 91.

19. Zhu Rongji, *Zhu Rongji Meets the Press* [Zhu rongji jianghua shilu] (Beijing: People's Press, 2011), 354.

20. Interview with Chinese official, Beijing, June 22, 2012.

21. John L. Campbell, "Institutional Analysis and the Role of Ideas in Political Economy," in *The Rise of Neoliberalism and Institutional Analysis*, ed. John L. Campbell and O. K. Pedersen (Princeton, NJ: Princeton University Press, 2001); Peter A. Hall, "Policy Paradigms, Social Learning, and the State: The Case of Economic Policymaking in Britain," *Comparative Politics* 25, no. 3 (April 1993): 275–96.

22. Deng's speech on December 24, 1990, "Seize the Opportunity to Develop the Economy" [Shanyu liyong shiji jiejue fazhan wenti], in Deng Xiaoping, *Selected Works of Deng Xiaoping* [Deng Xiaoping wenxuan], vol. 3 (Beijing: People's Press, 1993), 364.

23. Deng's speeches from January 18 to February 21, 1992. "Excerpts from Talks Given in Wuchang, Shenzhen, Zhuhai, Shanghai" [Zai Wuchang Shenzhen Zhuhai Shanghai dengdi de tanhua yaodian], in Deng Xiaoping, *Selected Works of Deng Xiaoping* [Deng Xiaoping wenxuan], vol. 3 (Beijing: People's Press, 1993), 373, 377.

24. Li Peng, *Market and Control: Economic Diary of Li Peng* [Shichang he tiaokong Li Peng jingji riji] (Beijing: Xinhua, 2007), 828; Jiang Zemin, *Selected Works of Jiang Zemin* [Jiang Zemin wenxuan] (Beijing: People's Press, 2006), 162.

25. Guo Shuqing, "A Series of Symposiums in 1991 to Discuss the Foals of Economic System Reform" [Huiyi 1991nian taolun jingjitizhi gaige mubiao de xilie zuotanhui], in *Jiangzemin and the Proposition of the Socialist Market Economy System* [Jiang Zemin he Shehuizhuyi Shichang Jingji de tichu], ed. Chen Jun and Hong Nan (Beijing: Central Party Literature Press, 2012), 72; Zhou Xiaochuan, "The Historical Significance of the 14th National Congress in Establishing a Socialist Market Economy as the Goal of Systemic Reform" [Shisida queli shuihuizhuyi shichangjingji wei tizhi gaige mubiao de lishi yiyi], in *Jiangzemin and the Proposition of the Socialist Market Economy System* [Jiang Zemin he Shehuizhuyi Shichang Jingji de tichu], ed. Chen Jun and Hong Nan (Beijing: Central Party Literature Press, 2012), 59.

26. Jiang Chunze, "An Internal Report on the Question of Planning and Market" [Guanyu shichang he jihua de yifen neibu baogao], *China Through the Ages* [Yanhuang chunqiu] 3 (2013): 13.

27. Chen Jun and Hong Nan, eds., *Jiangzemin and the Proposition of the Socialist Market Economy System* [Jiang Zemin he Shehuizhuyi Shichang Jingji de tichu] (Beijing: Central Party Literature Press, 2012).

28. Jiang Chunze, "The Birth of the Socialist Market Economy" [Shehuizhuyi shichangjingji de dansheng], *Shenzhen Commercial News*, August 2009.

29. Early on, Premier Li took a backseat in economic policy, citing health reasons. Vice Premier Zhu was de facto in charge of the day-to-day operation of the economic administration. His approach to learning had an outsized impact on policy practices.

30. Zhu, *Zhu Rongji Meets the Press*, 338.

31. Guo Shuqing, *The Transformation of the Model and the Transformed Model* [Moshi de biange he biange de moshi] (Shanghai: SDX Joint Publishing, 1989); Barry Sautman, "Sirens of the Strongman: Neo-Authoritarianism in Recent Chinese Political Theory," *China Quarterly* 129 (March 1992): 72–102.

32. Liu Hong, *The 1980s: The Glories and Dreams of Chinese Economists* [Bashi niandai zhongguo jingjixueren de guangrong yu mengxiang] (Nanning: Guangxi Normal University Press, 2010).

33. Chen and Nan, *Jiangzemin and the Proposition of the Socialist Market Economy System*, 72.

34. Inspection Team of Market Management to South Korea, "Introduction to the Macroeconomic System in South Korea" [Nanchaoxian hongguan jingjitizhi jieshao], *Internal Reference of Economic System Reform* 9 (1990): 38–47.

35. India was a curious case. It was rarely mentioned but was worthy of an exclusive trip by the vice director of the System Reform Commission to obtain firsthand knowledge of the role of the Indian state in the economy. The vice director reported

that even in the heyday of the planning era, Indian SOEs seldom received specific production plans but rather negotiated with industrial ministries to hammer out nonbinding "memos." Furthermore, he concluded that since the 1980s, the Indian government had refrained from directly undertaking construction projects and focused on managing the overall economy. Administrative intervention had been giving way to fiscal, credit, and exchange rate policies—that is, market levers. He Gu, "Report on India's Economic System" [Guanyu yindu jingjixitong de baogao], *Internal Reference of Economic System Reform* 12 (1990): 42–46.

36. The Italian and French governments ran their remaining SOEs according to the principle of separating ownership from control, providing another set of prime examples. The exercise of state ownership via state holding companies in Italy triggered particular interest in the idea that instead of intervening, the state could actually participate in the market.

37. Top leaders received distinguished guests at those meetings. Premier Li Peng met the vice president of the World Bank Attila Karaosmanoglu in 1990. Karaosmanoglu responded positively to Li's request to resume the bank's loans to China.

38. F. F. Ridley, "French Technocracy and Comparative Government," *Political Studies* 14, no. 1 (1966): 34–52.

39. Xiang Huaicheng, "Witness Fiscal System Reform" [Jianzheng caizheng tizhi gaige], in *Witness Major Reform Decisions: An Oral History of Reformers* [Jianzheng zhongda gaige juece: gaige qinlizhe zishu], ed. China Society of Economic Reform (Beijing: Social Sciences Academic, 2018), 517.

40. Xiang, "Witness Fiscal System Reform."

41. Zhu, *Zhu Rongji Meets the Press*, 365.

42. Central taxes, for example, would cover those tax categories that safeguarded national interests and implemented macrocontrol. Tax revenues generated by economic activities such as value-added taxes were to be shared between the central and local governments based on a 70/30 ratio. Tax revenues closely aligned with local jurisdictions, such as those generated by land and agricultural activities, were claimed by the local governments. See "Decision of the State Council on Implementing the Tax Sharing System and Financial Management System" [Guanyu shixing fenshuizhi caizheng guanli tizhi de jueding], December 1993, issued by the State Council.

43. Ministry of Finance, "The Framework of the Current Tax-Sharing Fiscal System" [Xianxing fenshuizhi caizheng tizhi kuangjia], May 14, 2014, http://www.mof.gov.cn /zhuantihuigu/czjbqk1/jbqk2/201405/t20140504_1074657.htm.

44. Xiang, "Witness Fiscal System Reform," 518.

45. Jiang Yonghua, "Experiencing Tax-Sharing Reform" [Qinli fenshuizhi gaige], in *Witness Major Reform Decisions: An Oral History of Reformers* [Jianzheng zhongda gaige juece: gaige qinlizhe zishu], ed. China Society of Economic Reform (Beijing: Social Sciences Academic, 2018), 535.

46. Interview with Chinese official, Beijing, June 21, 2013.

47. Xu Shanda, "Background and Decision-Making Process of the 1994 Tax Sharing Reform" [1994nian caizheng gaige de beijing he juece guocheng], in *Witness Major Reform Decisions: An Oral History of Reformers* [Jianzheng zhongda gaige juece: gaige qinlizhe zishu], ed. China Society of Economic Reform (Beijing: Social Sciences Academic, 2018), 555.

48. Brahm, *Zhu Rongji and the Transformation of Modern China*, 14–15.
49. Zhu Rongji's speech at the National Economic Work Conference in 1993.
50. Barry J. Naughton, *The Chinese Economy: Adaptation and Growth*, 2nd ed. (Cambridge, MA: MIT Press, 2018), 103.
51. Wu Xiaoling, "Practices and Explorations for Establishing Financial Market Order" [Chuangjian jinrong shichang zhixu de tansuo], in *Witness Major Reform Decisions: An Oral History of Reformers* [Jianzheng zhongda gaige juece: gaige qinlizhe zishu], ed. China Society of Economic Reform (Beijing: Social Sciences Academic, 2018), 573; Zhu, *Zhu Rongji Meets the Press*.
52. Stephen Bell and Hui Feng, *The Rise of the People's Bank of China: The Politics of Institutional Change* (Cambridge, MA: Harvard University Press, 2013), 76.
53. Bell and Feng, *The Rise of the People's Bank of China*, 182
54. See Dali Yang, *Remaking the Chinese Leviathan: Market Transition and the Politics of Governance in China* (Stanford, CA: Stanford University Press, 2004). After deliberating on whether China should also encourage mixed operations in financial industries and thus a synthesized framework of financial supervision, Zhu controversially vetoed this proposal and argued that "mixed operations will absolutely bring chaos." See the speech by Lou Jiwei, "The Chairman of the National Social Security Fund, Lou Jiwei's Speech at the 16th High-Level Forum on Enterprise Development," January 28, 2018, Beijing, http://finance.sina.com.cn/china/gncj/2018-01-30/doc-ifyqyqni5050209.shtml.
55. Zhu, *Zhu Rongji Meets the Press*, 482.
56. Isaac Ariail Reed, "Power: Relational, Discursive, and Performative Dimensions," *Sociological Theory* 31, no. 3 (October 2013): 193–218.
57. Brahm, *Zhu Rongji and the Transformation of Modern China*, 19–28.
58. Zhu, *Zhu Rongji Meets the Press*, 374.
59. The idea of macrocontrol was not an invention of the post-Tiananmen era. In the 1980s, young economists and think-tank researchers floated this idea when rethinking the appropriate role for the Chinese state in a market economy. During the groundbreaking Mogan Mountain meeting in 1984, much touted in the field of economics, young thinkers had the ears of officials and raised and discussed the idea of macrocontrol. Yet as I have explained, the bureaucratic condition in which macrocontrol could take root simply did not exist in the 1980s. It was an era in which reform was largely micro in its approach. The focus was on remodeling on-the-ground market participants such as enterprises and local governments and on working to unleash the economic incentives of producers and consumers. Microreform squeezed the space for thinking macroeconomically.
60. Fed Hu, "Zhu Rongji's Decade," *Wall Street Journal*, March 10, 2003.
61. Zhu, *Zhu Rongji Meets the Press*, 409.
62. Zhu, *Zhu Rongji Meets the Press*, 409.
63. Zeng Peiyan, *Zeng Peiyan on Development and Reform* [Zeng peiyan lun fazhan yu gaige], vol. 1 (Beijing: People's Press, 2014), 488.
64. Pierre Bourdieu, *Distinction* (London: Routledge, 1986).
65. The room for ministries to exercise agency in this field-style economic bureaucracy expanded with a new system of coordination installed among the ministries. Ministries that had once submitted policy proposals to the State Council could now proceed without having to coordinate with other agencies in advance, even if the policy

255

propositions they submitted directly implicated the cooperation of other agencies or associated changes in their policies. As a result, state councilors had to busy themselves with negotiating with the implicated agencies. Starting in 2000, Zhu implemented a ministry responsibility system, in which one ministry was expected to take the lead (*qiantou*) to negotiate with other agencies and have them sign onto the proposals prior to reporting to the State Council. The resultant decrease in the bureaucratic burden was apparent to the State Council. To the ministries, the absence of top-down authorization injected uncertainties into interagency relations, raising questions as to which ministries should be the leading agencies (*qiantou bumen*) and whether they had the authority to get other departments on board. The ministry responsibility system thus was poised to augment the autonomy of individual ministries while also intensifying the competition for authority.

66. Cheng, *China's Leaders*.
67. See Dali Yang, "Economic Transformation and State Rebuilding in China," in *Holding China Together: Diversity and National Integration in the Post-Deng Era*, ed. Barry J. Naughton and Dali L. Yang (New York: Cambridge University Press, 2004).
68. Calculated by the author from *China Finance Yearbook* [Zhongguo caizheng nianjian] (Beijing: China State Finance Magazine, 1994–2009).
69. Qu Jingdong, "The Project System: A New Form of State Governance" [Xiangmuzhi: yizhong xin de guojia zhili tizhi], *Social Sciences in China* 33, no. 4 (2012): 28–47.
70. Asian Development Bank, "Challenges and Opportunities in China's Local Finance Management" [Zhongguo caizheng difang guanli de tiaozhan he jiyu], 2014, Mandaluyong, Philippines, ADB, https://www.adb.org/zh/publications/local-public-finance -management-peoples-republic-china-challenges-and-opportunities-zh.

4. NATIONAL CHAMPIONS AND THE ORGANIZATIONAL APPROACH TO ENTERPRISES AND MARKETS

1. "Bulletin of the Fourth Economic Census," 2018, http://www.stats.gov.cn/zt_18555 /zdtjgz/zgjjpc/d4cjjpc_19207/.
2. In the 1980s, Chinese scholars and officials showed interest in enterprise reforms undertaken by fellow socialist countries. A considerable gap remained between theory and practice. Enterprise reform experiments in China in the 1980s traced their origins to indigenous inventions rather than emulation. It was precisely the mixed outcomes generated by enterprise reforms in Eastern Europe that led the Chinese reformers to choose their own path. As soon as post-Communist transitions showed signs of distress around 1995, Chinese reformers and economists alike immediately rejected shock therapies and radical privatization of SOEs as not being viable for China. For more details on intellectual exchanges between China and Eastern Europe, see Julian Gewirtz, *Unlikely Partners: Chinese Reformers, Western Economists, and the Making of Global China* (Cambridge, MA: Harvard University Press, 2017). For the articulation of a Chinese approach to SOE reform, see Wang Zhongyu, "Walk the Road of SOE Reform with Chinese Characteristics: Speech Excerpts of Wang Zhongyu at the 'International Symposium on Policy Choices of SOE Reform in China' " [Zou you zongguo tese de guoyouqiye gaige luzi: guojia jingmaowei zhuren wang zhongyu zai zhongguo guoyouqiye gaige zhengce xuanze

guoji yantaohui shang de fayanzhaiyao], *International Data and Information* [Guoji ziliao xinxi] 8 (1995): 8–10.

3. John F. Padgett, "The Politics of Communist Economic Reform: Soviet Union and China," in *The Emergence of Organizations and Markets*, ed. John F. Padgett and Walter W. Powell (Princeton, NJ: Princeton University Press, 2012), 271–315.

4. Monica C. Higgins and Edgar H. Schein, *Career Imprints: Creating Leaders Across an Industry* (San Francisco: Jossey-Bass, 2005); Christopher Marquis and András Tilcsik, "Imprinting: Toward a Multilevel Theory," *Academy of Management Annals* 7, no. 1 (June 2003): 195–245.

5. See, for example, Zhang Dicheng, *The Chronicle of State-Owned Enterprise Reform (1978–2005)* [Zhongguo guoyouqiye gaige biannianshi] (Beijing: Zhongguo Gongren, 2006).

6. Dylan Sutherland, *China's Large Enterprises and the Challenge of Late Industrialization* (London: Routledge, 2003), 42.

7. Interview with Chinese official, Beijing, July 22, 2013.

8. Chen Jian, *Corporate Governance in China* (London: Routledge, 2004), 125.

9. Xu Penghang, "To Develop Horizontal Linkages and Speed Up Economic Development of Huangshi" [Jiakuai huangshi jiangji fazhan bufa], *Study and Practice* [Xuexi he shijian] 2 (1986): 18.

10. Wang Zhongyu, "Major Breakthroughs and Comprehensive Advancement: Thinking Enterprise Organizational Structure Adjustment from the Formation of Jihua Enterprise Group" [Zhongdian tupo quanmian tuijin: cong jihua jituan de xingcheng kan qiye zuzhijiegou tiaozheng de silu], *China Economic System Reform* [Zhongguo jingji tizhi gaige] 3 (1991): 31–32; Li Rongrong, "The Deepening of Industrial Structural Adjustment in Suzhou City" [Suzhoushi gongyejiegou tiaozheng gongzuo buduan shenhua], *Economic Work Newsletter* [Jingji gongzuo tongxun] 11 (1992): 19–21.

11. Zhang, *The Chronicle of State-Owned Enterprise Reform*, 159.

12. Wang, "Major Breakthroughs and Comprehensive Advancement."

13. Lin Zhaomu, "Correctly Implement the Strategy of Developing Enterprise Groups" [Zhengque shishi fazhan qiye jituan zhanlue], in "Forum on Implementing the Spirit of 15th National Congress of the Communist Party of China and Speed Up the Reform of State-Owned Enterprises: An Excerpt" [Luoshi shiwuda jingshen jiakuai guoyouqiye gaige zuotanhui fayan zhaideng], *Qiushi* 8 (1998): 11–12.

14. Sutherland, *China's Large Enterprises*, 42.

15. Wang, "Major Breakthroughs and Comprehensive Advancement," 32.

16. Wang, "Major Breakthroughs and Comprehensive Advancement."

17. Chen, *Corporate Governance in China*, 141.

18. Xu Penghang, "The Advantage of Huangshi and Economic Developmental Strategy" [Huangshi de yoush he jingji fazhan zhanlue], *Industrial Economy* [Gongye jingji] 5 (1985): 17–23; Li Lawang, "Actively Develop Horizontal Connections to Enhance Urban Vitality" [Jiji fazhan hengxiang lianxi zengqiang chengshi huoli], in *China Urban Economic and Social Yearbook* [Zhongguo chengshi shehui jingji nianjian] (Beijing: China Urban Yearbook, 1986), 967.

19. Chen, *Corporate Governance in China*, 125.

20. Sutherland, *China's Large Enterprises*, 47.

21. "Work Meeting on Adjusting Enterprise Organizational Structure" [Quansheng qiye zuzhi jiegou tiaozheng gongzuo huyi], in *Jilin Yearbook* [Jilin nianjian], ed. Jilin

Provincial Local History Compilation Committee (Changchun: Jilin, 1992), 115–16; Xu Penghang, "Strengthen the Research on Hubei Product Strategy" [Jiaqiang dui hubei chanpin zhanlue de yanjiu], *Decision-Making and Consultancy* [Zixun yu juece] 2 (1989): 4–8.

22. Zhao Weichen, *At the Forefront of Economic Reform* [Zai jingji gaige qianyan] (Beijing: Central Party Literature, 2010), 197.

23. Wang Zhongyu, *Tackling State-Owned Enterprise Reform* [Guoqi gaige gongjian jishi] (Beijing: Enterprise Management Publishing, 2010), 750.

24. Yang Changji, "Explanation on Compiling and Implementing the Outline of Economic Operation Adjustment and Control Program in 1995" [Guanyu bianzhi 1995nian jingji yunxing he tiaokong fangan gangyao de shuoming], *National Economic Management and Planning* [Guomin jingji guanli yu jihua] 4 (1995): 71–72.

25. Wang Zhongu, "On the Macro-Adjustment and Control System of Market Economy" [Lun shichang jingji de hongguan tiaokong tixi], *Journal of Technical Economics and Management* [Jishu jingji yu guanli] 3 (1994): 4–5.

26. Zhao, *At the Forefront of Economic Reform*, 192–93.

27. Wang, *Tackling State-Owned Enterprise Reform*, 245.

28. Wang Zhongyu, "On Understanding Several Issues of Current Enterprise Work" [Tan dangqian qiye gongzuo de jige renshi wenti], *China Market* [Zhongguo shichang] 6 (1996): 4–5.

29. Wang, *Tackling State-Owned Enterprise Reform*, 492.

30. Yang, "Explanation on Compiling and Implementing the Outline of Economic Operation Regulation and Control Program in 1995," 71.

31. Interview with Chinese official, Beijing, June 8, 2013.

32. Wang, *Tackling State-Owned Enterprise Reform*, 722.

33. Wang, *Tackling State-Owned Enterprise Reform*, 429.

34. Wu Xiaobo, *The Gains and Losses of Past Economic Reforms* [Lidai jingji gaige deshi] (Hangzhou: Zhejiang University Press, 2013), 218–21.

35. SETC Vice Director Jiang Qiangui argues that, for example, strategic investors who could take on SOEs had yet to be cultivated. See Jiang Qiangui and Zhang Chunlin, "Reasons for the Formation of State-Owned Enterprise Debt and the Progress of Debt Restructuring" [Guoyou qiye zhaiwu xingcheng de yuanyinhe zhaiwuchongzu de jinzhan], *Economic Affairs* [Jingjijie] 6 (1996): 20–23.

36. Guo Dongle, *Debates on Theories of Socialist Market Economy in China, 1992–1995* [Zhongguo shehuizhuyi shichang jingji lilun zhengming 1992–1995] (Beijing: China Wujia Publisher, 1996), 22.

37. "Notice Regarding Opinions on Deepening the Pilot Work of Large Enterprise Groups" [Guanyu shenhua daxing qiye jituan shodden gongzuo de yijian], issued by the State Council, SETC, and the System Reform Commission, April 29, 1997.

38. See Lin, "Correctly Implement the Strategy of Developing Enterprise Groups."

39. Chen Jinhua, *Memories of the Eventful Years* [Guoshi yishu] (Beijing: History of Chinese Communist Party Publishing, 2005), 271–75.

40. The SRC was left supervising the reform of small SOEs, which were largely to be privatized or made into joint stock companies, thus ending their time as a constituency of the SRC. The agency also sought to institute a shareholding system in SOEs. While this line of initiatives failed to pick up momentum during the tenure of the SRC, it gained ground after the forging of enterprise groups was completed.

258

41. SETC and PBOC coissued document 492 in 1996: "Notice on Several Issues in the Trial Implementation of the Merger and Bankruptcy of State-Owned Enterprises" [Guanyu shixing guoyou qiye jianbing pochan zhong ruogan wenti de tongzhi].
42. Wang, *Tackling State-Owned Enterprise Reform*, 914.
43. Chen Qingtai, *Optimizing Capital Structure: Pilot City Work Manual* [Youhua ziben jiegou chengshi shidian gongzuo shouce] (Beijing: China Economic Press, 1996).
44. New listings were rationed and highly sought after by large enterprises. See the case studies provided by Gao Shangquan and Yang Qixian, *State-Owned Enterprise Reform in China* [Zhongguo guoyou qiye gaige] (Jinan: Jinan Press, 1999), 296–310.
45. See National Bureau of Statistics, *Research on State-Owned Enterprise Reform and Hot Issues* [Guoyou qiye gaige ji redian wenti yanjiu] (Beijing: China Statistics Press, 2001), 160.
46. Statistics are from *Yearbook of Large Corporations of China* (Beijing: China Statistics Press, 2003) and *China Enterprise Group Yearbook* (Beijing: Xinhua, 2003).
47. In a well-documented merger case, upon the request of Zibo and Fushun, cities in Shandong Province, the SETC persuaded the Qilu Petrochemical Company, a provincial SOE that originally supplied raw materials to Zibo Petrochemical Factory and Fushun Petrochemical Factory, to take over these two city enterprises, which had seen their supply allotments constricted and were heavily indebted. SETC officials hosted five coordination meetings and also reported the issue to the State Council to pressure Qilu. Together the central and local parties hammered out a plan that eventually allayed Qilu's concern by offering interest-rate holidays and state-assisted recapitalization opportunities. The expanded Qilu Petrochemical Company lengthened its internal production chains and ended up being more profitable than it had been in the premerger period. See Gao and Yang, *State-Owned Enterprise Reform in China*. For similar SETC-assisted merger cases, see also Wang Dongjiang and Cao Yuanzheng, *Tackling SOE Reform: A Practical Guide on Building Modern Enterprise Institutions and Restructuring Assets* [Guoyou qiye gaige gongjian xiandai qiye zhidu yu zichan chongzu shiwu] (Beijing: Reform, 1998).
48. Instances of takeovers cutting across provincial boundaries had been on the rise since the late 1990s. See Chen, *Corporate Governance in China*, 142.
49. Chen, *Optimizing Capital Structure*.
50. Wang, "On Understanding Several Issues of Current Enterprise Work."
51. Xu Penghang, "Unleashing Our Own Advantages and Accelerating Asset Restructuring: Promote the Coordinated Development of Coastal and Inland Economies" [Fahui zishen youshi jiakuai zichan chongzu cujin yanhai neidi jingji xietiao fazhan], *Economic Work Newsletter* 10 (1996): 3–4.
52. Sutherland, *China's Large Enterprises*, 50.
53. Li Xiaopeng and Zhang Guobiao, *China's Industrial Policy* [Zhongguo de chanye zhengce] (Beijing: China Development Press, 2017), 152.
54. Wang, *Tackling State-Owned Enterprise Reform*, 914.
55. In 1996, pilot cities merged 1,192 enterprises and bankrupted 1,099 enterprises. In 1997, pilot cities merged 1,022 enterprises and bankrupted 675 enterprises. Bankruptcy was a commonplace measure to restructure SOEs at the local level. The centrality of bankruptcy to SOE reform was unthinkable before the SETC assumed a leading role in SOE reform. Statistics are from *China Economic Yearbook 1997*

(Beijing: China Economic Yearbook, 1998), 680, and *China Economic Yearbook 1998* (Beijing: China Economic Yearbook, 1999), 707.

56. For Zhu's reversal, see Zhu Rongji, *Zhu Rongji Meets the Press* [Zhu rongji jianghua shilu] (Beijing: People's Press, 2011), 52, 392.

57. Jiang Qiangui, "Cultivating Large Enterprise Groups Requires the Promotion by Government and the Operation by Market" [Peiyang dajituan yao zhengfu tuidong shichang yunzuo], *People's Daily*, April 1, 2002.

5. THE REMAKING OF PUBLIC FINANCE IN CHINA AND THE FINANCIAL APPROACH TO ECONOMIC CONTROL

1. Jin Chongji, *Biography of Zhou Enlai* [Zhou Enlai Zhuan] (Beijing: Central Party Literature Press, 2008).

2. "1975 State Council's Report on the Work of the Government," http://www.gov.cn /test/2006-02/23/content_208796.htm.

3. Deng Jiarong and Zhang Yanhua, *The Pathfinder of China's Financial Reform: Liu Hongru* [Zhongguo jinrong gaige tanluren] (Beijing: China Financial Publishing, 2019), 167.

4. Zhou Zhengqing, "Questions on Contemporary Financial Situation and Financial Reform" [Guanyu dangqian jinrong xingshi he jinrong tizhi gaige wenti], in *Information Collection of National Trust and Investment Company Managers Seminar* [Quanguo xintuo touzi gongsi jingli yantaohui ziliao huibian], ed. Hunan Trust and Investment (Changsha: Hunan Trust and Investment, 1991), 25.

5. Deng and Zhang, *The Pathfinder of China's Financial Reform*, 162. Since interest rates for depositors were still kept artificially low by the State Council, bank credit remained a cheap source of financing for SOEs and public investment. The difference lies in the fact that now local governments, more than the central government, made decisions on credit allocation, which contained an even larger moral hazard. Cheap credit could be used to fund unsound local investments for the sole purpose of driving up short-term economic growth. The ineffectiveness, or lack, of central regulation of local credit expansion contributed to inflation in the 1980s.

6. Jia Kang, "Forty Years of Coordination Between Fiscal and Monetary Policies: Interview of Jia Kang," *21st Century Business Herald*, October 18, 2018.

7. Deng and Zhang, *The Pathfinder of China's Financial Reform*, 167.

8. See, for example, Yang Dali, *Remaking the Chinese Leviathan: Market Transition and the Politics of Governance in China* (Stanford, CA: Stanford University Press, 2004); Christine P. W. Wong, "Central-Local Relations in an Era of Fiscal Decline: The Paradox of Fiscal Decentralization in Post-Mao China," *China Quarterly* 128 (1991): 691–715.

9. Interview with former PBOC official, Beijing, July 21, 2012.

10. Stephen Bell and Hui Feng, *The Rise of the People's Bank of China: The Politics of Institutional Change* (Cambridge, MA: Harvard University Press, 2013), 77.

11. Liu Hong, *The 1980s: The Glories and Dreams of Chinese Economists* [Bashi niandai zhongguo jingjixueren de guangrong yu mengxiang] (Nanning: Guangxi Normal University Press, 2010).

12. Deng and Zhang, *The Pathfinder of China's Financial Reform*, 152.
13. Wu Xiaoling, "Practices and Explorations for Establishing Financial Market Order" [Chuangjian jinrong shichang zhixu de tansuo], in *Witness Major Reform Decisions: An Oral History of Reformers* [Jianzheng zhongda gaige juece: gaige qinlizhe zishu], ed. China Society of Economic Reform (Beijing: Social Science Academic, 2018).
14. Yu Jiang and Xia Li, "Liu Hongru: Wudaokou Is a Product of an Era" [Wudaokou shi yige shidai de chanwu], *Modern Bankers* [Dangdai jinrong jia] 9 (2011): 16–22.
15. Yu and Xia, "Liu Hongru," 18.
16. Liu Hongru, "Reviewing the Course of Financial System Reform in Our Country" [Huigu woguo jinrong tizhi gaige de lichen], *Bainianchao* 5 (2009): 24.
17. Deng and Zhang, *The Pathfinder of China's Financial Reform*, 212–30.
18. Zhou, "Questions on Contemporary Financial Situation and Financial Reform."
19. Liu Hongru, "On Economic System Reform" [Guanyu jingji tizhi gaige zhege wenti], in *Information Collection of National Trust and Investment Company Managers Seminar* [Quanguo xintuo touzi gongsi jingli yantaohui ziliao huibian], ed. Hunan Trust and Investment (Changsha: Hunan Trust and Investment, 1991), 30–42.
20. Bell and Feng, *The Rise of the People's Bank of China*, 79–80.
21. Liu Hongru, "Deepen Financial Theory Research in Deepened Financial Reform: Speech of Vice Governor Liu Hongru of PBOC at Financial Research Institute Director Meeting" [Zai Shenhua jinrong gaige zhong Shenhua jinrong lilun yanjiu: liuhongru fuhangzhang zai renminyinhang jinyansuo suozhang huiyishang de jianghua], *Northern China Finance* [Huabei jinrong] 6 (1998): 3–9.
22. Interview with Chinese official, Beijing, June 18, 2013.
23. For a survey of the field of economics and economic research, see Julian Gewirtz, *Unlikely Partners: Chinese Reformers, Western Economists, and the Making of Global China* (Cambridge, MA: Harvard University Press, 2017).
24. Gewirtz, *Unlikely Partners*, 12.
25. Interview with Chinese official, Beijing, May 30, 2013.
26. Wu Jinglian, *Collected Works of Wu Jinglian* [Wujinglian wenji], vol. 3 (Beijing: Central Compilation and Translation Bureau, 2015), 217–28.
27. Wu Jinglian and Zhou Xiaochuan, *A Comprehensive Design of China's Economic Reform* (Beijing: China Zhanwang, 1988).
28. Susan L. Shirk, *The Political Logic of Economic Reform in China* (Berkeley: University of California Press, 1993).
29. "Decision of the CPC Central Committee on Economic System Reform" [zhonggong zhongyang guanyu jingji tizhi gaige de jueding], 12th Central Committee of the Communist Party of China, Third Plenary Session, passed on October 20, 1984, https://www.gov.cn/test/2008-06/26/content_1028140.htm.
30. Yu and Xia, "Liu Hongru," 20.
31. Deng and Zhang, *The Pathfinder of China's Financial Reform*, 190.
32. Liu Hongru, "The Formation of China's Central Banking System," *China Finance* 23 (2013): 21–23.
33. Gao Xin and He Pin, *Biograph of Zhu Rongji: From Anti-Party Rightist to Successor of Deng Xiaoping* [Zhurongji zhuan: cong fandang youpai dao deng Xiaoping jiebanren] (Taipei: Journalist Cultural Enterprise, 1993).
34. Wu, "Practices and Explorations for Establishing Financial Market Order."

35. In hindsight, we know that Gao Xiqing was the only minister-level financial bureaucrat during Zhu's tenure who did not start his career in the government. Notably, he had begun his career on Wall Street. Yet even for Gao, his ties to the government dated back to the late 1980s, when he was briefly brought back to pioneer the design of China's stock market. Finance thus provides a strong case affirming the party's distrust of outsiders when it came to appointing key bureaucratic personnel, in spite of a powerful desire to learn from the West.

36. Gao Xin and He Pin, *Biograph of the Iron-Faced Prime Minister Zhu Rongji* [Tiemian zaixiang zhurongji dazhuan] (New York: Mirror Media, 1998).

37. Ronald Mckinnon, in his interview with Chinese financial media, attributed the origin of the internal expansion strategy to the fiscal expansion policy in 1998. "Mckinnon: China's 4 Trillion Yuan Fiscal Stimulus Package Is Exciting" [Maiijinnong: zhongguo siwanyi caizheng ciji fangan lingren zhenfen], *China Business News*, November 17, 2008.

38. Lou Jiwei and Gao Jianhong, "The Reform of Central Bank's Monetary Policy and the Development of the Bond Market" [Zhongyang yinhang huobi zhengce gongju de gaige yu guozhai shichang de xingcheng], *Finance and Insurance* 12 (1994): 99–104.

39. Former Premier Zhao Ziyang made similar comments, saying that the State Planning Commission represented the macroeconomy, the State Economic and Trade Commission represented the enterprises, and only the Ministry of Finance truly represented the central state. See Zhao Ziyang, *Prisoner of the State: The Secret Journal of Premier Zhao Ziyang*, ed. Bao Pu, Renee Chiang, and Adi Ignatius (New York: Simon & Schuster, 2010), 70.

40. Zhu Rongji, *Zhu Rongji Meets the Press* [Zhu rongji jianghua shilu] (Beijing: People's Press, 2011), 411–13.

41. "Gaojian: The History of Bond Capital Market Development I Experienced" [Gaojian: wosuojingli de zhongguo zhaiquan shichang de lishi], *Financial News*, August 30, 2017, https://www.sohu.com/a/166099859_481741.

42. Tang Linmin and Dehua Wang, "Review and Evaluation of Management Reform Since the Resumption of National Bond Insurance" [Guozhai huifu faxing yilai guanli gaige de huigu ji pingjia], *Contemporary China History Studies* 22, no. 2 (2015): 38–46.

43. Wei Fang, "A Brief Analysis of the Institutional Setup of the National Development and Reform Commission" [Guojia fagaiwei de jigou shezhi jianxi] (master's thesis, China Youth University of Political Studies, 2017), http://cdmd.cnki.com.cn/Article/CDMD-11625-1018036083.htm.

44. Xiao Meng, *Debt Restructuring and Bankruptcy Procedure in the Reconstruction of Corporate Governance: Revisting the Jinglun Conference* [Gongsi zhili jiegou zhaiwu chongzu he pochan chengxu: chongwen jinglun huiyi] (Beijing: Central Compilation and Translation, 1999).

45. Xiao, *Debt Restructuring and Bankruptcy Procedure*.

46. Wu Jinglian, "The Difficulties and Countermeasures of the Corporation Reform of State-Owned Large and Medium-Sized Enterprises" [Guoyou dazhognxing qiye gongsi gaige de nandina he duice], *Economic Daily* [Jingji Ribao], February 26, 1995.

47. Zeng Peiyan, *Zeng Peiyan on Development and Reform* [Zeng peiyan lun fazhan yu gaige], vol. 1 (Beijing: People's Press, 2014), 468.

48. Zhu Rongji, *Zhu Rongji Meets the Press* [Zhu rongji jianghua shilu] (Beijing: People's Press, 2011), 63, 182.

49. Carl Walter and Fraser Howie, *Red Capitalism: The Fragile Financial Foundation of China's Extraordinary Rise* (Hoboken, NJ: Wiley, 2012), 68–72.
50. Walter and Howie, *Red Capitalism*, 74.
51. Wang Yingyao, "The Rise of the 'Shareholding State': Financialization of Economic Management in China," *Socio-Economic Review* 13, no. 3 (July 2015): 603–25.
52. Sarah Ho and Thomas Marois, "China's Asset Management Companies as State Spatial-Temporal Strategy," *China Quarterly* 239 (September 2019): 728–51.

6. THE ASCENT OF THE INDUSTRIAL VIEW: INDUSTRIAL POLICY FOR MAKING A MANUFACTURING SUPERPOWER

1. Soohan Kim and Frank Dobbin, "Industrial Policy," in *The Palgrave Encyclopedia of Strategic Management*, ed. Mie Augier and David J. Teece (London: Palgrave Macmillan, 2016).
2. You Lin, Zheng Xinli, and Wang Ruipu, *A General History of National Affairs of People's Republic of China* [Zhonghua renmin gongheguo guoshi tongjian] (Beijing: Hongqi, 1999), 446.
3. Liu Hong, "The Structure Team Connecting the Past and the Future" [Chengqian qihou jiegou zu], *Economic Observer*, January 19, 2009.
4. Xue Baoding, Zhang Xuansan, and Li Boxi, "System Engineering and the Analysis of Society and Economy" [Xitong gongcheng he shehui jingji xitong], *Enterprise Economy* 11 (1982): 3–7; Zhu Xihao, "The Impact of Information, Control and System Theories on Methodology of Social Science" [Xinxi kongzhi he xitonglun dui shehuikexue fangfalun de yingxiang], *Modernization* 2 (1985): 6–8.
5. Wang Huijiong and Li Boxi, "Industrial Policy and Industrial Structure: A Research Design" [Chenye zhengce yu chanye jiegou keti de xitong sheji], *Study Materials for Economic Professionals* 1 (1986): 32–44.
6. Sebastian Heilmann and Lea Shih, "The Rise of Industrial Policy in China, 1978–2012" (Harvard-Yenching Institute Working Paper Series, Cambridge, MA, 2013), https://www.harvard-yenching.org/wp-content/uploads/legacy_files/featurefiles/Sebastian%20Heilmann%20and%20Lea%20Shih_The%20Rise%20of%20Industrial%20Policy%20in%20China%201978-2012.pdf.
7. Lv Dong, *Commemorative Anthology of Lv Dong* [Lv dong jinian wenji], ed. Commemorative Anthology of Lv Dong Editorial Board (Beijing: China Industrial Economic Federation, 2005).
8. Chen Jinhua, *Memories of the Eventful Years* [Guoshi yishu] (Beijing: History of Chinese Communist Party Publishing, 2005), 209–10.
9. The 2001 Government Work Report by Premier Zhu Rongji reflected on this segment of history and his approach to tackling macroeconomic instability. "2001 State Council Government Work Report" [2001nian zhengfu gongzuo baogao], delivered March 5, 2001, at the Fourth Session of the Ninth National People's Congress, https://www.gov.cn/test/2006-02/16/content_201157.htm.
10. State Planning Commission, *National Guidelines for Industrial Policy of the 1990s* [Jiushi niandai guojia chanye zhengce gangyao], no. 3, State Council, Beijing, 1994.
11. In particular, the SPC's *National Guidelines for Industrial Policy of the 1990s*.

12. See, for example, the "Tenth Five-Year Plan for Machinery Industry (2001)" and "Tenth Five-Year Plan for the Automobile Industry (2001)" issued by the State Economic and Trade Commission.

13. Huang Yasheng, "Between Two Coordination Failures: Automotive Industrial Policy in China with a Comparison to Korea," *Review of International Political Economy* 9, no. 3 (2002): 538–73.

14. Speech by the bureau chief of industrial policy of the NDRC at a news conference of the State Council, December 21, 2005, https://www.gov.cn/xwfb/2005-12/21/content _133196.htm.

15. National Development and Reform Commission, *Advancing the NDRC's Opinions on Withholding Blind Investment in Steel, Electrolytic Aluminum, and Cement Industries* [Guowuyuan bangongting zhuanfa fazhan gaigewei deng bumen guanyu Zhizhi gnagtgie dianjilv shuini hangye mangmu touzi ruogan yijian de tongzhi], no. 4, State Council, Beijing, 2005.

16. Zhao Ying, *Empirical Research on the Transformation of China's Industrial Policy, 2000–2010* [Zhongguo chanye zhengce biandong qushi shizheng yanjiu 2000–2010] (Beijing: Economy Management Publishing, 2010), 168.

17. Interview with Chinese official, Beijing, June 7, 2012.

18. Julian Gewirtz, "The Futurists of Beijing: Alvin Toffler, Zhao Ziyang, and China's 'New Technological Revolution,' 1979–1991," *Journal of Asian Studies* 78, no. 1 (2009): 115–40.

19. Liu Hong, "A Historical Event That Chooses National Developmental Mode" [Xuanze guojia fazhan moshi de yici lishixing shijian], *Economic Observer*, October 30, 2014.

20. Lin Justin Yifu, "Emancipating the Mind, Seeking Truth from Facts, Advancing with the Times, Seeking Truth and Being Pragmatic, Enhancing Theoretical Self-Confidence: Participation in 11 Symposiums in 1991 and Subsequent Work" [Jiefang sixiang shishiqiushi yushijujin qiuzhen wushi zengqiang lilun zixin canjia 1991nian 11zuotanhui he zhihou de gongzuo], in *Jiang Zemin and the Proposition of the Socialist Market Economy System* [Jiang Zemin he Shehuizhuyi Shichang Jingji de tichu], ed. Chen Jun and Hong Nan (Beijing: Central Party Literature Press, 2012).

21. "Looking Back at Socialist Market Economy in 22 Years" [22 nian shehuizhuyi shichang jingji huigu], *Caijing Magazine*, September 2, 2013, http://finance.sina.com .cn/china/20130902/090016634101.shtml.

22. Lin, "Emancipating the Mind."

23. "Interview with Dong Biqin, Former Major Technical Equipment Office of the State Council" [Zhunfang yuan guowuyuan zhongda jishu zhuangbei bangongshi dong-biqin], *China Business News*, January 11, 2010.

24. Bai Jie, "China's High-Tech Industry Is Growing Fast and Lacks International Competitiveness" [Woguo gaoxin jishu chanye zengzhang kuai quefa guoji jingzhengli], *Science News Weekly* 34 (2001): 10.

25. Bai Jie, "China's High-Tech Industry Is Growing Fast."

26. "Report from the 16th National Congress: Jiang Zemin Proposed Pursuing a New Style Industrialization, Vigorously Implementing the Strategy of Rejuvenating the Country Through Science and Education, and the Strategy of Sustainable Development" [Shiliuda xianchang baodao: Jiang Zemin tichu yaozou xinxing gongyehua daolu, dali shishi kejiaoxingguo he kechixu fazhan zhanlue], *Xinhua News*, November 8, 2002, https://news.sina.com.cn/c/2002-11-08/1002800216.html.

27. China has conducted three industrial censuses from 1949 to the present. They took place in 1950, 1986, and 1995. These Chinese industrial censuses surveyed aspects of industrial development related to total industrial assets, ownership structures, and product structures as well as to sectoral distributions of industrial firms, their production capacities, their productivity, the amount of equipment they used, and their technological conditions.

28. Wei Liqun, "Persist in Taking a New Road to Industrialization (2002)" [Jianchi zou xinxing gongyehua daolu], in *Cultivating a Road for Reform and Opening-Up* [Gaige kaifang gengyun lu] (Beijing: China Yanshi, 2018), 283–93.

29. Gao Bai, Guowu Li, and Zhihong Zhen, eds., *High-Speed Rail: An Analysis of the Chinese Innovation System* (Hackensack, NJ: World Scientific, 2021).

30. "Grand Integration: Li's Path to a Mega Industrial Ministry" [Dazhenghe dagongyebu lishi lujing], *Caifu Shibao*, March 24, 2008.

31. "State Commission Office for Public Sector Reform Affirms the Role of the Development and Reform Commission; Experts Say Its Functions May Be Readjusted" [Zhongbianban kending fagaiwei zuoyong zhuanjia cheng qi zhicheng huozai tiaozheng], *China Business News*, March 12, 2013, https://m.yicai.com/news/2547400 .html.

32. Wei Fang, "A Brief Analysis of the Institutional Setup of the National Development and Reform Commission" [Guojia fagaiwei de jigou shezhi jianxi] (master's thesis, China Youth University of Political Studies, 2017), http://cdmd.cnki.com.cn/Article /CDMD-11625-1018036083.htm.

33. "Notice of the Ministry of Industry and Information Technology on Issuing the Guidelines for the Development of Generic Technologies in the Industry (2011)" [Gongye he xinxihua bu guanyu yinfa 'chanye guanjian gongxing jishu fazhan zhi-nan de tongzhi'], no. 320, Ministry of Industry and Information Technology, Beijing, 2011.

34. "Solving the Predicament of Key Components, the Ministry of Industry and Information Technology Deliberates Supportive Policies" [Pojie guanjian lingbujian kunju, gongxinbu yunniang zhichi zhengce], *Shanghai Security News*, November 27, 2011.

35. "Notice of the Ministry of Industry and Information Technology on Applying for 'High-End CNC Machine Tool and Basic Manufacturing Equipment' 2013 Science and Technology Major Special Projects" [Gongye he xinxihuabu guanyu shenbao gaodang shukong jichuang yu jichu zhizao zhuangbei keji zhongda zhuanxiang 2013niandu keti de tongzhi], Ministry of Industry and Information Technology, Beijing, 2013, https://d .wanfangdata.com.cn/claw/Cg9MYXdOZXdTMjAyMzA5MDQSCkkcwMDAxMzc4 NDEaCHFlMTZwY3Rs. Previous industrial policy programs paid little attention to machine tool manufacturing. If they did, they stopped at doling out tax incentives to manufacturing enterprises.

36. MIIT's in-house research institute, China's Center for Information and Industry Development, put forward the idea of intelligent manufacturing around 2011. It was soon adopted as the official program of the MIIT.

37. References to Germany's Industry 4.0 were common in the speeches and writings of MIIT officials even before the MIIT rolled out its own intelligent manufacturing proposal. See, for example, Wang Xiwen (Center for International Economic and Technological Cooperation, MIIT), "Looking at the Future Smart Manufacturing

Industry from the Germany's 'Industry 4.0' Initiative" [Cong deguo gongye 4.0 zhanlue kan weilai zhineng zhizao], *Zhongguo Xinxihua* 15 (2014): 8–9; Zuo Shiquan, "German Integration of Industrialization and Industrialization" [Deyizhi lianghua ronghe], *China Equipment* [Zhungbei zhizao] 4 (2012): 84–88.

38. "Interpretation of 'The Action Plan for the Development of Smart Photovoltaic Industry (2018–2020)' " [Zhineng guangfu chanye fazhan xingdong jihua], Ministry of Industry and Information Technology, Beijing, April 11, 2018, https://d.wanfangdata.com.cn /claw/Cg9MYXdOZXdTMjAyMzA5MDQSCkcwMDAyNzc5OTIaCHRsMTllN3pt.

39. Data was accessed from annual department budget and financial accounts posted on the MIIT's official website: https://www.miit.gov.cn/zwgk/czzj/index.html.

40. Data were accessed on the NDRC's official website: National Development and Reform Commission Department Budget 2013, https://www.ndrc.gov.cn/xwdt/tzgg /201304/W020190905470739114016.pdf and National Development and Reform Commission Department Budget 2016, https://www.ndrc.gov.cn/fzggw/jgsj/bgt/sjdt /201604/P020191210505433096246.pdf.

41. "Notice of the Ministry of Industry and Information Technology, the Ministry of Science and Technology, the Ministry of Finance, and the State Administration of Taxation on the Issuance of the National Industrial Technology Policy" [Gongye-hexinxihuabu kexuejishubu caizhengbu guojiashuiwuzongju guanyu yinfa guojia chanye jishu zhengce de tongzhi], no. 232, Ministry of Industry and Information Technology, Beijing, 2009.

42. "Notice of the General Office of the Ministry of Industry and Information Technology on the Establishment of the Intelligent Manufacturing Expert Advisory Committee" [Gongyehexinxihuabu bangongting guanyu chengli zhineng zhizao zhuanjia zixun weiyuanhui de tongzhi], no. 267, Ministry of Industry and Information Technology, Beijing, 2017.

43. For example, one of the MIIT's key consultants, Zhu Sendi, the vice chairman of the China Machinery Industry Federation, was the director of the Technology and Development Bureau of the Ministry of the Machinery Industry. Zhu was a longtime observer of the CNC machine tools industry and had advocated for the importance of building China's indigenous capacity to manufacture this pivotal product.

44. For an example, see Andrew Scobell, Edmund J. Burke, Cortez A. Cooper Iii, Sale Lilly, Chad J. R. Ohlandt, Eric Warner, and J. D. Williams, *China's Grand Strategy: Trends, Trajectories, and Long-Term Competition* (Santa Monica, CA: RAND, 2020), https://www.rand.org/pubs/research_reports/RR2798.html.

45. Wei Ren, " 'Strategic Research on a Manufacturing Power' Released; Three Steps Towards a Manufacturing Power" [Zhizao qiangguo zhanlue yanjiu fabu sanbuzou maixiang zhizao qiangguo], *China Equipment* [Zhuangbei zhizao] 5 (2015): 2; Zhao Qiang et al., "Research on Optimization and Assessment of the Evaluation Index System for Manufacturing Power" [Zhizao qiangguo pingjia zhibiao tixi youhua yu ceping yanjiu], *China Engineering Science* 19, no. 13 (2017): 13–19.

46. Zhao et al., "Research on Optimization and Assessment of the Evaluation Index System."

47. Manufacturing Research Office of Chinese Academy of Engineering, " 'Made in China 2025' Series of Research Results Released," Beijing, June 17, 2016, https://www .cae.cn/cae/html/main/col4/2016-06/17/20160617165537858319768_1.html.

48. Lu Feng and Feng Kaidong, *The Policy Choice to Develop China's Automobile Industry with Independent Intellectual Property Rights* [Woguo fazhan zizhu zhishi chanquan qiche gongye de zhengce xuanze] (Beijing: Peking University Press, 2005); Yu Yongding and Lu Feng, " 'Double Surpluses,' Capacity Gap and Indigenous Innovation" [Shuang shuncha: nengli quekou he zizhu chuangxin], *Chinese Social Science* [Zhongguo shehui kexue] 6 (2012): 91–114.

49. Wang Xiwen, *New Industrial Policy* [Xin chanye zhengce] (Beijing: Xinhua, 2017), 192.

50. See Li Xiaopeng and Zhang Guobiao, *China's Industrial Policy* [Zhongguo de chanye zhengce] (Beijing: China Development Press, 2017), 258.

51. Wu Jing and Lu Nanfang, "Grand Narrative at History's Turning Point: A Political Analysis of the Internet Ideology of China's 'Industrial Party' " [Lishi zhuanzhe zhongde hongda xueshi: gongye dang wangluo sichao de zhengzhi fenxi], *Dongfang Journal* 1 (2018): 49–60.

52. See "Decision of the Guangdong Provincial Committee of the Communist Party of China and the People's Government of Guangdong Province on Promoting Industrial Transfer and Labor Transfer" [Zhonggong Guangdong shengwei guangdongsheng renmin zhegnfu guanyu tuijin chanye zhuanyi he laodongli zhuanyi de jueding], no. 4, Guangzhou, 2008; "Several Opinions of the People's Government of Zhejiang Province on Accelerating the 'Freeing of Cages and Changing Birds' to Promote Economic Transformation and Upgrading (for Trial Implementation)" [Zhejiangsheng renmin zhegnfu guanyu jiakuai tenglong huanniao cujin jingji zhuanxing shengji de ruoganyijian(shixing)], no. 49, Hangzhou, 2012.

53. "Guidelines from the High-Tech Industry Development Bureau of the National Development Planning Commission for National High-Tech Industrial Bases" [Guojia fazhan jihua weiyuanhui gaojishu chanye fazhansi guanyu guojia gaojishu chanye jidi fazhan zhidao yijian], National Development and Planning Commission, Beijing, January 16, 2003.

54. See "Notice of the Ministry of Industry and Information Technology on Launching the 2016 Special Action to Establish Pilot and Model Programs for Intelligent Manufacturing" [Gongye he xinxihua bu guanyu kaizhann zhinengzhizao shidian shifan 2016 zhuanxiang xingdong de tongzhi], no. 125, Ministry of Industry and Information Technology, Beijing, 2016.

CONCLUSION

1. Giovanni Arrighi, *The Long Twentieth Century: Money, Power and the Origins of Our Times,* updated ed. (London: Verso, 2010).

2. Mark Dincecco and Wang Yuhua, "State Capacity," in *Oxford Handbook of Historical Political Economy,* ed. Jeffery Jenkins and Jared Rubin (Oxford: Oxford University Press, 2022).

3. Development research shows that the selection of development goals is highly associated with the remolding of state structures and the engineering of state capacities. See Vivek Chibber, *Locked in Place: State-Building and Late Industrialization in India* (Princeton, NJ: Princeton University Press, 2006).

4. An example is Steven K. Vogel, *Marketcraft: How Governments Make Markets Work* (New York: Oxford University Press, 2018).

5. Karl Polanyi, *The Great Transformation: The Political and Economic Origins of Our Time* (Boston: Beacon, 2001).

6. David M. Lampton, *Following the Leader: Ruling China, from Deng Xiaoping to Xi Jinping* (Berkeley: University of California Press, 2014).

7. Michael W. Bauer and Stefan Becker, "Democratic Backsliding, Populism, and Public Administration," *Perspectives on Public Management and Governance* 3, no. 1 (March 2020): 19–31.

REFERENCES

Adams, Julia. *The Familial State: Ruling Families and Merchant Capitalism in Early Modern Europe.* Ithaca, NY: Cornell University Press, 2005.

Adams, Julia, and Mounira Maya Charrad, eds. *Patrimonial Power in the Modern World.* Los Angeles: SAGE, 2011.

Amsden, Alice H. *Asia's Next Giant: South Korea and Late Industrialization.* Oxford: Oxford University Press, 1989.

Andreas, Joel. *Rise of the Red Engineers: The Cultural Revolution and the Origins of China's New Class.* Stanford, CA: Stanford University Press, 2009.

Andreas, Joel. "The Structure of Charismatic Mobilization: A Case Study of Rebellion During the Chinese Cultural Revolution." *American Sociological Review* 72, no. 3 (June 2007): 434–58.

Ang, Yuen. "Beyond Weber: Conceptualizing an Alternative Ideal Type of Bureaucracy in Developing Contexts." *Regulation & Governance* 11, no. 3 (August 2017): 282–98.

Ang, Yuen. *China's Gilded Age.* Cambridge: Cambridge University Press, 2021.

Ang, Yuen. *How China Escaped the Poverty Trap.* Ithaca, NY: Cornell University Press, 2016.

Arrighi, Giovanni. *The Long Twentieth Century: Money, Power and the Origins of Our Times.* Updated ed. London: Verso, 2010.

Asian Development Bank. "Challenges and Opportunities in China's Local Finance Management" [Zhongguo caizheng difang guanli de tiaozhan he jiyu]. 2014, Mandaluyong, Philippines, ADB. https://www.adb.org/zh/publications/local-public-finance -management-peoples-republic-china-challenges-and-opportunities-zh.

Babb, Sarah. *Managing Mexico: Economists from Nationalism to Neoliberalism.* Princeton, NJ: Princeton University Press, 2001.

Bachman, David M. *Chen Yun and the Chinese Political System.* Berkeley, CA: Institute of East Asian Studies, 1985.

Bachman, David. "The Paradox of Analyzing Elite Politics Under Jiang." *China Journal* 45 (January 2001): 95–100.

Bai Jie. "China's High-Tech Industry Is Growing Fast and Lacks International Competitiveness" [Woguo gaoxin jishu chanye zengzhang kuai quefa guoji jingzhengli]. *Science News Weekly* [Kexue xinwen] 34 (2001): 10.

Bauer, Michael W., and Stefan Becker. "Democratic Backsliding, Populism, and Public Administration." *Perspectives on Public Management and Governance* 3, no. 1 (March 2020): 19–31.

Bell, Stephen, and Hui Feng. *The Rise of the People's Bank of China: The Politics of Institutional Change.* Cambridge, MA: Harvard University Press, 2013.

Berman, Elizabeth Popp. *Thinking Like an Economist: How Efficiency Replaced Equality in U.S. Public Policy.* Princeton, NJ: Princeton University Press, 2022.

Blyth, Mark. *Great Transformations: Economic Ideas and Institutional Change in the Twentieth Century.* New York: Cambridge University Press, 2002.

Bo Yibo. *A Memoir of Major Decisions and Events* [Ruogan zhongda juece yu shijian de huigu]. Beijing: History of Chinese Communist Party Publishing, 1991.

Bourdieu, Pierre. *Distinction.* London: Routledge, 1986.

Bourdieu, Pierre. *On the State: Lectures at the Collège de France, 1989–1992.* Cambridge: Polity, 2015.

Brahm, Laurence J. *Zhu Rongji and the Transformation of Modern China.* Singapore: Wiley, 2003.

Brink, Tobias ten. *China's Capitalism: A Paradoxical Route to Economic Prosperity*, trans. Carla Welch. Philadelphia: University of Pennsylvania Press, 2019.

Brugger, Bill. "Underdeveloped Socialism and Intensive Development." In *Chinese Marxism in Flux 1978–84: Essays on Epistemology, Ideology and Political Economy*, ed. Bill Brugger. London: Routledge, 2019.

Cai, Yongshun. "China's Moderate Middle Class." *Asian Survey* 45, no. 5 (September/October 2005): 777–99.

Campbell, John L. "Institutional Analysis and the Role of Ideas in Political Economy." In *The Rise of Neoliberalism and Institutional Analysis*, ed. John L. Campbell and O. K. Pedersen. Princeton, NJ: Princeton University Press, 2001.

Cao Yingwang. *Founding Commander-in-Chief of Economics and Finance Chen Yun* [Kaiguo jingji tongshuia chenyun]. Beijing: China Translation and Publishing, 2015.

Centeno, Miguel. *Democracy Within Reason: Technocratic Revolution in Mexico.* University Park: Pennsylvania State University Press, 1997.

Central Committee of the Chinese Communist Party. "A Summary of the Guangdong, Fujian Provincial Discussion Meeting" [Guangdong, Fujian liangsheng zuotanhui jiyao]. In *Compilation of Important Documents Since the Third Plenum of the 11th Central Committee* [San Zhong Quanhui Yilai ZhongyaoWenxian xuanibian], ed. Document Research Center of CCP CC, 1169–83. Vol. 3. Beijing: People's Publisher [Renmin chubanshe], 1986.

Central Party Literature Press. *Biography of Li Xiannian (1949–1992)* [Lixiannian zhuan]. Beijing: Central Party Literature Press, 2009.

Chen Jian. *Corporate Governance in China.* London: Routledge, 2004.

Chen Jinhua. *Memories of the Eventful Years* [Guoshi yishu]. Beijing: History of Chinese Communist Party Publishing, 2005.

Chen Jun and Hong Nan, eds. *Jiangzemin and the Proposition of the Socialist Market Economy System* [Jiang Zemin he Shehuizhuyi Shichang Jingji de tichu]. Beijing: Central Party Literature Press, 2012.

Chen Lixu. "Chen Yun and Li Xiannian" [Chenyun yu lixiannian]. *Century Elegance* [Shiji Fengcai] 3 (2014): 14–20.

Chen Qingtai. *Optimizing Capital Structure: Pilot City Work Manual* [Youhua ziben jiegou chengshi shidian gongzuo shouce]. Beijing: China Economic Press, 1996.

Chen Yun. "On the Relationship Between Planning and Market" [Jihua yu shichang wenti]. *Macroeconomic Research* [Hongguan jingji yanjiu] 32 (1982): 2–4.

Chen Yun. *Selected Works of Chen Yun* [Chen Yun Wenxuan]. Beijing: People's Press, 1995.

Chen Yun. "Several Explanations of the First Five Year Plan (06/30/1954)" [Guanyu diyige wunianjihua de jidian shuoming]. In *Selected Manuscripts of Chen Yun (1949–1956)* [Chenyun wengao xuanbian]. Hubei: Renmin, 1982.

Chen Yun's Former Residence and Qingpu Revolution History Memorial Hall, eds. *Getting Close to Chen Yun: Oral History Museum Collection Catalog* [Zoujin Chenyun: koushu lishi guancang ziliao jilu], 117. Beijing: Central Literature Publishing, 2008.

Cheng Zhongxuan. "My Years of Serving as a Secretary at the Guangdong Provincial Party Committee" [Wo zai guangdong shengwei dang mishu]. *China Through the Ages* [Yanhuang chunqiu] 4 (2013): 15–21.

Chibber, Vivek. *Locked in Place: State-Building and Late Industrialization in India.* Princeton, NJ: Princeton University Press, 2006.

"Decision of the CPC Central Committee on Economic System Reform" [zhonggong zhongyang guanyu jingji tizhi gaige de jueding]. 12th Central Committee of the Communist Party of China, Third Plenary Session, passed on October 20, 1984. https://www.gov.cn/test/2008-06/26/content_1028140.htm.

Deng Jiarong and Zhang Yanhua. *The Pathfinder of China's Financial Reform: Liu Hongru* [Zhongguo jinrong gaige tanluren]. Beijing: China Financial Publishing, 2019.

Deng Xiaoping. "Excerpts from Talks Given in Wuchang, Shenzhen, Zhuhai, Shanghai" [Zai Wuchang Shenzhen Zhuhai Shanghai dengdi de tanhua yaodian]. In *Selected Works of Deng Xiaoping* [Deng Xiaoping wenxuan]. Vols. 1–3. Beijing: People's Press, 1993.

Deng Xiaoping. "Seize the Opportunity to Develop the Economy" [Shanyu liyong shiji jiejue fazhan wenti]. In *Selected Works of Deng Xiaoping* [Deng Xiaoping wenxuan]. Vol. 3. Beijing: People's Press, 1993.

Deng Xiaoping. "The Urgent Task Facing the Third Generation of Leadership" [Disandai lingdao jiti de dangwuzhiji]. In *Selected Works of Deng Xiaoping* [Deng Xiaoping wenxuan]. Vol. 3. Beijing: People's Press, 1993.

Dickson, Bruce J. *Red Capitalists in China: The Party, Private Entrepreneurs, and Prospects for Political Change.* Cambridge: Cambridge University Press, 2003.

Dincecco, Mark, and Wang Yuhua. "State Capacity." In *Oxford Handbook of Historical Political Economy*, ed. Jeffery Jenkins and Jared Rubin. Oxford: Oxford University Press, 2022.

Dittmer, Lowell. "China in 1988: The Continuing Dilemma of Socialist Reform." *Asian Survey* 29, no. 1 (January 1989): 12–28.

Dittmer, Lowell, and Yu-Shan Wu. "The Modernization of Factionalism in Chinese Politics." *World Politics* 47, no. 4 (July 1995): 467–94.

Erikson, Emily. *Trade and Nation: How Companies and Politics Reshaped Economic Thought*. New York: Columbia University Press, 2021.

Evans, Peter B. *Embedded Autonomy*. Princeton, NJ: Princeton University Press, 1995.

Eyal, Gil, Ivan Szelenyi, and Eleanor R. Townsley. *Making Capitalism Without Capitalists: The New Ruling Elites in Eastern Europe*. London: Verso, 1999.

Fang, Wei. "A Brief Analysis of the Institutional Setup of the National Development and Reform Commission" [Guojia fagaiwei de jigou shezhi jianxi]. Master's thesis, China Youth University of Political Studies, 2017. http://cdmd.cnki.com.cn/Article/CDMD-11625-1018036083.htm.

Fewsmith, Joseph. *Dilemmas of Reform in China: Political Conflict and Economic Debate*. Armonk, NY: Routledge, 1994.

Fligstein, Neil. *The Transformation of Corporate Control*. Cambridge, MA: Harvard University Press, 1993.

Fourcade, Marion. *Economists and Societies: Discipline and Profession in the United States, Britain, and France, 1890s to 1990s*. Princeton, NJ: Princeton University Press, 2010.

Fourcade-Gourinchas, Marion, and Sarah L. Babb. "The Rebirth of the Liberal Creed: Paths to Neoliberalism in Four Countries." *American Journal of Sociology* 108, no. 3 (November 2002): 533–79.

Frickel, Scott, and Neil Gross. "A General Theory of Scientific/Intellectual Movements." *American Sociological Review* 70, no. 2 (April 2015): 204–32.

Fu Mingxian and Zhang Huaiping. *Market Economy and Government Functions and Institutional Setup* [Shichang jingji yu zhengfu zhineng ji jigou shezhi]. Wuhan: Hubei People's Press, 1997.

Gao Bai, Guowu Li, and Zhihong Zhen, eds. *High-Speed Rail: An Analysis of the Chinese Innovation System*. Hackensack, NJ: World Scientific, 2021.

"Gaojian: The History of Bond Capital Market Development I Experienced" [Gaojian: wosuojingli de zhongguo zhaiquan shichang de lishi]. *Financial News*, August 30, 2017. https://www.sohu.com/a/166099859_481741.

Gao Shangquan and Yang Qixian. *State-Owned Enterprise Reform in China* [Zhongguo guoyou qiye gaige]. Jinan: Jinan Press, 1999.

Gao Xin and He Pin. *Biograph of the Iron-Faced Prime Minister Zhu Rongji* [Tiemian zaixiang zhurongji dazhuan]. New York: Mirror Media, 1998.

Gao Xin and He Pin. *Biograph of Zhu Rongji: From Anti-Party Rightist to Successor of Deng Xiaoping* [Zhurongji zhuan: cong fandang youpai dao deng Xiaoping jiebanren]. Taipei: Journalist Cultural Enterprise, 1993.

Gewirtz, Julian. "The Futurists of Beijing: Alvin Toffler, Zhao Ziyang, and China's 'New Technological Revolution,' 1979–1991." *Journal of Asian Studies* 78, no. 1 (2009): 115–40.

Gewirtz, Julian. *Unlikely Partners: Chinese Reformers, Western Economists, and the Making of Global China*. Cambridge, MA: Harvard University Press, 2017.

Ghosh, Arunabh. *Making It Count: Statistics and Statecraft in the Early People's Republic of China*. Princeton, NJ: Princeton University Press, 2020.

Gorski, Philip S. *The Disciplinary Revolution: Calvinism and the Rise of the State in Early Modern Europe*. Chicago: University of Chicago Press, 2003.

Gu Mu. *A Memoir of Gu Mu* [Gumu huiyil]. Beijing: Central Party Literature Press, 2009.

Guan Mengjue. *The Economic Thoughts of Chen Yun* [Chenyun tongzhi de jingji sixiang]. Beijing: World Affair, 1984.

Guan Shan. "Ren Zhongyi on Deng Xiaoping and Guangdong's Reform and Open Up" [Ren Zhongyi tan Deng Xiaoping he guangdong de gaige kaifang]. *China Through the Ages* [Yanhuang chunqiu] 8 (2004): 8–17.

Guo Dongle. *Debates on Theories of Socialist Market Economy in China, 1992–1995* [Zhongguo shehuizhuyi shichang jingji lilun zhengming 1992–1995]. Beijing: China Wujia Publisher, 1996.

Guo Shuqing. "A Series of Symposiums in 1991 to Discuss the Foals of Economic System Reform" [Huiyi 1991nian taolun jingjitizhi gaige mubiao de xilie zuotanhui]. In *Jiangzemin and the Proposition of the Socialist Market Economy System* [Jiang Zemin he Shehuizhuyi Shichang Jingji de tichu], ed. Chen Jun and Hong Nan, 71–90. Beijing: Central Party Literature Press, 2012.

Guo Shuqing. *The Transformation of the Model and the Transformed Model* [Moshi de biange he biange de moshi]. Shanghai: SDX Joint Publishing, 1989.

Haggard, Stephan. *Developmental States.* Cambridge: Cambridge University Press, 2018.

Hall, Peter A. *Governing the Economy: The Politics of State Intervention in Britain and France.* Cambridge: Blackwell, 1986.

Hall, Peter A. "Policy Paradigms, Social Learning, and the State: The Case of Economic Policymaking in Britain." *Comparative Politics* 25, no. 3 (April 1993): 275–96.

Hallett, Tim, and Marc J. Ventresca. "Inhabited Institutions: Social Interactions and Organizational Forms in Gouldner's 'Patterns of Industrial Bureaucracy.'" *Theory and Society* 35, no. 2 (April 2006): 213–36.

Hamrin, Carol Lee. *China and the Challenge of the Future: Changing Political Patterns.* New York: Routledge, 2019.

Harding, Harry. *Organizing China: The Problem of Bureaucracy, 1949–1976.* Stanford, CA: Stanford University Press, 1968.

Harvey, David. *A Brief History of Neoliberalism.* Oxford: Oxford University Press, 2007.

He Gu. "Report on India's Economic System" [Guanyu yindu jingjixitong de baogao]. *Internal Reference of Economic System Reform* 12 (1990): 42–46.

He Yaowu and Wu Li. *Documenting Sixty Years of State Affairs* [Liushinian guoshi jiyao]. Hunan: Hunan People's Press, 2009.

Heilmann, Sebastian, and Elizabeth J. Perry. *Mao's Invisible Hand: The Political Foundations of Adaptive Governance in China.* Cambridge, MA: Harvard University Asia Center, 2011.

Heilmann, Sebastian, and Lea Shih. "The Rise of Industrial Policy in China, 1978–2012." Harvard-Yenching Institute Working Paper Series, Cambridge, MA, 2013. https://www.harvard-yenching.org/wp-content/uploads/legacy_files/featurefiles/Sebastian%20Heilmann%20and%20Lea%20Shih_The%20Rise%20of%20Industrial%20Policy%20in%20China%201978-2012.pdf.

Higgins, Monica C., and Edgar H. Schein. *Career Imprints: Creating Leaders Across an Industry.* San Francisco: Jossey-Bass, 2005.

Ho, Sarah, and Thomas Marois. "China's Asset Management Companies as State Spatial-Temporal Strategy." *China Quarterly* 239 (September 2019): 728–51.

Hu Deping. *Why Did China Need to Reform? In Memory of My Father Hu Yaobang* [Zhongguo weishenme xuyao gaige: siyi fuqin Hu Yaobang]. Beijing: People's Press, 2011.

274

REFERENCES

Hu, Fed. "Zhu Rongji's Decade." *Wall Street Journal*, March 10, 2003.

Huang Yasheng. "Between Two Coordination Failures: Automotive Industrial Policy in China with a Comparison to Korea." *Review of International Political Economy* 9, no. 3 (2002): 538–73.

Hung, Ho-fung. *The China Boom: Why China Will Not Rule the World*. New York: Columbia University Press, 2015.

Hung, Ho-fung. "Grandpa State Instead of Bourgeois State: Patrimonial Politics in China's Age of Commerce, 1644–1839." In *Patrimonial Capitalism and Empire*, ed. Mounira M. Charrad and Julia Adams, 115–36. Political Power and Social Theory, vol. 28. Bingley, UK: Emerald, 2015.

Inspection Team of Market Management to South Korea. "Introduction to the Macroeconomic System in South Korea" [Nanchaoxian hongguan jingjitizhi jieshao]. *Internal Reference of Economic System Reform* 9 (1990): 38–47.

Jia Kang. "Forty Years of Coordination Between Fiscal and Monetary Policies: Interview of Jia Kang." *21st Century Business Herald*, October 18, 2018.

Jia Kang, Shi Wei, and Liu Cuiwei. "Li Xiannian's Thoughts on Comprehensive Balance" [Li Xiannian de zonghe pingheng caizheng sixiang]. In *The History of Ideas on Public Finance in China* [Zhongguo caizheng sixiang shi], 74–86. Shanghai: Lixin Accounting Publishing, 2018.

Jiang Chunze. "The Birth of the Socialist Market Economy" [Shehuizhuyi shichangjingji de dansheng]. *Shenzhen Commercial News* [Shenzhen shangbao], August 2009.

Jiang Chunze. "An Internal Report on the Question of Planning and Market" [Guanyu shichang he jihua de yifen neibu baogao]. *China Through the Ages* [Yanhuang chunqiu] 3 (2013): 11–17.

Jiang Qiangui. "Cultivating Large Enterprise Groups Requires the Promotion by Government and the Operation by Market" [Peiyang dajituan yao zhengfu tuidong shichang yunzuo]. *People's Daily* [Renmin ribao], April 1, 2002.

Jiang Qiangui and Zhang Chunlin. "Reasons for the Formation of State-Owned Enterprise Debt and the Progress of Debt Restructuring" [Guoyou qiye zhaiwu xingcheng de yuanyinhe zhaiwuchongzu de jinzhan]. *Economic Affairs* [Jingjijie] 6 (1996): 20–23.

Jiang Yonghua. "Experiencing Tax-Sharing Reform" [Qinli fenshuizhi gaige]. In *Witness Major Reform Decisions: An Oral History of Reformers* [Jianzheng zhongda gaige juece: gaige qinlizhe zishu], ed. China Society of Economic Reform, 528–49. Beijing: Social Sciences Academic, 2018.

Jiang Zemin. *Selected Works of Jiang Zemin* [Jiang Zemin wenxuan]. Beijing: People's Press, 2006.

Jin Chongji. *Biography of Zhou Enlai* [Zhou Enlai Zhuan]. Beijing: Central Party Literature Press, 2008.

Johnson, Chalmers A. *MITI and the Japanese Miracle: The Growth of Industrial Policy, 1925–1975*. Stanford, CA: Stanford University Press, 1982.

Kim, Soohan, and Frank Dobbin. "Industrial Policy." In *The Palgrave Encyclopedia of Strategic Management*, ed. Mie Augier and David J. Teece. London: Palgrave Macmillan, 2016.

King, Lawrence, and Ivan Szelenyi. "Post-Communist Economic Systems." In *The Handbook of Economic Sociology*, ed. Neil J. Smelser and Richard Swedberg, 205–32. Princeton, NJ: Princeton University Press, 2005.

Kohli, Atul. *State-Directed Development: Political Power and Industrialization in the Global Periphery*. Cambridge: Cambridge University Press, 2012.

Kraus, Richard, and Reeve D. Vanneman. "Bureaucrats Versus the State in Capitalist and Socialist Regimes." *Comparative Studies in Society and History* 27, no. 1 (January 1985): 111–22.

Kuhn, Robert Lawrence. *The Man Who Changed China: The Life and Legacy of Jiang Zemin*. Shanghai: Shanghai Translation Publishing, 2004.

Kuhn, Thomas S. *The Structure of Scientific Revolutions*. Chicago: University of Chicago Press, 2012.

Lampton, David M. *Following the Leader: Ruling China, from Deng Xiaoping to Xi Jinping*. Berkeley: University of California Press, 2014.

Lau, Lawrence, Yingyi Qian, and Gerald Roland. "Reform Without Losers: An Interpretation of China's Dual-Track Approach to Transition." *Journal of Political Economy* 108, no. 1 (February 2000): 120–43.

Li Cheng. *China's Leaders: The New Generation*. Lanham, MD: Rowman & Littlefield, 2001.

Li Cheng and Lynn White. "The Fifteenth Central Committee of the Chinese Communist Party: Full-Fledged Technocratic Leadership with Partial Control by Jiang Zemin." *Asian Survey* 38, no. 3 (March 1998): 231–64.

Li Jie and Yu Jundao. *Records of Mao Zedong (1945–1957)* [Shilu maozedong]. Vol. 3. Beijing: Beijing Lianhe Publishing, 2018.

Li Lawang. "Actively Develop Horizontal Connections to Enhance Urban Vitality" [Jiji fazhan hengxiang lianxi zengqiang chengshi huoli]. In *China Urban Economic and Social Yearbook* [Zhongguo chengshi shehui jingji nianjian]. Beijing: China Urban Yearbook, 1986.

Li Peng. *Market and Control: Economic Diary of Li Peng* [Shichang he tiaokong Li Peng jingji riji]. Beijing: Xinhua, 2007.

Li Peng. *Memories of Li Peng* [Lipeng huiyilu]. Beijing: China Electric Power, 2014.

Li Rongrong. "The Deepening of Industrial Structural Adjustment in Suzhou City" [Suzhoushi gongyejiegou tiaozheng gongzuo buduan shenhua]. *Economic Work Newsletter* [Jingji gongzuo tongxun] 11 (1992): 19–21.

Li Xiannian. "Activating Rural Markets" [Huoyue nongcun shichang]. In *Li Xiannian on Public Finance, Banking, and Trade: 1950–1991* [Li Xiannian lun caizheng jinrong maoyi]. Vol. 2. Beijing: China Financial & Economic Publishing, 1992.

Li Xiannian. "Current Financial Situation and the Work of Banking, 1954" [Dangqian caizheng zhuangkuang he yinhang de gongzuo renwu]. In *Li Xiannian on Public Finance, Banking, and Trade: 1950–1991* [Li Xiannian lun caizheng jinrong maoyi]. Vol. 2. Beijing: China Financial & Economic Publishing, 1992.

"Li Xiannian's Speech in Chicago" [Lixiannian zai zhijiage de yanjiang]. *People's Daily* [Renmin ribao], July 27, 1985.

Li Xiaopeng and Zhang Guobiao. *China's Industrial Policy* [Zhongguo de chanye zhengce]. Beijing: China Development Press, 2017.

Liao Jili. "On the Question of Efficiency, Proportion and Speed" [Tantan xiaoyi bili he sudu wenti]. *National Economic Planning and Management* [Guomin jingji jihua yu guanli] 7 (1983): 17–23.

Lieberthal, Kenneth G., and David M. Lampton, eds. *Bureaucracy, Politics, and Decision Making in Post-Mao China*. Berkeley: University of California Press, 2018.

Lin Justin Yifu. *Demystifying the Chinese Economy*. Cambridge: Cambridge University Press, 2011.

Lin Justin Yifu. "Emancipating the Mind, Seeking Truth from Facts, Advancing with the Times, Seeking Truth and Being Pragmatic, Enhancing Theoretical Self-Confidence: Participation in 11 Symposiums in 1991 and Subsequent Work" [Jiefang sixiang shishiqiushi yushijujin qiuzhen wushi zengqiang lilun zixin canjia 1991nian 11zuo-tanhui he zhihou de gongzuo]. In *Jiang Zemin and the Proposition of the Socialist Market Economy System* [Jiang Zemin he Shehuizhuyi Shichang Jingji de tichu], ed. Chen Jun and Hong Nan. Beijing: Central Party Literature Press, 2012.

Lin Justin Yifu, Tao Ran, and Liu Mingxing. "Decentralization and Local Governance in China's Economic Transition." Paper prepared for the conference "The Rise of Local Governments in Developing Countries," London School of Economics, May 2003.

Lin Zhaomu. "Correctly Implement the Strategy of Developing Enterprise Groups" [Zhengque shishi fazhan qiye jituan zhanlue]. In "Forum on Implementing the Spirit of 15th National Congress of the Communist Party of China and Speed Up the Reform of State-Owned Enterprises: An Excerpt" [Luoshi shiwuda jingshen jiakuai guoyouqiye gaige zuotanhui fayan zhaideng]. *Qiushi* 8 (1998): 11–12.

Lippit, Victor D. "The Great Leap Forward Reconsidered." *Modern China* 1, no. 1 (January 1975): 92–115.

Litwak, Eugene. "Models of Bureaucracy Which Permit Conflict." *American Journal of Sociology* 67, no. 2 (September 1961): 177–84.

Liu Hong. "A Historical Event That Chooses National Developmental Mode" [Xuanze guojia fazhan moshi de yici lishixing shijian]. *Economic Observer* [Jingji guancha bao], October 30, 2014.

Liu Hong. *The 1980s: The Glories and Dreams of Chinese Economists* [Bashi niandai zhongguo jingjixueren de guangrong yu mengxiang]. Nanning: Guangxi Normal University Press, 2010.

Liu Hong. "The Structure Team Connecting the Past and the Future" [Chengqian qihou jiegou zu]. *Economic Observer* [Jingji guancha bao], January 19, 2009.

Liu Hongru. "Deepen Financial Theory Research in Deepened Financial Reform: Speech of Vice Governor Liu Hongru of PBOC at Financial Research Institute Director Meeting" [Zai Shenhua jinrong gaige zhong Shenhua jinrong lilun yanjiu: liuhongru fuhangzhang zai renminyinhang jinyansuo suozhang huiyishang de jianghua]. *Northern China Finance* [Huabei jinrong] 6 (1998): 3–9.

Liu Hongru. "The Formation of China's Central Banking System." *China Finance* 23 (2013): 21–23.

Liu Hongru. "On Economic System Reform" [Guanyu jingji tizhi gaige zhege wenti]. In *Information Collection of National Trust and Investment Company Managers Seminar* [Quanguo xintuo touzi gongsi jingli yantaohui ziliao huibian], ed. Hunan Trust and Investment, 30–42. Changsha: Hunan Trust and Investment, 1991.

Liu Hongru. "Reviewing the Course of Financial System Reform in Our Country" [Huigu woguo jinrong tizhi gaige de lichen]. *Bainianchao* 5 (2009): 22–28.

Lou Jiwei. "The Chairman of the National Social Security Fund, Lou Jiwei's Speech at the 16th High-Level Forum on Enterprise Development." January 28, 2018, Beijing. http://finance.sina.com.cn/china/gncj/2018-01-30/doc-ifyqyqni5050209.shtml.

Lou Jiwei and Gao Jianhong. "The Reform of Central Bank's Monetary Policy and the Development of the Bond Market" [Zhongyang yinhang huobi zhengce gongju de gaige yu guozhai shichang de xingcheng]. *Finance and Insurance* [Jinrong yu baoxian] 12 (1994): 99–104.

Lu Feng and Feng Kaidong. *The Policy Choice to Develop China's Automobile Industry with Independent Intellectual Property Rights* [Woguo fazhan zizhu zhishi chanquan qiche gongye de zhengce xuanze]. Beijing: Peking University Press, 2005.

Lv Dong. *Commemorative Anthology of Lv Dong* [Lv dong jinian wenji], ed. Commemorative Anthology of Lv Dong Editorial Board. Beijing: China Industrial Economic Federation, 2005.

Marquis, Christopher, and Kunyuan Qiao. *Mao and Markets: The Communist Roots of Chinese Enterprise.* New Haven, CT: Yale University Press, 2022.

Marquis, Christopher, and András Tilcsik. "Imprinting: Toward a Multilevel Theory." *Academy of Management Annals* 7, no. 1 (June 2003): 195–245.

McDonnell, Erin Metz. "Patchwork Leviathan: How Pockets of Bureaucratic Governance Flourish Within Institutionally Diverse Developing States." *American Sociological Review* 82, no. 3 (June 2017): 476–510.

McDonnell, Erin Metz. *Patchwork Leviathan: Pockets of Bureaucratic Effectiveness in Developing States.* Princeton, NJ: Princeton University Press, 2020.

"Mckinnon: China's 4 Trillion Yuan Fiscal Stimulus Package Is Exciting" [Maiijinnong: zhongguo siwanyi caizheng ciji fangan lingren zhenfen], *China Business News*, November 17, 2008.

Montias, J. M. "Planning with Material Balances in Soviet-Type Economies." *American Economic Review* 49, no. 5 (December 1959): 963–85.

Morgan, Kimberly J., and Ann Shola Orloff, eds. *The Many Hands of the State: Theorizing Political Authority and Social Control.* New York: Cambridge University Press, 2017.

Mudge, Stephanie L. *Leftism Reinvented: Western Parties from Socialism to Neoliberalism.* Cambridge, MA: Harvard University Press, 2018.

Myers, James T. "China: Modernization and 'Unhealthy Tendencies.'" *Comparative Politics* 21, no. 2 (January 1989): 193–213.

Narayanan, Raviprasad. "The Politics of Reform in China: Deng, Jiang and Hu." *Strategic Analysis* 30, no. 2 (April 2006): 329–53.

Nathan, Andrew J., and Kellee S. Tsai. "Factionalism: A New Institutionalist Restatement." *China Journal* 34 (July 1995): 157–92.

National Archives Administration of China. *The Central Committee of the Communist Party of China in Xibaipo* [Zhonggong Zhongyang zai xibaipo]. Shenzhen: Haitian Publisher, 1998.

National Bureau of Statistics. *Research on State-Owned Enterprise Reform and Hot Issues* [Guoyou qiye gaige ji redian wenti yanjiu]. Beijing: China Statistics Press, 2001.

Naughton, Barry J. *The Chinese Economy: Adaptation and Growth.* 2nd ed. Cambridge, MA: MIT Press, 2018.

Naughton, Barry. *Growing Out of the Plan: Chinese Economic Reform, 1978–1993.* Cambridge: Cambridge University Press, 1995.

"Notice Regarding Opinions on Deepening the Pilot Work of Large Enterprise Groups" [Guanyu shenhua daxing qiye jituan shodden gongzuo de yijian]. Issued by the State Council, SETC, and the System Reform Commission, April 29, 1997.

Pacewicz, Josh. *Partisans and Partners: The Politics of the Post-Keynesian Society.* Chicago: University of Chicago Press, 2016.

Pacewicz, Josh. "Tax Increment Financing, Economic Development Professionals and the Financialization of Urban Politics." *Socio-Economic Review* 11, no. 3 (July 2013): 413–40.

Padgett, John F. "The Politics of Communist Economic Reform: Soviet Union and China." In *The Emergence of Organizations and Markets*, ed. John F. Padgett and Walter W. Powell, 271–315. Princeton, NJ: Princeton University Press, 2012.

Party Documents Research of the Central Committee of CCP. "Around the Breakthrough of Price Liberalization in 1988" [1988nian wujia chuangguan qianhou]. *China Through the Ages* [Yanhuang Chunqiu] 10 (2005): 22–25.

Pei, Yuanxiu. "The Formation and Development of the Comprehensive Balance Theory" [Zonghe pingheng lilun de xingcheng he fazhan]. *Frontline* [Qianxian] 3 (1981): 54–57.

Perkins, Dwight H. "China's Economic Policy and Performance." In *The Cambridge History of China*. Vol. 15, *The People's Republic*, Part 2, *Revolutions Within the Chinese Revolution, 1966–1982*, ed. Roderick MacFarquhar and John K. Fairbank. Cambridge: Cambridge University Press, 1991.

Polanyi, Karl. *The Great Transformation: The Political and Economic Origins of Our Time*. Boston: Beacon, 2001.

Polillo, Simone. *The Ascent of Market Efficiency: Finance That Cannot Be Proven*. Ithaca, NY: Cornell University Press, 2020.

Qian, Yingyi. "The Process of China's Market Transition: The Evolutionary, Historical, and Comparative Perspectives." In *China's Deep Reform: Domestic Politics in Transition*, ed. Lowell Dittmer and Guoli Liu, 229–50. Lanham, MD: Rowman & Littlefield, 2006.

Qu Jingdong. "The Project System: A New Form of State Governance" [Xiangmuzhi: yizhong xin de guojia zhili tizhi]. *Social Sciences in China* [Zhongguo shehuikexue] 33, no. 4 (2012): 28–47.

Reed, Isaac Ariail. "Power: Relational, Discursive, and Performative Dimensions." *Sociological Theory* 31, no. 3 (October 2013): 193–218.

"Report from the 16th National Congress: Jiang Zemin Proposed Pursuing a New Style Industrialization, Vigorously Implementing the Strategy of Rejuvenating the Country Through Science and Education, and the Strategy of Sustainable Development" [Shiliuda xianchang baodao: Jiang Zemin tichu yaozou xinxing gongyehua daolu, dali shishi kejiaoxingguo he kechixu fazhan zhanlue], *Xinhua News*, November 8, 2002, https://news.sina.com.cn/c/2002-11-08/1002800216.html.

Ridley, F. F. "French Technocracy and Comparative Government." *Political Studies* 14, no. 1 (1966): 34–52.

Riskin, Carl. *China's Political Economy: The Quest for Development Since 1949*. Oxford: Oxford University Press, 1987.

Roll, Michael, ed. *The Politics of Public Sector Performance: Pockets of Effectiveness in Developing Countries*. London: Routledge, 2013.

Rothstein, Bo. "The Chinese Paradox of High Growth and Low Quality of Government: The Cadre Organization Meets Max Weber." *Governance* 28, no. 4 (November 2015): 533–48.

Sautman, Barry. "Sirens of the Strongman: Neo-Authoritarianism in Recent Chinese Political Theory." *China Quarterly* 129 (March 1992): 72–102.

Schneider, Ben Ross. *Politics Within the State: Elite Bureaucrats and Industrial Policy in Authoritarian Brazil.* Pittsburgh, PA: University of Pittsburgh Press, 1992.

Schurmann, Franz. *Ideology and Organization in Communist China.* Berkeley: University of California Press, 1969.

Scobell, Andrew, Edmund J. Burke, Cortez A. Cooper Iii, Sale Lilly, Chad J. R. Ohlandt, Eric Warner, and J. D. Williams. *China's Grand Strategy: Trends, Trajectories, and Long-Term Competition.* Santa Monica, CA: RAND, 2020.

Scott, James C. *Seeing Like a State: How Certain Schemes to Improve the Human Condition Have Failed.* New Haven, CT: Yale University Press, 1999.

Seabrooke, Leonard. "Epistemic Arbitrage: Transnational Professional Knowledge in Action." *Journal of Professions and Organization* 1, no. 1 (March 2014): 49–64.

Shambaugh, David. "The Dynamics of Elite Politics During the Jiang Era." *China Journal* 45 (January 2001): 101–11.

Shan, Xu. "Xue Muqiao: The Red Currency Struggle" [Xue Muqiao: Hongse huobi zhanzheng]. In *Oriental Outlook* [Dongfang liaowang zhoukan], August 24, 2009.

Shih, Victor. *Factions and Finance in China: Elite Conflict and Inflation.* Cambridge: Cambridge University Press, 2009.

Shirk, Susan L. *The Political Logic of Economic Reform in China.* Berkeley: University of California Press, 1993.

Silberman, Bernard S. *Cages of Reason: The Rise of the Rational State in France, Japan, the United States, and Great Britain.* Chicago: University of Chicago Press, 1993.

Smith, Chris. "Living at Work: Management Control and the Dormitory Labour System in China." *Asia Pacific Journal of Management* 20, no. 3 (September 2003): 333–58.

Song Ping. "The Speech of Comrade Song Ping on the Opening Ceremony of the National Conference of Macroeconomic Management" [Songping tongzhi zai quanguo hongguan jingji guanli wenti yantaohui kaimushi shang de jianghua]. *Planned Economy Research* [Jihua jingji yanjiu] 9 (1986): 3–7.

Sutherland, Dylan. *China's Large Enterprises and the Challenge of Late Industrialization.* London: Routledge, 2003.

Szelenyi, Ivan, and Eric Kostello. "The Market Transition Debate: Toward a Synthesis?" *American Journal of Sociology* 101, no. 4 (January 1996): 1082–96.

Tan, Yeling, and James Conran. "China's Growth Model in Comparative and Historical Perspectives." In *Diminishing Returns: The New Politics of Growth and Stagnation,* ed. Mark Blyth, Jonas Pontusson, and Lucio Baccaro, 143–66. New York: Oxford University Press, 2022.

Tang Linmin and Dehua Wang. "Review and Evaluation of Management Reform Since the Resumption of National Bond Insurance" [Guozhai huifu faxing yilai guanli gaige de huigu ji pingjia]. *Contemporary China History Studies* [Dangdai zhongguoshi yanjiu] 22, no. 2 (2015): 38–46.

Tian Jiyun. *The Great Practice of Reform and Open-Up* [Gaige kaifang de weida shijian]. Beijing: Xinhua, 2009.

Tian Jiyun. "Hu Yaobang in Our Hearts" [Women xinzhong de Hu Yaobang]. *China Through the Ages* [Yanhuang chunqiu] 11 (2015): 13–14.

Tsai, Wen-Hsuan, and Chien-Wen Kou. "The Party's Disciples: CCP Reserve Cadres and the Perpetuation of a Resilient Authoritarian Regime." *China Quarterly* 221 (March 2015): 1–20.

Tsou Tang. "Chinese Politics at the Top: Factionalism or Informal Politics? Balance-of-Power Politics or a Game to Win All?" *China Journal* 34 (July 1995): 95–156.

Vogel, Ezra F. *Deng Xiaoping and the Transformation of China*. Cambridge, MA: Belknap Press of Harvard University Press, 2013.

Vogel, Ezra F. *One Step Ahead in China: Guangdong Under Reform*. Cambridge, MA: Harvard University Press, 1990.

Vogel, Steven K. *Marketcraft: How Governments Make Markets Work*. New York: Oxford University Press, 2018.

Wacquant, Loïc. "Crafting the Neoliberal State: Workfare, Prisonfare, and Social Insecurity." *Sociological Forum* 25, no. 2 (June 2010): 197–220.

Wade, Robert. *Governing the Market: Economic Theory and the Role of Government in East Asian Industrialization*. Princeton, NJ: Princeton University Press, 2003.

Walter, Carl, and Fraser Howie. *Red Capitalism: The Fragile Financial Foundation of China's Extraordinary Rise*. Hoboken, NJ: Wiley, 2012.

Wan Li. "Further Develop New Agriculture." News release of Xinhua Press no. 4712, 1982.

Wang, Dayang. "The Origin of Crossing the River by Feeling for the Stones" [Mozhe shitou guohe de laili]. *Study Times* [Xuexi shibao], April 11, 2018. http://cpc.people.com.cn/n1/2018/0412/c69113-29921565.html.

Wang Dongjiang and Cao Yuanzheng. *Tackling SOE Reform: A Practical Guide on Building Modern Enterprise Institutions and Restructuring Assets* [Guoyou qiye gaige gongjian xiandai qiye zhidu yu zichan chongzu shiwu]. Beijing: Reform, 1998.

Wang, Hui, and Christopher Connery. "Depoliticized Politics, Multiple Components of Hegemony, and the Eclipse of the Sixties." *Inter-Asia Cultural Studies* 7, no. 4 (December 2006): 683–700.

Wang Huijiong and Li Boxi. "Industrial Policy and Industrial Structure: A Research Design" [Chanye zhengce yu chanye jiegou keti de xitong sheji]. *Study Materials for Economic Professionals* [Jingji gongzuozhe xuexi ziliao] 1 (1986): 32–44.

Wang Xiwen. "Looking at the Future Smart Manufacturing Industry from the Germany's 'Industry 4.0' Initiative" [Cong deguo gongye 4.0 zhanlue kan weilai zhineng zhizao]. *China Information Technology* [Zhongguo Xinxihua] 15 (2014): 8–9.

Wang Xiwen. *New Industrial Policy* [Xin chanye zhengce]. Beijing: Xinhua, 2017.

Wang Yingyao. "The Rise of the 'Shareholding State': Financialization of Economic Management in China." *Socio-Economic Review* 13, no. 3 (July 2015): 603–25.

Wang Yuhua. "Coercive Capacity and the Durability of the Chinese Communist State." *Communist and Post-Communist Studies* 47, no. 1 (March 2014): 13–25.

Wang Zhongyu. "Major Breakthroughs and Comprehensive Advancement: Thinking Enterprise Organizational Structure Adjustment from the Formation of Jihua Enterprise Group" [Zhongdian tupo quanmian tuijin: cong jihua jituan de xingcheng kan qiye zuzhijiegou tiaozheng de silu]. *China Economic System Reform* [Zhongguo jingji tizhi gaige] 3 (1991): 31–32.

Wang Zhongyu. "On the Macro-Adjustment and Control System of Market Economy" [Lun shichang jingji de hongguan tiaokong tixi]. *Journal of Technical Economics and Management* [Jishu jingji yu guanli] 3 (1994): 4–5.

Wang Zhongyu. "On Understanding Several Issues of Current Enterprise Work" [Tan dangqian qiye gongzuo de jige renshi wenti]. *China Market* [Zhongguo shichang] 6 (1996): 4–5.

Wang Zhongyu. *Tackling State-Owned Enterprise Reform* [Guoqi gaige gongjian jishi]. Beijing: Enterprise Management Publishing, 2010.

Wang Zhongyu. "Walk the Road of SOE Reform with Chinese Characteristics: Speech Excerpts of Wang Zhongyu at the 'International Symposium on Policy Choices of SOE Reform in China' " [Zou you zongguo tese de guoyouqiye gaige luzi: guojia jingmaowei zhuren wang zhongyu zai zhongguo guoyouqiye gaige zhengce xuanze guoji yantaohui shang de fayanzhaiyao]. *International Data and Information* [Guoji ziliao xinxi] 8 (1995): 8–10.

Weber, Isabella M. *How China Escaped Shock Therapy*. Abingdon, UK: Routledge, 2021.

Weber, Max. *Economy and Society: An Outline of Interpretive Sociology*, ed. Guenther Roth and Claus Wittich. Berkeley: University of California Press, 1978.

Weber, Max. *Politics as a Vocation*. Melbourne: Hassell Street, 2021.

Wei Liqun, "Persist in Taking a New Road to Industrialization (2002)" [Jianchi zou xinxing gongyehua daolu]. In *Cultivating a Road for Reform and Opening-Up* [Gaige kaifang gengyun lu], 283–93. Beijing: China Yanshi, 2018.

Wei Ren. " 'Strategic Research on a Manufacturing Power' Released; Three Steps Towards a Manufacturing Power" [Zhizao qiangguo zhanlue yanjiu fabu sanbuzou maixiang zhizao qiangguo]. *China Equipment* [Zhuangbei zhizao] 5 (2015): 2.

Whittaker, Hugh D., Timothy Sturgeon, Toshie Okita, and Tianbiao Zhu. *Compressed Development: Time and Timing in Economic and Social Development*. Oxford: Oxford University Press, 2012.

Wilson, Patrick. *Second-Hand Knowledge: An Inquiry Into Cognitive Authority*. Westport, CT: Greenwood, 1983.

Wong, Christine P. W. "Central-Local Relations in an Era of Fiscal Decline: The Paradox of Fiscal Decentralization in Post-Mao China." *China Quarterly* 128 (1991): 691–715.

Woo-Cumings, Meredith, ed. *The Developmental State*. Ithaca, NY: Cornell University Press, 1999.

"Work Meeting on Adjusting Enterprise Organizational Structure" [Quansheng qiye zuzhi jiegou tiaozheng gongzuo huyi]. In *Jilin Yearbook* [Jilin nianjian], ed. Jilin Provincial Local History Compilation Committee, 115–16. Changchun: Jilin, 1992.

Wu Guoyou. "To Look at the Practical Characteristics of Chen Yun's Idea of 'Seek Truth from Facts' from an Economic Perspective" [Cong jingji shijiao kan Chen Yun shishiqiushi sixiang de shijian tedian]. In *Chen Yun and Contemporary China* [Chenyun yu dangdai zhongguo], ed. Zhu Jiamu. Beijing: Contemporary China Publishing, 2010.

Wu Jing and Lu Nanfang. "Grand Narrative at History's Turning Point: A Political Analysis of the Internet Ideology of China's 'Industrial Party' " [Lishi zhuanzhe zhongde hongda xueshi: gongye dang wangluo sichao de zhengzhi fenxi]. *Dongfang Journal* 1 (2018): 49–60.

Wu Jinglian. *Collected Works of Wu Jinglian* [Wujinglian wenji]. Vol. 3. Beijing: Central Compilation and Translation Bureau, 2015.

Wu Jinglian. "The Difficulties and Countermeasures of the Corporation Reform of State-Owned Large and Medium-Sized Enterprises" [Guoyou dazhognxing qiye gongsi gaige de nandina he duice]. *Economic Daily* [Jingji Ribao], February 26, 1995.

Wu Jinglian and Ma Guochuan. "The Role of the 'Dual-Track' System and Its Consequences." In *Whither China: Restarting the Reform Agenda*, trans. Xiaofeng Hua and Nancy Hearst, 120–34. New York: Oxford University Press, 2016.

Wu Jinglian and Zhou Xiaochuan. *A Comprehensive Design of China's Economic Reform*. Beijing: China Zhanwang, 1988.

Wu Xiaobo. *The Gains and Losses of Past Economic Reforms* [Lidai jingji gaige deshi]. Hangzhou: Zhejiang University Press, 2013.

Wu Xiaoling. "Practices and Explorations for Establishing Financial Market Order" [Chuangjian jinrong shichang zhixu de tansuo]. In *Witness Major Reform Decisions: An Oral History of Reformers* [Jianzheng zhongda gaige juece: gaige qinlizhe zishu], ed. China Society of Economic Reform, 571–84. Beijing: Social Sciences Academic, 2018.

Xiang Huaicheng. "Witness Fiscal System Reform" [Jianzheng caizheng tizhi gaige]. In *Witness Major Reform Decisions: An Oral History of Reformers* [Jianzheng zhongda gaige juece: gaige qinlizhe zishu], ed. China Society of Economic Reform, 514–27. Beijing: Social Sciences Academic, 2018.

Xiao Gongqin. "China's Changing of the Guard: The Rise of the Technocrats." *Journal of Democracy* 14, no. 1 (January 2003): 60–65.

Xiao Meng. *Debt Restructuring and Bankruptcy Procedure in the Reconstruction of Corporate Governance: Revisiting the Jinglun Conference* [Gongsi zhili jiegou zhaiwu chongzu he pochan chengxu: chongwen jinglun huiyi]. Beijing: Central Compilation and Translation, 1999.

Xu Penghang. "The Advantage of Huangshi and Economic Developmental Strategy" [Huangshi de yoush he jingji fazhan zhanlue]. *Industrial Economy* [Gongye jingji] 5 (1985): 17–23.

Xu Penghang. "Strengthen the Research on Hubei Product Strategy" [Jiaqiang dui hubei chanpin zhanlue de yanjiu]. *Decision-Making and Consultancy* [Zixun yu juece] 2 (1989): 4–8.

Xu Penghang. "To Develop Horizontal Linkages and Speed Up Economic Development of Huangshi" [Jiakuai huangshi jiangji fazhan bufa]. *Study and Practice* [Xuexi he shijian] 2 (1986): 18–20.

Xu Penghang. "Unleashing Our Own Advantages and Accelerating Asset Restructuring: Promote the Coordinated Development of Coastal and Inland Economies" [Fahui zishen youshi jiakuai zichan chongzu cujin yanhai neidi jingji xietiao fazhan]. *Economic Work Newsletter* [Jingji gongzuo tongxun] 10 (1996): 3–4.

Xu Shanda. "Background and Decision-Making Process of the 1994 Tax Sharing Reform" [1994nian caizheng gaige de beijing he juece guocheng]. In *Witness Major Reform Decisions: An Oral History of Reformers* [Jianzheng zhongda gaige juece: gaige qinlizhe zishu], ed. China Society of Economic Reform, 550–70. Beijing: Social Sciences Academic, 2018.

Xu Xiaohong. "The Great Separation: The Cultural Revolution and the Political Origins of Ordoeconomism in China." Paper presented at the annual meeting of the Association for Asian Studies, Honolulu, HI, March 2022.

Xue Baoding, Zhang Xuansan, and Li Boxi. "System Engineering and the Analysis of Society and Economy" [Xitong gongcheng he shehui jingji xitong]. *Enterprise Economy* [Qiye jingji] 11 (1982): 3–7.

Xue Muqiao, *Memoirs of Xue Muqiao* [Xuemuqiao huiyilu]. Tianjin: Tianjin People's Press, 2006.

Yang Changji. "Explanation on Compiling and Implementing the Outline of Economic Operation Adjustment and Control Program in 1995" [Guanyu bianzhi 1995nian jingji yunxing he tiaokong fangan gangyao de shuoming]. *National Economic Management and Planning* [Guomin jingji guanli yu jihua] 4 (1995): 71–72.

Yang, Dali. "Economic Transformation and State Rebuilding in China." In *Holding China Together: Diversity and National Integration in the Post-Deng Era*, ed. Barry J. Naughton and Dali L. Yang. New York: Cambridge University Press, 2004.

Yang, Dali. *Remaking the Chinese Leviathan: Market Transition and the Politics of Governance in China*. Stanford, CA: Stanford University Press, 2004.

Yang Mingwei. *Late Years of Chen Yun* [Chen yun wannian suiyue]. Beijing: People's Press, 2005.

Yao Jin. *100-Day Interviews of Yao Yilin* [Yao Yilin baixi tan]. Beijing: History of Chinese Communist Party Publishing, 2008.

Yao Yilin. "On the Work of Commerce (1957)" [Guanyu shangye gongzuo wenti]. In *Selected Documents of Commerce and Economic Work* [Shangye jingji ziliao xuanbian], ed. Department of Management of Hangzhou School of Commerce. Hangzhou: Hangzhou College of Commerce Press, 1982.

Yao Yilin, *One-Hundred Nights Conversation with Yao Yilin* [Yao Yilin baixitan]. Beijing: History of Chinese Communist Party Publishing, 1988.

Yao Yilin. "Statistics Is the Basis for Making Policies" [Tongji shi zhiding zhengce de zhuyao yiju]. *Economics Digest* [Jingjixue Wenzhai] 4 (1984): 54–55.

You Lin, Zheng Xinli, and Wang Ruipu. *A General History of National Affairs of People's Republic of China* [Zhonghua renmin gongheguo guoshi tongjian]. Beijing: Hongqi, 1999.

Yu Jiang and Xia Li. "Liu Hongru: Wudaokou Is a Product of an Era" [Wudaokou shi yige shidai de chanwu]. *Modern Bankers* [Dangdai jinrong jia] 9 (2011): 16–22.

Yu Yiqing. "How Deng Xiaoping Resisted Oppositions and Promoted 'Dark Horse' Zhu Rongji" [Deng Xiaoping Ruhe Lipai Zhongyi Fuzhi Heima Zhu Rongji]. 2015. http://politics.people.com.cn/n/2014/1121/c1001-26067334.html.

Yu Yongding and Lu Feng. " 'Double Surpluses,' Capacity Gap and Indigenous Innovation" [Shuang shuncha: nengli quekou he zizhu chuangxin]. *Chinese Social Science* [Zhongguo shehui kexue] 6 (2012): 91–114.

Yuan Baohua. "Industrial Census Is an Important Part of Four Modernizations" [Gongye pucha shi sihuajianshe de yixiang zhongyao jichu gongzuo]. In *Economic Works of Yuan Baohua* [Yuan Baohua Jingji Wenji]. Beijing: China Economic Press, 1991.

Yuan Baohua, *A Memoir of Yuan Baohua* [Yuan Baohua huiyilu]. Beijing: People's University Press, 2008.

Zeng Peiyan. *Zeng Peiyan on Development and Reform* [Zeng peiyan lun fazhan yu gaige]. Vol. 1. Beijing: People's Press, 2014.

Zhang Dicheng. *The Chronicle of State-Owned Enterprise Reform (1978–2005)* [Zhongguo guoyouqiye gaige biannianshi]. Beijing: Zhongguo Gongren, 2006.

Zhang Jincai. "Chen Yun and the Transformation of Central Leading Organizations on Economics and Finance" [Chenyun yu Zhongyang caijing lingdao jigou de bianqian]. *Beijing Party History* [Beijing dangshi] 1 (2013): 24–28.

Zhang Yanning. "Experience of the Decision-Making Process of State-Owned Enterprise Reform" [Qinli guoyou qiye gaige de juece guocheng]. In *Witness Major Reform Decisions: An Oral History of Reformers* [Jianzheng zhongda gaige juece: gaige qinlizhe zishu], ed. China Society of Economic Reform, 241–51. Beijing: Social Sciences Academic, 2018.

Zhang Zheng, Zhang Dasheng, and Wang Xiaokuan, eds. *Full Record of the Economic Development of the People's Republic of China* [Zhonghua renmin gongheguo jingji fazhan quanjilu]. Vol. 1. Beijing: China Society Publishing, 2010.

Zhao Qiang, Wu Jin, Xia Peng, Wang Di, Liu Dan, Liu Yun, and Dong Han. "Research on Optimization and Assessment of the Evaluation Index System for Manufacturing Power" [Zhizao qiangguo pingjia zhibiao tixi youhua yu ceping yanjiu]. *China Engineering Science* [Zhongguo gongcheng kexue] 19, no. 13 (2017): 13–19.

Zhao Weichen. *At the Forefront of Economic Reform* [Zai jingji gaige qianyan]. Beijing: Central Party Literature, 2010.

Zhao Ying. *Empirical Research on the Transformation of China's Industrial Policy, 2000–2010* [Zhongguo chanye zhengce biandong qushi shizheng yanjiu 2000–2010]. Beijing: Economy Management Publishing, 2010.

Zhao Ziyang. *Collected Works of Zhao Ziyang* [Zhao Ziyang wenxuan]. Vol. 1. Hong Kong: Chinese University of Hong Kong Press, 2016.

Zhao Ziyang. *The Course of Reform*. Hong Kong: Century Publisher, 2009.

Zhao Ziyang. *Prisoner of the State: The Secret Journal of Premier Zhao Ziyang*, ed. Bao Pu, Renee Chiang, and Adi Ignatius. New York: Simon & Schuster, 2010.

Zhou Xiaochuan. "Financial Reform Should Allow Trial and Error" [Jinrong gaige yinggai yunxu shicuo]. *Securities Times* [Zhengquan shibao], November 19, 2012. http://money.sohu.com/20121119/n357973071.shtml.

Zhou Xiaochuan. "The Historical Significance of the 14th National Congress in Establishing a Socialist Market Economy as the Goal of Systemic Reform" [Shisida queli shuihuizhuyi shichangjingji wei tizhi gaige mubiao de lishi yiyi]. In *Jiangzemin and the Proposition of the Socialist Market Economy System* [Jiang Zemin he Shehuizhuyi Shichang Jingji de tichu], ed. Chen Jun and Hong Nan, 53–70. Beijing: Central Party Literature Press, 2012.

Zhou Xueguang. *The Logic of Governance in China*. Cambridge: Cambridge University Press, 2022.

Zhou Zhengqing. "Questions on Contemporary Financial Situation and Financial Reform" [Guanyu dangqian jinrong xingshi he jinrong tizhi gaige wenti]. In *Information Collection of National Trust and Investment Company Managers Seminar* [Quanguo xintuo touzi gongsi jingli yantaohui ziliao huibian], ed. Hunan Trust and Investment, 17–29. Changsha: Hunan Trust and Investment, 1991.

Zhu Jiamu. *A Biographical Chronicle of Chen Yun* [Chen Yun nianpu]. Beijing: Central Party Literature Press, 2000.

Zhu Rongji. *Zhu Rongji Meets the Press* [Zhu rongji jianghua shilu]. Beijing: People's Press, 2011.

Zhu Xihao. "The Impact of Information, Control and System Theories on Methodology of Social Science" [Xinxilun kongzhilun he xitonglun dui shehuikexue fangfalun de yingxiang]. *Modernization* [Xiandaihua zazhi] 2 (1985): 6–8.

Zou Huiqin. *The Study of Economic Thoughts of Li Xiannian* [Lixiannian jingji sixiang yanjiu]. Xining: Qinghai People's Press, 1993.

Zuo Shiquan. "German Integration of Industrialization and Industrialization" [Deyizhi lianghua ronghe]. *China Equipment* [Zhungbei zhizao] 4 (2012): 84–88.

INDEX

Anhui, 71
Asian Financial Crisis, 144, 175
asset management corporations, 176
authority: of bureaucracy, 8, 11, 30, 50–59, 113, 150, 153, 228; of central bank, 154–59, 162, 179; of central government, 99, 103, 226; of circulators, 44, 62–63, 73, 78, 102; cognitive, 20, 137; of local generalists, 71–73, 102; of local governments, 75–78, 173, 184; of MIIT, 205–7; monetary, 76–78, 155, 162, 167; of planning, 36; policy, 4, 12–17, 27, 132; of SOE reformers, 121, 124, 132–33, 137, 141–45; of technocrats, 85–86, 101, 107, 186
autonomy: of central bank, 103, 155; of circulators, 48; of commercial enterprises, 64, 120, 126; of economic bureaucrats, 14, 225; of industrial policy, 30, 182, 189; of local generalists, 68–69; of local governments, 74–75; of SEZs, 76; of the state, 6–7, 220

balance theory, 56, 82. See also circulators
Banking Regulatory Commission, 11–12
bank recapitalization, 175–80

bonds, 106–7, 142, 155, 159, 169–72, 176–77, 187; shifting accounting practices for, 170–71
Bourdieu, Pierre, 110
Brazil, 8, 80, 206
Britain, 7
budget, 45, 53, 68, 76–77, 79–80, 152, 170–71, 203; balanced, 150; soft constraints of, 76, 79, 103
bureaucracy: competition within, 61, 72–79, 199, 219–20; ethos of, 8; fragmentation of, 87, 182–86, 220; politics and, 13, 220; Weberian model of, 8–9
bureaucratic capitalism, 224
bureaucratic field, 110, 132, 136, 179, 199, 207, 213, 229
bureaucratic locations: of circulators, 47; definition of, 18; of local generalists, 63–64; in paradigm emergence, 25
bureaucrats, Chinese: educational backgrounds of, 14; fragmentation of, 86–87, 184; low turnover of, 35, 111; professionalization of, 13–15; reputation of, 40, 42, 55, 59, 135

capitalism, 5, 93, 217, 224
career backgrounds, 21, 72, 75, 81, 114,
    189, 197–98
careers: mobility of, 9; and policy
    making, 24; of reform elites, 65–66
career sequences: definition of, 19; of
    SOE reformers, 121
career trajectories: definition of, 19; in
    paradigm emergence, 25; of SETC
    directors, 122; of SPC, NDRC, and
    MIIT ministers, 198
Central Bank, 11, 30, 102–4, 154–56, 163,
    169. See also People's Bank of China
Central Financial-Economic
    Commission, 41–42
Central Huijin, 157, 166, 177–78
centralization, 40, 66, 81, 149–50,
    167; and the circulators, 88; and
    local generalists, 115–16; and local
    governments, 112–13; and tax reform,
    100–103; and the technocrats, 86, 97
central planning, 18, 29–30, 36, 44;
    circulators and, 28, 44–47, 50, 61;
    disposition of, 6; local generalists
    and, 68–74; local governments
    resist, 51–54. See also State Planning
    Commission
central specialists, 65–67
Cheng Li, 111
Chen Jinhua, 139
Chen Yun, 36, 41–42, 49–50, 77, 91; and
    SEZs, 78; as technocrat, 73–74
Chile, 7
China Construction Bank, 176
China Development Bank, 178
Chinese Academy of Engineering, 2, 206
Chinese Academy of Social Sciences, 159
Chinese Communist Revolution, 5,
    38–39, 50–51, 89
Chinese economic bureaucracy:
    entrepreneurship of, 10; history of,
    5–7; hybridity of, 9
Chinese Investment Corporation, 177–78
Chinese Marxism, 47
Chinese Nationalists, 40, 158
circulation perspective: on debt,
    151; development of, 44–45, 67;

implementation of, 47; programs and
    theory of, 57, 61
circulators, 44–61, 63, 81; age out of
    power, 85; and balance theory, 59–60,
    74, 78–79; criticism by Mao of, 54;
    definition of, 28; early years of, 36–44;
    and local generalists, 64, 70–75, 79,
    88; and macroeconomics, 78; network
    analysis of, 49; as technocrats, 73
comparative advantage theory, 192–94
competitiveness: industrial, 22–23, 30,
    195–96; technological, 186, 200, 203,
    212–13
Comprehensive Reform School, 30, 154,
    159–68, 177; coauthorship network of,
    161; core beliefs of, 160–63; introduces
    corporate control, 173; leaders in
    financial bureaucracy, 166
compressed development, 15–16, 231
concentration: in paradigm
    emergence, 25
consumer sector, 45–47, 66, 71, 192
consumption, 45–47, 123, 192, 230
contracting-out system, 71, 120, 162
convergence: in paradigm emergence, 25
coordination, 10, 45, 212; career-based,
    165; central, 45, 85, 128; inter-agency,
    87; lack of, 7, 124, 185; market-based,
    131, 134–36; political, 131; and SETC,
    141–42
corporate control, 172–75; and banking,
    177–78; and SOE restructuring, 23, 121
corruption, 10, 75–76, 105, 224
crisis management, 1, 55, 78, 112–13,
    167–69, 175–76, 187, 193
Cultural Revolution, 37, 50, 53–54, 87,
    90–91, 230; and linking up, 125
currency crisis, 38–42. See also money
    doctors

database: used for book's analysis, 26–27
debt: interenterprise, 134; and
    macrocontrol, 107; national, 106, 171;
    political perception of, 150; of SOEs,
    13, 167–69, 171–79
debt-driven development, 2, 179, 217
debt-to-equity swaps, 140, 174

decentralization, 22–23, 53–55, 66, 69, 75–76, 152, 162, 184; and the bureaucracy, 92; and inflation, 80
Deng Xiaoping, 35, 63; and local generalists, 68; and Maoist radicals, 70; and technocrats, 90
developmental state, 6–7, 12
dual circulation, 231
dual-track system, 75–76

East Asia: developmental states of, 6; economies of, 95, 175; industrialization model of, 193–94
Eastern Europe: as economic case study, 94–95; and shock therapy, 215
economic bureaucracy, Chinese. *See* Chinese economic bureaucracy
economic growth, 13, 21, 74–78, 80–81, 86, 103, 107, 169–71, 187, 211–12, 217, 231; export-led, 195, 219
Economic Reform and Opening Up, 35
economics, 14, 39, 98, 198; evolutionary, 207–8; industrial, 184; institutional, 173; Keynesian, 94, 170, 187; neoclassical, 208; Western, 155, 193. *See also* macroeconomics
educational backgrounds: 14, 39, 89, 97, 190, 198; in economics, 14, 97, 198; in engineering, 14, 22, 29, 97, 198
elite self-transformation, 37–38
engineers, 8, 14–15, 22, 29, 88–89, 97–98; and industrial policy, 218; and technocrats, 110, 116–17, 165–67, 182–83, 190
enterprise groups, 128–30; statistics on, 141
enterprises: and innovation, 201, 207–8; local, 102, 152, 223; private, 155; public, 6, 119, 129; reform of, 120–21, 137–42; and SEZs, 76. *See also* state-owned enterprises
epistemic resources, 18, 98, 135, 183, 200
exogenous shocks, 23–24
expansion: in paradigm emergence, 25

factionalism, 17, 29, 37, 72, 88, 220, 228
Federal Reserve, 103

financialization, 22–23, 30, 217; compared to industrial policy, 213; societal participation in, 209
financial markets, 16, 22–23, 102, 104–6, 150
financial reformers, 20, 22–23, 30, 94, 149–51, 159, 161–81
Five-Year Plan: First, 68; Thirteenth, 2
Ford Foundation, 173
foreign direct investment, 66, 76, 118, 194, 208, 225, 227
foreign exchange, 76, 106, 177
foreign ideas, 61, 94–95, 100, 173, 192
foreign models, 41, 93–94, 104, 117, 225
France, 7, 96, 206

Gang of Four, 35, 37, 56, 69
Gao Jian, 172
Gao Xiqing, 177
general-purpose technologies, 200–202
generations: of bureaucrats, 14; career histories of, 114–15; turnover of bureaucratic, 111
Germany, 202, 206
globalization, 76, 94, 224–26, 230–31
gold standard, 41
Great Leap Forward, 50–55, 79; and inflation, 79
Guangdong, 70, 80, 158, 211; negotiates tax compromise, 101
Guangzhou, 73
Guizhou, 170

Hayek, Friedrich, 94
heavy industry, 44–47, 53, 67
Hodgson, Geoffrey, 208
Huida, 177–78
Hu Jintao, 14, 189, 195
Hu Yaobang, 65, 67, 73, 90, 115, 163
hyperinflation, 101

imprint, 38, 122–23, 218
incrementalism, 74
India, 96, 206
indigenous innovation, 9, 181, 187, 207
industrial competitiveness, 22–23, 30, 131, 181–82, 187, 189, 191; and the MIIT, 195–96, 203, 205–8, 210, 212–13

industrialization, 192–96, 209–11, 227; new-style, 195; socialist, 122, 192; state-led, 51, 193; unfished, 15, 181

industrial ministries, 49, 87, 109, 124, 139, 185, 188, 190, 196–97, 200, 204

Industrial Party, 208–9

industrial policy, 21, 181–214; becomes a paradigm, 212; definition of, 182–83; evolution before competitiveness agenda, 189; turns to localities, 210

Industry 4.0, 202

inflation, 38–42, 79–80, 101–5, 169; falls due to macrocontrol, 107; sixteen points to fight, 105–6

intelligent manufacturing, 202–4, 210

interenterprise restructuring, 22–23. See also linking-up strategy

Internal Reference for Reform, 95

International Monetary Fund, 225

Intersectoral linkages, 77, 191, 124, 202, 217

intrabureaucratic struggle, 61–62

Italy, 96

Japan: as developmental state, 6; as economic case study, 93, 96, 100, 144, 206; role in currency crisis, 40

Jiang Zemin, 88–89, 91–94, 195, 212

keiretsu system, 144

Kissinger, Henry, 94

Korea, 6, 93, 95–96, 206

Kostello, Eric, 50

Kuhn, Thomas, 4

liberalization, 56, 119; economic, 77, 162, 215; financial, 16, 156–57, 227; ideological question of, 175; price, 67, 80; trade, 194

Li Fuchun, 41

Li Jiange, 164

Li Keqiang, 14

linking-up strategy, 19, 119, 123–28; mechanisms of, 125; through mergers and acquisitions, 128–29

Lin Yifu, 193

Li Peng, 88–89, 91, 93–94

Liu He, 183

Liu Hongru, 154, 161, 164

Liu Lanbo, 91

Li Xiannian, 36, 45–46, 50, 66–67; on public finance, 152

local generalists, 16–17, 20, 63, 65–66, 81; and centralization, 115–16; and circulators, 64, 70–75, 79, 88; and decentralization, 69–70, 75–77; definition of, 28; and growth, 75–77; and Tiananmen Square, 85

local governments, 10, 51, 75–76, 78; and centralization, 112–13; develop financial levers, 155; in the Great Leap Forward, 53; location in economic policy field, 136; and the MIIT, 210; resist tax reform, 100–101

local specialists, 66; and inflation, 80

locations, bureaucratic. See bureaucratic locations

Lou Jiwei, 161, 164, 166, 168–69, 177

macrocontrol paradigm, 85, 108–16; compared to macroeconomic policy, 107; definition of, 98; documents related to, 108; and industrial policy, 186–89, 212; undermines industrial ministries, 109

macroeconomics, 54–55, 61, 67, 71, 78, 133–34; compared to macrocontrol, 107; introduced to banking, 103; and the SETC, 134–35

Made in China 2025, 2, 181; authorship of, 205–7

Ma Hong, 193

managers-turned-bureaucrats, 19; in SOE reform, 119. See also local generalists

Mao era, 3, 36, 227

Mao Zedong, 35, 51–54; and the radicals, 69; rejects the idea of economic laws, 51

markets: constituencies of, 115, 223; efficiency of, 29, 117, 129, 144–45, 165, 167; integration of, 137, 183, 222; rationalization of, 85. See also financial markets

masses, 69, 81

Mexico, 7
ministers' career experiences and
   education, 198
Ministry of Commerce, 18, 46–48, 67
Ministry of Finance, 18, 30, 67, 99; and
   bank recapitalization, 177; and bond
   issuance, 169–72; on public finance, 153
Ministry of Foreign Economic Relations
   and Trade, 49
Ministry of Industry and Information
   Technology, 2, 21, 31; Bureaus of
   Equipment and Development
   Planning, 2; and industrial policy,
   182, 195–213; and local government
   penetration, 210–12
Ministry of Information, 196
Ministry of Science and Technology, 204,
   210
monetary policy, 29, 41, 75–76, 78, 104,
   107, 157–58, 164, 167, 169
money doctors, 102. See also circulators;
   currency crisis

Naisbitt, John, 192
national champions, 2, 118–45
National Development and Reform
   Commission, 189–211; foundation
   of, 189; and localities, 211; ministers'
   career experiences and education, 198;
   as superagency, 199
neoliberalism, 7, 96
networks: definition of, 20; in paradigm
   emergence, 25
new-style industrialization, 195
niches, 135–36, 199–202
nodal agency, 12, 182, 204
non-performing loans, 175–78

organizational approach, 138, 142–46
overcapacity, 190–91
overheating, 78, 81, 102, 151; industrial
   policy used to control, 186–87

party elite, 11
peasants, 39, 43, 46, 51, 54–55, 69–71, 81
People's Bank of China, 102–4, 110, 132,
   155; initiates commercial banking

wave, 158; location in economic policy
   field, 136; on public finance, 153; and
   Wudaokou, 157
personnel networks, map of, 49
piece-rate wages, 55, 58
planned economy, 6, 19, 28, 47, 56
planning: central, 6, 12, 18, 28–30, 36,
   44–45, 47–56, 61, 68–70, 74, 123–25,
   183–85, 212, 216–17; credit, 88, 104, 151,
   155; industrial, 16, 28, 48–52, 182–85,
   197, 200, 203, 212, 216; long-term, 18;
   new definition of, 109; yearly, 199
Polanyi, Karl, 3, 179, 222
policy authority, 4, 13, 16; and
   bureaucratic turf war, 132–33
policy, economic: in the 1980s, 67; as
   depoliticized field, 13; developed from
   socialist-era experiments, 58
policy experiment, 10, 44, 57–60, 103, 119,
   137, 140–44, 158, 210–11, 215
policy, industrial. See industrial policy
policy, monetary. See monetary policy
policy paradigms, 4, 150; co-existence
   between, 64, 213; competition
   between, 74–79, 190–95, 217;
   definition of, 21, 215–16; formation
   and emergence of, 22, 24–25, 72–74,
   98–101, 110–12, 137–42, 199–203,
   217–18; pattern and stages of, 25,
   216–17; shifts in, 91–93, 189, 196;
   timeline of, 22
populism, 69; in the Great Leap Forward,
   51–53
privatization, 6; and SOE reform, 119–20
proportionate development, 60
protectionism, 129, 146, 223, 231
public investment, 75–76, 102–3, 114, 150–51,
   172, 179, 187; and capital formation,
   107, 180; and stimulus package, 187

real estate, 102, 106, 108
recentralization, 22–23, 103, 216–18, 220
red and expert, 51, 160
reform elites, four types of, 65–66; major
   policy stances of, 67
Republican China, 101
Rostow, Walt Whitman, 192

sequences, career. *See* career sequences
Shanghai, 41–42, 89, 92, 158
shareholder, 174–78, 223, 226
shareholding, 128, 174, 175, 177–79, 227
Shenzhen, 158
shock therapy, 6, 138, 162, 215
Singapore, 93
Sinopec, 139
sixteen points, 105–8
socialism, 6, 3, 42, 53, 56, 58, 62, 90, 94, 123, 140; and capitalism, 93
SOE reformers, 118–46; career trajectories of, 122. *See also* state-owned enterprise reform
SOEs. *See* state-owned enterprises
Soviet Union, 6, 47, 53, 60, 116
Special Economic Zones, 66, 68, 76, 78, 80
state capacity, 13, 42, 53, 100–112, 184, 197, 220–21
State Council, 2, 11, 20, 136, 144, 154, 159–60, 172; and the CIC, 178; Finance and Trade Office of, 48–49; Financial Economic Committee of, 36, 64–65; on fiscal revenue versus banking, 163; and the MIIT, 197; Research Office of, 168, 196
State Economic and Trade Commission, 30; absorption of industrial ministries, 188; establishment of, 131; and linking up, 133–46; location in economic policy field, 136; overlapping mandate of, 132; revival due to macrocontrol, 109. *See also* SOE reformers
state-owned banks, 102–4, 152, 155, 158, 169; commercialization of, 178; and private banks, 158; recapitalization and restructuring of, 175–77
state-owned enterprise reform, 118–46; beginnings in Mao period, 124; lack of models for, 120; and the organizational approach, 146. *See also* linking-up strategy
state-owned enterprises, 68, 76; conglomeration of, 23; merger of, 128–31, 137–42; privatization of, 6

State Planning Commission, 132; and industrial policy, 183–86; location in economic policy field, 136; loses under macrocontrol, 109; ministers' career experiences and education, 198
State Security Commission, 140
supply chains: domestic, 230; local, 125, 130; and the SETC, 134, 139
System Reform Commission, 64–65, 93, 132, 166
Szelenyi, Ivan, 50

tax, 42–43, 45, 69, 99–101, 113–14, 153, 161–62, 170–71; value-added, 100, 120
technocracy, 51, 89, 91, 149
technocrats, 7, 28, 72, 91–117; 1990s rise of, 85, 90; confront tax crisis, 100; definition of, 89; and international learning, 93–96; and marketization, 96; political identity of, 111; respond to the Asian Financial Crisis, 175
Thailand, 96
think tanks, 20, 22, 87, 154, 159–60, 163, 165, 168, 179, 218
Third Wave, The, 192
Thirteenth Five-Year Plan, 2
Toffler, Alvin, 192
trade: domestic, 43–45, 125; international, 38, 75, 92, 138, 193–95
trajectories, career. *See* career trajectories

United States, 38, 173, 206, 230

Vietnam, 35, 96

Wanfang Laws and Regulations Database, 27
Wang Qishan, 227
Wang Yang, 211
Wang Zhongyu, 122, 129, 132, 142
Wan Li, 71
Washington Consensus, 225
Weber, Max, 7–10
Wei Liqun, 196

work style: definition of, 72
World Trade Organization, 138, 226
Wudaokou School, 30, 154–65, 177–78;
    compared with Comprehensive
    Reform School, 162–63; foundation
    and curriculum of, 156–57; graduates
    in financial bureaucracy, 157
Wu Jianlian, 164
Wu Xiaoling, 11, 157, 161, 164, 177

Xiang Huaicheng, 100
Xi Jinping, 14, 227–29
Xue Muqiao, 40–41
Xu Penghang, 122, 127

Yang Weimin, 184
Yao Yilin, 36, 45, 47–50, 73, 77, 79
Ye Jizhuang, 41

Zeng Peiyan, 109
Zeng Shan, 41
Zhang Ping, 190
Zhang Yanning, 87
Zhao Weichen, 131
Zhao Ziyang, 65–67, 70, 73–74, 80, 87, 90,
    115, 160, 163, 192
Zhou Enlai, 150
Zhou Jiannan, 160
Zhou Xiaochuan, 15, 160–61, 164, 166,
    176, 193
Zhu Rongji, 29, 88–89, 91–92, 94, 99–101,
    105–6, 165, 168; on bond issuance,
    171; halts bankruptcies, 144; interest
    in Western banking, 104; and local
    generalists, 115; and macrocontrol, 116;
    on non-performing loans, 176; and
    the SETC, 131

Printed in the USA
CPSIA information can be obtained
at www.ICGtesting.com
JSHW022029250324
59894JS00002B/10